KÖHLER · LINSE · BEZOLD

Übungsgrammatik · Englisch

Klaus Köhler · Erhard Linse
Rolf Bezold

Übungs-grammatik Englisch

Verlag Enzyklopädie Leipzig

Die Autoren
Dr. Klaus Köhler ⎫
Erhard Linse   ⎬ Technische Universität Dresden
Rolf Bezold   ⎭

Leitfaden, Komplexübungen: Köhler, Linse
Übungen Kapitel 1–4, 10–15, 17, 18: Köhler, Linse
Kapitel 5–9, 20: Köhler, Linse, Bezold

Köhler, Klaus:
Übungsgrammatik Englisch / Klaus Köhler ; Erhard Linse ; Rolf Bezold. –
2., unveränd. Aufl. – Leipzig : Verlag Enzyklopädie, 1990. – 270 S.

NE: Linse, Erhard:; Bezold, Rolf:
ISBN 3-324-00312-1

ISBN 3-324-00312-1

© Verlag Enzyklopädie Leipzig, 1990
0834/02026890
Printed in the German Democratic Republic
Satzherstellung: INTERDRUCK
Graphischer Großbetrieb Leipzig, III/18/97
Druck und buchbinderische Weiterverarbeitung:
Grafischer Großbetrieb Völkerfreundschaft Dresden
Einbandgestaltung: Rolf Kunze
Best.-Nr.: 578 117 0

Vorwort

Das vorliegende Buch ist eine grundlegende Neubearbeitung der erstmals 1972 erschienenen Englischen Übungsgrammatik. Bei der Umgestaltung des Leitfadens haben wir durch Straffung einiger Kapitel (vor allem Partizip und Infinitiv) bzw. Erweiterung anderer Komplexe (z. B. Anwendung der Zeiten, modale Hilfsverben, Pronomen) eine Akzentverlagerung vorgenommen, die uns aus unterrichtspraktischen Erwägungen angebracht schien. Die deskriptive Darbietung der Grammatik mit struktureller Gliederung ist beibehalten worden. Doch werden bei der Erklärung, danach bei der Einübung einer bestimmten grammatischen Konstruktion oft auch andere Ausdrucksmöglichkeiten angegeben, damit der Lernende sich nicht auf die gerade behandelte Form festgelegt fühlt.

Entscheidend für die Neufassung des Übungsteils war die Orientierung auf kommunikative Komponenten der Sprachvermittlung. In weitaus größerem Maße als im vorangegangenen Buch wurden kontextuale Übungen zu Themen des Alltags und des Allgemeinwissens einbezogen, um situatives Lernen zu stimulieren. Zur knappen Veranschaulichung sprachlicher Strukturen konnte und sollte auf Einzelsätze nicht verzichtet werden, doch ging es uns in diesen Fällen darum, nicht Sätze um der grammatischen Erläuterung willen zu bilden, sondern Grammatik in Satzbeispielen zu erläutern, die primär den täglichen Sprachgebrauch widerspiegeln, zum Teil auch den Stil der Fachsprache berücksichtigen.

Der Anhang enthält längere kohärente Texte wissenschaftsgeschichtlichen, kulturellen und literarischen Inhalts, die in Form grammatischer Querschnitte einer abschließenden Überprüfung der erworbenen Kenntnisse dienen sollen.

Wie ihr Vorläufer ist die Übungsgrammatik Englisch ihrer Anlage nach in erster Linie für die Erwachsenenbildung gedacht. Die im Schlüssel gegebenen Lösungen für eine Reihe von Beispielen sind vor allem dazu bestimmt, denjenigen die Arbeit mit dem Buch zu erleichtern, die es im Selbststudium benutzen wollen.

Wir danken Frau Theresa McGing, B.A. (London), für die Durchsicht des Manuskripts sowie Professor Dr. Manfred Gerbert, Dresden, und Dr. Karl Gräf, Ilmenau, für wertvolle Hinweise. Unser Dank gilt weiterhin Frau Wollgiehn vom Verlag Enzyklopädie Leipzig, Lektorat Fremdsprachen, Halle, für die Arbeit am Manuskript.

Dresden, im März 1987 *Die Autoren*

Abkürzungen

AE = Amerikanisches Englisch
BE = Britisches Englisch

A.D. (anno Domini) = u. Z.
a.m. / am (ante meridiem) = Zeit zwischen 0.00 Uhr und 12.00 Uhr mittags
B.C. (before Christ) = v. u. Z.
et al. (et alii) = and other persons / and co-workers
L = Leitfaden
o.s. = oneself
p.m. / pm (post meridiem) = Zeit zwischen 12.00 Uhr und 24.00 Uhr
sb = somebody
sth = something

Inhaltsverzeichnis

	Leitfaden	Übungen
Leitfaden	9	
0. Grundsätzliches zur englischen Wortstellung	9	
1. Interrogative and Negative Sentences – Frage und Verneinung	10	125
2. The Tenses – Die Zeitformen des Verbs	14	129
3. The Conditional – Der Konditional	25	151
4. The Passive Voice – Das Passiv	30	156
5. The Infinitive – Der Infinitiv	36	165
6. The Defective Auxiliaries and their Equivalents – Die unvollständigen Hilfsverben	48	174
7. Reported (Indirect) Speech – Die indirekte Rede	60	186
8. The Gerund – Das Gerundium	63	191
9. The Participles – Die Partizipien	72	201
10. The Subjunctive Mood – Der Konjunktiv	81	211
11. Complementation of the Verb – Ergänzung des Verbs	82	214
12. Question Tags/Short Answers/Additions to Statements – 'Frageanhängsel'/Kurzantworten/Ergänzende Feststellungen	84	215
13. Emphasis – Hervorhebung von Satzteilen	86	218
14. Conjunctions – Konjunktionen	88	219
15. The Pronouns – Die Pronomen	90	221
16. The Adjective – Das Adjektiv	103	
17. The Adverb – Das Adverb	105	233
18. The Comparison of Adjectives and Adverbs – Die Steigerung von Adjektiven und Adverbien	111	235
19. The Noun – Das Substantiv	114	
20. The Article – Der Artikel	121	237
Übungen	125	
Anhang	241	
Komplexübungen	241	
Schlüssel	251	
Unregelmäßige Verben	261	
Kontrahierte Formen	263	
Formen des Verbs im Aktiv	264	
Formen des Verbs im Passiv	265	
Register	266	
Bibliographie	270	

Leitfaden

0. Grundsätzliches zur englischen Wortstellung

0.1. Für das Englische gilt in Haupt- und Nebensatz die feste **Wortfolge**:
Subjekt – Prädikat – Objekt.[1]
Im Gegensatz zum Deutschen wird dabei das zusammengesetzte Prädikat (= Hilfsverb + Vollverb) nicht getrennt. Diese Wortfolge bleibt auch erhalten, wenn der Satz durch eine adverbiale Bestimmung eingeleitet wird, oder wenn dem Hauptsatz ein Nebensatz vorausgeht.

> I know him.
> Eve can translate English texts.
> We have read this article.
> Yesterday I repeated the test.
> If I see Jean I'll inform her.
> Before we can carry out the experiment
> we must consult our professor.

0.2. Verben mit zwei Objekten (*indirect object* + *direct object*)

Nach einigen Verben, z. B. **give, tell**[2], sind – wie im Deutschen – zwei Objekte möglich: ein *'indirect object'* (meist auf Personen bezogen) und ein *'direct object'* (meist Sachbezug). Ist das *indirect object* ein **Substantiv**, so kann es **vor** dem *direct object* stehen oder mit *to* dem *direct object* **folgen** (a). Ist das *indirect object* ein **Pronomen**, so steht es in der Regel **vor** dem *direct object* (b). Das *indirect object* steht jedoch **nach** *it* und wird dann meist mit *to* angeschlossen (c).
I gave Tom the book. (a) (oder:) I gave the book to Tom. (a)
I gave him the book. (b)
I don't have the book, I gave it (to) Tom. / I gave it to him. (c)

Das *indirect object* steht immer **mit** *to*, wenn es bei einer Gegenüberstellung hervorgehoben wird.
I gave the book to John, not to Mary. (bzw. ... not to him but to her)

---

[1] s. auch Kapitel 13.
[2] Weitere Verben mit 2 Objekten s. 4.2.

L 1.

Anmerkung:
Ist das *indirect object* wesentlich länger als das *direct object*, oder wird es näher erläutert, so wird es ebenfalls mit *to* angeschlossen:
John showed the photos to most of his friends. – I'll tell the story to everybody I know.

1. Interrogative and Negative Sentences – Frage und Verneinung

1.1. The Question – Der Fragesatz

In der Frage bleibt im Englischen die feste Wortstellung
Subjekt – Prädikat (Vollverb) – Objekt
erhalten. Daraus ergeben sich folgende Regeln:

1.1.1. Ist das Interrogativpronomen Subjekt bzw. Teil des Subjekts (= Subjektfrage), so ist analog zum Deutschen die **Wortstellung S – P – O** von vornherein gegeben. Sie bleibt im Gegensatz zum Deutschen auch erhalten, wenn das Prädikat sich aus Hilfsverb und Vollverb zusammensetzt.
Who knows him? – Who can answer this question? – What causes the tides?

Who (wer) fragt nach Personen, *what* (was) nach Sachen. Mit *which* (welche, -r, -s) oder *which of* (wer von ..., welche, -r, -s von ...) kann nach einer Person oder Sache bzw. nach Personen oder Sachen aus einer bestimmten Anzahl heraus gefragt werden.
Who is that? – What happens in this film? – Which is your English teacher, Mr Brown or Mrs Green? – Which is your car, the big one or the small one? – Which of you speaks English? – Which of these cars is yours? – Which of you wants to read this book?

What und *which* können Teil des Subjekts sein. Beachten Sie Verbindungen wie:
what (which) kind/sort/type of[1] (was für).
Ebenfalls als Teil des Subjekts kommen *whose* (wessen), *how much/how many* (wieviel/wie viele) vor.
What[2] building is this? – What flowers grow in your garden? – Which bus goes to the airport? – What kind of trees are these? – What sort of weather is it today? – What type of machinery is produced in your factory? – Whose house is this? (auch: Whose is this house?) – How much money is in the safe? – How many students study at the Dresden University of Technology?
Unterscheiden Sie:
What kind *of* professor is he? – (He is a professor of physics.)
What kind *of a* professor is he? – (He is quite a strict but popular professor.)

---

[1] Vorzugsweise bei technischen Begriffen
[2] Bei Ausrufen steht vor zählbaren Begriffen im Singular *What a*: What a pretty girl Rose has become. (Was für ein hübsches Mädchen Rose geworden ist!) **Aber:** What fine weather we are having today!

1.1.2. Wird nicht nach dem Subjekt gefragt, aber ein Hilfsverb erscheint als Teil des Prädikats, dann bleibt die **Wortstellung S – P (= Vollverb) – O** ebenfalls gewahrt. Wie im Deutschen leitet das Hilfsverb den Fragesatz ein, während das Vollverb im Gegensatz zum Deutschen vor das Objekt tritt:
Wortfolge: Hilfsverb – Subjekt – Vollverb – Objekt.
Can you translate this text? – May I ask a question? – Will you be here tomorrow? – Have you seen the film? – Is he an engineer? – Was she at home?

Der Fragesatz kann durch ein Frageadverb – *why, when, where, how* – oder ein Interrogativpronomen – *whom* (umgangssprachlich oft: *who*), *what, which, whose* – eingeleitet werden.
Where are my shoes? – Why is he angry? – What can I do for you? – Who(m) must I inform? – When will the meeting take place?

1.1.3. Wird nicht nach dem Subjekt gefragt und ist kein Hilfsverb vorhanden, so erfolgt bei der direkten Frage[3] im Präsens und Präteritum eine Umschreibung mit *do/does* (Präsens), *did* (Präteritum), damit die **Wortstellung S – P (= Vollverb) – O** erhalten bleibt:
do/does/did **– Subjekt – Infinitiv (ohne** *to*) **– Objekt.**
Do you speak English? – Does Anne like modern art? – Did you see Fred at the conference? – What do you want? – Who(m) did they consult? – Which do you prefer, wine or champagne? – Where does Jim work? – When did Tom arrive?[4] – Why does John want to stay at home?

1.1.4. *Have* kann die Funktion eines Hilfsverbs (a) oder eines Vollverbs (b) haben.[5] In der Funktion eines Vollverbs wird es in Frage und Verneinung mit *do/does/did* umschrieben.
Have you met him? (a) – Did you have a conversation with her? (b)
Im heutigen Englisch wird, vor allem in der Umgangssprache, häufig *have got*, seltener die Vergangenheitsform *had got*, (jeweils ohne *do*-Umschreibung!) verwendet, besonders, wenn nach einem Besitz oder Verwandtschaftsverhältnis oder nach dem körperlichen Befinden gefragt wird. Unter dem Einfluß des AE findet sich in diesen Fällen auch *have* mit *do*-Umschreibung.
Have you got a brother? = Do you have a brother? – Has he got a car? = Does he have a car? – Have you got toothache? = Do you have toothache? – Had you got an umbrella with you yesterday? (häufiger:) Did you have an umbrella with you yesterday?

In etwas formalerem Stil wird *have* im Präsens, seltener im Präteritum, auch ohne Umschreibung verwendet.
Have you a sister? – Have you an appointment?

Wird nach einer sich wiederholenden oder gewohnheitsmäßigen Situation gefragt,

---
[3] Zur indirekten Frage s. 7.3.
[4] **Aber:** I don't know when Tom arrived. (s. 7.3.)
[5] Zu *have* als Umschreibung für *must* s. 6.6.1.
have = veranlassen s. 5.7.1. und 9.5.

L 1.1.5.

so steht häufig *have* mit *do*-Umschreibung (a); *have got* bezieht sich mehr auf den Einzelfall (b). Unter dem Einfluß des AE wird auch beim Einzelfall oft mit *do* umschrieben (c)[6].
Do you often have time to go to the movies? (a) – Have you got time to go to the movies tonight? (b) – Do you sometimes have headaches? (a) – Have you got a headache now? (b) – Have you got Scotch Whisky today? (b) = Do you have Scotch Whisky today? (c) – Have you got time for a walk? (b) = Do you have time for a walk? (c)

In **feststehenden Wendungen** erfolgt in Frage und Verneinung immer Umschreibung mit *do*; die Verlaufsform ist möglich, *have got* wird nicht verwendet. Beispiele sind:
have breakfast / lunch / dinner / supper / brunch / tea;
have (a cup of) tea / coffee / chocolate; have (a glass of) beer / wine / champagne / juice / lemonade etc;
have a holiday / a day off / a good time[7];
have a conversation / a talk / a chat; have trouble / difficulty; have a break; have a look at; have a walk / a stroll etc; have a bath / a shower / a swim; have a try; have a lesson.
When did you have breakfast? – How many glasses of wine did Anne have last night? – Do you have a bath every day? – Did you have a pleasant holiday? – How often do you have a day off? – Did they have a talk with her about it? – Did you have a good time at the seaside? – Do you often have trouble with your car? – Are you having trouble with your car again?

1.1.5. In Fragesätzen steht – abweichend vom Deutschen – die Präposition im modernen Sprachgebrauch gewöhnlich hinter dem Verb, zu dem sie bedeutungsmäßig gehört (a), in Verbindung mit *be* auch nach einem Adjektiv oder dem Subjekt (b). Zwischen Verb und Präposition kann ein Objekt stehen (c), in der Regel aber keine adverbiale Bestimmung (d).
What did they talk *about*? (a) (Worüber haben sie sich unterhalten?) – *What* does this novel deal *with*? (a) (Wovon handelt dieser Roman?) – *What* does this alloy consist *of*? (a) (Woraus besteht diese Legierung?) – *Who* do you want to speak *to*? (a) (Mit wem wollen Sie sprechen?) – *Where* do these machines come *from*? (a) (Woher kommen diese Maschinen?) – *What* is Rita afraid *of*? (b) (Wovor hat Rita Angst?) – *What* is this film *about*? (b) (Wovon handelt dieser Film?) – *Who(m)* do you want to discuss this matter *with*? (c) (Mit wem willst du über diese Angelegenheit sprechen?) – *What* do you need these data *for*? (c) (Wozu brauchst du diese Daten?) – *What* topics did they speak *about* at the conference? (d) (Über welche Themen haben sie auf der Versammlung gesprochen?)
In Fällen, wo die Präposition bedeutungsmäßig nicht unmittelbar zum Verb oder

---

[6] Die unter 1.1.4. genannten Anwendungsmöglichkeiten von *have* und *have got* treffen natürlich auch auf den bejahenden Satz und für die Verneinung zu: Tom has got three brothers. (oder:) Tom has three brothers. – They haven't got a car of their own. (oder:) They don't have a car of their own. – We hadn't got an umbrella with us yesterday. Häufiger: We didn't have an umbrella ... – I haven't got a sister.

[7] *have time* auch mit *have got* möglich: Have you got time to come with us?

Adjektiv gehört, kann sie auch **vor** dem Fragewort stehen (a). Hat sie **keinen** Bezug zum Verb, bleibt sie immer vor dem Fragewort (b).
Which house does she live in? (oder:) In which house does she live? (a) – Who(m) do you intend to spend your holidays with? (oder:) With whom do you intend to spend your holidays? (nicht: With who) (a) – Under which conditions does this process take place? (b)

1.2. Negative Sentences – Die Verneinung

1.2.1. Zur Verneinung wird *not* verwendet. Kommt ein Hilfsverb im Satz vor, dann folgt *not* diesem unmittelbar. Die in der Umgangssprache übliche kontrahierte Form *n't* für *not* wird immer mit dem jeweiligen Hilfsverb zusammengeschrieben.[8] (s. Übersicht, Seite 263)
This test is not/isn't very difficult. – He is not/isn't a good driver. – I cannot/can't come today.

Befindet sich nur ein Vollverb im verneinten Satz, so wird es im Präsens und Präteritum mit der entsprechenden Form von *do* umschrieben (kontrahierte Formen: don't/doesn't/didn't).[9] Für *have* und *have got* gelten die unter 1.1.4 angeführten Regeln.
I do not/don't know him. – Bob does not/doesn't speak French. – We did not/didn't meet Eric yesterday. – I don't think Fred will come tomorrow. – We do not/don't have any trouble with our new TV-set. – I haven't got time now to read this article. = I don't have time ...

1.2.2. Bei der verneinten Frage folgt *not* unmittelbar dem Subjekt, wenn ein Hilfsverb vorhanden ist; die kontrahierte Form *n't* wird dagegen mit dem Hilfsverb zusammengeschrieben. Ist kein Hilfsverb vorhanden, wird mit der entsprechenden Form von *do* umschrieben. Das gilt auch für die **verneinte Subjektfrage**.
Isn't Fred/Is Fred not one of your colleagues? – Can't you/Can you not help us? – Doesn't Hugh/Does Hugh not live in London? – Why didn't Liz/did Liz not come?[10] – Why didn't you/did you not have a talk with Peg? – Which of you doesn't/does not know Gary?

1.2.3. Der verneinte Imperativ[11] wird stets mit *don't* ... bzw. *do not* ... umschrieben, auch bei *be*.

---

[8] Beachten Sie: Betontes *not* wird nicht kontrahiert: It isn't true. – It's not true. – I haven't asked him. – I've not asked him. – This problem's not difficult; I think it's rather simple.

[9] Wird eine durch *think, suppose, believe, imagine* eingeleitete Aussage verneint, so werden diese Verben mit *do/does/did* umschrieben: I don't suppose Tom speaks English. (nicht: I suppose Tom doesn't speak English). – **Aber:** I hope Joan won't be too late (nicht: I don't hope Joan will be late.)

[10] Auch bei der indirekten Rede bleibt hier die Umschreibung mit do bestehen: I don't know why Sarah didn't come.

[11] Der Imperativ wird im Englischen durch den Infinitiv ohne *to* gebildet; es gibt für Singular und Plural nur eine Form: Open the window. (Öffne/Öffnet/Öffnen Sie das Fenster!) – Be careful. (Sei/Seid/Seien Sie vorsichtig!) – Keep the temperature constant. (Die Temperatur ist konstant zu halten.) – Let's ask Roy. (Fragen wir Roy.)

Don't/Do not switch off the light. (Schalte/Schaltet/Schalten Sie das Licht nicht aus!) – Don't be late. (Komm/Kommt/Kommen Sie nicht zu spät!)

2. The Tenses – Die Zeitformen des Verbs

Im Englischen unterscheidet man zwei Zeitformen:
Die **einfachen Zeitformen** *(Simple Tenses)* und
die **Verlaufsformen** *(Continuous Tenses)* (Bildung s. Seite 264f.).
Mit den **einfachen Zeitformen** wird zum Ausdruck gebracht,
– daß eine Feststellung allgemeingültig ist
– daß ein Vorgang gewohnheitsmäßig oder wiederholt stattfindet.
Das heißt, der Verlauf der Handlung an sich ist für die Aussage nicht wesentlich.

Durch die **Verlaufsform** wird ausgedrückt,
– daß Handlungen oder Vorgänge zu einem Zeitpunkt in der Gegenwart, Vergangenheit oder Zukunft schon begonnen haben; sie werden irgendwann zwischen Anfang und Ende in ihrem Ablauf dargestellt
– daß ein Vorgang, der schon abgeschlossen ist, innerhalb einer bestimmten Zeitspanne stattgefunden hat.

Simple Tenses	*Continuous Tenses*
Water boils at 100°C.	Get the teabags, the water is boiling.
Do you often read English books?	What book are you reading?
My uncle lived in Berlin.	My uncle was living in Berlin when World War II broke out.
I have read this book twice.	I have been reading all afternoon.
We'll often dine out in the next few weeks.	Don't come tomorrow, I'll be dining out.

Die Verlaufsform kann auch eine allmählich stattfindende Entwicklung oder den Übergang in einen anderen Zustand ausdrücken, z.B. im Zusammenhang mit *gradually, increasingly, by degrees, more and more*.
The situation is becoming more and more complicated. (Die Situation wird immer komplizierter.) – Modern industry is increasingly using robots. (Die moderne Industrie verwendet in zunehmendem Maße Roboter.)

Außerdem kann mit der Verlaufsform einer Feststellung besonderer Nachdruck verliehen werden (s. auch 13.2.). Das erklärt die Verwendung dieser Form auch im Konditional.
You are always making the same mistake. (Du machst doch immer wieder denselben Fehler.) – Tom was being impolite, when I asked him a favour. (Tom war wirklich unhöflich, als ich ihn um einen Gefallen bat.) – If I were you I would be trying to come to an agreement with Jim. (An deiner Stelle würde ich doch versuchen, mich mit Jim zu einigen.)

Bestimmte Verben, die einen **Zustand**, nicht eine Tätigkeit ausdrücken (oft statische Verben genannt), werden **nicht** in der **Verlaufsform** verwendet, z.B.: ***know,***

understand, recognize, realize (begreifen, sich bewußt werden), *seem, (dis)like, prefer, lack, possess, own, resemble, belong to, exist, consist of, contain, include, incorporate, involve, depend on, rely on, constitute, satisfy, mean, suppose, hear*[1], *sound*.
We know Jim very well. – Do you understand what Tom is talking about? -- I realize now what you mean. – Fred likes Paula very much. – Matter exists in different forms. – The ordinary hydrogen atom consists of two particles, a proton and an electron.

Bei einigen Verben, z. B. *feel* (fühlen); *look forward to* (sich freuen auf); *hurt/ache* (schmerzen) besteht kaum ein Unterschied zwischen den einfachen Zeiten und der Verlaufsform.

How do you feel today?	How are you feeling today?
Do you look forward to her visit?	Are you looking forward to her visit?
My eyes hurt.	My eyes are hurting.

Manche Verben bilden eine Verlaufsform nur, wenn sie in übertragener Bedeutung vorkommen, z. B.: *appear* (auftreten); *taste* (eine Speise kosten); *see* (jmd. sehen, im Sinne von: jmd. treffen); *see sb off* (jmd. irgendwohin begleiten).[2]
The famous Leningrad ballet is appearing at our opera-house this week. (aber:) The hypothesis appears (= seems) to be correct.
Mother is tasting the pudding. (aber:) The pudding tastes good.
Jane is smelling the egg. It smells bad.
I'm seeing Liz this weekend. (aber:) Did you see John leave?
They want to take the 6.30 train; will you be seeing them off?

2.1. The Present Tense – Das Präsens

2.1.1. Die einfache Form des Präsens *(Present Simple Tense)* bezeichnet gewohnheitsmäßig stattfindende bzw. sich häufig wiederholende Vorgänge oder auch aufeinanderfolgende Tätigkeiten. Sie wird verwendet zur Darstellung allgemeingültiger Vorgänge, häufig in der Wissenschaftssprache, oder wenn man den Inhalt eines Buches, Films etc. schildert, sowie bei Sportreportagen.
John goes to the theatre once a month. – Engineers make designs of machines. – Paula reads a lot. – When do you usually have your lunch? – Does this bus go on Sundays? – I come home from work at about half past four, then I have tea and read the newspaper.
Hydrogen and oxygen combine to form water. – The action of the play takes place in the 18th century.

2.1.2. Mit der **Verlaufsform des Präsens** *(Present Continuous)* wird zum Ausdruck gebracht, daß Handlungen oder Vorgänge zu einem Zeitpunkt der Ge-

---

[1] Anstelle der nicht üblichen Verlaufsform steht bei "hear" häufig "can". Das trifft auch für "see" = sehen (im Sinne einer optischen Wahrnehmung) zu: I can hear her laugh. – I can see him cleaning the car.
[2] Auf "feel" in übertragener Bedeutung (= think) trifft das nicht zu: I feel (= I think) we should give him a chance.

genwart bereits begonnen haben und weiter andauern (a). Finden zwei Handlungen zeitlich parallel statt, so erscheinen gewöhnlich beide in der Verlaufsform (b).
What are you doing? – I'm writing a letter. (a) (Was tust du? – Ich schreibe einen Brief.)
Wait a minute, they are making an important experiment. (a)
Henry is working, and his brother is reading the paper. (b)

Mit der Verlaufsform des Präsens kann auch etwas ausgedrückt werden, das während eines längeren, aber doch begrenzten Zeitraums geschieht, jedoch nicht im Augenblick des Sprechens.

You can't have the book before next week, Jane is reading it. – I don't have much spare time this summer, I'm finishing my diploma thesis.

Ebenso können sich wiederholende Handlungen im *Present Continuous* erscheinen, wenn sie zeitlich begrenzt sind.

Henry is taking lunch at a restaurant as long as his wife is abroad.

Mit der Verlaufsform des Präsens kann auch eine Handlung ausgedrückt werden, die in naher Zukunft stattfinden soll, meist im Zusammenhang mit einer Zeitbestimmung.

Ruth is coming tomorrow. – We're going on holiday next week.

2.2. The Past Tense – Das Präteritum

2.2.1. Die **einfache Form des Präteritums** *(Past Simple Tense)* bezieht den geschilderten Vorgang oder Zustand auf einen in der Vergangenheit abgeschlossenen Zeitpunkt oder Zeitraum[3] – häufig in Verbindung mit Zeitangaben oder Frageadverbien wie

yesterday; the day before yesterday; last week/month/year/summer etc; five weeks/ three months ago (vor fünf Wochen/drei Monaten); *in 1979; in March/April etc; on Monday/Tuesday etc; at that time/at the time/then* (damals); *the other day* (neulich); *when?/what time?*

Did you meet Sue yesterday? – I talked to Bob some minutes ago. – How long were you ill? – When did Tina arrive? – I was abroad at that time.

2.2.2. Mit der **Verlaufsform des Präteritums** *(Past Continuous)* wird zum Ausdruck gebracht, daß Vorgänge zu einem bestimmten Zeitpunkt oder innerhalb einer Zeitspanne der Vergangenheit stattgefunden haben.

I was working between eight and eleven last night. (Ich habe gestern abend zwischen acht und elf Uhr gearbeitet.) – We could not speak to them because they were having a meeting. – I didn't have much spare time last year because I was working on my doctoral thesis.

Die Verlaufsform des Präteritums wird ebenfalls verwendet bei Vorgängen, die zeitlich parallel stattgefunden haben (häufig durch *while* verbunden).

---

[3] Im Deutschen werden solche Sätze meist im Perfekt gebildet, die Unterscheidung zwischen Präteritum und Perfekt ist nur ein Stilproblem. Im Englischen dagegen ist zwischen Past Tense und Present Perfect Tense genau zu unterscheiden.

Mother was preparing dinner while father was watching TV.⁴ – Jack was reading and his sister was writing a letter.

Auch Vorgänge, die sich innerhalb einer bestimmten Zeitspanne wiederholt haben, werden in der Regel mit der Verlaufsform des Präteritums ausgedrückt.
Tom was taking lunch at a restaurant as long as his wife was abroad.

Die Verlaufsform des Präteritums wird auch verwendet, um etwas auszudrücken, das schon im Gange war, als etwas anderes passierte.
The postman brought your telegram when we were having breakfast.

Beachten Sie den Unterschied: When we came, Mary was making tea. (= Mary was already making tea, when we came.) (aber:) When we came, Mary made tea. (= After we had come, Mary made tea.)

2.3. The Present Perfect – Das Perfekt

Wie schon in der englischen Bezeichnung zum Ausdruck kommt, wird durch das *Present Perfect*⁵ mit seinen beiden Formen – *Simple* und *Continuous* – eine **Beziehung zwischen Vergangenheit und Gegenwart** hergestellt.

2.3.1. Die **einfache Form des Perfekts** *(Present Perfect Simple)* beschreibt etwas, das zu einem nicht erwähnten oder nicht näher bestimmten Zeitpunkt der Vergangenheit geschehen ist, aber sich in der Gegenwart noch auswirkt. In Fragesätzen wird danach gefragt, ob etwas stattgefunden hat; bei Verneinung wird ausgedrückt, daß etwas (noch) nicht stattgefunden hat.
I have read a lot of modern English novels. (= I know a lot of ...) – Somebody has left the door open. (= The door is still open.) – The situation has changed completely. (= ... is completely different now.) – John has broken his leg. (= He has a broken leg now.)
I have caught a cold. – Mike's bicycle has been stolen. – Your taxi has arrived. – Have you finished your translation? – John has gone without his coat, it is still here. – Have you seen 'Hamlet'?⁶ Yes, I have.

---

⁴ Es finden sich aber auch Sätze wie: While the driver changed the tyre, we tried to find a restaurant. – What did you do while I was repairing the device?

⁵ Das Present Perfect wird mit "have" gebildet, auch bei den Verben, die im Deutschen mit "sein" verwendet werden: Tom has come. (Tom ist gekommen.) – Where have you been? (Wo bist du gewesen?) (ebenso:) arrive, drive, run, walk, leave, swim, jump etc.
Beachten Sie, daß bei "go" auch "be" möglich ist: be gone = etw./jmd. ist nicht mehr da (= Zustand): When I came back, my bicycle was gone. (aber:) Peter has just gone home. "have/be finished": kein Bedeutungsunterschied, wenn kein Objekt folgt: Wait a minute, we have/are nearly finished. (... wir sind fast fertig.) – "be finished" bedeutet auch "be very tired": I have had a very busy day, I'm completely finished. – (aber nur:) Have you finished reading the book?

⁶ (aber:) Did you see "Hamlet"? (= Did you see the production on TV/at the theatre last night?)
Das Present Perfect wird nicht verwendet, wenn man an einen bestimmten Zeitpunkt in der Vergangenheit denkt, selbst wenn man ihn nicht direkt erwähnt.

L 2.3.1.

Der Bezug zur Gegenwart wird häufig hervorgehoben durch Zeitbestimmungen wie: *so far/up to now/until now/till now/as yet/*(vorwiegend Fachsprache:) *hitherto* bisher, bis jetzt; *to this day/up* (oder: *down) to the present (day)/to date* bis zum heutigen Tag; *already* (vorzugsweise in bejahenden Sätzen)/*yet* (in Fragesätzen, nachgestellt) schon; *not yet* noch nicht; *just* gerade, soeben; *only just*[7] gerade erst; *ever*[8] (in Fragesätzen) schon einmal, jemals; *never*[8] niemals; *these three (four etc) days/weeks etc* in den letzten drei (vier usw.) Tagen/Wochen usw.; *before*[9] schon früher; *lately/recently*[10] in letzter Zeit.

In Verbindung mit diesen Zeitbestimmungen findet sich die einfache Form des Perfekts häufiger als die Verlaufsform.

They have not contacted me so far. – I have already written to Tom. – Have you phoned Eve yet? – We haven't asked Jim yet[11]. – Jack has just left. – Have you ever been abroad? – Have you talked to Tom lately? – I have seen/I've been seeing Liz a lot recently/lately. – It has rained/It has been raining most of the time recently.

Das Present Perfect ist auch möglich bei *today, this morning/afternoon/week/month/year/summer etc.*

Bei *this morning/afternoon, this spring/summer/autumn/winter* wird das Present Perfect nur verwendet, wenn der genannte Zeitabschnitt noch nicht vorüber ist, sonst steht das Präteritum.

Mary has phoned this morning. (It's 11 a.m. now.) (aber:) Mary phoned this morning. (It's 3 p.m. now.)

Bei *today, this week/month/year* wird mit dem *Present Perfect* ausgedrückt, daß offen bleibt, wann oder wie oft innerhalb des **noch nicht** abgeschlossenen Zeitraums der Vorgang sich ereignet hat; das Präteritum deutet an, daß bekannt ist, wann etwas geschehen ist oder geschehen sein könnte.

Have you seen Lucy today? (= at *any* time today)
Did you see Lucy today? (= It's afternoon now and you want to know if the speaker met her in the morning.)

Anmerkung 1

Wird ohne nähere Zeitbestimmung in einer Gesprächssituation nach etwas gefragt, das jemand erlebt hat, so stehen Frage und Antwort oft im *Present Perfect,* die sich anschließende Unterhaltung geht dann im *Past Tense* weiter (a). Wird etwas im Perfekt berichtet, so stehen Ergänzungen oder sich anschließende Fragen oft im Präteritum (b).

'Where have you been?' – 'I have been to the cinema.' – 'Did you like the film?' – 'Yes, it was rather good.' (a)

---

[7] (aber:) just now = "gerade" mit Präteritum: Tom came just now. Im AE steht auch bei "just" meist das Präteritum.
[8] Auch mit Past Tense: Did you ever hear this word? – I never spoke to Iris.
[9] Present Perfect bei Bezug zur Gegenwart: I think we have met before. – Past Perfect bei Vergangenheitsbezug: When I saw Eve I knew I had seen her before.
[10] Mit Past Tense verweisen "recently" und "lately" auf einen Zeitpunkt innerhalb der letzten Zeit (= the other day: neulich, kürzlich): They moved into a new flat recently/lately.
[11] (oder:) We have not yet asked Jim. – We have not asked Jim yet.

We've spent our holidays at a small place where they didn't have a pub or café. (b)
'I've spent my holidays at the seaside this year.' – 'Did you stay at a hotel?' – 'No, I stayed in a caravan on a camping site.' (b)

Anmerkung 2
Auch aktuelle Informationen der Massenmedien werden häufig im *Present Perfect* mitgeteilt[12], wobei weitere Einzelheiten im *Past Tense* folgen.
Heavy rainfalls have flooded several roads. (= Several roads are under water now.) – The French Foreign Minister has arrived in Rome for talks with the Italian government. – One of the town's biggest banks has been robbed. The burglars cracked several safes and stole nearly £30,000. The police arrived too late on the scene.

Anmerkung 3
Nicht immer ist bei Verwendung des *Present Perfect* eine direkte Auswirkung auf die Gegenwart eindeutig gegeben, z. B. im Zusammenhang mit Häufigkeitsadverbien wie *often, seldom, sometimes, once, twice, three times* usw. Eine sich anschließende Frage oder eine Ergänzung steht dann meist im *Past Tense*.
We have been to Bulgaria several times.
I have talked to her often. (= I can talk to her again.) (aber:) I talked to her often. (= I can't talk to her again.)
We have visited the Tretyakov Gallery twice, it was very impressive each time. (aber:) I visited …, when I was in Moscow.

Anmerkung 4
Beachten Sie: This is the first/second etc time (that) I have been to Hungary. (Es ist das erste/zweite etc. Mal, daß ich in Ungarn bin.)

2.3.2. Mit *Present Perfect Continuous* und *Present Perfect Simple* kann ausgedrückt werden, daß etwas, das in der Vergangenheit begonnen hat, bis zum gegenwärtigen Zeitpunkt geschehen ist bzw. kurz zuvor beendet wurde.
We have been thinking/We have thought about your proposal, we think it is rather good. – I must have a break, I have been working/I have worked very hard. – We know Tom's opinion, we have been talking/have talked to him.

Besonders durch die Verlaufsform kann ausgedrückt werden, daß ein kürzerer, nicht unterbrochener Vorgang gerade zu Ende gegangen ist (a) oder zu Ende geht (b), außerdem, daß etwas über den gegenwärtigen Zeitpunkt hinaus weiter andauern kann (c) (vor allem in Verbindung mit *for, since, how long* – s. 2.3.3.).
Die einfache Form dagegen wird oft verwendet, wenn etwas, das zum gegenwärtigen Zeitpunkt schon abgeschlossen ist (d) oder bis dahin andauert (e), wiederholt oder mit Unterbrechungen stattgefunden hat.
Sorry, my trousers are dirty, I've been cleaning my car. (a)
I think I've been waiting long enough, I'll go now. (b)
I have been reading your article but I haven't finished it yet. (c) (aber:) I've read your book; I finished it yesterday.

---
[12] Im AE wird Past Simple verwendet.

We have discussed the problem several times, we won't discuss it again. (d) – We have checked most of the results until now. (e)

Beachten Sie den Unterschied zwischen unterbrochener und kontinuierlicher Tätigkeit:
I have written four letters this afternoon. (aber:) I have been writing letters this afternoon.

2.3.3. Die Beziehung zwischen Vergangenheit und Gegenwart kann besonders verdeutlicht werden durch *for/since* = seit; *how long* = wie lange schon; (weniger oft:) *since when* = seit wann. Mit *for*[13] wird die Zeitspanne zwischen Vergangenem und Gegenwärtigem ausgedrückt; *since* verweist auf den Zeitpunkt, zu dem ein Vorgang begonnen hat. Das *Present Perfect* bringt dabei zum Ausdruck, daß etwas in der Vergangenheit begonnen hat und noch andauert.[14] Sehr häufig wird hier die Verlaufsform verwendet.[15] Bei Verben, die keine Tätigkeit bezeichnen, z. B. *know, like, understand* usw. (s. Seite 14f.), ist nur das *Present Perfect Simple* möglich. Im Deutschen steht im bejahenden Aussagesatz und in der Frage meist das Präsens.

'How long have you been working in this factory?' – 'I have been working here for three years/since 1980.' ('Wie lange arbeitest du schon in diesem Betrieb?' – 'Ich arbeite (schon) seit drei Jahren/seit 1980 hier.')
'How long has Bob been abroad?' – 'He has been abroad for two months (now)/since Easter.' ('Wie lange ist Bob schon im Ausland?' – 'Er ist seit zwei Monaten/seit Ostern im Ausland.')
'How long has Rita been studying?' – 'She has been studying for five terms/since last year.'
'How long have they been living/have they lived in Berlin?' – 'They have been living/They have lived there for nearly five years.'
'How long has Rose been married?' – 'She has been married since May.'
Nora hasn't written to Tom for some months. – I have had my new car for some days/since Tuesday.[16] – Fred has known his wife since he was a student. – Jim has loved Liz since he has known her. = ... as long as he has known her.[17] (... seitdem er sie kennt.)

---

[13] "for" entfällt auch manchmal: Leo has been with us three days. – I have been here a fortnight.
[14] Gelegentlich kann der Vorgang auch kurz vor dem Zeitpunkt des Sprechens zum Abschluß gekommen sein: We haven't met for ages, how nice to see you again. – I have been waiting for more than an hour, I'm glad you are here now. – (aber:) I have been waiting for more than an hour, and she still hasn't come.
[15] Die einfache Form des Present Perfect (mit oder ohne "for, since, how long") beschreibt oft Situationen, die sich über einen langen Zeitraum erstrecken: The city hall has stood here since the 15th century.
[16] "have" im Sinne von "own, possess" (besitzen) nur mit Present Perfect Simple. "have" in feststehenden Wendungen (1.1.4.) ist auch mit Present Perfect Continuous möglich: We've been having a lot of fun since Tom came. (Wir haben viel Spaß gehabt, seit Tom kam.)
[17] Ein durch "since" oder "as long as" eingeleiteter Nebensatz steht auch im Present Perfect, wenn sich die beschriebene Handlung bis in die Gegenwart erstreckt.

Daß etwas noch andauert, kann auch durch *always* (schon immer); *all the time*; *all my life* usw. ausgedrückt werden.
I have always liked Sheila. (Ich mag Sheila schon immer.)

2.3.4. Beachten Sie folgende Gegenüberstellung von **Present Perfect** und *Past*:
He has lived here for many years. (= He still lives here.) (aber:) He lived here for many years. (= He doesn't live here any more.)
Dr Turner has been a university teacher for 10 years (and he still is). (aber:) Dr Turner was a university teacher for 20 years (and now he has been pensioned).
How long has Jane been ill? (= She is still ill.) (aber:) How long was Jane ill? (= She isn't ill any more.)
John has always helped us (and he still helps us). (aber:) John always helped us when we asked him.
They have been talking for hours (and they are still talking). (aber:) They were talking for hours last night.

2.4. The Past Perfect Tense – Das Plusquamperfekt

Mit dem **Plusquamperfekt** wird etwas ausgedrückt, das schon stattgefunden hatte, ehe etwas anderes geschah.
It had been raining before we started on our excursion. (Es hatte geregnet, ehe wir zu unserer Exkursion aufbrachen.) – We met our foreign friends for the first time last summer, but we had been exchanging letters with them before. (Wir trafen unsere ausländischen Freunde vorigen Sommer zum ersten Mal, aber wir hatten vorher schon mit ihnen korrespondiert.)

Das *Simple Past Perfect* wird zuweilen auch ohne direkten Bezug zu einem anderen Vorgang verwendet.
I had left my umbrella in the tram.

Häufig findet sich das *Past Perfect* mit *after* nachdem; *before* ehe, bevor, zuvor, vorher; *when* als, nachdem; *once* sobald, nachdem; *as soon as* sobald; *until/till/by*[18] bis; *by the time (that)* bis zu der Zeit als; *by that time* bis dahin.
After we had finished our work, we went to a restaurant.[19] – I had been watching TV before you came. – We had not seen Glen before. – Once we had found the mistake it was easy to solve the problem. – By eight o'clock they had reached an agreement. – By the time (that) the police arrived the bank robbers had already got away.
Im Plusquamperfekt werden die einfache Form und die Verlaufsform oft ohne Unterschied verwendet (a). Bei der **einfachen Form** liegt der Nachdruck mehr auf dem

---

[18] "until" und "till" werden verwendet, wenn über etwas gesprochen wird, das bis zu einem bestimmten Zeitpunkt dauerte. "by" wird verwendet, wenn davon die Rede ist, daß etwas zu oder vor einem bestimmten Zeitpunkt stattgefunden hat (= not later than): I had waited until four o'clock, but Lucy didn't turn up. – By twelve o'clock we had finished the experiment.

[19] Oder auch: We finished our work, and then we went to a restaurant.

Ergebnis der Handlung (b); mit der **Verlaufsform** kann zum Ausdruck gebracht werden, daß etwas eine Zeitlang ohne Unterbrechung stattgefunden hatte, ehe etwas anderes geschah (c).
We had been working/We had worked before the TV show began. (a) – Before I gave the lecture I had read lots of books on the subject. (b) – We had been waiting for twenty minutes when the bus came at last. (c).

2.5. The Future – Das Futur

Wenn etwas ausgedrückt werden soll, das in der Zukunft stattfinden wird oder beabsichtigt ist, gibt es folgende Möglichkeiten:
– I think my friend will visit me this weekend. (*shall/will*-Futur)
– My friend is going to visit us soon. (*be going to*-Konstruktion)
– My friend is visiting me tonight. (*Present Continuous*)
– Will your friend be visiting you this weekend? (*Future Continuous*)
– The Leipzig Fair starts next Sunday. (*Present Simple*).

2.5.1. *going to – will/shall*

2.5.1.1. In vielen Fällen kann sowohl *shall/will* als auch *going to* verwendet werden, dabei ist *going to* die in der Umgangssprache bevorzugte Form.
I am going to ring you up tomorrow./I shall ring you up tomorrow. – Are you going to take part in the conference?/Will you take part in the conference? – These machines will be replaced by new ones./These machines are going to be replaced ...

Doch gibt es auch Unterschiede in der Anwendung von *will/shall* und *going to*:

2.5.1.2. Mit *will/shall* kann etwas ausgedrückt werden, das unabhängig vom Willen oder Einfluß des Sprechenden geschehen wird (a). Deshalb findet sich diese Form häufig in der Fachsprache (b) und in Mitteilungen der Massenmedien (c).
Our train will arrive in Prague at 10.33. (a) – Betty will be thirty next month. (a) – The meeting won't take long. (a)
The new process will permit a considerable increase in labour productivity. (b) – Completely new problems will be solved by future generations of computers. (b)
The foreign ministers of the two countries will sign the treaty tomorrow. (c) – A collection of Picasso's early paintings will be shown in the Dresden Art Gallery from July to October. (c)

Andererseits wird mit dem *will/shall*-Futur häufig eine subjektive Reaktion – Gefühl, Wunsch, Erkenntnis – zum Ausdruck gebracht, z. B. bei *be glad/pleased, be happy, be surprised, be astonished; want/wish; know, understand, recognize.*
I'll be glad to meet Ruth again. – I think Bob will want to read the book. – Tomorrow we shall know more.

Steht ein Konditional- oder Temporalsatz im Präsens (oder Perfekt), dann wird im Hauptsatz meist das *shall/will*-Futur verwendet.
If we hurry up we'll catch the train. – Hugh will inform you as soon as the results of the tests are known. – I shall wait until you have finished your work.

Mit *shall/will* wird eine spontan entstandene Absicht oder eine Reaktion auf eine bestimmte Situation ausgedrückt.[20]
'Somebody is ringing, I'll[21] look who it is.'
'Wait a moment, we'll come with you.'
'It has begun to rain, I'll give you my umbrella.'
'Where's my watch?' – 'It's in the living room; I'll get it for you.'

2.5.1.3. Mit *going to* wird neben dem Hinweis auf die Zukunft eine Absicht ausgedrückt. Meist handelt es sich dabei um einen Entschluß, der schon vor der Gesprächssituation gefaßt worden ist.
John has sold his motorbike because he is going to buy a car. (..., weil er sich ein Auto kaufen wird/will.) – I am not going to talk to Jim about this matter again.[22]
'Why are you decorating the room?' – 'We are going to give a party.'
I am going to buy a new TV set. (= a decision already taken) (aber:) 'This is a nice TV set, I'll take it.' (= a decision taken at the moment of speaking)
Beachten Sie auch den Unterschied zwischen *going to* und *want/wish to*:
Glen is going to build a house. (= He wants to build a house, and it is quite certain that he will do it.)
Glen wants to build a house. (= It is his wish to build a house, but it is still uncertain if he can do it.)

2.5.1.4. Wird eine Voraussage bzw. eine Überzeugung, das etwas geschieht, zum Ausdruck gebracht, so steht *going to* oder auch das *will/shall*-Futur.
Don't forget your umbrella; I think it's going to rain. (oder:) Don't forget your umbrella; I think it will rain.
I am afraid our team is not going to win the match. (oder:) I am afraid our team will not win the match.

2.5.1.5. *was/were going to* bezeichnet einen Vorgang, der zu einem bestimmten Zeitpunkt der Vergangenheit beabsichtigt war oder bevorstand, aber noch nicht begonnen hatte. (= *Future in the Past*)
I was going to have lunch when Tom came. (Ich wollte gerade zu Mittag essen, ...) – You were going to change your job, when I talked to you last time. (Du wolltest doch deine Arbeitsstelle wechseln, als ...) – Bob knew that something was going to happen that might be very important for his future life. (Bob wußte, daß etwas geschehen würde, das möglicherweise für sein künftiges Leben sehr wichtig sein könnte.)

2.5.2. Das *Present Continuous* wird verwendet, um eine bevorstehende Handlung darzustellen, die bereits feststeht oder sehr wahrscheinlich ist, bzw. um

---

[20] Bei einem Versprechen ist neben "will/shall" auch "going to" möglich: I promise I'll help Liz. (oder:) I promise I'm going to help Liz. – I promise I won't do it again. (oder:) I promise I'm not going to do it again.
[21] Meist Kurzform oder auch "will". "shall" ist hier und in den folgenden Sätzen nicht üblich.
[22] Auch die Verlaufsform ist mit "going to" möglich: I think they are going to be talking for hours.

L 2.5.3.

nach einer Absicht zu fragen. Der Zeitpunkt liegt gewöhnlich in der nahen Zukunft und ist meist angegeben. Diese Form ist typisch für die Umgangssprache und findet sich vor allem bei Verben, die eine Tätigkeit ausdrücken.[23]
We are seeing her tomorrow. – I am probably going on a business trip next week. 'What are you doing tonight?' – 'We're going to the theatre.'

2.5.3. Mit dem *Future Continuous* wird etwas ausgedrückt, das zu einem Zeitpunkt oder innerhalb einer bestimmten Zeitspanne der Zukunft stattfinden wird.[24] Meist ist eine Zeitbestimmung angegeben.
Our guest-lecturer will be repeating his paper at the same time next Monday. – I suggest that we meet tomorrow, because I shall be working tonight. – Who will be watering your flowers when you are on holiday?

In Fragesätzen stellt die Verlaufsform des Futurs eine Möglichkeit dar, sich in sehr höflicher Form nach der Absicht des Gesprächspartners (oder anderer Personen) zu erkundigen.
Will you be staying here long? – Where will you be spending the weekend? – When will John be going abroad?

2.5.4. Bei offiziellen Bekanntmachungen und Ankündigungen von Reisen, Veranstaltungen usw. kann die **einfache Form des Präsens** verwendet werden.
On Friday the Swedish Foreign Minister returns home from a three-day visit to Italy. – The summer holidays begin next week. – A relief train (Entlastungszug) to Berlin leaves at 10.30 am today.

Die einfache Form des Präsens steht in Nebensätzen nach Konjunktionen, die eine Zeit oder Bedingung angeben.
We'll be happy when the exam is over. – We'll inform Tom if we see him. – I'll phone you as soon as Bob comes.

2.5.5. Vor allem im Stil der Massenmedien wird bei der Ankündigung von bevorstehenden offiziellen Ereignissen oft *be* + **Infinitiv** verwendet.
Representatives of the Soviet Union and the United States are to resume their disarmament talks in Geneva next week.

2.5.6. Die Formen *be about to* sowie *be on the point/verge of* (s. auch: 8.2.1.3.) bezeichnen eine vom Standpunkt der Gegenwart oder Vergangenheit aus unmittelbar bevorstehende Handlung.
Get up, we are about to have breakfast. (Steh auf, wir wollen gleich frühstücken.) –

---

[23] Besteht kaum ein Unterschied zwischen einem momentan oder bereits vorher getroffenen Entschluß, so können "will/shall"-Futur, die "going to"-Form oder Present Continuous verwendet werden: I think I'll go/I'm going to go/I'm going to the cinema tonight.
[24] Oft ist auch das Present Continuous möglich. Present Continuous oder Future Continuous wird verwendet, wenn etwas schon festgelegt ist (a), Future Continuous auch, wenn etwas ohne besondere Vereinbarung geschehen wird (b): John is giving/will be giving a party on Saturday. (a) – I can give Jack the book, I'll be meeting him at the pub on Saturday evening. (b) (= He is always there on Saturday evenings.)

Eve was on the point of leaving, when we arrived. (Eve wollte gerade weggehen, als wir kamen.)

be likely to kann zum Ausdruck bringen, daß etwas wahrscheinlich geschehen wird, ***be certain/sure to***, daß etwas mit Bestimmtheit zu erwarten ist.
I am likely to be on a business trip on Friday. (= I'll probably be on a business trip ...) – Bill is not likely/Bill is unlikely to ask us for support. (= Probably Bill won't ask us ...) – You are certain/sure to enjoy this film. (= You will certainly enjoy this film.)

2.6. The Future Perfect – Das Futur II

Das *Future Perfect* bezeichnet einen Vorgang, der zu einem bestimmten Zeitpunkt der Zukunft abgeschlossen sein wird oder noch andauern kann. Die Verlaufsform im *Future Perfect* verweist darauf, daß die Handlung weiter andauern wird.

Das *Future Perfect* steht immer in Verbindung mit einer Zeitbestimmung, z. B.: ***by the end of*** bis Ende; ***by ... o'clock*** bis ... Uhr; ***by Monday/Tuesday etc*** bis Montag/Dienstag usw.; ***by the time (that)*** bis; ***in (two ...) weeks'/months'/years' time*** in (zwei ...) Wochen/Monaten/Jahren – auch im Zusammenhang mit einem Temporalsatz.
We shall have analyzed the results of these tests by the end of the week. – Jack says he will have finished his work by Saturday. – I hope we shall have completed the translation by the time (that) Bob comes. – We'll have settled the matter before you come back. – Roy hopes he will have finished his doctoral thesis in three years' time. – On May 12th our parents will have been married for 30 years.
By the end of this year Mr King will have been teaching at the university for 20 years. (Am Ende dieses Jahres unterrichtet Mr King bereits 20 Jahre an der Universität.)

Die einfache Form des *Future Perfect* kann auch eine auf die Gegenwart bezogene Erwartung oder Annahme zum Ausdruck bringen, oft in Verbindung mit ***by now/meanwhile/in the meantime*** (inzwischen).
I'm sure you will have noticed by now that you have made a mistake. – I think John will have informed Mike in the meantime.

3. The Conditional – Der Konditional

3.1. Es gibt **zwei Formen** des Konditionals:

Conditional Present (**Konditional I**): I would[1] ask her.
Conditional Perfect (**Konditional II**): I would[1] have asked her.

Das *Conditional Present* bezieht die Aussage auf die **Gegenwart** oder **Zukunft**[2] (a), das *Conditional Perfect* auf die **Vergangenheit** (b).

---

[1] In der 1.Pers. Sing. sind "should" und "would" möglich, doch findet sich "would" häufiger als "should"; kontrahierte Form: "-'d".
[2] Bei Formen wie "I would like/prefer/love to" handelt es sich nicht um eine Bedingungs-

L 3.2.

It would be better to discuss this matter at once. (a) (Es wäre besser, die Angelegenheit sofort zu besprechen.) – I would wait until Bob comes. (a) (Ich würde warten, bis Bob kommt.)
I am sure Tom would have helped us. (b) (Tom hätte uns sicher geholfen.) – It would have taken much longer to solve this problem without your help. (b) (Ohne deine Hilfe hätte es viel länger gedauert, dieses Problem zu lösen.)

Um einer Feststellung besonderen Nachdruck zu verleihen, kann auch **be + -ing** (Verlaufsform) verwendet werden. (s. 13.2.)
I thought you would be staying another week. (Ich dachte, du würdest doch noch eine Woche bleiben.)
If you hadn't helped me I'd have been having trouble translating this text. (Wenn du mir nicht geholfen hättest, wäre es mir wirklich schwer gefallen, diesen Text zu übersetzen.)

3.2. Conditional Clauses – Konditionalsätze

Konstruktionen mit Konditionalsätzen werden verwendet, um auszudrücken, daß unter bestimmten Bedingungen etwas geschehen kann (a), geschehen könnte, aber vom Sprechenden für nicht sehr wahrscheinlich gehalten wird (b), oder daß etwas nicht geschehen ist (c). Der Bedingungssatz kann vor dem Hauptsatz stehen oder diesem folgen.
If I have time I shall go out tonight. (a = Typ I)
If I had time I would go out tonight. (b = Typ II)
If I had had time I would have gone out. (c = Typ III)

Bedingungssätze werden eingeleitet durch:
if[3] wenn, falls; *if not/unless* wenn nicht; *provided (that)/providing (that)/on condition that* vorausgesetzt, daß; *in case (that)*[4] falls; *supposing (that)* angenommen, daß; *even if* selbst wenn.

---

form im eigentlichen Sinne, sondern es wird ein Wunsch zum Ausdruck gebracht. Das trifft auch zu bei "would you mind …?" (s. 8.3.), "I would ask / request you; I would suggest / propose; I would say (think, recommend etc)", um eine Bitte, einen Vorschlag, einen Hinweis oder eine Meinung höflich zu formulieren. I would like to see this film. – Would you like another cup of tea? – I'd have liked to study architecture. (oder:) I'd have liked to have studied architecture. (oder:) I'd like to have studied architecture.
I would prefer to stay at home. – Would you prefer white wine or champagne? – I would have preferred to have a private talk with Eve.
'Will you have a look at these photos?' – 'I'd love to.'
Would you mind closing the door? (= Would you be kind enough to close the door?) – I would ask you to be punctual. – We would suggest that you come tomorrow. – I would say that this is a good proposal.

[3] Beachten Sie: "if" wird verwendet, um auszudrücken, daß etwas geschehen kann, "when" dagegen, daß etwas zu einem gewissen Zeitpunkt geschehen wird: If I see her, I shall ask her. (= Provided that I see her …) – When I see her I shall ask her. (= I'll see her and then I'll ask her.)
"Unless" steht häufig bei Warnung vor möglichen Konsequenzen: Unless we take a taxi we'll be late.

3.2.1. Typ I: Nebensatz: **Präsens** – Hauptsatz: **Futur**
If we miss the bus we shall be late.

Etwas wird geschehen, wenn die genannte Bedingung erfüllt wird; daß sie erfüllt wird, ist durchaus möglich.
If I see Jim I shall inform him about our agreement. – You won't catch the train if you don't hurry up/unless you hurry up. – We shall sign the contract provided the terms (Bedingungen) are favourable. – Gary will buy the yacht even if it is very expensive. – If[4] I have time I'll read the book tomorrow.

3.2.2. Typ II: Nebensatz: **Präteritum** – Hauptsatz: **Konditional I**
If we missed the bus we would be late.

Etwas wird geschehen, falls die genannte Bedingung erfüllt werden sollte. Daß sie erfüllt wird, ist möglich, oft nicht sehr wahrscheinlich oder auch unmöglich.
If we repeated the test we would perhaps get better results. (Wenn wir den Versuch wiederholten, würden wir vielleicht bessere Ergebnisse erhalten.)
If Mark gave me the book today I would return it tomorrow. (Wenn Mark mir das Buch heute gäbe, würde ich es morgen zurückgeben.)
I would write to Tom if I knew his address. (Ich würde Tom schreiben, wenn ich seine Adresse wüßte.)

Außerdem kann eine Wunschvorstellung (a), ein konkreter Wunsch (b) oder ein Vorschlag (c) zum Ausdruck gebracht werden.
If I had a car I would save a lot of time. (a) (Wenn ich ein Auto hätte, würde ich viel Zeit sparen.) – We would be glad if you came. (b) (Wir würden uns freuen, wenn du kämst.) – Would it be convenient if I came tomorrow? (c) (Würde es passen, wenn ich morgen komme?)

Anstelle von *I/he/she/it was* steht vor allem im formalen Stil oft *I/he/she/it were*.
If I was/were you I should accept his offer. (An deiner Stelle würde ich sein Angebot annehmen.)

3.2.3. Typ III: Nebensatz: **Plusquamperfekt** – Hauptsatz: **Konditional II**
If we had missed the bus we would have been late.

Etwas ist nicht geschehen, da die genannte Bedingung nicht erfüllt worden ist.
I would have met you at the station if you had sent me a telegram. (Ich hätte dich am Bahnhof abgeholt, wenn du mir ein Telegramm geschickt hättest.) – We don't know what would have happened if we had had a breakdown. (Wir wissen nicht, was geschehen wäre, wenn wir eine Panne gehabt hätten.)

---

[4] "in case" und "if" sind nicht austauschbar. "if" gibt ein mögliches Ereignis an, auf das reagiert werden kann, "in case" dagegen ein mögliches Ereignis, für das etwas im voraus getan werden kann. If there is a train delay we shall meet immediately before the performance begins. – I suggest that we meet immediately before the performance begins in case there is a train delay.

3.3. Zu den drei Grundtypen ergeben sich mehrere Variationsmöglichkeiten:

3.3.1. Zu Typ I:
if-Satz: Präsens – Hauptsatz: Präsens
Bei allgemeingültigen Feststellungen oder gewohnheitsmäßigen Reaktionen:
If you heat ice it melts. – If (= whenever) we ask him he usually helps us.

if-Satz: Präsens – Hauptsatz: Imperativ
If you are cold take my sweater.

if-Satz: Präsens – Hauptsatz: *can, may/might, must, should/ought to, needn't* + Infinitiv Präsens
If we don't want to be late we should go now. – If you wait a little longer you may/might talk to him.

if-Satz: *can* etc – Hauptsatz: Präsens, Futur
If I can't come I shall let you know in time.

if-Satz: *can* etc – Hauptsatz: *can* etc
If you can't come you needn't inform us.

if-Satz: *should*[5] – Hauptsatz: Präsens, Futur, Imperativ; *can* etc.
Wenn etwas möglich, aber nicht sehr wahrscheinlich ist.
If we should miss the train, we shan't/can't be there before midnight. (Falls wir den Zug verpassen sollten, ...) – If anybody should phone, tell them I'll be back tomorrow.

if-Satz: *will* (häufig: *'ll*)/ *would* – Hauptsatz: Futur oder *can* etc.
Nur bei höflicher Aufforderung oder Bitte um Zustimmung.[6]
If you'll make the tea I'll prepare some sandwiches. (= If you are ready to make the tea I'll ...) (Wenn du bitte den Tee kochst ...)
If you will/would wait a moment I'll look up Tom's telephone number. (= If you don't mind waiting a moment, I'll ...) (Wenn Sie bitte einen Augenblick warten wollen, ...)

3.3.2. Zu Typ II:
if-Satz: *would* – Hauptsatz: Konditional I
Nur zum Ausdruck einer höflichen Bitte oder Aufforderung.
If you would let me know your decision soon, I'd be very grateful. (Wenn Sie mir bald Ihre Entscheidung mitteilen würden, wäre ich ...)

if-Satz: *were to* – Hauptsatz: Konditional I
Wenn etwas möglich, aber nicht sehr wahrscheinlich ist.

---

[5] Hier keine Kurzform möglich.
[6] Im if-Satz können "will" und "would" auch bei der indirekten Rede verwendet werden, wenn "if" die Bedeutung von "whether" (= ob) hat. I don't know if they will come tomorrow. – Can you tell me if it would be more convenient to go by car or to take the train?

If we were to miss the train, we wouldn't arrive before midnight. (Falls wir den Zug verpassen sollten, ...)

if-Satz: Präteritum – Hauptsatz: *could, might, should/ought to* + Infinitiv Präsens
He could/might help us if he were here. – If you asked her she might go out with you. – You should/ought to forgive Bob if he apologized to you.

if-Satz: *could, should* – Hauptsatz: Konditional I
If I couldn't come I would tell you in time. (Wenn ich nicht kommen könnte, ...) – I would inform you if I should be prevented. (..., wenn ich verhindert sein sollte.)

3.3.3.   Zu Typ III:

if-Satz: Plusquamperfekt – Hauptsatz: *could/might, should/ought to* + Infinitiv Perfekt
You could have avoided these mistakes if you had been more careful. (Du hättest diese Fehler vermeiden können, ...) – You should/ought to have waited even if it had got very late. (Du hättest warten sollen, selbst wenn es sehr spät geworden wäre.)

3.3.4.   Zu Typ II + III:

if-Satz: Plusquamperfekt – Hauptsatz: Konditional I
Wenn zum Ausdruck gebracht wird, daß etwas möglich wäre, falls die im *if*-Satz genannte Bedingung erfüllt worden wäre.
If you had taken the medicine you would probably feel better now. – If we had bought a map we would know which route to take.

3.3.5.   Zu Typ I, II + III: *if only*

Soll ein Wunsch oder eine Hoffnung zum Ausdruck gebracht werden, daß etwas geschehen möge, so kann *if only* mit folgendem Präsens (gelegentlich auch Futur) verwendet werden.
If only he is punctual. (= I do hope he will be punctual.) (Hoffentlich ist er pünktlich.)
If only she will listen to reason. (= We do hope she will listen to reason.) (Hoffentlich ist sie einsichtig.)

Wird bedauert, daß etwas geschieht (a) oder geschehen ist (b), so steht *if only* mit folgendem Präteritum (a) bzw. Plusquamperfekt (b).
If only she didn't talk so much. (a) (Wenn sie nur nicht so viel reden würde.) – If only you had told the truth. (b) (Wenn du doch nur die Wahrheit gesagt hättest.)

Mit *if only* + *would* kann ein Wunsch zum Ausdruck gebracht werden, daß etwas geschieht bzw. nicht geschehen soll.
If only it would stop snowing. (Wenn es doch aufhören wollte zu schneien.) – If only he wouldn't drink so much. (Wenn er nur nicht so viel trinken würde.)

3.4.   Zuweilen wird der Bedingungssatz nicht durch *if* eingeleitet, dann steht das Hilfsverb vor dem Subjekt, d. h. es ergibt sich Inversion (s. 13.5.1.). Diese

Inversion findet sich vor allem mit *should, were* (nicht: *was*) und beim **Plusquamperfekt**.
Should something unforeseen happen I shall inform you. (= If something unforeseen should happen ...) (Sollte etwas Unvorhergesehenes geschehen, werde ich dich informieren.)
Were the meeting to take place tomorrow I would not be able to attend it. (= If the meeting were to take place ...) (Sollte die Versammlung morgen stattfinden, könnte ich sie nicht besuchen.)
Had we known all the facts it would have been easier for us to make a decision. (= If we had known ...) (Wenn wir alle Fakten gekannt hätten, wäre es einfacher gewesen, eine Entscheidung zu treffen.)

3.5.   Beachten Sie, daß *should* in der 1. Pers. Sing. und Plur. je nach Absicht des Sprechenden konditionale Bedeutung haben kann (a) oder als Modalverb zum Ausdruck bringt, daß etwas geschehen sollte oder müßte (b). Der folgende Satz enthält die doppelte Möglichkeit:
If you rang me up tonight, I should (= would) be able to tell you more details. (a) (..., würde ich dir mehr Einzelheiten mitteilen können.)
If you rang me up tonight, I should (= ought to) be able to tell you more details. (b) (... müßte ich eigentlich in der Lage sein ...)

Meist ergibt der Kontext, ob *should* als Konditionalform oder als Modalverb anzusehen ist.
We should go to the theatre tonight if we had tickets. (= We would go ...) (Wir würden ... gehen)
We should go to the theatre instead of watching TV. (= We had better go ...) (Wir sollten lieber ... gehen ...)
I should have gone to the theatre tonight if I had got a ticket. (= I would have gone ...) (Ich wäre ... gegangen ...)
I should have gone to the theatre instead of watching TV. (= I ought to have gone ...) (Ich hätte ... gehen sollen)

4.   The Passive Voice – Das Passiv

4.1.   Das **Passiv** wird gebildet durch (die entsprechende Form von)
be + Past Participle (+ *by* + Object).
Football is played all over the world. – The conference will be opened by the President of the Academy at 10 a.m.

Passivkonstruktionen sind im Englischen sehr häufig. Sie werden vor allem verwendet, wenn für die Aussage primär von Interesse ist, was getan wird bzw. mit einer Sache oder Person geschieht, nicht so sehr aber, durch wen oder wodurch es geschieht. Sie kommen häufig in der Fachsprache vor, vor allem wenn Prozesse oder Entwicklungen beschrieben werden.
Die Passivkonstruktion wird generell bevorzugt, wenn unerwähnt bleibt, wer oder

was die Handlung verursacht, d. h. im Aktivsatz würde ein Indefinitpronomen – z. B. *one, somebody, someone, people* (dt.: man) – stehen. Ist das, was den Vorgang auslöst – Person oder Sache – für die Information wichtig, so wird es durch *by* angeschlossen.
My umbrella has been stolen. (= Somebody has stolen my umbrella.) (Mein Regenschirm ist gestohlen worden.)
What is produced in this plant? (Was wird in diesem Betrieb hergestellt?)
The transistor came to be introduced after 1947. (Der Transistor wurde nach 1947 eingeführt.)
Plastics have been used since the early 1930s. (Plaste werden seit Anfang der dreißiger Jahre verwendet. / Man verwendet Plaste ...)
The results should be checked exactly. (Die Ergebnisse müßten genau überprüft werden.)
The radioactivity of uranium was discovered by Henri Becquerel. (Die Radioaktivität des Urans wurde von Henri Becquerel entdeckt.)
Lignite is won in open-cast mining. (Braunkohle wird im Tagebaubetrieb gewonnen.)

Im Passiv wird eine Aufforderung oder Anordnung weniger direkt oder persönlich formuliert als durch direkte Anrede mit Aktivsatz:
The car must be cleaned. (= *indirect order*) – You must clean the car. (= *direct order*)

4.2.   Im Englischen besteht eine Möglichkeit der Passivbildung, die vom Deutschen abweicht. Das gilt für Verben, die ein Objekt regieren, dem im Deutschen ein Dativobjekt entspricht. Solche Verben sind:
tell sagen, mitteilen; *approach* herantreten, herangehen an; *believe* glauben; *contradict* widersprechen; *follow* folgen, befolgen; *forbid* verbieten; *help/aid/assist* helfen; *obey* gehorchen, beachten; *oppose/resist* sich widersetzen; *pardon/forgive* verzeihen; *trust* vertrauen; etc.
I have been told that he is abroad. (Man hat mir gesagt, daß er im Ausland ist.)
We have not yet been approached in this matter. (Man ist in dieser Angelegenheit noch nicht an uns herangetreten.) – The lecture was followed by a lively discussion. (Dem Vortrag folgte eine lebhafte Diskussion.)
Zwei Passivkonstruktionen sind möglich bei Verben, die im Aktivsatz zwei Objekte regieren. Dazu gehören vor allem:
award (*a prize* etc) verleihen; *give* geben; *grant* gewähren; *hand* geben, überreichen; *lend* (*money* etc) leihen; *offer* anbieten; *pay* (*a sum* etc) zahlen; *promise* versprechen; *refuse/deny* verweigern; *save/spare* (*trouble* etc) ersparen; *send* schicken; *show* zeigen; *tell* erzählen, mitteilen; etc.
(Aktiv:)   They have offered him an interesting job.
(Passiv:) He has been offered an interesting job.
           An interesting job has been offered (to) him.
Die erste Variante ist die häufigere. (a) Nur wenn es hervorgehoben werden soll, erscheint das Sachobjekt als Subjekt der Passivkonstruktion. (b) Das Personalobjekt wird in diesem Falle mit **to**, als Personalpronomen auch **ohne** *to* angeschlossen.

L 4.3.

During our visit to Leningrad we were shown some of the beautiful castles in the vicinity of the town. (a) (Während unseres Besuches in Leningrad zeigte man uns einige der schönen Schlösser in der Nähe der Stadt.)
He will be awarded a prize for his invention. (a) (Ihm wird für seine Erfindung ein Preis verliehen.) – A special prize will be awarded to the winner of the competition. (b) (Der Sieger des Wettbewerbs wird mit einem Sonderpreis ausgezeichnet.)

4.3.   Bei Verben, die **unmittelbar mit einer Präposition** verbunden sind, findet sich ebenfalls eine vom Deutschen abweichende Passivkonstruktion. Die Präposition folgt auch im Passivsatz unmittelbar dem Verb. Beispiele sind u. a.:
account for erklären; *act (up)on* einwirken auf; *agree (up)on* sich einigen auf; *agree to* zustimmen; *attend to* sich kümmern um; bedienen; *come to/arrive at* erzielen, erreichen; *comment on* kommentieren; *comply with* erfüllen; *cope with* (etw.) bewältigen; *deal with* behandeln, sich beschäftigen mit; *dispense with/do without* auskommen ohne; *inquire into* untersuchen, erforschen; *insist (up)on* bestehen auf; *interfere with* sich einmischen in, stören; *keep to/adhere to/stick to* festhalten an; *look into* prüfen, untersuchen; *object to* sich wenden gegen; *provide against* Vorkehrungen treffen gegen; *provide for* Vorsorge treffen für, (etw.) vorsehen; *refer to* sich beziehen auf; *refer to sb/sth as* jmd./etw. bezeichnen als; *rely/depend (up)on* sich verlassen auf; *research into* erforschen; *send for* schicken nach; *speak about/of /to* sprechen über/von/mit; *talk about* sprechen von, sich unterhalten über; *tink of sb/sth as* halten für.
This matter must be talked about today. (Über diese Angelegenheit muß heute gesprochen werden.)
What topics will be dealt with at the conference? (Was für Themen werden auf der Konferenz behandelt?)
Can he be relied (up)on? (Kann man sich auf ihn verlassen?)
Their request should be complied with. (Man sollte ihre Bitte erfüllen.)
Eine analoge Konstruktion ist möglich bei den Verbindungen:

Verb + Adverb (*Phrasal Verbs*), z. B.:
allow for berücksichtigen; *bring about* bewirken, herbeiführen; *bring up* erziehen, (Probleme) aufwerfen; *carry on* fortsetzen; *carry out* durchführen; *close down* schließen; *cut down* verringern; *draw up* aufsetzen, -stellen; *fill in* ausfüllen; *give up* aufgeben; *go into* eingehen auf; *hand in* einreichen; *leave out* weglassen; *let sb down* jmd. im Stich lassen; *look after* sich kümmern um; *look through/go through* durchsehen; *look up* nachschlagen; *look (up)on sth/sb as* halten für; *make out (a prescription)* (ein Rezept) ausstellen; *mix up* verwechseln; *operate on* operieren; *pick up* aufgreifen, jmd. mitnehmen; *pull down* abreißen; *put forward* vortragen, unterbreiten; *put off* verschieben, jmd. hinhalten; *rule out* ausschließen, (Mißverständnis) ausräumen; *see to* sich kümmern um, untersuchen; *size up* einschätzen; *slow down* verlangsamen; *speed up* beschleunigen; *step up* steigern; *sum up* zusammenfassen; *switch/turn on* einschalten; *switch/turn off* ausschalten; *take up (a proposal)* (einen Vorschlag) aufgreifen; *turn down* ablehnen.
The meeting has been put off until next week. (Die Versammlung ist auf nächste Woche verschoben worden.) – The most important details should be summed up

once again. (Die wichtigsten Einzelheiten sollten noch einmal zusammengefaßt werden.) – Children of working women are looked after in crèches and kindergartens. (Die Kinder berufstätiger Frauen werden in Kinderkrippen und Kindergärten betreut.) – Different theories about the origin of the earth have been put forward throughout the centuries. (Verschiedene Theorien über den Ursprung der Erde sind im Laufe der Jahrhunderte aufgestellt worden.)

Verb + Adverb + Präposition, z. B.:
do away with abschaffen, beseitigen; *face up to (a problem)* sich (einem Problem) stellen; *get rid of* loswerden; *look down upon* herabsehen auf; *look forward to* sich freuen auf; *make up for* (Zeit) aufholen; *put up with* sich abfinden mit, dulden.
These outdated regulations should be done away with. (Diese veralteten Vorschriften sollte man abschaffen.) – The new situation has to be faced up to. (Man muß sich der neuen Situation stellen.)

Verb + Substantiv + Präposition, z. B.:
lose sight/track of aus den Augen verlieren; *make use of* Gebrauch machen von; *make a (great) fuss about* (viel) Aufhebens machen von; *make fun of* sich lustig machen über; *put an end/a stop to* etw. beenden; *take advantage of* ausnutzen; *take care of* sich kümmern um, verantwortlich sein für, pflegen; *take notice of* Kenntnis/Notiz nehmen von.
The new technique will soon be made use of. (Das neue Verfahren wird bald angewendet werden.) – This controversy should be put a stop to at once. (Diesen Streit sollte man sofort beenden.) – The details of the arrangement will be taken care of by our secretary. (Unsere Sekretärin wird sich um die Einzelheiten der Vereinbarung kümmern.)

Auch mit bestimmten Verbindungen **Verb + Präposition**, bei denen die Präposition nicht unmittelbar zum Verb gehört, ist ein Passiv möglich.
This house has not been lived in for some years. (Dieses Haus ist seit einigen Jahren nicht bewohnt.) – These glasses are quite new, they have not yet been drunk out of. (Diese Gläser sind ganz neu; es ist noch nicht daraus getrunken worden.)

4.4. Eine Passivkonstruktion mit *it* + *that*-Satz findet sich vor allem in Wendungen wie:
it has been agreed[1] es ist vereinbart worden; *it has been announced* es ist bekanntgegeben worden; *it has been arranged*[1]; *it is assumed/believed/thought*; *it is claimed* es wird behauptet; *it has been decided*[1]; *it has been demonstrated*; *it has been denied* man hat in Abrede gestellt; *it is/has been estimated* man schätzt; *it is expected*; *it is (to be) feared*; *it has been found*; *it is (to be) hoped*; *it has been pointed out* es ist darauf hingewiesen worden; *it has been proved* man hat bewiesen; *it has been reported*; *it is said*; *it has been shown* es hat sich gezeigt; *it has been stated*; *it can/may be taken for granted* es kann vorausgesetzt werden.

Besonders typisch für die Fachsprache sind Wendungen wie:
it should be added außerdem ist zu erwähnen; *it should be taken into consideration/account* man sollte in Betracht ziehen; *it should be noted* man sollte beachten; *it*

---
[1] Mit folgendem that-Satz oder Infinitiv.

L 4.5. 34

should/must be remembered man sollte/muß beachten; *it has been suggested* es ist darauf hingewiesen worden.
It is (to be) hoped that the remaining difficulties will be ruled out before long. (Es ist zu hoffen, daß die noch bestehenden Schwierigkeiten bald ausgeräumt werden.) – It has been estimated that the costs for the research project will amount to some $5,000. (Man hat geschätzt, daß die Kosten für das Forschungsprojekt ungefähr $ 5 000 betragen.)

4.5.   Auch im Passiv wird die **Verlaufsform** verwendet, um eine Handlung zu kennzeichnen, die zu einem bestimmten Zeitpunkt oder innerhalb einer bestimmten Zeitspanne stattfindet, sie ist hier aber auf Präsens und Präteritum beschränkt.
The new shopping centre is being designed by some architects from the Dresden University of Technology. (Das neue Einkaufszentrum wird von einigen Architekten der Technischen Universität Dresden entworfen.)
We could not visit the whole castle, because some of the rooms were being repapered. (Wir konnten nicht das gesamte Schloß besichtigen, weil einige Räume neu tapeziert wurden.)

4.5.1.   Um die Handlung vom Zustand abzugrenzen, wird die Verlaufsform verwendet.
The test was being finished the moment we arrived. (Der Versuch wurde gerade abgeschlossen, als wir kamen.) (aber:) The test was already finished when we arrived. (Der Versuch war schon beendet, als wir kamen.)
A new residential area is being built on the outskirts of our town. (Ein neues Wohngebiet wird zur Zeit am Rande unserer Stadt gebaut.) – (aber:) Most of the old houses in this part of the town are built of brick. (Die meisten alten Häuser in diesem Stadtteil sind aus Ziegeln gebaut.)

4.6.   Bei einigen Verben kann die Passivkonstruktion das Ergebnis der Handlung oder die Handlung selbst beschreiben, z. B.:
build; *break*; *close*; *complete*; *damage*; *destroy*; *equip/provide with* ausrüsten/versehen mit; *finish*; *hurt/injure*; *involve*; *prepare*; *open*; *shut*; *type*; *write*; *wound* etc.
The museum was closed. (Das Museum war/wurde geschlossen.) – When we arrived, the museum was closed. (Als wir ankamen, war das Museum geschlossen.) – The museum was closed by the municipal authorities for purposes of restoration. (Das Museum wurde von der Stadtverwaltung zwecks Restaurierung geschlossen.)
The vase is broken. (Die Vase ist zerbrochen.) – The vase was broken by my sister. (Die Vase wurde von meiner Schwester zerbrochen.)
The greater part of the town was destroyed after the earthquake. (Der größte Teil der Stadt war nach dem Erdbeben zerstört.) – The greater part of the town was destroyed by the earthquake. (Der größte Teil der Stadt wurde durch das Erdbeben zerstört.)
The letter is typed; you may sign it. (Der Brief ist geschrieben; Sie können ihn unterschreiben.) – The letter was typed by our secretary. (Der Brief wurde von unserer Sekretärin geschrieben.)

4.6.1. Um einen entstehenden Zustand von einem bereits bestehenden zu unterscheiden, wird in einigen Fällen **get**[2] + **Past Participle** verwendet, z. B.: *get excited/annoyed/confused/worried/frightened/involved/dressed*, sowie: *get engaged/married/divorced*.
Sue was very excited yesterday. She got excited when she read Peter's letter. (Sue war gestern sehr aufgeregt. Sie regte sich auf, als sie Peters Brief las.) – Mike is married. He got married last month. (Mike ist verheiratet. Er hat vorigen Monat geheiratet.)

4.6.2. Bei einigen Verben kann sowohl *get* als auch *be* verwendet werden, um eine Handlung auszudrücken, z. B.: *be/get broken, be/get damaged/destroyed, be/get caught, be/get injured/hurt/wounded, be/get killed, be/get hit, be/get invited, be/get bitten/stung*, etc.
Did you get invited / Were you invited to Eve's birthday party? (Bist du zu Eves Geburtstagsfeier eingeladen worden?)
The thief got/was caught by the police. (Der Dieb wurde von der Polizei gefaßt.)
How many people got/were injured in the accident? (... wurden ... verletzt?)

4.6.3. Beachten Sie die Bedeutungsunterschiede in Fällen, wo das Partizip wie ein Adjektiv verwendet wird, z. B.: *be known* bekannt sein, *become known* bekannt werden; *be acquainted with* bekannt sein mit, *become/get acquainted with* bekannt werden mit; *be interested in* interessiert sein an, *become interested in* Interesse gewinnen an; *be used/accustomed to* gewöhnt sein an, *get used/accustomed to* sich gewöhnen an.
Top athletes are accustomed to hard training. – Young athletes soon become accustomed to hard training.

Beachten Sie die passivische Form bei bestimmten Wendungen, z. B.: **be based/founded on** beruhen auf; **be annoyed/irritated at** sich ärgern über; **be pleased/delighted** sich freuen.
The book is based on facts. – I'm pleased to hear that you are well.

4.7. In Aktivsätzen ohne Objekt kann bei einigen Verben das Subjekt das Ziel (nicht der Träger) der Handlung sein, das Verb beschreibt eine bestimmte Eigenschaft des Subjekts und hat so eine dem Passiv entsprechende Bedeutung, z. B.: *read (well, badly)* sich (gut, schlecht) lesen; *sell (well, badly)* sich (gut, schlecht) verkaufen; *wash* sich waschen lassen; *show* gezeigt werden; *play* gespielt werden; *compare with* sich vergleichen lassen mit; *drive* sich fahren; *feel* sich anfühlen; *take/photograph well* sich gut fotografieren lassen.
Diese Konstruktion findet sich relativ häufig in der modernen Fachsprache, z. B. bei: *handle* sich handhaben/bearbeiten lassen, sich anfühlen; *assemble* sich montieren/zusammenstellen lassen; *weld* sich schweißen lassen; etc.
This book reads well. (Dieses Buch liest sich gut.) – At the moment, an interesting film is showing at our cinema. (Zur Zeit wird in unserem Kino ein interessanter

---

[2] Oft ist auch "become" möglich.

L 5.

Film gezeigt.) – This type of cassette recorder sells rather badly. (Dieser Kassettenrecorder verkauft sich ziemlich schlecht.) – Tom's girl-friend takes/photographs well. (Toms Freundin ist fotogen.)
This material handles easily. (Dieses Material läßt sich leicht bearbeiten.) – Some metals weld better than others. (Manche Metalle lassen sich besser schweißen als andere.)

5. The Infinitive – Der Infinitiv

Der Infinitiv kommt im Englischen **mit und ohne** *to* vor und hat die folgenden Formen:

	Active	Passive
Present Simple	(to) write	(to) be written
Present Continuous	(to) be writing	– – –
Perfect Simple	(to) have written	(to) have been written
Perfect Continuous	(to) have been writing	– – –

He can *read* English books. – I want *to write* a letter now. – We shall *try not to be late.* – You do not seem *to be listening.* – Jack hasn't come yet, he may still *be working* in the office.
She must *have missed* the train. – Sorry *to have troubled* you. – Tom seems *to have been working* all night.
This method cannot *be applied* here. – The document has *to be typed* right away. – They ought *to have been informed.*

5.1. Der Infinitiv **mit** *to* steht u. a. nach Verben:

z. B.: *afford* (es) sich leisten können; *agree*[1] sich einigen; *appear/seem* scheinen; *arrange*[1] festlegen; *claim*[1] behaupten; *decide*[1]/*determine*[1]/*resolve*[1]/*make up one's mind* sich entschließen; *expect* erwarten; *fail* nicht können; *hope*[1] hoffen; *manage* zustande bringen; *offer* anbieten; *plan*[1] planen; *pretend*[1] vorgeben; *promise*[1] versprechen; *refuse* sich weigern; *threaten*[1] drohen; *want/wish.*
My friend wants to go to the theatre tonight. – John doesn't seem to be at home. (oder:) John seems not to be at home.[2]

---

[1] Nach diesen Verben ist auch (that +) Nebensatz möglich: I hope to see Anne tomorrow. = I hope (that) I'll see Anne tomorrow. – Peter has promised to be back by ten. = ... that he will be back by ten.

[2] Bei "seem/appear" kann zur Verneinung das Verb selbst mit "do/does/did" oder der folgende Infinitiv mit "not" ohne Bedeutungsunterschied verneint werden. Bei anderen Verben ergibt sich ein Bedeutungsunterschied, je nachdem, ob das Verb selbst oder der folgende Infinitiv verneint wird, z. B. I didn't ask Tom to lock the door. (Ich habe Tom nicht gebeten, die Tür abzuschließen.) (aber:) I asked Tom not to lock the door. (Ich habe Tom gebeten, die Tür nicht abzuschließen.)

sowie nach **Adjektiven** und **Substantiven:**[3]
The text is easy to translate. – I had no opportunity to talk to Jack.

außerdem nach: *too* + **Adjektiv**; **Adjektiv** oder **Substantiv** + *enough*; *enough* + **Substantiv**.
It's too late to go out. – Would you be kind enough to lend me your dictionary? (Wären Sie so freundlich, mir Ihr Wörterbuch zu leihen?) – Eve is intelligent enough to see through this pretext. (Eve ist intelligent genug, um diesen Vorwand zu durchschauen.) – I'm not expert enough / I'm not enough of an expert to decide this question. (Ich kenne mich nicht genügend aus, um diese Frage zu entscheiden.) – We don't have enough time to discuss this problem now.

Beachten Sie auch den Infinitiv nach Substantiven oder Indefinitpronomen in Sätzen wie: I have some shopping to do. – Can you give me something to eat. – I have a lot to do.

5.1.1.   Wird durch den Infinitiv eine Absicht oder ein Zweck zum Ausdruck gebracht, so steht oft *in order to* oder *so as to*; verneint muß *in order not to* oder *so as not to* stehen.
Iris attends an English course for advanced learners in order to improve her fluency of conversation. (Iris besucht einen Englischkurs für Fortgeschrittene, um ihre Gesprächsfertigkeit zu verbessern.) – We should go by car in order not to be late for the concert. (Wir sollten mit dem Auto fahren, um nicht zu spät zum Konzert zu kommen.) – I have decided to buy a car so as to be independent of trains and buses. (Ich habe mich entschlossen, mir ein Auto zu kaufen, um nicht auf Eisenbahn und Bus angewiesen zu sein.) – We had better leave now so as not to miss the bus. (Wir sollten jetzt lieber gehen, damit wir den Bus nicht verpassen.)
Nach *(not) so* + **Adjektiv** und *(not) such* + **Substantiv** steht *as to*. Be so good as to come early. (Sei so gut und komm zeitig.) – Bob is not such a good tennis player as to have a real chance of winning this tournament. (Bob spielt nicht so gut Tennis, um wirklich eine Chance zu haben, dieses Turnier zu gewinnen.)

5.1.2.   Um die Wiederholung eines Infinitivs zu vermeiden, steht oft nur *to*[4].
We asked Jim to lend us his cassette recorder but he didn't want to. – My wife asked me to repair the washing-machine, but I was not able to. 'Will you come with us?' – 'Oh, yes, I'd like to.' (Ja, gern.)

5.1.3.   Zwischen *to* und das **Verb** kann ein **Adverb** treten. Man spricht dann von einem *Split Infinitive*.
It is not quite easy to really understand a novel like 'Ulysses' by James Joyce. – This method makes it possible to considerably raise labour productivity.

---

[3] Zum Gerundium nach Verben, Adjektiven und Substantiven s. Kapitel 8.
[4] Nach Substantiven oder Adjektiven entfällt "to" oft, auch nach "want" und "like" im Nebensatz: We wanted to talk to him, but so far we've had no chance (to). – You can have the book as long as you like.

L 5.2.

5.2. Der Infinitiv ohne *to* steht:

- nach den **unvollständigen Hilfsverben** (außer *ought to*, **used to**): Can we help you? – I must go now. – You shouldn't miss this film.
- nach einigen **Verben** in der Konstruktion **Objekt mit Infinitiv** (s. 5.7.1.): We saw him leave.
- nach einigen **idiomatischen Redewendungen** wie:

(you) had / 'd better ...	Es wäre besser, wenn (du) ..., (du) solltest lieber ...
(you) had / 'd best ...	Es wäre am besten, wenn (du) ...
(I) would / 'd rather[5] ... (than ...)	(Ich) würde lieber ... (als ...)
(I) would (just) as soon ... (as ...)	(Ich) würde ebenso gern ... (wie) ...
Why ...?	Warum sollte man ...?
Why not ...?	Warum sollte man nicht ...?
(One) cannot / could not (help) but ... (formaler Stil)[6]	(Man) muß / mußte ... (Man) kann / konnte nicht umhin ...

You had better ask him first. – We'd better not go by car today. – I'd rather go to the cinema than watch TV.[7] – We may go out tonight, but I would as soon stay at home. – I think we have said enough about this topic; why start it again? – Why not make a decision at once? – One cannot (help) but admire Peg's knowledge of English.

5.3. *help* (helfen) – *need* (brauchen, müssen) – *dare* (wagen)

Nach *help* ist der Infinitiv mit oder ohne *to* möglich.
Donald will help us (to) complete the design.

need und *dare* können als Hilfsverben oder als Vollverben vorkommen. Werden sie als **Hilfsverben** verwendet (6.6.1.), folgt der **Infinitiv ohne** *to*; *need* kann nur im Präsens als Hilfsverb benutzt werden.
I dare not take / I do not dare (to) take this decision by myself. (Ich wage es nicht, diese Entscheidung selbst zu treffen.)
Ted has said he daren't tell Jane the truth / ... he doesn't dare (to) tell ...
I dared not ask Roy for money / I didn't dare (to) ask ...
How dare Nora say such a thing? / How does Nora dare to say ...?
I dare to say that Tom's arguments are not convincing. – (aber:) I daresay it will be a good thing to have Jack on our side. (Ich glaube durchaus, ...)
Ben need not wait / Ben doesn't need to wait. (= Ben doesn't have to wait.)
Need[8] I come this evening? / Do I need to come ...? (= Do I have to come this evening?)

---

[5] Zuweilen auch: (I) would sooner ... (than ...)
[6] Häufiger: (I) can't / couldn't help + Gerundium (s. 8.4.)
[7] Beachten Sie: Nach "rather than" (anstatt, ... und nicht) kann Infinitiv ohne oder mit "to" und auch das Gerundium stehen: It is advisable to introduce new machines rather than overhaul / to overhaul / overhauling the old ones. (Es ist ratsam, neue Maschinen einzuführen und nicht die alten zu überholen.)
[8] Nach Fragewort jedoch "must": Why must I come?

Did you really need to ask this question? (= Did you really have to ask ...?)
I need to apply for a visa.[9] (= I have to apply .../I must apply ...)
The calculations need to be checked.[9] (= ... have to be checked.)
You'll need to work hard if you want to finish the manuscript on time / You'll have to work hard ...

5.4. Abweichend vom Deutschen steht der **Infinitiv des Passivs**, wenn durch den Infinitiv eine passivische Bedeutung zum Ausdruck gebracht wird, d. h. das Subjekt des Satzes verursacht nicht etwas, sondern etwas geschieht mit der Person oder Sache, die Subjekt des Satzes ist.
Lots of problems are to be discussed today. (= It is necessary to discuss ...) – (aber:) We have lots of problems to discuss today.
This questionnaire is to be filled in very carefully. – (aber:) I have a long questionnaire to fill in.
During summertime a great number of foreign tourists are to be seen in our town. (= During summertime one can see ...)
A loud noise was to be heard. – The book is nowhere to be found. – Plenty of work remains to be done. (= It is still necessary to do a lot of work.) – The test is to be repeated at once.
Nach *there is/was* ist der Infinitiv des Aktivs oder Passivs möglich.[10]
There is no time to lose / to be lost.
In Verbindung mit Adjektiven wie *easy, difficult, hard, interesting, nice*, sowie bei *let* (hier: vermieten) und *blame* (hier: schuldig sein) steht gewöhnlich der Infinitiv des Aktivs.
This text is easy to translate. – What Tom says is hard to believe. – Rooms to let. – The driver of the lorry is to blame for the accident.

5.4.1. Die Konstruktion **Substantiv + passivischer Infinitiv** – im Deutschen oft durch Relativsatz wiederzugeben – bringt eine Notwendigkeit zum Ausdruck.
The problems to be dealt with today will take a lot of time. (Die Probleme, die heute zu behandeln sind, werden viel Zeit erfordern.)

5.5. Anstelle eines **indirekten Fragesatzes** steht der Infinitiv häufig nach Fragewörtern wie *what, where, when, how, who(m)* und nach der Konjunktion

---

[9] Im bejahenden Satz folgt nach "need" der to-Infinitiv.
Wenn ein verneintes Verb vorausgeht, z. B. "don't think / suppose etc", oder ein Zweifel zum Ausdruck gebracht wird, ist auch der Infinitiv ohne "to" möglich. Nach "need hardly" steht nur der Infinitiv ohne "to".
I don't think we need (to) wait any longer. – I wonder if I need (to) repeat the examination. – I need hardly stress how important this meeting is. (= I think it is hardly necessary to stress ...)
[10] Gelegentlich kann sich ein Bedeutungsunterschied ergeben: There was nothing to do in the little village where we spent our holidays. (= There were no opportunities of entertainment ...) (aber:) There is nothing to be done about this situation. (= It is impossible to change this situation.)

L 5.6.

whether – vor allem in Verbindung mit Verben wie ***ask, decide, explain, find out, inform, know, show, tell, wonder*** (gern wissen wollen) – sowie nach Ausdrücken wie ***be at a loss*** (nicht wissen), ***have no idea*** (keine Vorstellung haben), ***be uncertain/ not sure*** (nicht sicher sein), ***make up one's mind*** (sich entschließen) oder nach Substantiven, z. B. ***question (of), problem (of)***. Im Deutschen ist ein Nebensatz erforderlich, oft mit "können, sollen, müssen".

Mark should tell us what to do. (= ... what we can do/must do/ought to do.)
We explained to Bob how to solve the problem. (= ... how he could/should solve the problem.)
Do you know who(m) to apply to for further information? (= ... who(m) I/we/one could apply to ...)
Ask Liz how to spell this word. (= ... how this word is spelt.)
I wonder where to find Frank. (= ... where I can find Frank.)
We were at a loss what to do. (= We didn't know what we could/should do.)
I couldn't make up my mind whether to stay another few days. (= ... if I should stay ...)
The problem of how to reduce environmental pollution is very urgent. (= The problem how environmental pollution can be reduced ...)
I'm thinking about when to take a holiday this year.

5.6.   Der **Infinitiv anstelle eines Relativsatzes** steht häufig nach **Ordnungszahlen** sowie nach ***the last, the only (one), the next*** und nach **Superlativen**.
Who was the first to finish (= who finished) the translation? (Wer war als erster mit der Übersetzung fertig?) – Paul will be the only one to help us in this situation. – This is one of the most interesting books to have been published on robotics recently.

Vor allem in Fragesätzen und in verneinten Sätzen findet sich der Infinitiv auch nach **Substantiven** sowie nach ***anybody, anyone, nobody, no-one, anything, nothing, something, someone, somebody***.
Glen is not the man to change his mind very often. – I don't have anybody/I have nobody (oder: no-one) to talk to in this matter.

5.7.   Object with Infinitive – Objekt mit Infinitiv

Die Konstruktion ***Object with Infinitive***[11]
We assume ***this hypothesis to be*** correct.
dient der Verkürzung eines Satzgefüges:
We assume that this hypothesis is correct.
Im Deutschen wird häufig ein Nebensatz verwendet, eingeleitet durch "daß" oder "wie".

Es können alle Formen des Infinitivs vorkommen – je nach vorausgehendem Verb **mit oder ohne** *to*. Die *Continuous Forms* sind verhältnismäßig selten.
We often see him *work* in the garden. (Wir sehen ihn oft im Garten arbeiten.) – I

---

[11] Sie entspricht dem lateinischen Accusativus cum Infinitivo.

have never heard her *complain*. (Ich habe nie gehört, daß sie sich beklagt.) – We want you *to be* punctual. (Wir möchten, daß du pünktlich bist.) – The introduction of the new process will allow labour productivity *to be increased*. (Die Einführung des neuen Verfahrens wird eine Erhöhung der Arbeitsproduktivität ermöglichen.) – I don't consider his arguments *to have been* convincing. (Ich bin nicht der Meinung, daß seine Argumente überzeugend waren.) – We assume the values *to have been checked* before. (Wir setzen voraus, daß die Werte vorher geprüft worden sind.)

Im modernen Englisch sind in vielen Fällen anstelle des **Object with Infinitive** andere Konstruktionen möglich, zum Teil auch zu bevorzugen, auf die bei den entsprechenden Verben hingewiesen wird.

5.7.1. Bei der **Object with Infinitive**-Konstruktion steht der **Infinitiv ohne** *to* vor allem nach den Verben

see sehen; *hear*[12] hören; *feel*[13] fühlen; *watch/observe* beobachten, zusehen; *listen to*[12] (vor allem AE) zuhören, wenn sie eine Sinneswahrnehmung zum Ausdruck bringen.[14]
We often hear them argue. (Wir hören sie oft heftig debattieren.)
Did you see Bill go upstairs? (Hast du gesehen, daß Bill nach oben gegangen ist?)
The policeman watched the thief come out of the department store. (Der Polizist beobachtete, daß der Dieb aus dem Kaufhaus kam.)

make/have (veran)lassen, auffordern; *let* (zu)lassen.
The assistant made/had the students describe the test. (Der Assistent ließ die Studenten den Versuch beschreiben.) – What made you change your mind? (Was hat

---

[12] Beachten Sie: Did you hear the thunder? – We heard an interesting concert/lecture etc. – (aber:) I listened to some records/their conversation etc.
[13] "feel" in der Bedeutung "glauben, halten für" erfordert Infinitiv mit "to": We felt the situation to be rather complicated.
[14] Bei "see" in der Bedeutung "verstehen, einsehen", "hear" = "erfahren" steht immer ein Nebensatz. Nach "notice" findet sich gelegentlich Object with Infinitive, häufiger ein Nebensatz.
I see that you are right. – We have heard that Bert is abroad.
Nach den Verben "see, hear, feel, watch" ist, wenn sie eine Sinneswahrnehmung ausdrücken, neben dem Infinitiv auch ein Partizip möglich. Dabei können sich gewisse Bedeutungsnuancen ergeben. Man verwendet in der Regel den Infinitiv, um auszudrücken, daß eine Handlung von Anfang bis Ende wahrgenommen wird, die "ing-Form" dagegen, wenn nur ein Teil des Vorgangs wahrgenommen wird.
I often watch Peter repair household gadgets. – For about half an hour I watched Peter repairing household gadgets.
Der Infinitiv steht auch meist, wenn mehrere aufeinanderfolgende Handlungen beschrieben werden: I heard Jane open the front door, come upstairs and go into the room.
In Verbindung mit "can/could" steht nach "see, watch, hear" in der Regel die ing-Form: I could hear them talking.
Wird der wahrgenommene Vorgang im Passiv dargestellt, so ist nur das Present Participle Passive oder das Past Participle möglich.
We watched the engine being repaired. – I have seldom heard the word "psyche" pronounced correctly.

dich veranlaßt, deine Meinung zu ändern?) – We'll let you go a little earlier. (Wir werden dich etwas früher gehen lassen.)
Die Verben *make* und *have* können nur mit folgendem Infinitiv im Aktiv verwendet werden.[15]

5.7.2. Der Infinitiv **mit** *to* steht vor allem nach folgenden Verben:

– *want*[16]/(seltener:) *wish* wünschen, wollen; *(I) would like*[16] (Ich) möchte gern; *expect*[17] erwarten; *cause/induce* veranlassen; *order*[18] auffordern; *allow/permit* erlauben, ermöglichen, dürfen.
Do you want me to help you? (Willst du, daß ich dir helfe?/Soll ich dir helfen?) – I would like you to have a look at these photos. (Ich möchte gern, daß du dir diese Fotos ansiehst.) – We can't expect this question to be settled today. (Wir können nicht erwarten, daß diese Frage heute gelöst wird.) – Our chief editor has caused your article to be printed. (Unser Chefredakteur hat veranlaßt, daß Ihr Artikel gedruckt wird.) – The doctor ordered Jim to stay in bed for some days. (Der Arzt verordnete Jim einige Tage Bettruhe.) – The head nurse didn't allow us to talk to the patient. (Die Oberschwester erlaubte uns nicht, mit dem Patienten zu sprechen.)

– *tell (sb to do sth)* (jmd.) auffordern (etw. zu tun), (jmd.) sagen (er solle etw.tun); *urge* dringend bitten, auffordern; *force/compel* zwingen, veranlassen; *get* (vor allem umgangssprachlich) veranlassen, überreden; *forbid* verbieten; *ask* bitten; *request* bitten, ersuchen; *advise* raten; *recommend*[18] empfehlen; *warn (sb to do sth)* (jmd.) auffordern/ermahnen (etw. zu tun); *warn sb not to do sth* jmd. warnen etw. zu tun.
Nach diesen Verben steht in der Regel der Infinitiv des Aktivs.
I told Fred to buy something for our guests. (Ich sagte Fred, er solle etwas für unsere Gäste kaufen.) – You should get Tom to read this book. (Du solltest Tom dazu bringen, dieses Buch zu lesen.)

---

[15] Beachten Sie: You should make the firm supply the goods at once. (Sie sollten veranlassen, daß die Firma die Waren sofort liefert.) – (aber:) You should cause the goods to be supplied at once. (Sie sollten veranlassen, daß die Waren sofort geliefert werden.)
Nach "have" ist auch das Präsenspartizip möglich: Tom had us laughing. (Tom brachte uns zum Lachen.)
Zu "have + Objekt + Past Participle" s. 9.5.
Gelegentlich finden sich auch die Formen "(I) won't have" = (Ich) möchte nicht; "(I) would have" = (Ich) möchte gern:
I won't have you pass on this piece of information. (auch:) I won't have you passing on ... (Ich möchte nicht, daß du diese Information weitergibst.)
I would have Tom take part in our talk. (häufiger:) I would like Tom to take part in our talk. (s. 5.7.2.)
[16] Anstelle eines folgenden passivischen Infinitivs ist auch das Past Participle möglich. (s. 9.6.): I want this done at once. (Ich möchte, daß das sofort gemacht wird.)
[17] Wird "expect" im Sinne einer Vermutung verwendet, so folgt ein Nebensatz: I expect you will be very busy tomorrow. (Ich vermute ...)
[18] s. auch 10.1.

– (vor allem in der Fachsprache:) *enable sb to do sth* jmd. befähigen / es ermöglichen, etw. zu tun; *enable sth to be done* ermöglichen, etw. zu tun; *require*[19] erfordern.
This dictionary of basic English will enable you to make yourself understood in everyday situations. (Dieser englische Sprachführer wird es dir ermöglichen, dich in Alltagssituationen zu verständigen.) – The new production technology will enable better and cheaper goods to be produced. (Die neue Technologie wird es ermöglichen, bessere und billigere Waren herzustellen.) – The present situation requires a decision to be taken immediately. (Die gegenwärtige Lage erfordert es, sofort eine Entscheidung zu treffen.)

5.7.2.1. Bei einigen Verben findet sich die *Object with Infinitive*-Konstruktion besonders in der Schriftsprache, vor allem wenn als Infinitiv *be* (zuweilen auch: *have been*) folgt. In der Umgangssprache wird ein **Nebensatz mit** *that* vorgezogen.

assume annehmen, voraussetzen; *consider*[20] betrachten als, der Meinung sein; *believe*[20] / *suppose* / *think*[20] denken, vermuten, halten für; *hold* halten für; *judge*[20] halten für; *show* / *prove* zeigen, beweisen; *declare*[20] erklären; *understand* als sicher annehmen; *know* wissen.
Let us assume Tom's hypothesis to be valid. (Wir wollen annehmen, daß Toms Hypothese richtig ist.) – I consider it (to be) my duty to help them. (Ich halte es für meine Pflicht, ihnen zu helfen.) – The experimental results prove our assumption to have been correct. (Die Versuchsergebnisse zeigen, daß unsere Annahme richtig war.)
I think him to be reliable. (häufiger:) I think (that) he is reliable. (Ich halte ihn für zuverlässig.) – Nowadays everybody knows radioactive substances to be of great use for medical purposes. (= Nowadays everybody knows that radioactive substances are of great use for ...)

Bei den folgenden Verben ist die *Object with Infinitive*-Konstruktion **neben** dem *Gerund* möglich:
imagine / *fancy*[20] sich vorstellen / einbilden; (gelegentlich auch:) *like* mögen; *hate* / *dislike* nicht mögen.
Fancy him to win the prize. / Fancy him winning the prize. (Stell dir vor, er gewinnt den Preis.)
I like people to be frank. / I like people being frank. (Mir gefällt es, wenn Menschen offen und ehrlich sind.)

5.7.3. Bezieht sich das Objekt in der *Object with Infinitive*-Konstruktion zurück auf das **Subjekt**, so steht das entsprechende **Reflexivpronomen**.
Peg fancies herself (to be) more attractive than all her friends. (Peg bildet sich ein, daß sie hübscher als alle ihre Freundinnen ist.)

---

[19] s. auch: 8.5. und 10.1.
[20] Bei diesen Verben entfällt häufig der Infinitiv "to be", besonders im Zusammenhang mit "it" als Objekt.

5.7.4. *for* + Objekt + Infinitiv mit *to*

Die Konstruktion *for* + Objekt + Infinitiv mit *to* kann man als eine der *Object with Infinitive*-Konstruktion verwandte Form betrachten, die häufig einen Zweck, eine Absicht oder eine Erwartung zum Ausdruck bringt. Sie steht meist nach

Adjektiven, wie *(un)necessary, (un)important, essential, (ir)relevant, (in)significant, (im)possible, (un)usual, (un)common, normal, anxious, difficult, useful, useless, desirable, convenient;*

too, enough;

nach **Verben**, wie *wait, arrange, take (dauern), remain.*

Auch nach **Substantiven** wie *(high) time, possibility/chance/opportunity* ist diese Konstruktion möglich.

It is necessary for scientists to know foreign languages. – It's important for us to be informed about all the details of the plan.

This problem is too difficult for us to solve at once. (Dieses Problem ist zu schwierig, als daß wir es sofort lösen könnten.)

It is essential for there to be sufficient time to discuss the papers that will be read in the plenary session. (Es ist wichtig, daß zur Diskussion der Vorträge, die auf der Plenarsitzung gehalten werden, genügend Zeit zur Verfügung steht.)

Lots of people were waiting for the box-office to be opened. (Viele Menschen warteten darauf, daß die Kasse geöffnet wurde.)

You should arrange for two rooms to be reserved for Tuesday and Wednesday. (Du solltest dich darum kümmern, daß zwei Zimmer für Dienstag und Mittwoch reserviert werden.)

Because of the fog it took us a lot of time to get to the airport. (oder:) ... it took a lot of time for us to get ... (Wegen des Nebels dauerte es sehr lange, bis wir zum Flughafen kamen.)

It is high time for me to leave. (Es ist höchste Zeit, daß ich gehe.)

Die *for*-Konstruktion ist auch ohne direkten Bezug auf ein Adjektiv, Verb oder Substantiv möglich.

For production to be increased we must raise labour productivity. (Damit die Produktion erhöht werden kann, müssen wir die Arbeitsproduktivität steigern.)

5.8. Subject with Infinitive – Subjekt mit Infinitiv

Die Konstruktion *Subject with Infinitive*[21]

They are expected to come today.
(Subjekt – Verbform im Passiv – Infinitiv mit *to*[22])

verkürzt ein Satzgefüge:

It is expected that they will come today.

Gegenüber der Form *Object with Infinitive* hat sich der Anwendungsbereich der *Subject with Infinitive*-Konstruktion im modernen Englisch beträchtlich erweitert.

---

[21] Sie entspricht dem lateinischen Nominativus cum Infinitivo.
[22] Einzige Ausnahme: "let": He was let go. (Man ließ ihn gehen.)

Sie ist vor allem in der heutigen Schriftsprache ein häufig verwendetes Stilmittel, speziell bei Informationen der Massenmedien und in der Fachsprache, kommt aber auch in der Umgangssprache vor.
In der *Subject with Infinitive*-Konstruktion finden sich **alle Formen des Infinitivs**.
Für die Übertragung ins Deutsche bieten sich unterschiedliche Möglichkeiten an.
Eve is thought *to be* ill. (Man nimmt an, daß Eve krank ist./Vermutlich ist Eve krank.)
The negotiations are scheduled *to be resumed* next month. (Es ist geplant, die Verhandlungen nächsten Monat wieder aufzunehmen./Die Verhandlungen sollen nächsten Monat wieder aufgenommen werden.)
Newton is known *to have discovered* the laws of gravity. (Es ist bekannt, daß Newton die Gravitationsgesetze entdeckt hat./Bekanntlich hat Newton die Gravitationsgesetze entdeckt.)
Several passengers are reported *to have been injured* in the train accident. (Es wird berichtet, daß mehrere Fahrgäste bei dem Zugunglück verletzt worden sind./Berichten zufolge sollen bei dem Zugunglück mehrere Fahrgäste verletzt worden sein.)
Ted is said *to be staying* abroad. (Man sagt/Es heißt, Ted sei z. Zt. im Ausland./Ted soll sich z. Zt. im Ausland aufhalten.)
The health of the patient who had a liver transplantation last month is reported *to have been making* good progress these days. (Es wird berichtet, daß der Gesundheitszustand des Patienten, bei dem vorigen Monat eine Lebertransplantation vorgenommen wurde, sich in den letzten Tagen wesentlich gebessert hat.)

Beachten Sie bei der Übersetzung vom Deutschen	ins Englische
Subjekt des Nebensatzes	→ Subjekt der Infinitivkonstruktion
Prädikat des Hauptsatzes	→ Verbform im Passiv
Prädikat des Nebensatzes	→ Infinitiv
Man nimmt an, daß seine Berechnungen richtig sind.	His calculations are supposed to be correct.

5.8.1. Die *Subject with Infinitive*-Konstruktion findet sich vor allem nach folgenden Verben:
say (s. auch: 6.5.3.3.) sagen, sollen; *know* wissen, kennen; *think*[23]/*believe*[23] glauben, annehmen, halten für; *consider*[23] ansehen als, halten für, der Meinung sein; *assume* (häufig in der Fachsprache)/*presume* annehmen, voraussetzen; *hold* annehmen; *allege* behaupten, annehmen; *repute*[23] gelten als; *understand* als sicher annehmen, wissen; *rumour* (als Gerücht) verbreiten, sollen.
Broadway is known to be the most famous street in New York. (Der Broadway ist bekanntlich die berühmteste Straße in New York.)
Bob is said to have specialized in radiology. (Bob soll sich auf dem Gebiet der Radiologie spezialisiert haben.)

---

[23] Der Infinitiv "to be" kann entfallen.

L 5.8.1.

In this equation a is assumed to be greater than b. (In dieser Gleichung wird vorausgesetzt, daß a größer ist als b.)
The films of Ingmar Bergman are considered to be among the best of our time. (Die Filme von Ingmar Bergman zählen zu den besten unserer Zeit.)
Asta Nielsen is reputed to have been one of the greatest stars of the silent film era. (Asta Nielsen gilt als einer der größten Stars der Stummfilmzeit.)

expect = erwarten, sollen (als Ausdruck einer Erwartung oder Aufforderung; verneint, um die Ungewißheit oder Unwahrscheinlichkeit auszudrücken, daß eine bestimmte Erwartung erfüllt wird).

suppose = sollen zum Ausdruck einer Aufforderung oder Erwartung; verneint im Sinne einer eindringlichen Ermahnung oder eines Tadels; gelegentlich auch "sollen" im Sinne einer Annahme (= vermuten).

Mark's new book is expected to become a best-seller. (Man erwartet, daß Marks Buch ein Bestseller wird.) – I am expected to finish this work within the next days. (= I am to finish ...)[24] (Man erwartet von mir, daß ich diese Arbeit in den nächsten Tagen abschließe./Ich soll diese Arbeit ... abschließen.) – Joan cannot be expected to make such an important decision at once. (Man kann nicht erwarten, daß Joan solch eine wichtige Entscheidung sofort trifft.)
You shouldn't be watching TV now, you are supposed to be working. (Du solltest jetzt nicht fernsehen, du müßtest arbeiten.) – Scientists are supposed/expected to keep abreast of the latest developments in their fields of research. (Von Wissenschaftlern wird erwartet, daß sie sich über die neuesten Entwicklungen ihres Forschungsgebietes auf dem laufenden halten.) – What are we supposed to do now? (= What are we to do now?/What shall we do now?) (Was sollen wir jetzt tun?)
You are not supposed to smoke in this restaurant. (= Smoking is not allowed here.) (Sie dürfen hier nicht rauchen. = allgemeines Verbot) – Put out your cigarette, you are not supposed to be smoking here. (Mach die Zigarette aus, du darfst hier nicht rauchen. = spezielle Situation)
Peggy has taken a holiday; she is supposed to have gone to the seaside. (= ... probably she has gone ...) (Peggy hat Urlaub genommen, vermutlich ist sie an die See gefahren.)

Anmerkung
Ob *be supposed to* eine Aufforderung oder Erwartung bzw. eine Vermutung zum Ausdruck bringt, muß sich aus dem Kontext ergeben:
Why are you still at home? You are supposed to be in the laboratory. (= ... You ought to be ...) (... Du müßtest doch im Labor sein.)
Jim is not at home; he is supposed to be in the laboratory. (= ..., he is probably in the laboratory.) (..., er ist vermutlich im Labor.)

tell jmd. auffordern etw. zu tun; jmd. sagen, er solle etw. tun; *make/cause/induce* veranlassen; *order* auffordern, anordnen; *ask/request* bitten, ersuchen; *allow/permit* (s. auch: 6.3.) erlauben, zulassen, dürfen; *forbid* verbieten.
Glen should be told to apologize. (Man sollte Glen auffordern, sich zu entschuldi-

---
[24] s. 6.5.3.1.

gen.) – Jane was told not to eat too much. (Man sagte Jane, sie solle nicht so viel essen.) – Do you think Fred might be made/caused/induced to change his mind? (Glaubst du, daß man Fred veranlassen könnte, seine Meinung zu ändern?) – Visitors are requested not to touch the exhibits. (Die Besucher werden gebeten, die Ausstellungsstücke nicht zu berühren.) – Were you allowed/permitted to talk to the patient? (Durftet ihr mit dem Patienten sprechen?)

report[25] berichten; *estimate* schätzen, veranschlagen; *intend/mean/design* (s. auch: 6.5.3.4.) beabsichtigen, bestimmen, sollen (im Sinne einer Absicht); *find/discover* feststellen; *show/prove* zeigen, nachweisen, sich erweisen als; *schedule/plan* planen, vorsehen; *state* feststellen, darlegen; *declare* erklären (als, zu); *point out* hinweisen auf.

Last night the French Foreign Minister was reported to be having talks with the Soviet government in Moscow. (Gestern abend wurde mitgeteilt, daß der französische Außenminister Gespräche mit der sowjetischen Regierung in Moskau führt.)
Expenses for the redevelopment of these tenement houses are estimated to amount to about $1,000,000. (Schätzungen zufolge belaufen sich die Kosten für die Sanierung dieser Mietshäuser auf etwa eine Million Dollar.)
This article is intended/meant to give a survey of new trends in biogenetics. (Dieser Artikel soll einen Überblick über neue Trends in der Biogenetik geben.)
In 1898, polonium was found by the Curies to be a radioactive substance. (Im Jahre 1898 stellten die Curies fest, daß Polonium ein radioaktiver Stoff ist.)
For a long time X-rays have been shown to play an important part in medicine. (Seit langem ist nachgewiesen, daß Röntgenstrahlen eine wichtige Rolle in der Medizin spielen.)
The new power plant is scheduled to be put into operation at the end of this year. (Es ist vorgesehen, das neue Kraftwerk Ende dieses Jahres in Betrieb zu nehmen.)
In the final communiqué the relations between the Soviet Union and India were stated to have been improving steadily within the last few years. (In dem Abschlußkommuniqué wurde festgestellt, daß sich die Beziehungen zwischen der Sowjetunion und Indien in den letzten Jahren stetig verbessert haben.)

see[26] (sehen); *hear*[26] (hören); *observe* (nur Schriftsprache = beobachten); *feel* (halten für, der Meinung sein).
The burglars were seen to drive off in a lorry. (Man hat gesehen, daß die Einbrecher in einem LKW wegfuhren.)
Our neighbours can often be heard to quarrel. (Man kann oft hören, wie sich unsere Nachbarn streiten.)
The situation of the defendant was felt to be rather critical. (Man war der Meinung, daß die Lage des Angeklagten ziemlich kritisch sei.)

---

[25] Statt Infinitiv Passiv kann auch Past Participle stehen (s. 9.4.)
[26] Nach "see" und "hear" ist anstelle des Infinitivs auch das Partizip möglich (9.4.): They were heard quarrelling. (Man hörte, wie sie sich stritten.)

L 6.

6. The Defective Auxiliaries and their Equivalents – Die unvollständigen Hilfsverben und ihre Äquivalentformen

Die unvollständigen Hilfsverben, im Englischen *Defective Auxiliaries*, *Defectives* oder *Modal Verbs* genannt, weisen eine Reihe von Besonderheiten auf:
- es **entfällt das -s der 3. Pers. Sing.**: She can type.
- in Frage und Verneinung erfolgt **keine Umschreibung mit** *do*: May I ask a question? – You should not be late.
- der folgende Infinitiv wird **ohne** *to* angeschlossen (Ausnahmen: ought to, used to): We must work now. – You ought to inform him.
- es ist **kein unmittelbarer Objektbezug** möglich, d. h. das Objekt kann nur über ein Vollverb angeschlossen werden: He can speak Dutch.
- die Formen *might, should, ought to* haben nur **konjunktivische** Bedeutung; *could* kann im **Indikativ** und **Konjunktiv** verwendet werden.
- im Indikativ des Präteritums und in allen zusammengesetzten Zeiten werden die unvollständigen Hilfsverben mit sinnverwandten Formen umschrieben. Diese Äquivalentformen können natürlich auch im Präsens verwendet werden.

6.1. *can* – (verneint:) *cannot/can't*
could – (verneint:) *could not/couldn't*

6.1.1. *can* bezeichnet

- eine **Fähigkeit** (geistig oder physisch). – Äquivalentformen: be able to, be capable of[1] (vorzugsweise Schriftsprache), verneint: not be able to, be unable to[2], be incapable of[1].
Pete can speak Spanish. (= Pete speaks Spanish.) – I cannot play the guitar. (= I don't play the guitar.) – I hope I shall be able to translate this text. – We have not been able to find the mistake so far. – Can you repair/Are you able to repair the radio yourself?

- eine **Möglichkeit** allgemeiner oder theoretischer Art (s. auch 6.2.): Going by car in the rush hours can be a nuisance. – You should take warm clothes with you, it can be very cold in Siberia. – The telephone is ringing, can it be Peter?

Wird statt der Möglichkeit die **Gelegenheit** betont, so findet sich als Äquivalentform *have an opportunity/a chance to do/of doing sth* (s. 8.2.1.3.):
I hope I'll have a chance to read this book soon. – We've had an opportunity of seeing some interesting films recently.

- eine **allgemeine Eigenschaft**: She can be very amiable (liebenswürdig).

---

[1] Gerundium s. 8.2.1.3.
[2] Im Sinne von "nicht können" gelegentlich auch "fail to": She failed to answer most of the questions. = She was not able to answer ...
Sehr oft bringt "fail to" eine bloße Negation zum Ausdruck: Neil failed to realize his mistake. = Neil didn't realize his mistake.

can kann ausdrücken, daß man sich erkundigt, ob etwas **erlaubt** ist:
Can I use your cassette recorder? (= May I use your cassette recorder?) – Can we park in this street? (= Is parking allowed in this street?)
can kann eine höfliche **Frage**, eine **Bitte** oder ein **Angebot** zum Ausdruck bringen.
Can I help you? – Can I have another cup of coffee? – I can carry your trunk if it's too heavy for you.

6.1.2. *could* bezeichnet als Präteritum von *can* eine **allgemeine**, nicht auf eine spezielle Situation bezogene **Fähigkeit**.
Äquivalentform: *be able to.*
Eve could dance very well when she was young. / Eve was able to dance ...

Bezieht sich die Fähigkeit auf eine **bestimmte Handlung** oder **Situation**, so wird meist mit *be able to*[3] oder auch mit *manage to*, *succeed in* umschrieben.[4] Bei *hear, see, feel* steht *could*.
How many tickets were you able to get / did you manage to get? – Finally we were able to reach an agreement / ... we managed to reach ... / ... we succeeded in reaching an agreement.

In verneinten Sätzen ist jeweils *could* oder Äquivalentform möglich:
The examinee was so excited that he could not answer the question. / ... that he was unable to answer the question.

Could kann auch ausdrücken, daß etwas durchaus **möglich**, aber **nicht unbedingt wahrscheinlich** ist, und entspricht oft *might*.
You could / might be right. – The weather could / might change today.
Could kann in konditionaler Bedeutung in der indirekten Rede vorkommen (= would be able to).
I could do the translation if I had a good dictionary. (s. 3.3.2.)
Could kann ausdrücken, daß sehr höflich um **Erlaubnis gefragt** wird (a) oder daß in der Vergangenheit eine **generelle Erlaubnis** bestand (b). Es kann außerdem eine höfliche **Frage** (c), einen **Vorschlag** (d) oder eine **Anregung** (e) zum Ausdruck bringen.
'Could I have your car today?' – 'Of course, you can.' (nicht: could) (a) – When I was a little boy I could go to the cinema once a week.[5] (b) – Could you tell me the way to the station? (c) – We could go to the theatre tomorrow. (d) – You could help Jane to prepare lunch. (e)

Could als Präteritum von *can* bezeichnet auch eine **allgemeine Eigenschaft**: He could get very angry when he was contradicted.

---

[3] Vor allem in der Umgangssprache findet sich aber auch in diesem Falle "could": We are glad you could come.
[4] "manage to, succeed in" verweisen auf den Erfolg (verneint: Mißerfolg) einer Handlung, wobei angedeutet wird, daß es schwierig war, etwas zu tun. Natürlich können beide Verben auch bei Gegenwarts- und Zukunftsbezug verwendet werden. "succeed in + Gerundium": 8.2.1.1.
[5] Bei einer einmaligen Erlaubnis in der Vergangenheit kann nur "was / were allowed to" (s. 6.3.) verwendet werden: We were allowed to see the patient yesterday.

L 6.2.

6.2. *may/might* zum Ausdruck einer **Möglichkeit**

Soll zum Ausdruck gebracht werden, daß etwas möglicherweise der Fall ist oder geschehen wird, so wird *may* (deutsch oft: vielleicht) verwendet.[6] Die Möglichkeit kann auch durch *perhaps*, *maybe*, *it is possible*, oder *possibly* wiedergegeben werden.

Wird nach einer Möglichkeit **gefragt**, so steht **nicht** *may*, sondern *can* (s. 6.1.1.), oder es wird umschrieben mit *do you think (that)...?; is it possible (that)...?*
Sue may be right. (= Perhaps/Maybe Sue is right.)
They haven't come yet, they may still be in the university. (= ..., it is possible that/perhaps/maybe they are still in the university.) – He may be ill. (aber Frage:) Can he be ill? (= Do you think he's ill?).

6.2.1. *might* schränkt gegenüber *may* die Möglichkeit etwas ein und entspricht dann *could* (6.1.2.)

It might/could snow this afternoon. (Es könnte heute nachmittag schneien.) – I might/could be mistaken. (Ich könnte mich irren.)

might steht auch in der indirekten Rede.
Alice said she might come this week. (= Alice said she would perhaps/possibly come this week.)

might kann auch bei höflichen Fragen oder Anregungen verwendet werden (6.1.2.); gelegentlich deutet es eine Ermahnung an.
'Might I ask a question?' (= Would it be possible to ask a question?) – 'Of course, you may.' (nicht: might)
You might inform Tom if you see him. (= It would be nice of you to inform Tom if ...) – You might be more friendly to Susan. (= You had better be more friendly to Susan.)

6.2.2. *may not/cannot*

Durch *may not* wird eine Möglichkeit eingeschränkt, durch *cannot* wird sie ausgeschlossen.
This may not be true. = Perhaps this is not true. (Das stimmt vielleicht nicht.) – This cannot be true. = It's impossible that this is true. (Das kann nicht stimmen.)

6.2.3. *may* kann auch einen Wunsch oder eine Hoffnung ausdrücken.
May all your wishes come true. (Mögen sich alle deine Wünsche erfüllen.)

---

[6] Mit "may" wird hauptsächlich ausgedrückt, daß etwas geschehen kann und möglicherweise geschieht: I may see Jane tomorrow. = Perhaps I'll see her tomorrow.
Dagegen drückt "can" aus
– daß etwas generell möglich ist, schließt aber nicht ein, daß es auch geschieht: You can meet Tom at the club every Sunday. = It is possible to meet Tom at the club every Sunday.
– daß es mehrere Möglichkeiten gibt, etwas zu tun: We can discuss this problem now or we can talk about it tomorrow.

6.3. *may* zum Ausdruck der **Erlaubnis**

Mit *may* kann um eine Erlaubnis gebeten oder eine Erlaubnis erteilt werden. Ein Verbot wird durch *must not/mustn't*, weniger kategorisch durch *may not* (vorzugsweise in Antworten) zum Ausdruck gebracht. In Fragen ist *may* höflicher als *can*.
Äquivalentformen: *be allowed/permitted to*.
'May I come in?' – 'Yes, you may./No, you may not.' – You may visit us as often as you like. (oder: You can visit ...) – My father is in hospital, we are allowed to visit him every day. – You must not/mustn't smoke here. (= You are not allowed/permitted to smoke here.) – Were you allowed to be present at the experiment? – My friend will be allowed to take part in an exchange practical for students in Sofia.

Beachten Sie: *can* – nicht *may* – wird bei einer bereits erteilten, generellen Erlaubnis verwendet.
My uncle has told us that we can always spend our holidays in his bungalow.

might im Sinne einer **Erlaubnis** findet sich im **Konditionalsatz** und in der **indirekten Rede**.
I asked if I might come a little later. – The engineer said we might have a look at the new machine.

6.4.   *will* – (verneint:) *will not/won't*
     would – (verneint:) *would not/wouldn't*

6.4.1.   Mit *will* und *would* kann eine höfliche Frage oder Bitte, mit *won't* auch eine Einladung einem Gesprächspartner gegenüber zum Ausdruck gebracht werden.
Will you have a cup of tea? – Will somebody close the window, please? – Would you tell me the time, please? – 'Won't you have a glass of wine with us?' (= Would you like to have ...) – 'Yes, I will.' (nicht: I'll.) (oder:) I'd like to.

6.4.2.   In bestimmten Fällen kann *will* auch einen **Wunsch** ausdrücken:
I will/I'll have orange juice not coffee for breakfast.
Meist jedoch werden zum Ausdruck eines Wunsches Äquivalentformen verwendet: *want to*; *(I) would like to*; (formal:) *wish to*; (verneint auch:) *refuse to*. In der Vergangenheit findet sich auch *would not*.
Why do you want to study mathematics? – I would like to read this book. (Ich möchte gern ...) – We don't want to go out tonight. – I want to be woken at 6 a.m. – Fred would not tell us details about his project. (= Fred didn't want to/refused to tell us ...)

6.4.3.   *will* kann eine feste Absicht ausdrücken, *won't* bzw. *wouldn't* eine Weigerung.
Äquivalentformen: *be determined to, intend to, mean to, be going to, be willing to*; verneint bei Personen auch *refuse to*.
I will[7] write this letter whether you like it or not. = I am determined to write ... (Ich

L 6.4.4.

will/bin entschlossen ...) – Eve won't come with us. = Eve doesn't want to come with us.) – He wouldn't tell us the truth. = He refused/didn't want to tell us the truth. (Er wollte uns die Wahrheit nicht sagen.)
Bei Sachbezug bringt *won't* bzw. *wouldn't* eine Funktionsunfähigkeit zum Ausdruck.
The key won't/wouldn't fit. (Der Schlüssel paßt/paßte nicht.)

6.4.4. *will* kann einen gewohnheitsmäßigen Vorgang oder eine allgemeine Eigenschaft zum Ausdruck bringen; im Deutschen steht dann das Präsens. Bezieht sich eine gewohnheitsmäßige Handlung auf die Vergangenheit, kann *would* oder *used to* (+ Infinitiv)[8] verwendet werden, bei einem gewohnheitsmäßigen Zustand nur *used to*. Bei *used to* wird in der Frage meist, in der Verneinung sehr häufig mit *did* umschrieben, also: did you use to ...?; I didn't use to ...[9] (Im Deutschen meist mit "früher")
He will/He'll change his mind rather frequently. (= He changes...). Water will boil/Water boils at 100 °C. – Wet wood won't burn. (= ... does not burn.) – Hugh would smoke/used to smoke a lot when he was young. (= Hugh smoked a lot ...) – The Tower of London, which used to be a prison for a long time, is now a famous museum. – Locomotives used to be driven by steam before the diesel engine was developed. – 'Didn't your aunt use to live in Berlin?' – 'Yes, she did,/Yes, she used to, but two years ago she moved to Dresden.' – Gary didn't use to/Gary used not to enjoy ballets until he got to know a girl who was a dancer. (= Gary didn't enjoy ...)

6.4.5. *will* mit folgendem Infinitiv Präsens oder Perfekt kann eine **begründete Vermutung** oder eine **Wahrscheinlichkeit** zum Ausdruck bringen. (deutsch etwa: "wird wohl" oder "wahrscheinlich")
Let's go home, lunch will be ready. (= ..., lunch is likely to be ready.)
Don't disturb my brother, he will be working. (= ..., he is probably working.)
They will have noticed the mistake in the meantime. (= It is quite likely that they have noticed ...)
Ted will have completed the translation by now. (= I think Ted has completed ...)

6.5. *shall – should/ought to*

6.5.1. *shall* im Sinne von "sollen"[10] kommt vorwiegend in der **Frageform der 1. Pers.** Sing. und Plur. vor[11], wenn der angesprochenen Person ein Vorschlag oder

---
[7] "will" zum Ausdruck der Absicht ist betont und hat deshalb keine Kurzform.
[8] Peter used to/would speak English a lot when he was abroad. (aber:) Peter is used to speaking English. (s. 8.2.1.3.)
[9] Im AE auch: Did (you) used to, (I) didn't used to.
[10] shall-Futur s. 2.5.1.
[11] In der 2. und 3. Person kann "shall" eine Anordnung, eine angedrohte Konsequenz, zuweilen auch ein Versprechen bezeichnen. Diese Anwendung von "shall" wirkt im heutigen Englischen sehr formal, in der Umgangssprache etwas altmodisch: Each applicant shall submit a curriculum vitae. (besser:) ... must/is to submit ... = muß einreichen.

Angebot unterbreitet werden soll oder von ihr eine Anordnung bzw. Empfehlung erwartet wird.
Shall we come tomorrow? – Shall I help you? – What shall we do now?

6.5.2. *should* (im Sinne von "sollte/müßte"[12]) und **ought to** haben annähernd gleiche Bedeutung. Mit folgendem **Infinitiv Präsens** bezeichnen sie eine auf die Gegenwart oder Zukunft bezogene Aufforderung, Verpflichtung oder Empfehlung.
You should/ought to eat more vitamins. – Eric should/ought to repay the money at once. – Lisa should not/shouldn't (oder: ought not to/oughtn't to) take this matter too seriously.
Mit *ought to* kann zusätzlich betont werden, daß etwas objektiv notwendig ist.
You should read this book. (= I recommend you to read ...) – You ought to read this book for your examination. (= It is really advisable that you read ...)
should/ought to können außerdem eine **große Wahrscheinlichkeit** oder **starke Vermutung** zum Ausdruck bringen.
They should/ought to be back by noon. (= It is quite probable that they will be back by noon.) – The telephone is ringing, that should/ought to be my girl-friend.
should kommt häufig – anstelle von *must* – bei **Gebrauchs-** oder **Bedienungsanweisungen** in der Fachsprache vor.
Morphine should be used in small doses only. (Morphium sollte/darf nur in geringer Dosis verwendet werden.) – This type of machinery should not be operated by unskilled workers. (Ungelernte Arbeiter sollten solche Maschinen nicht bedienen.)
Im Fragesatz kann *should* auch ein **höfliches Angebot** oder eine **Bitte um Rat** zum Ausdruck bringen.
Should I help you with the translation? (Soll/Kann ich dir bei der Übersetzung helfen?) – Should we discuss the matter with Fred?

6.5.3. Für das deutsche Hilfsverb **sollen**, dessen unterschiedliche Bedeutungen sich nur zum Teil mit den Anwendungsmöglichkeiten von *shall, should, ought to* decken, ergeben sich **folgende Umschreibungen**:

6.5.3.1. *be to* = "sollen" im Sinne einer **Aufforderung, Anordnung, Festlegung**[13], **Erwartung** (häufig als Frage); verneint als Aufforderung, etwas nicht zu tun. In dieser Bedeutung kommt *be to* nur im Präsens und Präteritum vor. (s. auch: 6.5.3.1.1.)
You are to type this letter at once. – Frank is to give a lecture today. – The French ambassador is to open an exhibition of impressionist paintings by Monet and Cézanne in the Moscow Tretyakov Gallery this week. (Im Zeitungsstil bei Überschriften häufig verkürzt zu: French ambassador to open an exhibition ...) – The test is to be repeated next week. – When am I to come? (= When shall I come?) – What

---

[12] s. auch "should" als Konditionalform (Kapitel 3) und als Umschreibung eines Konjunktivs (Kapitel 10).
[13] Festlegung oder Verpflichtung wird zuweilen auch mit "be due to" umschrieben: Roy is due to start teaching at our school next spring.

are we to do now? (= What shall we do now?) – You are not to leave before they have phoned.

Beachten Sie: Die Konstruktion *be to* + **Infinitiv Passiv** kann unterschiedliche Bedeutungen haben:
– einmal entsprechend dt. "sollen" im Sinne einer Erwartung oder Aufforderung:
  The problem was to be solved yesterday (but it was not);
– zum anderen zur Darstellung eines bloßen Sachverhalts:
  Unfortunately, no solution to the problem was to be found yesterday (that's why we must continue our efforts);
– oder auch als Formulierung einer Anweisung:
  The questionnaire is to be filled in very carefully. (= ... must/should be filled in ...).

6.5.3.1.1. *was/were to* mit folgendem **Infinitiv Präsens** bezieht eine Aufforderung, Anordnung oder Festlegung auf die **Vergangenheit**, ohne darauf zu verweisen, ob sie erfüllt wurde.
was/were to mit folgendem **Infinitiv Perfekt** verweist immer darauf, daß eine Aufforderung, Anordnung oder Festlegung **nicht** erfüllt wurde. Tom *was to sign* the contract yesterday; do you know if he did? (aber:) Tom *was to have signed* (oder: was to sign) the contract yesterday, but he didn't. (deutsch in beiden Fällen: Tom sollte ... unterschreiben, ...)
(Ebenso:) Have you got a message from John? He *was to inform* us about his decision this morning. (aber:) John *was to have informed* us about his decision until last night, but he didn't leave a message.

Durch *was/were to* wird auch auf eine **Entwicklung** oder **Folgeerscheinung** verwiesen, die zu einem bestimmten Zeitpunkt in der Vergangenheit noch nicht absehbar war.
After the presentation of his first plays nobody would have thought that Tennessee Williams was to become one of the most famous playwrights of the 20th century. (..., daß Tennessee Williams ... werden sollte.)

6.5.3.1.2. Zwischen *was/were to* und *should, ought to* mit folgendem Infinitiv Präsens muß in der Anwendung genau unterschieden werden. Während bei *was/ were to* ein Bezug auf die **Vergangenheit** gegeben ist, verweisen *should, ought to* auf **Gegenwart oder Zukunft**.
Bob was to ring back half an hour ago. (Bob sollte vor einer halben Stunde zurückrufen.) – Bob should/ought to ring back any moment. (Bob müßte jeden Augenblick zurückrufen.) –
The talks were to be continued last week. – The talks should/ought to be continued next week.

6.5.3.2. *be expected to*[14] = "sollen" im Sinne einer **Erwartung**.
They are expected to start work on the new project next week. (Sie sollen mit dem neuen Projekt nächste Woche beginnen.)

---
[14] s. auch 5.8.1.

L 6.6.1.

be supposed to[14] = "sollen" wird verwendet,
– um eine **Erwartung** auszudrücken, die eine gewisse **Verpflichtung** einbezieht (a);
– um einen **kritischen Hinweis** oder eine **Ermahnung** zu geben, daß eine bestimmte Erwartung noch nicht erfüllt worden ist (b);
– (verneint:) um jemanden zu ermahnen, etwas nicht zu tun[15] (c);
– gelegentlich auch, um eine **Vermutung** auszudrücken (d).
You are supposed to (= ought to) assist Tom in preparing the experiment. (a) (Du sollst Tom bei der Vorbereitung des Versuchs unterstützen.) – How can you be doing a crossword puzzle now; you are supposed to be washing the dishes. (b) (= ... you ought to be washing ...) (Wie kannst du jetzt Kreuzworträtsel lösen; du solltest doch jetzt abwaschen.) – You are not supposed to talk about the arrangement before it has been accepted. (c) (= You are not to talk ...) (Du sollst nicht über die Vereinbarung sprechen, ehe sie akzeptiert ist.) – Paul is supposed to have inherited a lot of money from his uncle. (d) (= Paul is said to have inherited ...) (Paul soll ... geerbt haben.)

Beachten Sie: Wird "sollen" verwendet, um nach einer bestimmten Erwartung seitens des Gesprächspartners zu **fragen**, so kann es auch mit *want to* (5.7.2.) umschrieben werden.
Do you want me to meet you at the station?

6.5.3.3. *be said to*[14] = "sollen" im Sinne einer **Vermutung** oder einer auf Wissen bzw. Erfahrung gestützten Annahme.
Eve is said to be ill. = It is believed that Eve is ill. (Eve soll krank sein.) – Dr King is said to be an excellent surgeon. = People say Dr. King is an excellent surgeon.

Wird *be said to* zur Angabe einer **bekannten Eigenschaft** verwendet, entspricht es nicht deutsch "sollen": People who cannot distinguish between colours are said to be colour-blind. (... nennt man ...)

6.5.3.4. *be intended/meant/designed to*[14] = "sollen" im Sinne einer **Absicht** oder einer **Funktionsbestimmung**.
The present paper is intended/meant to give a survey of recent findings in cancer research. (Der vorliegende Artikel soll eine Übersicht über neue Erkenntnisse in der Krebsforschung geben.) – The new theatre is designed to (= is to) seat about 1 000 people. (Das neue Theater soll etwa 1 000 Sitzplätze haben.)

6.6. *must* und *need* (verneint:) *need not/needn't/(don't need to)*

6.6.1. *must* bezeichnet eine **Notwendigkeit** oder eine **Verpflichtung**, die

---

[15] Eine Aufforderung, etwas nicht zu tun, kann ausgedrückt werden durch: "ought not to/should not" = dringende Empfehlung; "am/is/are not to" oder "am/is/are not supposed to" = nachdrückliche Aufforderung; "am/is/are not allowed/permitted to" oder "must not" = Verbot.
You should not pass on this information. – You are not (supposed) to pass on this information. – You are not allowed/permitted to pass on this information. = You must not pass on this information.

L 6.6.1.

stärker ist als im Falle von *should/ought to*. Es kommt in der Regel nur im Präsens vor.[16]

Äquivalentformen sind: *have to/have got to*[17].

have to kann in allen Zeiten verwendet werden und wird im modernen Englisch bei Frage und Verneinung im Präsens und Präteritum mit *do* umschrieben.

have got to kommt im Präsens, gelegentlich auch im Präteritum, vor, wird nicht mit *do* umschrieben und findet sich vor allem in der Umgangssprache.

Peter must/has to repeat the examination. – We must apologize to her. – When must I come this afternoon? – You don't have to hurry up. – We had to repeat the test. – Some tests had to be repeated. – Do you have to/Have you got to translate the text at once? – The letter has (got) to be typed at once. – Did you have to wait long? – Fortunately I didn't have to stay in hospital for a long time. – We'll have to work a lot over the weekend. – Glen told us he had had to postpone his trip. (... er habe seine Reise verschieben müssen.) – The calculations will have to be checked exactly. (Man wird die Berechnungen überprüfen müssen.)

Beachten Sie: Zwischen *must* und *have (got) to* im Präsens kann sich ein Unterschied in der Anwendung ergeben: Bei *must* beruht die Notwendigkeit meist auf einer Entscheidung des Sprechenden selbst, bei *have (got) to* geht die Notwendigkeit auf äußere Umstände zurück (Vereinbarung, Verpflichtung, Vorschrift usw.).

I must go to the doctor, I don't feel well today.
I've got to go to the doctor, I've got an appointment today.
I must talk to Tom. = I think it's necessary that I talk to Tom.
We've (got) to talk to Tom. = I'm expected to talk to Tom.
We've (got) to leave now, because there is a seminar at 4 p.m.
I must work on Sunday because I've got to finish some designs by Monday. (That means: I've decided to work on Sunday, because the designs have to be ready by Monday.)

In der Bedeutung von *must* oder *have (got) to* kommt gelegentlich auch *need* als **Vollverb** vor.

You have to have an invitation if you want to attend the conference. (= You need to have an invitation ...)
The matter has (got) to be settled today. (= ... needs to be settled today.)
Did you really have to come home so late? (= Did you really need to come home so late?)
I'll have to think the matter over. (= I'll need to think ...)

---

[16] Als Präteritalform kann "must" in der indirekten Rede stehen: We realized that we must give up the plan.

[17] Im BE wird vor allem "have got to" verwendet, wenn eine spezielle Verpflichtung vorliegt, bei einer allgemeinen Verpflichtung wird "have to" vorgezogen: I've got to leave now. (aber:) I have to leave home at six on workdays. – Have you got to speak French at the conference? (aber:) Do you often have to speak French?
Im AE kann "have to" in beiden Fällen verwendet werden; diese Tendenz deutet sich auch im BE an.
In der amerikanischen Umgangssprache entfällt bei "have got to" zuweilen "have": I got to do it at once.

In Fragesätzen **ohne** Fragewort steht im Präsens gelegentlich *need* als **Modalverb**, häufiger jedoch finden sich die Formen *do (I) have to ...?* bzw. *have (I) got to ...?* Do we have to leave now? / Have we got to leave now? / Must we leave now? (oder auch:) Need we leave now? / Do we need to leave now?

Aber **mit** Fragewort nur: When do we have to leave? / When have we got to leave? (oder:) When must we leave?

Neben *(I) don't have to/haven't got to* kann eine Notwendigkeit verneint werden durch *(I) need not/(I) needn't* oder *(I) don't need to*[18]: You don't have to / haven't got to tell us all the details. = You needn't / don't need to tell us ... (Du brauchst nicht ...)

6.6.2. Verpflichtung, Notwendigkeit oder Zwang auf Grund äußerer Umstände kann auch ausgedrückt werden durch *be obliged to,* (stärker:) *be forced / compelled to.* Eine unvermeidbare Konsequenz wird auch durch *be bound to* ausgedrückt.
If the agreement is not accepted in its present form, we shall be obliged to make some concessions. (= ..., we shall have to make ...) – In 1633, Galileo was forced to recant his heliocentric conception of the universe before the Inquisition. (= In 1633, Galileo had to recant ...)
My friend was compelled by illness to interrupt his studies for one year.
Such a thing was bound to happen. (= ... simply had to happen.)

6.6.3. *must* kann auch eine starke Wahrscheinlichkeit zum Ausdruck bringen; durch *cannot / can't* wird die Wahrscheinlichkeit verneint.
The Millers have got two cars, they must make a lot of money. – You ate three sandwiches an hour ago, you can't be hungry again.

6.7. *may, can, might, could, should, ought to, must* und *need not* mit folgendem **Infinitiv Perfekt** beziehen die Aussage auf die **Vergangenheit**.

– *may* bezeichnet eine **Möglichkeit oder Vermutung** (a), *may not* schränkt die Möglichkeit ein (b), *cannot* schließt sie aus (c). Wird nach einer Möglichkeit gefragt, so steht nicht *may* sondern *can* (d).
– *might* bringt eine im Vergleich zu *may* vagere Vermutung (e) oder auch eine nicht verwirklichte Möglichkeit (f) zum Ausdruck.
– *could* bezeichnet eine nicht genutzte Fähigkeit oder Möglichkeit (g) oder auch eine Möglichkeit, bei der es offen ist, ob sie genutzt wurde (h); es kann auch einen leichten Vorwurf beinhalten (i).

---

[18] "don't have to / needn't" bringt zum Ausdruck, daß etwas nicht zu geschehen braucht, "should not / ought not to", daß etwas eigentlich nicht geschehen dürfte oder sollte, "must not", daß etwas nicht geschehen darf:
We don't have to / needn't talk about the project at the moment. (= It isn't necessary that we talk about ...)
We shouldn't / ought not to talk about ... (= It is most advisable not to talk about ...)
We must not talk about ... (= We are not allowed to talk about ...)

L 6.7.

– *could not* verweist auf eine verneinte Möglichkeit bzw. Fähigkeit (j); eine negative Schlußfolgerung kann durch *could not* oder auch *can't* ausgedrückt werden (k).

Bill may have missed the train.[19] (a) (= Bill has probably missed the train.) (Bill hat vielleicht den Zug verpaßt.)
Liz may not have recognized me. (b) (= Perhaps Liz didn't recognize me.) (Vielleicht hat Liz mich nicht erkannt.)
They can't have got the letter yet. (c) (= It is impossible that they have already got the letter.) (Sie können den Brief unmöglich schon bekommen haben.)
Where can I have put my umbrella? (d) (Wo kann ich meinen Regenschirm hingelegt haben?)
They might have stayed with their friends overnight.[19] (e) (= It might be possible that they stayed ...) (Sie haben möglicherweise bei ihren Freunden übernachtet.)
(aber:) They might/could have stayed with their friends overnight. (f, g) (= It would have been possible for them to stay ..., but they didn't.) (Sie hätten bei ihren Freunden übernachten können.)
I could have informed you (if you had asked me). (g) (= It would have been possible for me ...) (Ich hätte dich informieren können.)
Eve could have drunk the whisky. (h) (= Eve had an opportunity to drink the whisky.) (Eva könnte den Whisky getrunken haben.)
You could have been more careful. (i) (Du hättest wirklich vorsichtiger sein können.)
I couldn't have advised you on this matter. (j) (= I wouldn't have been able to advise you ...) (Ich hätte dich in dieser Angelegenheit nicht beraten können.)
I think somebody has helped Tom, he couldn't/can't have solved the problem himself. (k) (= ...Tom would have been unable to solve ...) (Ich denke, jemand hat Tom geholfen, er hätte das Problem nicht selbst lösen können.)

should/ought to mit folgendem **Infinitiv Perfekt** drücken aus,
– daß eine Verpflichtung oder Erwartung nicht erfüllt worden ist,[20] (a)
– daß eine notwendige Handlung unterlassen wurde (b) oder
– daß etwas inzwischen sehr wahrscheinlich geschehen ist. (c)

Mit *should not/ought not to* wird etwas in der Vergangenheit Geschehenes mißbilligt. (d)

---

[19] Beachten Sie bei der Verwendung von "may" und "might":
He may have stolen the car. = It is possible that he has stolen the car (but we don't know if he did).
He might have stolen the car. = It is possible that he has stolen the car (but it's not very probable).
He might have stolen the car kann außerdem bedeuten: It would have been possible for him to steal the car (but he didn't).
[20] Neben "should/ought to + Infinitiv Perfekt" kann "was/were to + Infinitiv Perfekt" verwendet werden, wenn es sich um eine Festlegung oder Vereinbarung handelt, die nicht eingehalten wurde (s. 6.5.3.1.1): The plane from Cairo should have landed/was to have landed at 3.15 (but it was delayed).

I ought to/should have submitted the manuscript yesterday. (a) (= I was supposed to submit ...) (Ich hätte das Manuskript gestern einreichen sollen.)
You should/ought to have left a message. (a) (= We had expected you to leave ...) (Du hättest eine Nachricht hinterlassen sollen.)
His hints should/ought to have been taken into consideration. (b) (= It was wrong not to take his hints into consideration.) (Man hätte seine Hinweise berücksichtigen sollen.)
Jim should/ought to have arrived by now.[21] (c) (= It is quite likely that Jim has arrived by now./Jim may well have arrived by now.) (Jim müßte inzwischen angekommen sein.)
You should not/ought not to have kept Eve waiting so long. (d) (= It was very impolite to keep Eve waiting so long.) (Du hättest Eve nicht so lange warten lassen sollen.)

must + **Infinitiv Perfekt** bringt eine starke Wahrscheinlichkeit oder Gewißheit zum Ausdruck. (a)

need not/needn't drückt aus, daß etwas in der Vergangenheit hätte nicht zu geschehen brauchen oder vermeidbar gewesen wäre. (b)

don't have to drückt aus, daß nicht sicher ist, ob etwas wirklich geschehen ist. (c)

can't verweist darauf, daß etwas unter keinen Umständen geschehen konnte. (d)

It must have been nice to see her again. (a) (= I'm sure it was nice to see her again.) (Es muß schön gewesen sein, sie wiederzusehen.)
They haven't come yet, something must have kept them. (a) (= ..., most probably something has kept them.) (Sie sind noch nicht gekommen, etwas muß sie aufgehalten haben.)
Bob looks tired, he must have been working a lot. (a) (Bob sieht müde aus, er hat offenbar viel gearbeitet.)
These details need not have been gone into. (b) (= It was not necessary to go into these details.) (Auf diese Einzelheiten hätte man nicht einzugehen brauchen.)
The accident doesn't have to have happened the way the witness described it. (c) (= It is not certain whether the accident happened the way ...) (Der Unfall braucht sich nicht so ereignet zu haben, wie der Zeuge ihn beschrieben hat.)
I saw you at the cinema this morning, you can't have worked much today. (d) (..., du kannst heute nicht viel gearbeitet haben.)

Unterscheiden Sie:
Jim must have done it. (= I'm sure he did it.)
Jim can't have done it. (= It is impossible that Jim did it.)
Jim needn't have done it. (= There was no reason for Jim to do it.)
Jim doesn't have to have done it. (= It is not certain whether Jim did it.)

---

[21] Zuweilen muß der Kontext entscheiden, welcher Sinn zugrunde liegt: Bill ought to/should have finished the test in the meantime (he started it several hours ago). (Bill müßte den Versuch inzwischen beendet haben.) – (aber:) Bill should/ought to have finished the test (but he didn't). (Bill hätte den Versuch beenden sollen.)

7. Reported (Indirect) Speech – Die indirekte Rede

Aussagen können in der **direkten** oder **indirekten** Rede formuliert werden, z. B.:
He says, '*I* am busy.' → He says (that)[1] *he* is busy.
She says, 'It is raining.' → She says (that) it is raining.
She asks, 'Why isn't Tom in the office?' → She asks why Tom isn't in the office.
He asks, 'Do you know *my* friend?' → He asks if I know *his* friend.
They say, 'We can help her.' → They say (that) they can help her.

Bei der indirekten Rede gibt es bestimmte Grundmuster für die zeitliche Beziehung zwischen Hauptsatz und Nebensatz. Prinzipiell gilt dabei, daß im Gegensatz zum Deutschen eine indirekte Rede nicht im Konjunktiv formuliert wird.

Die häufigsten Verben, durch die eine indirekte Rede eingeleitet wird, sind: *say*[2], *tell*[2], *think, believe, suppose, know, hope, point out, report, state*; weiterhin: *announce, declare, promise, admit, deny, write, read, be sure, be afraid, fear, notice, answer, prove.*

7.1. Steht das Verb des Hauptsatzes im **Präsens**, so findet sich in der indirekten Rede dieselbe Zeitform wie in der direkten Rede.
They say, 'We like him.' → They say they like him.
He says, 'They have just left.' → He says they have just left.
She says, 'They left yesterday.' → She says they left yesterday.
They say, 'The test will be repeated.' → They say the test will be repeated.

7.1.1. Das gilt auch bei **Perfekt** oder **Futur** im Hauptsatz:
He has often said, 'I love her.' → He has often said he loves her.
He will say, 'I had no time to attend the meeting.' → He will say he had no time to attend the meeting.

7.2. Steht das Verb des Hauptsatzes im **Präteritum**, so ergeben sich folgende **Grundtypen**:

7.2.1. Hauptsatz: *Past Tense* – Nebensatz: *Past Tense*, um auszudrücken, daß etwas geschah oder gültig war zu dem Zeitpunkt, wo es erwähnt wurde, d. h. es handelt sich um eine auf die Gesprächssituation bezogene Gleichzeitigkeit, wobei offen bleiben kann, ob die Aussage noch auf die Gegenwart zutrifft.

---

[1] Der Nebensatz wird oft ohne "that" eingeleitet.
[2] Bei der indirekten Rede steht in der Regel nach "say" kein Personalobjekt, nach "tell" muß es stehen: Bob said (that) he would go abroad. (aber:) Bob told me (that) he would go abroad.
Bei der **direkten Rede** ist "say" mit Personalobjekt nur möglich, wenn es mit "to" angeschlossen wird; findet sich bei "tell" ein Personalobjekt, so steht es immer ohne "to".
He said (to me), 'See you tomorrow.' – He told me 'You needn't wait.'

He said, 'She is not at home.' → He said she was not at home. (Er sagte, sie sei nicht zu Hause.)
He said, 'It is raining.' → He said it was raining. (Er sagte, es regne.)
She said, 'I don't know him.' → She said she didn't know him. (Sie sagte, sie kenne ihn nicht.)
He said, 'I'm going to read a paper at the conference.' → He said he was going to read a paper at the conference. (2.5.1.5.) (Er sagte, daß er einen Vortrag auf der Konferenz halten werde.)
Mary said, 'Peter has to / must work.' → Mary said Peter had to / must work.[3] (Mary sagte, Peter müsse arbeiten.)
He said, 'You needn't come.' → He said I didn't have to come. (Er sagte, ich brauche nicht zu kommen.)
The doctor told me / said to me, 'You must not smoke any more.' → The doctor told me I must not / I was not allowed to smoke any more. (= The doctor told me not to smoke any more. s. 5.7.2.) (Der Arzt hat mir gesagt, ich dürfe nicht mehr rauchen.)

7.2.2.   Hauptsatz: *Past Tense*[4] – Nebensatz: *Past Perfect*, um auszudrücken, daß etwas stattgefunden hat oder gültig war, ehe es erwähnt wurde, d. h. es handelt sich um eine auf die Gesprächssituation bezogene Vorzeitigkeit.[5]
He said, 'I have made a mistake.' → He said (that) he had made a mistake. (Er sagte, er habe einen Fehler gemacht.)
He said, 'I was abroad.' → He said he had been abroad. (Er sagte, er sei im Ausland gewesen.)
She said, 'I was working on my doctoral thesis for five years.' → She said (that) she had been working on her doctoral thesis for five years. (Sie sagte, sie habe fünf Jahre an ihrer Dissertation gearbeitet.)
They said, 'We had to wait a long time.' → They said they had had to wait a long time. (Sie sagten, daß sie lange warten mußten.)

7.2.3.   Hauptsatz: *Past Tense*[6] – Nebensatz: *Conditional*, um auszudrücken, daß etwas geschehen wird.
He said, 'I shall / will go on a business trip tomorrow.' → He said he would go on a business trip tomorrow. (Er sagte, er werde morgen auf Dienstreise gehen.)

7.2.4.   Bei allgemeingültigen Feststellungen – auch subjektiver Natur – sowie Angaben von Eigenschaften, wissenschaftlichen Aussagen, Mitteilungen der Massenmedien findet sich im Nebensatz auch anstelle des *Past Tense* das *Present Tense*, anstelle des *Past Perfect* das *Present Perfect*, anstelle des *Conditional* das *Future*.

---

[3] Zu "have to / must" s. 6.6.1., Fußnote 16
[4] Gelegentlich auch Past Perfect: We had always believed the problem had been solved long ago.
[5] Ist der zeitliche Bezug zwischen Haupt- und Nebensatz durch eine entsprechende Zeitbestimmung eindeutig gegeben, so kann vor allem im gesprochenen Englisch im Nebensatz auch Past Tense stehen: He said he was ill last month.
[6] Gelegentlich auch Past Perfect: She had said she would come.

L 7.3.

We were told that there are/were two trains from Dresden to Rostock a day. (Man sagte uns, daß täglich zwei Züge von Dresden nach Rostock fahren.) − Susan said that roses are/were her favourite flowers. (Susan sagte, daß Rosen ihre Lieblingsblumen sind.) − We knew already that Peter is/was an excellent chess player. (Wir wußten schon, daß Peter ein ausgezeichneter Schachspieler ist.) − Galileo proved that the sun is/was the centre of the universe. (Galilei wies nach, daß die Sonne das Zentrum des Universums ist.) − It was reported yesterday that a new Soviet satellite has/had been put into orbit. (Gestern wurde berichtet, daß die SU einen neuen Satelliten auf eine Erdumlaufbahn gebracht hat.) − It was announced in the news that the Italian Prime Minister will/would be visiting Romania next week. (In den Nachrichten wurde bekanntgegeben, daß der italienische Ministerpräsident nächste Woche Rumänien besuchen wird.)

7.3. Die **Zeitenfolge der indirekten Rede** gilt auch für die **indirekte Frage**. Der indirekte Fragesatz wird durch Fragewörter oder die Konjunktionen *if/whether* eingeleitet; dabei bleibt die Wortstellung **S − P − O** erhalten.
She often says, 'Why do you drink so much coffee?' → She often asks why I drink so much coffee.
He often says, 'Do you want to be a teacher?' → He often asks if/whether I want to be a teacher.
I said to Bob, 'Are you still working in a design office?' → I asked Bob if/whether he was still working in a design office.
She said, 'How does John feel after his operation?' → She asked how John felt after his operation.
Peggy said, 'Where have you been?' → Peggy wanted to know where I had been.
They said, 'Will you attend the conference?' → They inquired if I would attend the conference.

Anmerkung: Der Logik des zeitlichen Bezugs entsprechend muß zuweilen eine Zeit- oder Ortsbestimmung verändert werden, z. B.:
She said, 'I talked to him a fortnight ago.' → She said (that) she talked/had talked to him a fortnight ago. (aber:)
Last week she said, 'I talked to him a fortnight ago.' → Last week she said (that) she had talked to him a fortnight before.
She said, 'Did you go dancing last night?' → She asked me if I went/had gone dancing last night. (aber:)
Yesterday she asked me, 'Did you go dancing last night?' → Yesterday she asked me if/whether I had gone dancing the night before.
When I saw Alice in a café yesterday she said, 'We'll meet here again tomorrow.' → When I saw Alice in a café yesterday she said we would meet there again the next day/(oder:) the following day.

8. The Gerund – Das Gerundium

	Active	Passive
Present	writing	being written
Perfect	having written	having been written

Die Präsensformen des Gerundiums bezeichnen eine Gleichzeitigkeit, gelegentlich auch eine Vorzeitigkeit, die Perfektformen nur eine Vorzeitigkeit in Bezug auf den Kontext des Satzes.
(Gleichzeitigkeit:) I must apologize for *being* late. – Did you succeed in *passing* the driving test? – Hugh dislikes *being criticized*.
(Vorzeitigkeit:) After *finishing* our work we went to the cinema. – Peter denied *having stolen* the car. – Clare can be proud of *having been awarded* the first prize in the contest.

8.1.   Im Satzzusammenhang kann das Gerundium substantivischen oder verbalen Charakter haben.

Hat das Gerundium die Funktion eines **Substantivs**, so kann es **Subjekt** (a) und **Objekt** (b) oder **prädikative Ergänzung** zu **be** (c) sein. Es kann ein Artikel + *of*-Genitiv (d), ein Adjektiv (e), ein Possessivpronomen (f) oder ein *s*-Genitiv (g) hinzutreten.
Swimming is healthy. (a) (Schwimmen ist gesund.)
Bess enjoys dancing. (b) (Bess tanzt sehr gern.)
My favourite pastime is reading. (c) (Meine Lieblingsbeschäftigung in der Freizeit ist Lesen.)
The restoring of the castle[1] took ten years. (d) (Die Restaurierung des Schlosses dauerte 10 Jahre.)
Her permanent talking is getting on my nerves. (f, e) (Ihr ständiges Reden geht mir auf die Nerven.)
We were annoyed at John's unreasonable arguing. (g, e) (Wir waren über Johns unvernünftiges Argumentieren verärgert.)

Wird dem Gerundium ein Objekt angefügt (a), so nimmt es verbale Funktion an; es kann im Perfekt (b) und Passiv (c) stehen oder auch durch ein Adverb (d) näher bestimmt werden.
I dislike writing letters. (a) (Ich schreibe nicht gern Briefe.) – Visiting the Berlin Pergamon Museum is always worthwhile. (a) (Der Besuch des Berliner Pergamonmuseums lohnt sich immer.)
Three terrorists of hitherto unknown nationality are suspected of having hijacked the airliner. (b) (Drei Terroristen bisher unbekannter Nationalität werden verdächtigt, das Verkehrsflugzeug entführt zu haben.) – Betty hates being criticized. (c)

---

[1] Gelegentlich kein Artikel, aber of-Genitiv: Rusting of metals is a well-known chemical phenomenon. (Das Rosten von Metallen ist ...)

(Betty läßt sich nicht gern kritisieren.) – I regret not having been invited. (c) (Ich bedaure, daß ich nicht eingeladen worden bin.) This article is worth reading carefully. (d) (Es lohnt sich, diesen Artikel sorgfältig zu lesen.)

8.2. Das Verb steht in der Form des Gerundiums nach **allen Präpositionen**, nach **bestimmten Verben**, nach **Verb-Adverb-Verbindungen** *(Phrasal Verbs)* und nach **einigen feststehenden Wendungen**:
She went away *without leaving* a message. – Have you *finished reading* the article? – You should *give up smoking*. – *It's no use discussing* the matter again.

8.2.1. Nach Präpositionen steht das Verb in der Form des Gerundiums. Möglich sind die Verbindungen **Verb + Präposition, Adjektiv/** *Past Participle* **+ Präposition, Substantiv + Präposition**.
Die Präposition kann auch ohne vorangehendes Bezugswort stehen.

8.2.1.1. **Verb (im Aktiv) + Präposition**, z. B.:

abstain/desist/refrain from sich enthalten, unterlassen; *apologize for* sich entschuldigen wegen; *boast of/brag of, about/pride o.s. on* sich rühmen; *complain of/ about* sich beschweren; *confine/limit/restrict o.s. to*[2] sich beschränken; *contribute to* beitragen; *decide against* sich entscheiden gegen; *depend (up)on* abhängen von; *dream of* träumen (von); *insist (up)on/persist in* bestehen auf; *object to* Einspruch erheben/etw. einwenden gegen; *rely/depend/count/reckon (up)on* sich verlassen auf; *result in* zur Folge haben; *shrink from* zurückschrecken vor; *speak/talk about, of* sprechen über/von; *succeed in* gelingen, können; *think of* vorhaben, daran denken daß, halten von.
They are thinking of spending their holidays abroad this year. (Sie haben vor, ihre Ferien dieses Jahr im Ausland zu verbringen.) – Did you succeed in settling the matter? (Konntest du die Angelegenheit klären?) – Bert insists on being consulted in this matter. (Bert besteht darauf, in dieser Angelegenheit befragt zu werden.) – I shall confine myself to outlining some aspects of the problem. (Ich werde mich darauf beschränken, einige Aspekte des Problems darzulegen.)

8.2.1.2. **Verb + Objekt**[3] **+ Präposition** bzw. **Verb im Passiv + Präposition**, z. B.:

accuse sb of anklagen; *blame sb for/reproach sb for, with* tadeln; *charge sb with* (häufig im Passiv) beschuldigen; *criticize sb for* kritisieren; *excuse/forgive/pardon sb for* entschuldigen, vergeben; *inveigle/deceive sb into* verleiten; *keep/prevent/*

---
[2] Beachten Sie, daß "to" Teil des Infinitivs oder Präposition sein kann: I want to go now. (aber:) You should limit yourself to smoking five cigarettes a day.
Als Unterscheidungskriterium gilt: Ist "to" Präposition, so kann ein Substantiv (oder Pronomen) folgen: Tom is used to good food.
Folgt ein Verb, so steht es in der Form des Gerundiums: Tom is used to eating very well.
(aber:) He used to eat a lot until recently.
[3] Das Gerundium bezieht sich auf das Objekt des Satzes. (Vergleiche dazu jedoch: 8.6.)

stop sb **from** hindern; *protect sb/sth* **against, from** schützen; *save sb from* retten, schützen; *suspect sb of* verdächtigen; *talk/persuade sb into* überreden; *talk sb out of/dissuade sb from* abraten.
They criticized me for being much too late. = I was criticized for being much too late. (Man hat mich kritisiert, weil ich viel zu spät kam.) – A nineteen-year-old motorist is accused of having caused the traffic accident. (Ein 19-jähriger Kraftfahrer steht unter Anklage, den Verkehrsunfall verursacht zu haben.) – It is impossible to talk Tom into accepting our offer. (Es ist unmöglich, Tom zu überreden, unser Angebot anzunehmen.)

8.2.1.3. **Adjektiv/Past Participle/Substantiv + Präposition**, z. B.:

be accustomed[4] */used to* gewöhnt sein an; *get used/accustomed to* sich gewöhnen; *be aimed at* zielen auf; beabsichtigen; *be bent/intent/keen (up)on* sehr interessiert sein; *be (in)capable of* (nicht) können; *be charged with* beauftragt sein mit, beschuldigt werden; *be convinced of* überzeugt sein von; *be experienced in* erfahren sein in; *be far from* weit davon entfernt sein; *be fond of* mögen, etw. gern tun; *be good/bad at* etw. gut/nicht gut können; *be justified in* berechtigt/gerechtfertigt sein; *be mistaken/wrong in* sich irren; *be proud of* stolz sein auf; *be right in* recht haben (mit); *be tired of* überdrüssig sein;
difficulty/trouble[5] *in* Schwierigkeiten (bei); *experience in* Erfahrung (in); *hope of*[6] Hoffnung (auf); *interest (in)* Interesse (an); *key/approach to* Schlüssel (für); Ansatz zu; *method of/approach to* Methode/Verfahren zu; *objection to* Einwand gegen; *opportunity/chance of*[6] Gelegenheit zu; *possibility/way of*[6] Möglichkeit zu; *precondition/requirement for* Voraussetzung/Bedingung für; *prerequisite to/for* Voraussetzung für; *reason for*[6] Grund für; *starting point for* Ausgangspunkt für.
Außerdem **Wendungen** wie: *there is an/there is no alternative to* es besteht eine/keine Alternative zu; *it is a matter of* es handelt sich um; *there is little/no point in* es hat wenig/keinen Zweck; *be on the point/verge of* (2.5.6.) im Begriff sein; *there is some/little/no probability of* es ist möglich/wenig wahrscheinlich/unwahrscheinlich; *run the risk of* das Risiko eingehen; *take pleasure in* Gefallen finden an, sich erfreuen an.
I'm not used/accustomed to staying up late. (Ich bin nicht daran gewöhnt, lange aufzubleiben.) – Dora is fond of listening to classical music. (Dora hört gern klassische Musik.) – I'm far from doubting your words. (Es liegt mir fern, deine Worte zu bezweifeln.) – We had some difficulty/trouble in getting accommodation at a hotel. (Es war ziemlich schwierig, eine Hotelunterkunft zu finden.) – So far we haven't found an approach/a key to solving the problem. (Bis jetzt haben wir keinen Ansatz zur Lösung des Problems gefunden.) – There is little point in continuing this debate. (Es hat wenig Zweck, diese Debatte fortzusetzen.)

---

[4] Anstelle des Gerundiums findet sich gelegentlich auch der Infinitiv.
[5] "in" entfällt oft: I had trouble (in) finding out Tom's address.
[6] Auch der Infinitiv möglich.

L 8.2.1.4.

8.2.1.4. Präpositionen ohne vorangehendes Bezugswort:

after nachdem, nach; *before* bevor, vor, ehe; *by* dadurch daß, indem; *on* als, wenn, bei; *through* dadurch daß; *in* indem, wenn, bei; *for* weil, um zu; *without* ohne zu; und nach Ausdrücken wie: *instead of* anstatt zu; *in spite of* obwohl; *aside/apart from* neben, abgesehen von; *in addition to* neben, außer; *with a view to* um zu; *be close/near to, to come close/near to* nahe daran sein.
After finishing[7] our work we went to the cinema. (Nachdem wir unsere Arbeit beendet hatten, gingen wir ins Kino.) – By reading English books Mary has been steadily increasing her word power. (Mary hat ihren Wortschatz ständig erweitert, indem sie englische Bücher liest.) – Don't leave without apologizing to Jean. (Geh nicht weg, ohne dich bei Jean zu entschuldigen.) – On coming home[8] we found the door unlocked. (Als wir nach Hause kamen, stellten wir fest, daß die Tür nicht verschlossen war.) – Instead of working Glen went dancing. (Anstatt zu arbeiten, ging Glen tanzen.) – Jane came close to winning a prize in the competition. (Jane hätte bei dem Wettbewerb beinahe einen Preis gewonnen.)

8.2.2. Das Gerundium steht auch nach **Verb + Adverb** *(Phrasal Verb)* und **Verb + Adverb + Präposition:**

give up aufgeben; *go on/keep on* etw. immer wieder/weiter tun; *leave off* aufhören; *look forward to* sich freuen auf; *put off* auf-, verschieben; *take to* Gefallen finden an, sich zuwenden.
We had to put off discussing this problem. (Wir mußten die Besprechung dieses Problems verschieben.) – If Frank doesn't answer the phone, keep on trying. (Wenn sich Frank nicht am Telefon meldet, versuche es immer wieder.)

8.3. Ein folgendes Verb steht in der Form des Gerundiums nach:

avoid vermeiden; *consider*[9]*/contemplate* erwägen, vorhaben; *defer/delay/postpone* aufschieben; *detest* verabscheuen; *dislike* nicht mögen; *enjoy* etw. sehr gern tun; *escape* entgehen, -kommen; *finish* aufhören; *keep*[10] etw. immer wieder/weiter tun; *mind*[11] (nur in Frage und Verneinung) etw. dagegen haben; *miss* verpassen; *resent* übelnehmen; *resist* widerstehen; *risk* wagen, riskieren; *stop* aufhören.
Stop quarrelling. (Hört auf, euch zu streiten!) – I enjoy listening to records. (Ich höre gern Schallplatten.) – Have you finished analysing the results? (Sind Sie mit der Analyse der Ergebnisse fertig?) – Keep moving! (Nicht stehenbleiben!) – Would you mind closing the window? (Würdest du bitte das Fenster schließen?) – Do you mind showing our guests the town? (Zeigst du bitte unseren Gästen die Stadt?) – Mary does not mind being questioned about her private life. (Mary hat nichts dagegen, wenn man sie nach ihrem.Privatleben fragt.)

---

[7] Seltener: After having finished our work we went to the movies. In der Umgangssprache oft Nebensatz: After we had finished our work ...
[8] In der Umgangssprache häufiger Nebensatz: When we came home we ...
[9] "consider" im Sinne von "halten für" s. 5.7.2.1.
[10] "keep" entspricht häufig "keep on": He kept (on) talking.
[11] Anstelle des Gerundiums steht oft ein if-Satz: Do you mind if I smoke?

Nach mehreren Verben kann anstelle des Gerundiums auch ein Nebensatz stehen, z. B.: *admit* zugeben; *appreciate* (zu) schätzen (wissen); *deny* leugnen; *imagine/ fancy* (5.7.2.1.) sich (etw.) vorstellen; *include/involve* einschließen, beinhalten; *mean* bedeuten; *remember/recall/recollect* sich erinnern; *suggest*[12] vorschlagen. Ted denied having anything to do with the affair. (Ted leugnete, etwas mit der Angelegenheit zu tun zu haben.) – I remember meeting[13] Sue before. (Ich erinnere mich, daß ich Sue schon einmal begegnet bin.) – We appreciate having such a reliable co-worker. (Wir wissen es zu schätzen, daß wir einen so zuverlässigen Mitarbeiter haben.) – The change-over of production in our factory means saving a lot of labour. (Die Produktionsumstellung in unserem Betrieb bedeutet eine Einsparung vieler Arbeitskräfte.)

8.4. Das Gerundium steht nach **bestimmten Wendungen**:

it is no good/use es hat keinen Zweck; *is it any good/use...?* hat es irgendeinen Zweck...? *it is worth* (+ Gerundium im Aktiv) es lohnt sich; *(I) have done* (Ich) bin fertig mit; *what/how about...?* Wie wäre es, wenn ...? *(I) can't help* (ich) kann nicht umhin; *(I) can't stand* (ich) kann es nicht ertragen; *there is no* man kann nicht; *look like* aussehen, als ob; *feel like/feel up to* Lust haben zu, in der Stimmung sein; *it is like* es ist, als ob; *there is nothing like* es geht nichts über; *like* wie, z. B.; *besides/as well as* neben, außer; *be busy* beschäftigt sein und in Ausdrücken wie: *go shopping/swimming/dancing*, etc; *do some shopping/ cleaning/washing/typing*, etc.
It is worth seeing this film./This film is worth seeing. (Dieser Film ist sehenswert.) – It's no use/good waiting any longer. (Es hat keinen Zweck, noch länger zu warten.) – What about going to the theatre tonight?/How about going ...? (Wie wäre es, wenn wir heute abend ins Theater gingen?) – I don't feel like working this afternoon. (Ich habe keine Lust, heute nachmittag zu arbeiten.) – The weather looks like changing. (Es sieht aus, als ob sich das Wetter ändert.) – To see the film version of Hemingway's 'The Old Man and The Sea' is like reading the book a second time. (Wenn man die Verfilmung von Hemingways "Der alte Mann und das Meer" sieht, so ist es, als ob man das Buch zum zweiten Mal liest.) – We could do something special today like going to a cabaret. (Wir könnten heute etwas Besonderes unternehmen, z.B. in ein Kabarett gehen.) – As well as/Besides being very well illustrated the book is written in a brilliant style. (Das Buch ist in einem glänzenden Stil geschrieben und außerdem sehr gut illustriert.)

8.5. Nach *want, need, require* "erforderlich sein, müssen" steht das Gerundium im Aktiv, nach *need, require* auch der passivische Infinitiv.
The roof of our house needs repairing/to be repaired. (Das Dach unseres Hauses muß repariert werden.) – My car wants overhauling. (Mein Wagen muß überholt werden.)

---

[12] Bei "suggest" ergeben sich folgende Möglichkeiten: I suggest informing Bob. – I suggest (that) Bob should inform them/that Bob inform(s) them. (10.1.)
[13] Seltener: I remember having met Jane before.

8.6. Objekt + Gerundium

Bezieht sich die durch das Gerundium ausgedrückte Handlung oder Situation auf ein Objekt, das dem Verb (a) bzw. einem Verb/Adjektiv/Past Participle/Substantiv + Präposition (b) unmittelbar folgt, so steht das entsprechende Pronomen oder Substantiv im Objektkasus **direkt vor dem Gerundium** – wobei bekanntlich nur das Personalpronomen besondere Formen für den Objektkasus hat.
Do you mind me asking another question? (a) (= Do you mind if I ask another question?) (Haben Sie etwas dagegen, wenn ich noch eine Frage stelle?)
You can rely on me helping you. (b) (Du kannst dich darauf verlassen, daß ich dir helfe.) – The assistant insisted on the test being repeated. (b) (= ... insisted that the test should be repeated.) – We are proud of her having won the contest. (b) (Wir sind stolz darauf, daß sie den Wettbewerb gewonnen hat.) – I am used to Mary being late. (b) (Ich bin daran gewöhnt, daß Mary zu spät kommt.) – There is no chance of the damage being repaired. (b)

Anmerkung: Vergleiche dagegen die Form Verb + Objekt + Präposition + *-ing* (s. 8.2.1.2.):
Our head of department charged me with carrying out the investigations.

Beachten Sie: bei *prevent/stop* (hindern an) sind beide Formen möglich:
It is impossible to prevent/stop him interfering. (s. 8.6.a)
It is impossible to prevent/stop him from interfering. (s. 8.2.1.2.)

8.6.1. Anstelle des Personalpronomens im Objektkasus kann auch das **Possessivpronomen** stehen. Bei Personen, zuweilen auch bei Länder- und Ortsnamen, findet sich gelegentlich der *s*-Genitiv, der jedoch im modernen Sprachgebrauch als formal empfunden wird.
Excuse my disturbing you. (= Excuse me disturbing you.) (Entschuldigen Sie, daß ich Sie störe.) – I think you can rely on his assisting you. (= ... rely on him assisting you.) (Ich glaube, du kannst dich darauf verlassen, daß er dich unterstützt.) – Roy denies their having lent him any money.[14] (Roy leugnet, daß sie ihm Geld geliehen haben.) – Do you object to my sister's taking part in our excursion? (Hast du etwas dagegen, daß meine Schwester an unserer Exkursion teilnimmt?) – The majority of the Irish people have never been happy about Britain's interfering in their domestic affairs. (Die Mehrheit der Iren hat sich nie recht wohl gefühlt, daß sich England in ihre inneren Angelegenheiten einmischt.)

8.7. Nach einigen Verben und Adjektiven sind **Gerundium und Infinitiv** möglich, wobei sich oft Unterschiede in der Bedeutung ergeben.

---

[14] Nach "deny" und "risk" steht meist das Possessivpronomen.

8.7.1. Nur geringe Bedeutungsunterschiede bestehen bei den folgenden Verben: *like, love, prefer, hate; begin, start, cease, continue*; sowie nach **be afraid, be sorry**.[15]

like, love, prefer, hate + Gerundium oder Infinitiv bezeichnen eine allgemeine Vorliebe für etwas oder eine Abneigung gegen etwas (a). Wird auf eine spezielle Situation verwiesen, so steht in der Regel der Infinitiv (b). Deshalb findet sich z. B. nach **would like/love/prefer** nur der Infinitiv (c). Bei **prefer sth to sth** folgt ein Verb immer in der Form des Gerundiums (d).
I like going/to go to the theatre. (a) – Bess loves taking/to take long walks. (a) – I would love to spend my holidays in the Caucasus next year. (c) – Would you like to come with us or would you prefer to stay here? (c) – Jim hates getting up/to get up early, because he prefers working/to work late in the evening. (a) – I didn't go out last night because I preferred to watch TV. (b) – I don't like/I hate to interrupt you, but there is a phone call for you. (b) – Donald prefers travelling by air to going by car. (d)

Nach *begin* und *start* kann Gerundium oder Infinitiv stehen (a). Nur der Infinitiv ist möglich im Zusammenhang mit Verben, die eine Einsicht oder Erkenntnis ausdrücken, z. B.: *realize, understand, see, feel* (b), oder wenn *begin* und *start* in der Continuous Form verwendet werden (c). Das Gerundium ist üblich, wenn auf den Beginn einer längeren oder gewohnheitsmäßigen Handlung verwiesen wird (d).
We start working/to work at 7 a.m. (a) – I have just begun reading/to read the book. (a) – When did you begin to realize your error? (b) – The situation is beginning to become complicated. (c) – I started learning English at the age of ten. (d)

Das Gerundium nach *cease* bezeichnet das Ende eines Vorgangs (a), der Infinitiv die Beendigung eines Zustandes oder einer Situation. (b)
Nach *continue* kann Gerundium oder Infinitiv stehen. (c)
Fred has ceased collecting stamps. (a) (Fred hat aufgehört, Briefmarken zu sammeln.) – Some widespread forms of superstition such as fortune-telling have not yet ceased to exist. (b) (Einige weitverbreitete Formen des Aberglaubens, z. B. das Wahrsagen, sind noch nicht ausgestorben.) – We continued discussing/to discuss the topic after Tom had left. (c) (Wir diskutierten weiter über das Thema, nachdem Tom gegangen war.)

Nach *afraid* ist *of* + **Gerundium** oder *to*-**Infinitiv** oft ohne Bedeutungsunterschied möglich (a). Nur *afraid of* + **Gerundium** wird verwendet, wenn befürchtet wird, daß jemandem etwas widerfahren kann. (b)

---

[15] Ohne Bedeutungsunterschied kann Gerundium oder Infinitiv verwendet werden bei "aim" = beabsichtigen; "decide/determine" = beschließen; und nach Ausdrücken wie "it's a pleasure/a great honour" etc: We aim at finishing/to finish the test today. We decided/determined to postpone the meeting. (auch:) We decided/determined on postponing the meeting. – It's a pleasure seeing/to see you again.

L 8.7.2.

Mark is afraid of telling/to tell Sheila the truth. (a) – Rose does not like driving, because she is afraid of having an accident.[16] (b)

sorry + *for* + **Gerundium** (auch: + Infinitiv Perfekt oder *that*-Satz) wird verwendet, wenn man sich für etwas entschuldigt (a), *sorry* + **Infinitiv Präsens** drückt aus, daß man sich für etwas entschuldigt, das man gerade tut oder tun wird. (b)
I'm sorry for disturbing/having disturbed you this morning. (oder:) I'm sorry to have disturbed you/that I disturbed you this morning. (a) – Sorry to disturb you, I would like to ask you a question. (b)

8.7.2. Zwischen der Anwendung des Gerundiums und des Infinitivs ist grundsätzlich zu unterscheiden bei: *go on, stop, remember, forget, regret, try, propose, mean; be certain/sure, be interested.*

go on + **Gerundium** bezeichnet das Andauern einer Tätigkeit oder eines Zustandes (= *continue*), *go on* + **Infinitiv** verweist darauf, daß eine neue Handlung begonnen wird.
Hugh went on talking about the model of the shopping centre because the audience wanted to know a lot of further details. (Hugh sprach noch weiter über das Modell des Einkaufszentrums, da die Zuhörer viele weitere Einzelheiten wissen wollten.) – After introducing the model in general, Hugh went on to explain details. (Nachdem Hugh das Modell ganz allgemein vorgestellt hatte, ging er dazu über, Details zu erläutern.)

stop + **Gerundium** bezeichnet die Beendigung einer Tätigkeit (= *finish*); *stop* + **Infinitiv** drückt aus, daß man eine Tätigkeit abbricht, um etwas anderes zu tun.
The two secretaries stopped talking when their boss came in. (Die beiden Sekretärinnen hörten auf, sich zu unterhalten, als ihr Chef hereinkam.) – Each time Ruth has typed ten pages she stops to have a smoke. (Jedesmal wenn Ruth 10 Seiten geschrieben hat, unterbricht sie ihre Arbeit, um zu rauchen.)

remember + **Gerundium** verweist auf einen Vorgang in der Vergangenheit, *remember* + **Infinitiv** bezeichnet eine Aufforderung an jemanden, etwas, das noch getan werden muß, nicht zu vergessen.
I remember writing Eve some weeks ago. (Ich erinnere mich, daß ich Eve vor einigen Wochen geschrieben habe.) – Please, remember to write to Eve. (Denke bitte daran/Vergiß bitte nicht, Eve zu schreiben.)

forget + **Gerundium** verweist darauf, daß man etwas, das man getan hat, vergessen hat; **verneint:** daß man es nicht vergessen hat bzw. nicht vergessen wird (a); *forget* + **Infinitiv** drückt aus, daß man etwas vergessen hat, das zu tun war (b). **Verneintes** *forget* + **Infinitiv** entspricht *remember* + **Infinitiv** (c).

---

[16] afraid + Nebensatz – oft mit "may/might" – ist möglich, wenn eine Befürchtung zum Ausdruck gebracht wird, daß etwas geschehen könnte oder geschehen sein könnte: I'm afraid Joan might get angry. – I'm afraid I may have offended Tom. – I'm afraid Liz has missed the train.
"afraid" + Nebensatz findet sich auch im Sinne von "I'm sorry (but)", um auszudrücken, daß man etwas nicht tun kann oder nicht tun will: I'm afraid I can't help Paula.

Susan has forgotten meeting Jim before. (a) (Susan hat vergessen, daß sie Jim schon einmal getroffen hat.)
We shall never forget visiting the Hermitage in Leningrad. (a) (Wir werden nie unseren Besuch in der Leningrader Eremitage vergessen.)
Unterscheiden Sie: I have forgotten making an appointment with Tom. (a) (Ich habe vergessen, daß ich mich mit Tom verabredet habe.) – I have forgotten to make an appointment with Tom. (b) (Ich habe vergessen, mich mit Tom zu verabreden.)
Don't forget to send Bill a telegram. (= You should remember to send Bill a telegram.) (c) (Denke bitte daran, Bill ein Telegramm zu schicken.)

regret + **Gerundium**[17] bezeichnet ein Bedauern über etwas, das geschehen ist (a) oder nicht geschehen kann (b); *regret* + **Infinitiv** bringt zum Ausdruck, daß man bedauert, etwas tun zu müssen (c).
I regret telling (having told) Mark about my mishap. (a) (= I regret that I told Mark ...) (Ich bedaure, daß ich Mark etwas von meinem Mißgeschick erzählt habe.)
I regret not being able to attend the conference. (b) (Ich bedaure, daß ich die Konferenz nicht besuchen kann.)
We regret to inform you that you have failed the exam. (c) (= We regret we have to inform you ...) (Wir bedauern, Ihnen mitteilen zu müssen, daß Sie die Prüfung nicht bestanden haben.)

try + **Gerundium** etw. versuchen/ausprobieren (um festzustellen, was dabei zustande kommt); *try* + **Infinitiv** versuchen, sich bemühen (= attempt).
The tea is rather thin, try adding some milk and sugar. – I shall try to contact Fred tomorrow.

propose + **Gerundium** vorschlagen (= suggest);
propose + **Infinitiv** vorhaben (= intend).
The chairman proposed adjourning the meeting. (Der Vorsitzende schlug vor, die Versammlung zu vertagen.) – They propose (= intend) to leave tonight. (Sie beabsichtigen, heute abend abzureisen.)

mean + **Gerundium** bedeuten (im Sinne von "zur Folge haben": involve)
mean + **Infinitiv** beabsichtigen (= intend).
If you want to get tickets for the Kirov ballet this may mean queueing up for hours. (Wenn du Karten für das Kirow-Ballett haben möchtest, kann das bedeuten, daß du dich stundenlang anstellen mußt.)
I didn't mean to offend you. (Ich wollte Sie nicht beleidigen.)

be certain/sure + *of* + **Gerundium** jmd. ist sicher, daß er selbst etwas erlebt oder erreicht (a);
be certain/sure + **Infinitiv** der Sprechende ist sicher, daß die genannte Person etwas erlebt oder erreicht (b).
George is certain/sure of winning the contest. (a) (George ist sicher, daß er den Wettkampf gewinnen wird.) – George is certain/sure to win the contest. (b) (Sicher wird George den Wettkampf gewinnen.) (2.5.6.)

---

[17] Auch bei Vergangenheitsbezug sehr oft in der Präsensform.

L 8.7.3.

be interested in + **Gerundium** daran interessiert sein, etwas zu tun (a);
be interested + **Infinitiv** es interessant finden, daß man etwas erfährt oder erfahren hat (b).
Bess is interested in learning French. (a) (Bess ist daran interessiert, Französisch zu lernen.) – I was interested to hear something about your work. (b) (Es hat mich interessiert, etwas über deine Arbeit zu erfahren.)

8.7.3. Nach *advise, recommend, allow, permit, forbid* steht das Gerundium, um einen Rat, eine Empfehlung, Erlaubnis oder ein Verbot allgemein zu formulieren, ohne daß eine Bezugsperson genannt wird. Wenn die Bezugsperson erwähnt wird, so folgt diesen Verben die Objekt mit Infinitiv-Konstruktion.
There are many restaurants that do not permit/allow smoking during lunch hours. (aber:) My colleague does not allow me to smoke in his study. – Doctors advise taking sedatives only in urgent cases. (aber:) Gary advised me to consult an expert.

9. The Participles – Die Partizipien

Im Englischen gibt es folgende Formen des Partizips:

writing	*Present Participle Active* (= Präsenspartizip)
being written	*Present Participle Passive*
written	*Past Participle* (= Perfektpartizip)
having written	*Perfect Participle Active*
having been written	*Perfect Participle Passive*

In Verbindung mit *be* bilden das *Present Participle Active* und *Present Participle Passive* die Verlaufsform (a, b). Das *Past Participle* bildet die Perfektformen des Aktivs (c) und die Zeitformen des Passivs (d).
We are **making** an experiment. (a) – An experiment is **being made**. (b) – I have/had/will have/would have **read** the book. (c) – The test is/was/has been/had been/will be/will have been/would be/would have been **repeated**. (d)
Das *Present Participle Active* und das *Past Participle* haben **adjektivische** oder **verbale Funktion**.
Das *Present Participle Active*, das einen Zustand oder eine Eigenschaft beschreibt, hat die Merkmale eines **Adjektivs**: Es kann attributiv (a) und prädikativ (b) verwendet werden; es läßt sich steigern (c) und kann ein Adverb bilden (d).
Das *Present Participle*, das eine Tätigkeit bezeichnet, kann attributiv (e) verwendet, aber weder gesteigert noch zu einem Adverb umgebildet werden.
Das *Past Participle* in adjektivischer Funktion kann ebenfalls attributiv (f) und prädikativ (g) verwendet werden. Beschreibt es eine Eigenschaft oder einen Zustand, so kann es gesteigert werden (h) und zuweilen ein Adverb bilden (i).
A charming girl (a). – Eve is very charming (b). – Liz is the most charming girl I know (c). – A surprisingly good answer (d).

A crying child (e). – A complicated problem (f). – The problem is very complicated (g). – The problem is becoming more and more complicated (h). – They were talking excitedly (i).

Partizipien in verbaler Funktion verkürzen Relativ- und Adverbialsätze. Dabei bringen beide Formen des **Present Participle** eine **Gleichzeitigkeit** zur Zeitebene des Hauptsatzes zum Ausdruck (a). Das **Perfect Participle Active** und die relativ seltene Form des **Perfect Participle Passive** drücken eine **Vorzeitigkeit** aus (b). Das **Past Participle** bezeichnet je nach Kontext eine Handlung, die vollzogen worden ist (c) oder noch vollzogen wird (d).
Die Verkürzung von Nebensätzen durch Partizipien ist vor allem ein Merkmal der Schriftsprache, im gesprochenen Englisch findet sich häufig ein entsprechender Nebensatz. Nebensatzverkürzungen durch *Present Participle Passive* und *Perfect Participle Passive* kommen in der Umgangssprache kaum vor.
Reacting with a base an acid forms a salt and water. (a) (= When an acid reacts with a base it forms ...)
Yesterday we attended a lecture *dealing* with the development of modern English literature. (a) (= ... a lecture which dealt with ...)
The substances now *being investigated* by our lab assistant contain several impurities. (a) (= The substances which are now being investigated ...)
Having talked to Tom I was convinced he would support our plan. (b) (= After I had talked / After talking – 8.2.1.4. – to Tom I was convinced ...)
Having been heated for several hours the substance began to melt. (b) (= After the substance had been heated for several hours it began to melt.)
The tests *performed* by the students have been analysed in detail. (c) (= The tests which *were* performed ...)
The tests *performed* by the students are usually analysed in detail. (d) (= The tests which *are* performed by the students are usually analysed in detail.)

9.1. Als Attribut zum Subjekt und Objekt oder zu prädikativen Ergänzungen nach *be* können *Present Participle Active, Present Participle Passive* und *Past Participle* Relativsätze verkürzen und stehen dann hinter ihrem Bezugswort.[1,2]
The process *taking place* under these conditions is called polymerization. (= The process which takes place ...) (Der Prozeß, der unter diesen Bedingungen stattfindet, heißt Polymerisation.)
It is hoped that the techniques now *being developed*[3] in our plant will meet interna-

---

[1] Die Verkürzung von Relativsätzen, in denen eine Vorzeitigkeit zur Zeitform des Prädikats zum Ausdruck gebracht wird, ist nur mit dem Past Participle möglich. Konstruktionen mit dem Perfect Participle Active und dem Perfect Participle Passive kommen hier nicht vor. The proposals made by Tom are acceptable. (= The proposals which have been made by Tom ...) (aber:) Do you know the author who has written this book? (Falsch wäre: Do you know the author having written ...?)
[2] In der Schriftsprache steht das Past Participle zuweilen auch **vor** seinem Bezugswort: Considered a milestone in the history of the modern theatre, Arthur Miller's play "Death of a Salesman" has been produced again and again. (Arthur Miller's play 'Death of a Salesman', which is considered a milestone ...)
[3] "being" kann Relativsätze nur als Teil des Present Participle Passive verkürzen.

L 9.1.1.

tional demands. (= ... the techniques which are now being developed ...) (Man hofft, daß die Verfahren, die jetzt in unserem Betrieb entwickelt werden, internationalen Ansprüchen genügen.)
Some of the problems *discussed* are still unsolved. (= Some of the problems which have been discussed ...) (Einige der erörterten Probleme sind noch nicht gelöst.)
The assistant gave a report on the test series *carried out* last week. (= ... the test series which had been carried out ...) (Der Assistent gab einen Bericht über die Versuchsreihe, die vorige Woche durchgeführt worden war.)
Control engineering is a scientific discipline *applied* in many fields of technology. (= ... a discipline which is applied ...) (Die Regelungstechnik ist eine wissenschaftliche Disziplin, die in vielen Bereichen der Technik angewendet wird.)
Smoking at work is a habit complained about by many non-smokers. (= ... a habit which is complained about ...) (Rauchen während der Arbeit ist eine Gewohnheit, über die viele Nichtraucher klagen.)

Auch nach einleitendem *there, here*; *this, that*; *it* + Form von *be* folgt *Present Participle* oder *Past Participle* unmittelbar seinem Bezugswort; dabei handelt es sich jedoch nicht immer um die Verkürzung eines Relativsatzes.
This is the bus going to Piccadilly Circus. (Das ist der Bus, der zum Piccadilly Circus fährt / ... der Bus zum ...) – There is our professor coming. (Dort kommt unser Professor.) – There were some important problems discussed at the meeting. (Es wurden einige wichtige Probleme auf der Versammlung besprochen.)

9.1.1. Zur Stellung des *Past Participle*

Das *Past Participle* steht **nach** seinem Bezugswort, wenn
– es sich aus Verb + Präposition zusammensetzt (a)
– es durch eine Orts- und / oder Zeitbestimmung ergänzt wird (b)
– die Person oder Sache, die den Vorgang auslöst, durch *by* angeschlossen wird (c)
The measures *agreed upon* should be put into practice as soon as possible. (a) (Die vereinbarten Maßnahmen sollten sobald wie möglich verwirklicht werden.)
The paper *read* in the plenary session this morning was a highlight of the conference. (b) (Der in der Plenarsitzung heute morgen gehaltene Vortrag war ein Höhepunkt der Konferenz.)
I know most of the plays *written* by Shakespeare. (c) (Ich kenne die meisten Stücke von Shakespeare.)

Darüber hinaus läßt sich die Stellung des *Past Participle* nicht eindeutig in Regeln fassen. (Vergleiche: Michael Swan, Practical English Usage, Seite 453: "This is a complicated area of English grammar which has not yet been completely analysed.")
Meist steht jedoch das *Past Participle* **nach** dem Bezugswort, wenn es auf eine Handlung[4] verweist, die vollzogen worden ist oder noch vollzogen wird:

---

[4] Das Past Participle steht **vor** seinem Bezugswort, wenn es einen **Zustand** ausdrückt als Ergebnis von etwas, das mit der entsprechenden Person oder Sache geschehen ist:
a broken vase (= a vase **which has been broken**, d.h.: a vase **which is broken**) – (aber:) the vase broken yesterday (= the vase which got / was broken yesterday).
(Fortsetzung s. Seite 75)

The solution *found* is quite satisfactory. (Die gefundene Lösung ist durchaus zufriedenstellend.);
ebenso: *the tests made*; *the process described*; *the calculations performed*; *the steps taken*; *the comparison drawn*; *the changes effected*; *the measures taken*; *the results obtained*; *the points mentioned*[5]; *the examples given*[6].

Anmerkung 1: Gelegentlich kann ein *Past Participle*, das durch ein Adverb näher bestimmt ist, vor **oder** nach seinem Bezugswort stehen, z. B.: the recently built bridge (oder:) the bridge recently built; (ebenso:) a frequently asked question.
In anderen Fällen ist die Stellung **vor** dem Bezugswort üblich; z. B.: a much discussed book; a highly developed country, etc.
Auch einige Verbindungen Verb + Adverb stehen vor dem Bezugswort, z. B.: the broken-down car; a closed-down factory, (aber:) the experiments carried out; the hypothesis put forward, etc.
Einige Verbindungen Verb + Präposition können vor dem Bezugswort stehen, z. B.: the looked-for solution; the longed-for holidays; the hoped-for decision, etc.

Anmerkung 2: Gelegentlich kann das *Past Participle* unterschiedliche Bedeutung haben, je nachdem, ob es nach oder vor seinem Bezugswort steht, z. B.: the people concerned / Those concerned (die Betreffenden) – a concerned mother (eine besorgte Mutter);
the difficulties involved (die dabei auftretenden Schwierigkeiten) – an involved construction (= a complicated construction).

Beachten Sie: be concerned with sth = deal with sth; be concerned about sth = be worried about sth; be involved in = be mixed up in (trouble, a crime, etc.)

9.2.   Partizipien können **Adverbialsätze** verkürzen.
Ein Partizip, das sich auf das Subjekt des Satzes bezieht, wird als Related Participle (verbundenes Partizip) bezeichnet (a). Hat das Partizip ein eigenes Substantiv oder Pronomen als Bezugswort, so nennt man es Unrelated Participle (unverbundenes Partizip) (b).
Unrelated Participles sind im gesprochenen Englisch selten:
Coming home I found his telegram. (a) (= When I came home I found ...)
Having forgotten my identity card I had to go back to the hotel. (a) (= As I had forgotten my identity card I had to go ...)

Ebenso: a lost object; an established fact (= eine allgemein anerkannte Tatsache); a forgotten author; the arrested hijacker; reduced / increased prices; a generally accepted rule; a closely defined expression; a widely read author; a poorly attended performance.
Diese Konstruktion ist auch bei einigen Verben möglich, die kein Passiv bilden, z. B. the disappeared document (= a document *which has disappeared*).
Ebenso: an escaped prisoner; the recently arrived goods; a grown-up son; a far / much travelled man; faded colours; fallen rocks; a retired businessman etc.

[5] (aber:) the above-mentioned points = the points mentioned above.
[6] (oder:) the given examples. – Auch in anderen Fällen findet sich das Past Participle vor oder hinter seinem Bezugswort, z. B.: the quoted results / the results quoted; (ebenso:) the listed values, the desired effects, the proposed alterations.

L 9.2.1.   76

We talked a long time *discussing* modern English literature. (a)
Given fresh water regularly these flowers will keep more than a week. (a) (= If these flowers are given ..., they will keep ...)
The rain *having stopped*, we continued our walk. (b) (= After/Since the rain had stopped we continued our walk.)
Acids react with oxides of all metals, a salt and water *being formed*. (b)

9.2.1.   Partizipien können **Temporalsätze** verkürzen, dabei können die Konjunktionen *when*, *while* hinzutreten, mit *Past Participle* auch *once* (= nachdem, sobald), *until*. Nach *when* und *while* entfällt meist die Partizipform *being*.
Waiting for the tram this morning, we met our former teacher. (= When we were waiting ..., we met ...) (Als wir heute morgen auf die Straßenbahn warteten, trafen wir unseren früheren Lehrer.)
Having finished the book I went to bed. (= After I had finished the book I went to bed./After finishing the book I went ...) (Nachdem ich das Buch gelesen hatte, ging ich ins Bett.)
Checked carefully, the values were found to be incorrect.⁷ (= After the values had been checked carefully, they were found ...) (Nachdem die Werte genau überprüft worden waren, zeigte es sich, daß sie ungenau waren.)
(When) *crossing* the road I almost ran into a lorry. (= When I was crossing the road I ...) (Als ich die Straße überquerte, wäre ich beinahe in einen LKW gelaufen.)
(While) *staying* in the Caucasus, we climbed several high mountains. (= While we were staying in ...) (Während unseres Aufenthaltes im Kaukasus bestiegen wir mehrere hohe Berge.)
Once *deprived* of oxygen the brain dies. (= Once the brain has been deprived ..., it dies.) (Sobald dem Gehirn der Sauerstoff entzogen wird, ist es nicht mehr funktionsfähig.)
Metals do not melt until *heated* to a definite temperature. (= ... until they are heated ...) (Metalle schmelzen erst, wenn sie auf eine bestimmte Temperatur erhitzt werden.)
While/When in Berlin we visited the TV-tower. (= When we were in Berlin .../During our stay in ...) (Während unseres Aufenthaltes in Berlin besichtigten wir den Fernsehturm.)

9.2.2.   Partizipien können **Kausalsätze** verkürzen:
Being short of money, I cannot afford a trip abroad this year. (= Because I am short of money I ...) (Da ich nicht genug Geld habe, kann ich mir dieses Jahr keine Auslandsreise leisten.)
Not *knowing* what to do we asked his advice. (= Because we didn't know what to do we ...) (Da wir nicht wußten, was wir tun sollten, fragten wir ihn um Rat.)
Not *having received* an answer I wrote again. (= As I had not received an answer I ...) (Da ich keine Antwort erhalten hatte, schrieb ich noch einmal.)

---

[7] Das Past Participle steht oft anstelle des Perfect Participle Passive: Having been checked carefully the values ... (Die Werte erwiesen sich als falsch, nachdem sie genau überprüft worden waren.)

Durch *as* + **Personalpronomen** + *do/does/did* wird der kausale Zusammenhang besonders betont.
Hugh's article was much criticized, containing as it did a lot of inaccuracies. (= ... because it contained ...) (Hughs Artikel wurde sehr kritisiert, da er eine Menge Ungenauigkeiten enthielt.)

9.2.3. Ob es sich bei der Verkürzung um einen Temporal- oder Kausalsatz handelt, kann oft nur aus dem Kontext ermittelt werden.
Having finished our work we went to the pictures. (= After we had finished ... oder: Because we had finished our work we went ...) (Nachdem/Da wir unsere Arbeit beendet hatten, gingen wir ins Kino.)

9.2.4. Vorwiegend in der Schriftsprache können **Konditionalsätze** durch das *Past Participle* verkürzt werden, häufig in Verbindung mit *if* (verneint: *unless*, seltener *if not*).
(If) *recognized* early, cancer is curable in many cases. (= If cancer is recognized early, it is ...) (Wird Krebs rechtzeitig erkannt, so ist er in vielen Fällen heilbar.)
Unless completely *overhauled*, these machines cannot be used any more. (= These machines..., unless they are completely overhauled.) (Wenn diese Maschinen nicht vollständig überholt werden, können sie nicht mehr verwendet werden.)

9.2.5. In der Schriftsprache können **Konzessivsätze**, eingeleitet durch *(al)though/*(formal auch:) *albeit* (= obwohl), durch Partizipien verkürzt werden. Die Partizipform *being* entfällt meist.
Although *trying* hard, I was not able to meet the deadline. (= Although I was trying hard, I ...) (Obwohl ich mich sehr bemühte, konnte ich den Abgabetermin nicht einhalten.)
Though slightly injured Tom went on playing. (= Though Tom was slightly injured, he ...) (Obwohl Tom leicht verletzt war, spielte er weiter.)

9.2.6. Das Partizip kann als **Modalbestimmung** verwendet werden, um eine Situation näher zu erläutern oder um auszudrücken, wie etwas geschehen ist (oft durch *thus* verstärkt). Es steht dann gewöhnlich hinter dem Hauptsatz. Übersetzungsmöglichkeiten: "wobei", "dabei"; "und".
Bob is in the garage, *repairing* his car. (Bob ist in der Garage und repariert sein Auto.) – The lecturer discussed techniques of house-building, *stressing* the advantages of prefabricated parts. (Der Vortragende behandelte Methoden des Wohnungsbaus, wobei er die Vorteile der Fertigbauweise betonte.) – Our factory has introduced robots for different working processes, thus *raising* the output considerably. (Unser Betrieb hat für verschiedene Arbeitsprozesse Roboter eingeführt und so die Produktion beträchtlich erhöht.) – We spent ten days on the Black Sea *visiting* several well-known seaside resorts. (Wir verbrachten zehn Tage am Schwarzen Meer und besuchten mehrere bekannte Badeorte.)

9.2.7. Das *Unrelated Participle* bezieht sich nicht auf das Subjekt des Satzes, sondern hat ein **eigenes Bezugswort**. Es kann Kausal-, Temporal- und Modalsätze

gelegentlich auch Konditionalsätze verkürzen.[8] Diese Konstruktion findet sich vorwiegend in der Schriftsprache; besonders charakteristisch ist sie für die Fachsprache.
The nucleus of an atom contains one or more particles called protons, *each of them having* a definite positive charge. (Der Atomkern enthält ein oder mehrere Teilchen, genannt Protonen, von denen jedes eine bestimmte positive Ladung hat.)
The necessary preparations made, the experiment can be performed today. (Da/Nachdem die notwendigen Vorbereitungen getroffen sind, kann der Versuch heute stattfinden.)
The accused having confessed, the jurors passed a verdict of guilty. (Weil/Nachdem der Angeklagte gestanden hatte, fällten die Geschworenen den Schuldspruch.)
The car came to a standstill, *there being* no fuel left in the tank. (Der Wagen blieb stehen, weil kein Benzin mehr im Tank war.)
Weather permitting, we shall make an excursion tomorrow. (Wenn es das Wetter erlaubt, machen wir morgen eine Exkursion.)
The little girl ran down the street, *a big dog following* her. (Das kleine Mädchen rannte die Straße hinunter, ein großer Hund folgte ihr.)

9.2.7.1. Ein durch ein **Unrelated Participle** verkürzter Nebensatz wird oft durch **with** eingeleitet.
With one of the engines failing, the plane had to land at the nearest airport. (= Since one of the engines failed, the plane had to ...) (Da eines der Triebwerke ausfiel, mußte das Flugzeug auf dem nächstgelegenen Flughafen landen.)
The reconstruction of the city centre is making rapid progress *with a shopping arcade being built* as the main attraction. (Der Wiederaufbau des Stadtzentrums macht rasche Fortschritte, als Hauptattraktion wird eine Ladenstraße gebaut.)
With Tina gone, we resumed our work. (= After Tina had gone, we ...) (Als Tina weggegangen war, nahmen wir unsere Arbeit wieder auf.)

9.2.8. In bestimmten Wendungen findet sich das Partizip, obwohl es sich weder auf das Subjekt des Satzes bezieht noch ein eigenes Bezugswort hat. (sog. *'Dangling Participle'*)
z. B.: *generally/broadly speaking* im allgemeinen, im großen und ganzen; *strictly/properly speaking* genau genommen; *frankly speaking* offen gesagt; *roughly speaking* ungefähr; *depending on* abhängig von, je nachdem ob; *provided/providing that* vorausgesetzt, daß; *taking into consideration/into account/considering (that)* wenn man in Betracht zieht; *assuming (that)* vorausgesetzt, daß; *supposing (that)* angenommen, daß; *including* einschließlich; *concerning/regarding* was ... betrifft; *granting (that)* wenn auch, zugegeben daß; *talking of* da gerade von ... die Rede ist; *judging from/(by)* nach ... zu urteilen.
Generally speaking, this novel is rather tedious. (Im großen und ganzen ist dieser Roman ziemlich langweilig.) – The resolution will now be put to the vote *provided that* no further alterations are proposed. (Über die Resolution wird jetzt abgestimmt,

---

[8] Zuweilen entfällt die Partizipform "being": The medical check-up over, the patient was allowed to go home. (Nach der ärztlichen Untersuchung durfte der Patient nach Hause gehen.)

vorausgesetzt, daß keine weiteren Änderungen vorgeschlagen werden.) – *Considering the results our efforts have been rather successful.* (Wenn man die Ergebnisse betrachtet, sind unsere Bemühungen recht erfolgreich gewesen.)

Beachten Sie: Neben dem *Related Participle*, dem *Unrelated Participle* und dem *Dangling Participle* kommt beim nachlässigen Sprechen manchmal auch ein falsch bezogenes, also fehlerhaftes Partizip *(Misrelated Participle)* vor: Coming home the door was locked. (Das würde bedeuten, daß die nach Hause kommende Tür verschlossen war!)

9.3. Als prädikative Ergänzung zum Subjekt steht *Present Participle Active* oder *Past Participle* nach den Verben *sit, stand, lie; come, remain; feel.*
Bert *came running* down the street. (Bert kam die Straße heruntergerannt.) – Bess *was lying* on the couch *reading*. (Bess lag auf der Couch und las.) – The department store *remained closed* for some weeks. (Das Kaufhaus blieb einige Wochen geschlossen.) – We *felt impelled* to reconsider our decision. (Wir fühlten uns veranlaßt, unsere Entscheidung noch einmal zu überdenken.)

9.4. Auf das Objekt – im Passiv auf das Subjekt – bezogen, kann das Partizip stehen nach *see, hear*, nur auf das Objekt bezogen nach *watch, feel, listen to*.
We saw them coming out of the factory. (Wir sahen sie aus der Fabrik kommen.) – They were seen coming out of the factory. (Man sah sie aus der Fabrik kommen.) – They were heard quarrelling. (Man hörte, wie sie sich stritten.) – I watched Tom repairing the machine. (Ich sah zu, wie Tom die Maschine reparierte.) – It's a pleasure to listen to Paula speaking French. (Es ist ein Vergnügen, Paula französisch sprechen zu hören.)

Beachten Sie: We saw John *walking* down the street. = John was walking down the street when we saw him. – We saw John *walk* down the street. (i. e. from one end to the other.) (s. auch: 5.7.1.)

Nach *see, hear* im Passiv besteht kein Bedeutungsunterschied zwischen Partizip und Infinitiv: Anne was seen entering / to enter the house.

Nach *see, hear, watch* ist nur das Partizip möglich, wenn ein passivischer Sachverhalt beschrieben wird: We watched the car being repaired. – I heard my name called.

Ebenfalls auf das Objekt, im Passiv auf das Subjekt bezogen, steht das Partizip nach *keep*[9]*/leave*[9] = jmd./etw. (in einem Zustand) lassen; *catch* = (hier:) jmd. überraschen/ertappen; *set* = (hier:) etw./jmd. dazu bringen, daß; *find*; *report*.
Don't keep Lucy waiting. (Laß Lucy nicht warten.) – Have you been kept waiting? (Hat man dich warten lassen?) – Keep me informed. (Haltet mich auf dem laufenden.) – The liquid should be left cooling for one hour. (Man muß die Flüssigkeit eine Stunde abkühlen lassen.) – They left me wondering what to do. (Sie ließen

---

[9] Beide Verben kommen bei nahezu gleicher Bedeutung in unterschiedlichen Wendungen vor, z. B.: keep sth going / running, keep sb waiting; leave sth standing / running, leave sb wondering.

mich im Ungewissen, was ich tun sollte.) – Ted was caught trying to break into the shop. (Ted wurde ertappt, als er versuchte, in das Geschäft einzubrechen.) – The engine was set going. (Die Maschine wurde angelassen.)

9.5. **Have/get + Objekt + *Past Participle*** bringt zum Ausdruck: jemand veranlaßt, daß etwas getan wird (deutsch: lassen). Bei Frage und Verneinung wird in **Präsens** und **Präteritum** mit *do/does* bzw. *did* umschrieben.
I *have/get my hair cut* every three weeks. (Ich lasse mir alle drei Wochen die Haare schneiden.) – Where *did you have/get this dress* made? (Wo hast du dieses Kleid machen lassen?) – I must have/get my watch repaired.[10] (Ich muß meine Uhr reparieren lassen.) – We had/got our flat repapered. (Wir haben unsere Wohnung neu tapezieren lassen.)

Diese Konstruktion kann auch ausdrücken, daß jemandem etwas auf Grund äußerer Umstände oder persönlichen Verhaltens widerfährt, oder sie kann ganz allgemein einen passivischen Sachverhalt wiedergeben.
Dora had/got her thumb broken. (= Dora broke her thumb.) (Dora hat sich den Daumen gebrochen.)
If Mark goes on drinking so much, I'm afraid he will have his health ruined. (= ... he will ruin his health.) (Ich befürchte, Mark wird seine Gesundheit ruinieren, wenn er weiter so viel trinkt.)
The satellite had to have/get its trajectory corrected. (= The trajectory of the satellite had to be corrected.) (Die Flugbahn des Satelliten mußte korrigiert werden.)

Anmerkung: *get* **+ Objekt +** *Past Participle* kann auch ausdrücken, daß vom Subjekt selbst etwas getan wird oder getan werden soll:
I hope I can get the engine started. (Ich hoffe, ich kann den Motor anwerfen.)

9.6. Besonders in Fachtexten findet sich *as* **+** *Present Participle/Past Participle*. Das *Present Participle* bleibt dabei meist unübersetzt.
We may describe heat as consisting of the motion of molecules. (Man kann Wärme als eine Bewegung der Moleküle beschreiben.) – As indicated in table 1, the values obtained from the two experiments are almost identical. (Wie in Tabelle 1 angegeben, sind die aus beiden Versuchen erhaltenen Werte fast gleich.) – Mass is generally defined as being the property of a body of matter to offer a resistance to changes in its motion as well as to attract, and to be attracted by, another body. (Masse wird allgemein als die Eigenschaft eines materiellen Körpers definiert, Änderungen seines Bewegungszustandes einen Widerstand entgegenzusetzen sowie einen anderen Körper anzuziehen und von ihm angezogen zu werden.)

---

[10] (oder:) I have to have/get my watch repaired. (oder:) I've got to have/get my watch repaired.

10. The Subjunctive Mood – Der Konjunktiv

Mit dem Konjunktiv wird ausgedrückt, daß etwas möglichst geschehen sollte, weil es vorgeschlagen, erbeten, empfohlen oder gefordert wird. Der Konjunktiv findet sich vorwiegend in der Schriftsprache, in der Umgangssprache wird meist mit *should* umschrieben. Der Konjunktiv hat folgende, vom Indikativ abweichende Formen:

- bei Vollverb entfällt das *-s* der 3. Pers. Sing. Präsens:
  I suggest that he come tomorrow.
- das Präsens von *be* ist für alle Personen *be*.
  They insisted that the matter be discussed at once.
- die 3. Pers. Sing. Präsens von *have* lautet *have*:
  It is essential that every member of society have the same chance to develop his personality.
- im Präteritum von *be* steht für alle Personen *were*:
  If I were[1] you I would ask him. – I wish it were possible to go on holiday now.

10.1. Der Konjunktiv findet sich oft nach den Verben *suggest/propose* vorschlagen, anregen; *insist/urge* (darauf) bestehen, drängen, daß; *demand/require* (er)fordern; *order* anordnen; *recommend* empfehlen; *ask/request* bitten.
They have suggested that Jim talk (oder: should talk/talks) the matter over with Sue. (Sie haben vorgeschlagen, daß Jim die Angelegenheit mit Sue bespricht.) – Gary proposed that some items of the contract be changed (oder: should be changed). (Gary schlug vor, daß einige Punkte des Vertrags geändert werden sollten.)

Nach Wendungen wie *it is necessary*; *it is important*; *it is impossible*; *it is essential* wesentlich; *it is urgent/vital/imperative* dringend erforderlich; *it is desirable* wünschenswert; *it is advisable* ratsam ist der Konjunktiv möglich. Häufig werden auch Umschreibungen mit *should*[2] oder der Indikativ verwendet.
It is essential that they be informed at once. (= ... that they should be informed at once./... that they are informed at once. (oder:) It is essential to inform them at once./... for them to be informed ...)

Beachten Sie bei Verneinung die Stellung von *not*: It is vital that the decision not be put off any longer.

---

[1] Neben "were" auch "was". Nur "were" ist möglich bei folgendem Infinitiv: If Tom were to tell us details it would be easier to judge the situation. (Sollte Tom uns Einzelheiten mitteilen ...)

[2] "should" steht vor allem in der Schriftsprache oft nach "it is surprising; it is funny/strange/curious; it is our wish; I'm sorry", um die emotionale Reaktion zu betonen. Im gesprochenen Englisch wird Präsens oder Präteritum bevorzugt.
It is strange that he should refuse our invitation. = ... that he refuses ... – I am sorry I should have insulted you. = ... I insulted ...

L 10.2.

10.2. Nach *I wish (that)* ich wünschte, (daß); *if only* wenn nur; *as if/as though* als ob; *it's (high) time*[3] es ist (höchste) Zeit; *I would rather* es wäre mir lieber steht das Verb bei Bezug auf die Gegenwart, zuweilen auch auf die Zukunft, im Präteritum, nach *suppose/what if* wie wäre es, wenn im Präsens oder Präteritum.
I wish Tom didn't talk so much. – I wish you were more helpful. – I'd rather you came tomorrow. – Suppose we invited/invite Eve to our club.

Bei diesen Ausdrücken findet sich nach *I/he/she/it* häufig *were* zur Bezeichnung des Konjunktivs.
I wish it were/was Sunday. – If only Tom were more careful. – Suppose this were (was, is) true.

10.2.1. Der Konjunktiv findet sich auch in bestimmten feststehenden Wendungen.
Long *live* the friendship between our two countries. – God *save* the Queen/King. – As it *were* = so to speak.

11. Complementation of the Verb – Ergänzung des Verbs

11.1. Einige Verben können nur in Verbindung mit einem Substantiv oder Adjektiv bzw. Partizip verwendet werden, damit eine Aussage über das Subjekt möglich wird. Um eine auf das **Subjekt** bezogene Aussage handelt es sich nach Verben wie:
become + Substantiv oder Adjektiv/Partizip = werden: Nora has become a teacher. – The situation has become difficult/complicated.
Ebenso in der Bedeutung von "werden":
get + Adjektiv: It's getting late.
grow + Adjektiv (allmähliche Veränderung): It's growing dark.
turn + Adjektiv (bei Lebewesen, Nahrungsmitteln, Farben): Tom turned pale. – The tea has turned cold. – The leaves have turned yellow.
turn + Substantiv: Dorothy turned Catholic.
fall + Adjektiv (z. B.: *ill, silent*): Sarah has fallen ill.

---

[3] Nach "it's (high) time" kann auch Infinitiv oder "for + Infinitiv" stehen: It's time (for you) to phone John.
Nach "as if/as though" und nach "suppose" steht das Plusquamperfekt, wenn auf etwas Vergangenes hingewiesen wird: Peter looks as if he had been told something unpleasant.
Mit "I wish" und "if only" + Präteritum wird zum Ausdruck gebracht, daß etwas nicht so ist, wie man es sich wünscht. (a)
"I wish" und "if only" + would verweisen darauf, daß etwas noch nicht so ist, wie man es sich wünscht. (b)
Mit "I wish" und "if only" + Plusquamperfekt wird bedauert, daß etwas in der Vergangenheit geschehen bzw. nicht geschehen ist. (c)
I wish John were more reliable. (a) (Ich wünschte, John wäre zuverlässiger.) – I wish Jane would write soon. (b) (Ich wünschte, Jane würde bald schreiben.) – I wish you had informed me in time. (c) (Ich wünschte, du hättest mich rechtzeitig informiert.) – If only the weather had not been so bad. (c) (Wenn nur das Wetter nicht so schlecht gewesen wäre.)

go + Adjektiv (z. B.: *crazy/mad*; *blind, deaf, wrong*).
prove (to be)/turn out (to be) = sich erweisen als: This method has proved useful. – The test has turned out a success.
seem (to be)/appear (to be): Jane seems (to be) a nice girl. – John appears to be well informed.
look/look like = aussehen (wie): Mary looks very elegant in her new dress. – Peter looks like his brother.
sound (like) = klingen, sich anhören (wie): The idea sounds reasonable. (oder:) This sounds like a reasonable idea.
taste (of)[1] = schmecken (nach): The cake tastes delicious. – The icecream tastes of strawberries.
smell (of)[1] = riechen (nach): The soup smells good. – The whole room smells of her perfume.
remain/keep = bleiben: *Some seats remained empty. – Keep quiet.*

11.2. Einige Verben müssen in bestimmter Bedeutung durch ein Substantiv oder Adjektiv ergänzt werden, damit eine Aussage über das **Objekt** – im **Passiv** über das **Subjekt** – möglich wird, z. B.:

call/term + Substantiv oder Adjektiv = bezeichnen als, halten für: I would call him reliable. – Words with nearly the same meaning are called/termed synonyms. – Alex calls/terms himself an expert in art.
name + Substantiv = nennen, ernennen: They named their daughter Mary. – A physicist was named President of the Academy.
make + Substantiv = ernennen zu: They made Jim captain of the team.
make/(formal auch: *render*) + Adjektiv = machen: Eve's promise made Tom happy. – (häufig:) make/(render) it possible = es ermöglichen.
declare + Substantiv oder Adjektiv = erklären zu/für: The jury declared John winner of the contest. – The chairman declared the session open/closed.
proclaim + Substantiv = jmd. erklären zu: In 1804, Napoleon was proclaimed emperor.

Nach einigen Verben kann ein Substantiv – nach *prove* oft auch ein Adjektiv – die Aussage über das Objekt – im Passiv das Subjekt – näher erläutern, z. B.: *elect* wählen zu; *appoint* ernennen, berufen zu; *crown* krönen zu; *prove* nachweisen, daß. Who was elected chairman yesterday? – Did they appoint Donald professor? – It's difficult to prove you wrong.

11.3. Nach einigen Verben steht *as* oder *for* vor dem Substantiv bzw. Adjektiv, z. B.: *regard/look upon as* halten für; *recognize/acknowledge as* (an)erkennen als; *describe as* beschreiben als; *refer to as* bezeichnen als; *(mis)take for* (irrtümlich) halten für.
The discovery of radioactive elements can be regarded/looked upon as a milestone in the development of modern physics.
Nach einigen Verben kann *as* vor dem Substantiv bzw. Adjektiv stehen, z. B.:

---
[1] Auch mit Objekt möglich, z. B.: She tasted/smelled the soup.

L 11.4.

nominate (as) ernennen zu; *consider (as)* halten für; *designate (as)* bezeichnen als; *choose (as, for)* wählen zu: Whole numbers are designated (as) integers. – We consider the hypothesis (as) correct.

11.4. Bei einigen Verben mit zwei Objekten wird das *'indirect object'* entweder mit *for* angeschlossen, oder es steht vor dem *'direct object'*, z.B.: *buy, make, pay*: She made me a cup of coffee. – She made a cup of coffee for me. – I bought her a present. – I bought a present for her. (nur:) I bought it for her.

Nach einigen Verben wird das *'indirect object'* mit *to* bzw. *from* angeschlossen, z.B.: *describe to, dictate to, explain to, mention to, read to, report to, submit to* (unterbreiten, vorlegen), *steal from*: He explained the problem to me. – Somebody stole the bicycle from her. (oder:) Somebody stole her bicycle.

12. Question Tags / Short Answers / Additions to Statements – 'Frageanhängsel' / Kurzantworten / Ergänzende Feststellungen

12.1. **Frageanhängsel** kommen in der Umgangssprache vor, wenn man sich über die Richtigkeit einer Feststellung vergewissern will.
Bildung: Es wird das Hilfsverb wiederholt, bei Vollverb die entsprechende Form von *do* verwendet, jeweils mit folgendem Subjekt in der Form des Personalpronomens. Bei positiver Aussage steht das Hilfsverb bzw. *do/does/did* in der verneinten Form, bei verneinender Aussage in der bejahten Form.[1]
Your mother *is* an actress,, *isn't she*? (Ihre Mutter ist Schauspielerin, nicht wahr?) – Ted *has* got a car, *hasn't he*? (Ted hat doch sicher ein Auto?) – You *know* Tom, *don't you*? (Du kennst doch Tom?) – You *didn't meet* Mark yesterday, *did you*? (Du hast Mark gestern wohl nicht getroffen?) – John *can dance, can't he*? – Clare *used to smoke* a lot, *didn't she*? (6.4.4.) – Nice girl, *isn't she*?[2]

Beachten Sie: *I am* right, *aren't I*? – *Everybody is* ready, *aren't they*? – *Somebody informed* you, *didn't they*?

Will you nach einem **Imperativ** bewirkt, daß eine Anordnung höflich klingt; **won't you** drückt eine höfliche Aufforderung oder Einladung aus. Nach **verneintem Imperativ** kann nur *will you* verwendet werden.
Nach *let us/let's* steht *shall we*.
Open the window, will you? (Öffnen Sie doch bitte das Fenster!) – Have another glass of wine, won't you? (Trinken Sie doch noch ein Glas Wein.) – Don't be late, will you? (Komm doch bitte nicht so spät!) – Let's go now, shall we? (Gehen wir doch jetzt.)

---

[1] Wird Zustimmung erwartet, d.h. es ist keine Antwort nötig, so werden Question Tags mit fallender Intonation gesprochen (a); handelt es sich um eine Frage, so werden sie mit steigender Intonation gesprochen (b): Jane is pretty, isn't she? (a) – 'You will come with us, won't you?' – 'Yes, I will./No, I won't.' (b)

[2] Ist das Subjekt ein Pronomen, so kann es umgangssprachlich zusammen mit der entsprechenden Form von "be" entfallen: Good film, wasn't it? = It was a good film, wasn't it?

12.1.1. Nach positiver Aussage können *Question Tags* in der bejahenden Form, nach verneinender Aussage in der Verneinung stehen, um Interesse, Verwunderung etc. auszudrücken:
Betty has got engaged, has she? (ausgedrückt wird etwa: I'm glad / surprised to hear that.) – Paul doesn't want to study, doesn't he? (= etwa: How strange that he doesn't want to study.)

12.2. **Kurzantworten:** Bei *yes/no*-Antworten wird oft das Subjekt des Fragesatzes als Personalpronomen mit dem Hilfsverb, nach Vollverb mit der entsprechenden Form von *do* wiederholt:[3]
'Is your friend a teacher?' – 'Yes, he is. / No, he isn't.'
'Do you like classical music?' – 'Yes, I do. / No, I don't.'
'Can we help you?' – 'Of course, you can.'

Auch als Antwort auf Subjektfragen wird das Hilfsverb wiederholt, bei Vollverben *do/does/did* verwendet:
'Which of you can answer the question?' – 'I can.'
'Who wrote Oliver Twist?' – 'Dickens did.'
'Which of you didn't see the play?' – 'I didn't.'

Kommen mehrere Hilfsverben in der Frage vor, so wird nur das erste wiederholt:
'Have you been informed?' – 'Yes, I have.'

Bei Gefühlsreaktionen auf etwas Gehörtes wird das Hilfsverb in der Frageform wiederholt, nach Vollverben die entsprechende Form von *do* verwendet. 'My sister is getting married.' – 'Oh, is she?' (= Tatsächlich?)
'Peter wants to learn Japanese.' – 'Does he?'

12.2.1. Bei Kurzantworten steht nach Verben wie *hope, think, suppose, believe, say, tell sb, be afraid* immer *so* (dt. "es")
'Will we be seeing Tom tomorrow?' – 'I hope so.'
'Is Donald an engineer?' – 'Yes, I think so.' (= I think he is.)
'Has Bob failed the exam?' – 'I'm afraid so.' (= I'm afraid he has.)
'The film was boring.' – 'I told you so.'
Bei verneintem *think, suppose, believe* ergeben sich zwei Möglichkeiten:
'Is Fred an architect?' – 'I don't think so.' / 'I think not.'
'Does Eric know Spanish?' – 'I don't suppose so.' / 'I suppose not.'
(aber nur:) 'Will the train be late?' – 'I hope not.'

12.3. Soll zum Ausdruck gebracht werden, daß eine Handlung oder ein Zustand auch für eine andere Person oder andere Personen gilt, so ergeben sich folgende Möglichkeiten:
'Eve enjoys dancing.' – 'So do I.' (= 'Ich auch.')
Eve enjoys dancing and so do I. (= ... and I do as well.)

---

[3] Das trifft auch auf Aussagesätze allgemein zu: We can't make the test today, but we can tomorrow.
Auch wenn sich das Hilfsverb ändert, braucht das Vollverb nicht wiederholt zu werden: They said they would help us but they haven't.

L 13.

'Eve doesn't enjoy dancing.' – 'Nor/Neither do I.' (oder:) 'I don't, either.' (= 'Ich auch nicht.')
Eve doesn't enjoy dancing and neither do I. (oder:) ... and I don't, either.
Weitere Beispiele: They liked the film and so did I. – They didn't like the film and neither did I. – Ruth can speak English well and so can her brother. (oder:) ... and her brother, too.
'I'll go abroad this summer.' – 'So will/shall we.'
'I won't go abroad this summer.' – 'Nor will/shall we.' (oder:) 'We won't/shan't, either.'

13. Emphasis – Möglichkeiten zur Hervorhebung von Satzteilen

13.1. In bejahenden Sätzen kann das Prädikat durch (betontes) *do* hervorgehoben werden, um der Aussage Nachdruck zu verleihen, oder um eine emotionale Reaktion auszudrücken. Das gilt auch für den **Imperativ mit Vollverb** oder *be*.[1]
I do hope that Tom will come. (Ich hoffe sehr, daß Tom kommt.) – We did ask them. (Wir haben sie doch gefragt.) – Do help me! (Hilf mir doch bitte!) – Do be reasonable! (Seien Sie doch vernünftig!)

13.2. Soll eine Feststellung betont oder eine emotionale Reaktion auf wiederholte Handlungen bzw. Verhaltensweisen zum Ausdruck gebracht werden – oft mit *always, forever, continually, constantly, permanently* –, so wird häufig die *Continuous Form* verwendet.
Believe me, I am telling the truth. (Glauben Sie mir, ich sage wirklich die Wahrheit.) – You are always making the same mistakes. (Du machst doch immer wieder die gleichen Fehler.) – I am always paying for the coffee, why don't you today, for a change?

13.2.1. Bei *be* kann die *Continuous Form* verwendet werden, wenn von Verhaltensweisen die Rede ist, nicht aber zum Ausdruck von Zuständen oder Gefühlen:
Paula was being helpful in every way. (Paula war wirklich in jeder Weise hilfsbereit.) – You are being impolite. (Du bist aber wirklich unhöflich.) – (aber:) I am really happy. (Ich bin wirklich glücklich.) (nicht: I am being happy.)

13.3. Jeder Satzteil – außer dem Prädikat – kann durch einleitendes *it is/ was ... that* hervorgehoben werden. Bei Hervorhebung des Subjekts steht bei **Personen** neben *that* auch *who*.
Ausgangssatz: Darwin developed the theory of evolution in his book 'On the Origin of Species'.

---

[1] Im Anschluß an eine Frage kann "do" eine Zustimmung oder Aufforderung des Gesprächspartners zum Ausdruck bringen, auch bei Hilfsverben im Fragesatz.
'Can/May I go now?' – 'Do.' ('Kann ich jetzt gehen?' – 'Bitte.')
'Shall I spell the word?' – 'Please do.'

Mögliche Hervorhebungen:
- It was Darwin that/who developed the theory of evolution ...
- It was the theory of evolution that Darwin developed ...
- It was in his book 'On the Origin of Species' that Darwin developed ...

Weitere Beispiele: It was your friend who told me the story. – It was my brother that Jane borrowed the money from. – It was the transistor that made possible the modern computer. – It was on Monday that I met Donald.

Beachten Sie: It was not until ... that .... (Erst ....):
It was not until 1888 that Hertz succeeded in proving the hypothesis of Maxwell concerning the electromagnetic nature of the light waves.

13.4. Eine Hervorhebung ist auch durch *what ... is/was* möglich:
What annoys us is Peter's unreliability. – What I am afraid of is that some unexpected difficulties may arise. – What I wanted to do was (to) make you realize the importance of this problem.

Beachten Sie: *What matters is that* you hand in your manuscript this week. (Das Wesentliche/Worauf es ankommt, ist ...)

13.5. **Betonung durch Veränderung der üblichen Wortfolge**

13.5.1. Die Hervorhebung durch **Inversion** (Verb vor Subjekt)

13.5.1.1. Nach satzeinleitendem *here/there* steht das Verb vor dem Subjekt, wenn das Subjekt kein Pronomen ist. Im literarischen Stil ist diese Form der Inversion auch bei betonten satzeinleitenden Adverbialbestimmungen des Ortes möglich:
Here comes John's girl-friend. (aber:) Here she comes. – There lives our English teacher. – Round the corner came a car at top speed. – On the couch lay a big cat.
Ohne besondere Hervorhebung findet sich die Inversion bei *there/here* + *be* oder Vollverb (z. B. *exist, follow, come, remain*).
There are many people waiting outside. (= Many people are waiting outside.) – Let's go to the market-place, there is a nice wine-cellar there. – Here is a leaflet about travels to Hungary. – After the presentation of the paper there followed a lively discussion. – There remained little to be done.

13.5.1.2. Vor allem im literarischen Stil findet sich Inversion nach Ausdrücken wie: **hardly** (oder: *scarcely*) ... *when* kaum; *no sooner ... than* kaum; *only* erst; *seldom/rarely* selten; *never/at no time* niemals; *under no circumstances* unter keinen Umständen; und bei Vergleichen nach *so* + **Adjektiv**. Das (erste) Hilfsverb bzw. *do/does/did* bei Vollverben tritt vor das Subjekt:
Hardly/Scarcely had we got home when the thunderstorm broke out. – Only after a long and heated debate did they reach an agreement. – Never/At no time were the team's chances of winning the championship greater than now. – Under no circumstances can such a decision be accepted. – Rarely have I met such a beautiful

L 13.5.2.

girl. – Never have I been happier than now. – So great was Anne's joy that she was at a loss for words.

13.5.2. Ein Satz kann mit dem betonten Satzteil beginnen:
Such a problem I have never come across before. – To some of the questions no answer could be given. – Essential in this case is the following.

14. Conjunctions – Konjunktionen

Konjunktionen verbinden Sätze, Satzteile oder einzelne Wörter.

14.1. Konjunktionen, die Temporal-, Kausal-, Konditional-, Konzessiv-, Objekt- und Finalsätze einleiten:

Temporalsätze: *after* nachdem; *before* bevor, ehe; *until/till* bis; *when* als, wann, wenn; *now (that)* jetzt da; *once* sobald, nachdem; *since* seit; *while/as/when* während, als; *as soon as* sobald; *as long as* solange:
After Tom had gone we began to work. – I'll phone you before you leave. – They will wait until/till Peter comes. – It was raining when we left. – I don't know when Jim wants to visit us. – We'll show you the photos when you return. – You'll understand me now that you know the facts. – Once the problem is/has been solved, we'll feel better. – Tom has been working at the Humboldt University since he came to Berlin. – While/As/When we were taking a walk through the park we met some friends.

Kausalsätze: *as*[1]*/since/because*[1] da, weil; *for*[2] denn: John can't go out because he is ill. – As/Since one of the speakers can't come, we shall have to change our programme. – They stopped at a restaurant, for they were feeling hungry and thirsty.

Konditionalsätze (s. Kapitel 3): *if* wenn, falls; *unless* wenn nicht, außer wenn; *in case (that)* falls; *provided/providing (that)* vorausgesetzt, daß; *on condition that* unter der Bedingung, daß; *supposing (that)* angenommen, daß; *as long as* sofern.
We would be glad if you came. – Let's go out unless you're tired. – Please inform us in case (that) you should be prevented. – You can have the book provided/providing (that) you return it tomorrow. – I'll lend you this large sum on condition that you repay me by the end of the year. – Supposing you were single (= unmarried), would you marry Joan? – We can turn to the next topic, as long as you agree.

Konzessivsätze: *(al)though*[3] obwohl; *even if/even though* selbst wenn, wenn auch. I'll have a walk (al)though it is rather late. – We'd like to go to the jam session even if/even though it may be difficult to get tickets.

---

[1] Der Nebensatz mit "because" folgt meist dem Hauptsatz. Nebensätze mit "since" und "as" stehen oft vor dem Hauptsatz.
[2] Der durch "for" eingeleitete Kausalsatz – vorwiegend Schriftsprache – gibt eine zusätzliche Begründung und folgt immer dem Hauptsatz.
[3] In der Schriftsprache zuweilen auch "albeit".

Objektsätze: *that* "daß" nach Verben wie *say, tell, know, think, suppose, believe* und Adjektiven wie *glad, surprised* etc.[4]
I know that he is a teacher.

Finalsätze: *in order that/so that* damit.
We should make some concessions in order that/so that an agreement can be reached quickly.

14.2. Konjunktionen, die zum Ausdruck bringen, daß

– etwas gegenübergestellt wird: *whereas/while/(whilst)* während, wohingegen: Tom is rather stout, whereas/while his wife is very slim.
– etwas verglichen oder miteinander in Beziehung gebracht werden soll: *as* wie; *the way (that)/as* (so) wie; *as if/as though* als ob: As you know Bob is an engineer. – As/The way (that) the situation looks now, it will be difficult to find a compromise. – It seemed as if/as though Judith were/was angry.
– eine Schlußfolgerung gezogen wird: *that's why/therefore/so*[5] deshalb, so: Jim has often helped us, that's why/therefore we should help him now. – The weather was bad, so we stayed at home.

14.3. Daß etwas in Beziehung gesetzt oder gegenübergestellt wird, kann auch ausgedrückt werden mit: *both ... and* sowohl ... als auch, und; *as well as* sowie, und auch; *not only ... but also* nicht nur ... sondern auch; *rather than* lieber als, und nicht (= anstatt); *but* aber, außer, als; *except* außer; *yet* doch; *however*[6] jedoch; *no matter what/who/how/whether* ganz gleich was/wer/wie/ob; *either ... or* entweder ... oder; *neither ... nor* weder ... noch; *nevertheless/all the same* dennoch, trotzdem; *otherwise/or (else)* andernfalls.
Jane plays both the violin and the piano. – My friend has got a house as well as a big garden.[7] – Jim is not only an excellent student but also a good sportsman. – I like to take my holidays in summer rather than in winter. – We want to phone Bill rather than send a letter. – The text is very special but easy to understand. – We can't do anything but/except wait.[8] – Paul says he doesn't earn much, yet he has a big yacht.
I quite agree, however, I would add .../(oder:) ... I would add, however, ...

---

[4] "that" entfällt hier oft umgangssprachlich, selten aber nach bestimmten Verben der Schriftsprache wie "reply, object, conclude, remark, mention, doubt etc"; "that" kann nicht entfallen, wenn der Objektsatz von dem dazugehörigen Verb getrennt wird: Everybody realized, I think, that they had made a mistake.
[5] In der Schriftsprache auch "hence" und "thus", z. B.: Hence it follows that ... = daraus folgt, daß ...; hence we conclude that ... = daraus können wir schlußfolgern ...; thus it was proved that ... = so wurde bewiesen ...
[6] Beachten Sie die Bedeutung von "however" als Adverb im Sinne von "selbst wenn, ganz gleich wie": I'll finish this work however late it will get. = ... no matter how late it will get.
[7] Beachten Sie: Joan sings as well as playing the guitar. (s. 8.4.) (Joan singt und spielt Gitarre.) – (aber:) Joan sings as well as she plays the guitar. (Joan singt ebenso gut wie sie Gitarre spielt.)
[8] Nach "but" und "except" Infinitiv ohne "to".

No matter what happens I shall be on your side. – I shall stay up no matter when you come. – Sue will leave either today or tomorrow. – Frank neither smokes nor drinks. – Neither my colleague nor I knew anything about this arrangement. The task is very difficult, nevertheless/all the same we won't give up. – We must leave now, otherwise we won't catch the train.

14.4. Konjunktionen mit mehreren Bedeutungen:

as = da: As I was ill I couldn't come.
 = als: I met Tom as I was leaving the office.
 = wie: As I have said before ...
 = in dem Maße wie: The short-time memory decreases as we grow old.
 = obwohl (nur wenn es dem Bezugswort folgt): *Hot as* it was, Betty was wearing a coat. (= Although it was hot, Betty ...)

since = da: We bought the house since it was rather cheap.
 = seit: I haven't been skiing since I was twelve.

while = während (zeitlich): While Mark was reading his girl-friend was cooking.
 = während, wohingegen: Lots of people like seeing films on TV, while (= whereas) others prefer to go to the cinema.

14.4.1. Konjunktionen mit gleicher Bedeutung aber teilweise unterschiedlicher Anwendung: **if/when**; **if/whether**

if/when: *if* drückt eine Bedingung oder Voraussetzung aus, *when* einen zeitlichen Bezug:
We won't take a walk if it rains. – I'll see you in September when I'm back from my holiday.

Sind Bedingung und zeitlicher Bezug nicht eindeutig zu unterscheiden, kann sowohl *if* als auch *when* verwendet werden:
If/When a metal is heated it expands.

if/whether ob: In der indirekten Rede kann *if* oder *whether* verwendet werden:
I don't know if/whether this answer is correct.

Nach Präpositionen und vor Infinitiv kann nur *whether* stehen: We talked about whether we should go to the theatre. – I didn't know whether to wait any longer.

15. The Pronouns – Die Pronomen

15.1. The Personal Pronouns – Die Personalpronomen

| Subjektform: | I | you | he | she | it | we | you | they |
| Objektform: | me | you | him | her | it | us | you | them |

In der Umgangssprache wird in bestimmten Fällen die Objektform gegenüber der Subjektform des Personalpronomens bevorzugt, z. B.:

- nach einer Form **von be**: The phone is ringing; that must be *her* (oder: she). – If I were him (oder: he) I would think the matter over.
- bei Hervorhebungen durch *it is/was ... who(m)/that...*, wenn das Personalpronomen nicht das logische Subjekt ist: It was me (oder: I) whom they wanted to send to the conference. (Mich wollten sie zu der Konferenz schicken.) – (aber:) It was *she who* made that suggestion. (Sie hat diesen Vorschlag unterbreitet.)
- bei Vergleichen mit *than* und *as*: Do you think she knows more about it than him? (= than he). He is as old as me/as I (am).
- in kurzen Sätzen ohne Verb: 'Peter, will you wash the car, please?' – 'No! Not *me* again!'

Die Objektform **muß** stehen in Wendungen wie: *the two of us* wir beide; *all of them* sie alle.

15.2. The Demonstrative Pronouns – Die Demonstrativpronomen

this + Substantiv im Singular = dies(-e, -er, -es): this house
these + Substantiv im Plural = diese: these houses
that + Substantiv im Singular = jene(-r, -s): that house
those + Substantiv im Plural = jene: those houses

This – these verweisen auf etwas Näherliegendes (räumlich im Sinne von "dies hier"; zeitlich im Sinne von "jetzig, gegenwärtig").
That – those verweisen auf etwas Fernerliegendes (räumlich im Sinne von "das dort"; zeitlich im Sinne von "damalig").
This photo is good. – These photos are good. – That photo is bad. – Those photos are bad.
These are good photos. (Dies sind ...) – Those are bad photos. (Das sind ...)
I want to phone him this morning/afternoon/evening. – Tom was not at home that morning/afternoon/evening.
Beachten Sie: (in) these days = at present (jetzt); in those days = at that time (damals); those who = diejenigen, die; those present = die Anwesenden.

15.3. The Possessive Pronouns – Die Possessivpronomen

15.3.1. Das **adjektivische Possessivpronomen** hat folgende Formen:

my, your, his, her, its; our, your, their.
This is *his* book. – I don't know *her* father.
Die unpersönliche Form des adjektivischen Possessivpronomens lautet *one's*. Sie steht im Wörterbuch in Verbindung mit dem Infinitiv und wird im Kontext durch das entsprechende Possessivpronomen ersetzt:
One should try one's best. Man sollte sein Bestes versuchen.
make up one's mind sich entschließen; *change one's mind* seine Meinung ändern; *lose one's life* ums Leben kommen; *take one's time* sich Zeit nehmen.
I haven't made up my mind yet. – Tom often changes his mind. – Three people lost their lives. – Take your time.

L 15.3.2.

Beachten Sie auch Wendungen wie *of one's own*: Jack has got a car of his own. (... einen eigenen Wagen.) – *on one's own*: Can you do it on your own? (= by yourself) – *on the tip of one's tongue*: The word is on the tip of my tongue. (Das Wort liegt mir auf der Zunge.)

Das adjektivische Possessivpronomen findet sich in Verbindung mit Körperteilen und Kleidungsstücken.
She shook *her* head. – He raised *his* hand. – I've cut *my* finger. – Put *your* coat on.
Bei präpositionalem Objekt steht in der Regel der bestimmte Artikel: He took her *by the* hand.

15.3.2. Das **substantivische Possessivpronomen** hat folgende Formen:

mine, yours,[1] his, hers; ours, yours, theirs.

Das substantivische Possessivpronomen kann seinem Bezugswort folgen oder ihm vorausgehen.
This glass is mine, yours is over there. – Yours is the best translation. (= Your translation is the best.)

Ein substantivisches Possessivpronomen kann mit seinem Bezugswort durch *of* verbunden sein; vor dem Bezugswort steht dann der unbestimmte Artikel oder ein Indefinitpronomen.
Tom is a friend of mine (= Tom is one of my friends.) (Tom ist ein Freund von mir.) – Is Paula a colleague of yours? (= one of your colleagues?) (... von dir?) – Some friends of ours have seen this film. (... von uns ...)
In Verbindung mit *that/those* kann eine Abwertung zum Ausdruck gebracht werden: I don't like that dress of hers.

15.4. **The Reflexive Pronoun – Das Reflexivpronomen**

Die Formen des Reflexivpronomens sind:

Singular	myself	yourself	himself, herself, itself	oneself
Plural	ourselves	yourselves	themselves	

Abweichend vom Deutschen steht bei vielen Verben **kein** Reflexivpronomen, z.B. *agree* sich einigen; *apologize* sich entschuldigen; *approach* sich nähern; *behave*[2] sich verhalten; *boast/brag* sich rühmen; *complain* sich beschweren; *deal with* sich beschäftigen mit; *dress*[2] sich anziehen; *hurry (up)* sich beeilen; *imagine/fancy* sich vorstellen; *interfere* sich einmischen; *lie down* sich hinlegen; *long for* sich sehnen nach; *look forward to* sich freuen auf; *recover* sich erholen; *refrain/abstain (from)*

---

[1] Die folgenden Formen erscheinen als Briefschluß: Yours (in Privatbriefen); Yours sincerely / Sincerely yours; Yours truly / Yours faithfully (sehr formal).
[2] Bei einigen Verben kann das Reflexivpronomen hinzutreten, vor allem im Imperativ, z.B. "wash (oneself); dress (oneself); behave (oneself)": Eve usually washes (herself) in cold water. – Behave yourself. – Dress yourself before you have breakfast.

sich enthalten; *relax* sich entspannen; *rely/depend on* sich verlassen auf; *remember/ recall/recollect* sich erinnern an; *shave*² sich rasieren; *sit down* sich setzen; *talk* sich unterhalten; *turn/apply to* sich wenden an; *wash*² sich waschen:
What did you talk about? – You can rely/depend upon Roy. – I think we are now approaching the solution of the problem.

Einige Verben kommen in transitiver und reflexiver Bedeutung vor, z. B.: *change/ alter* (sich) ändern; *decrease* (sich) verringern; *deteriorate* (sich) verschlechtern; *develop/evolve* (sich) entwickeln; *form* (sich) bilden; *hide* (sich) verstecken; *improve* (sich) verbessern; *increase* (sich) erhöhen; *meet* (sich) treffen; *move* (sich) bewegen; *refer/relate to* (sich) beziehen auf; *separate* (sich) trennen; *worry/trouble/ bother* (sich) beunruhigen.
We have improved the conditions. – The conditions have improved.

In einigen Fällen muß das Verb mit dem Reflexivpronomen stehen, z.B.: *avail o.s. of sth* sich einer Sache bedienen; *concern o.s. with* sich befassen mit; *content o.s. with* sich begnügen mit.
I shall concern myself with this matter tomorrow. – Do you content yourself with this answer?

Einige Verben können auch in reflexiver Bedeutung vorkommen, die dann durch das Reflexivpronomen ausgedrückt wird.
I have hurt my finger. (Ich habe mir den Finger verletzt.) – aber: I have hurt myself. (Ich habe mich verletzt.)

Ebenso: *assert (o.s.)* (sich) behaupten; *betray (o.s.)/give (o.s.) away* (sich) verraten; *commit (o.s.)* (sich) verpflichten; *confine (o.s.) to/limit (o.s.) to/restrict (o.s.) to* (sich) beschränken auf; **convince** *(o.s.)* (sich) überzeugen; *devote (o.s.) to* (sich) widmen; *inform (o.s.)* (sich) informieren; *injure (o.s.)* (sich) verletzen.
We have convinced ourselves that this method is the best. – I shall confine myself to the main facts.

In einigen Fällen hat das Verb in reflexiver Form eine abweichende Bedeutung, z.B.: *control* steuern, regeln; kontrollieren; *control o.s.* sich beherrschen; *deny* leugnen; *deny o.s. sth* sich etwas versagen; *enjoy* mögen; *enjoy o.s.* sich amüsieren; *lend* (ver)leihen; *lend o.s. to* sich eignen für.
Did you enjoy yourself at the party? – This hall lends itself to poster conferences.

Beachten Sie die Wendungen: Help yourselves. (Bedienen Sie sich!) – Suit yourself. (Halten Sie es, wie Sie wollen.)

15.4.1. Durch das Reflexivpronomen kann ein Substantiv oder Pronomen hervorgehoben werden.
She told me the story *herself./She herself* told me the story. (Sie selbst hat mir die Geschichte erzählt.) – Did you talk to the *manager himself?* (Hast du mit dem Direktor selbst gesprochen?) – (aber:) Did *you* talk to the manager *yourself?* (Hast du selbst mit dem Direktor gesprochen?)

L 15.5.

15.5. The Reciprocal Pronoun – Das reziproke Pronomen

Das reziproke Pronomen, das eine wechselseitige Beziehung zum Ausdruck bringt (dt.: "uns, euch, sich" im Sinne von "einander"), hat zwei Formen, *each other* und *one another*, die meist unterschiedslos verwendet werden können.
We should help each other / one another. – They know each other / one another.

One another findet sich bei allgemeinen Feststellungen oder Definitionen:
'to converse' is the same as 'to talk to one another'.

15.6. The Indefinite Pronouns – Die Indefinitpronomen

Die indefiniten Pronomen lauten:
some, any; *much, many*; *little, few*; *all*; *each, every*; *both*; *no, none*; *either, neither*; *other(s), another*; *one*.
Bei einigen dieser Pronomen gibt es Zusammensetzungen.

15.6.1. some – any

some steht vorzugsweise in **bejahenden** Sätzen, *any* in **verneinten** Sätzen und in Fragesätzen, wenn die Antwort ungewiß ist oder eine negative Reaktion erwartet wird.

some + Bezugswort im Plural = einige
 + nichtzählbares Substantiv = etwas
 + zählbares Substantiv im Singular = irgendein

any + Bezugswort im Plural oder Singular:
 im verneinten Satz = kein(-e, -er, -es)
 im Fragesatz = irgendwelche(-r, -s) – (bleibt oft unübersetzt)

'I need some books on modern European architecture. Have you got any literature on this subject?' – 'Sorry, we haven't got any books in this field.'
We wanted to buy some bottles of Soviet champagne, but they didn't have any.
'I think there is some beer in the refrigerator.' – 'Sorry, I can't find any.'
We've got enough wine, you can have some more. – Tom lives in some little village near Rostock.[3]

In Fragesätzen kommt *some* bei einem Angebot vor, oder wenn eine positive Antwort erwartet wird.
The coffee is excellent. Wouldn't you like *some*?
Could we have *some* more tea?

Some hat auch die Bedeutung von "ungefähr, etwa":
Agatha Christie, Britain's 'Queen of Crime', wrote some eighty detective novels.

---

[3] Unterscheiden Sie: You have made some mistakes (einige Fehler). – (aber:) There must be some mistake in our calculation (irgendein Fehler).
I don't know any of these plays. (Ich kenne keines dieser Stücke.) – (aber:) I don't know some of these plays. (Ich kenne einige dieser Stücke nicht.)
I hope we shall meet again some time. (... irgendwann einmal) – (aber:) I meet him sometimes. (... manchmal.)

Beachten Sie: Some hundred people attended the meeting. (Etwa hundert Menschen ...) – (aber:) Several hundred people attended the meeting. (Mehrere hundert Menschen besuchten die Versammlung.)
Steht *any* in **bejahenden Sätzen**, so bedeutet es: "jeder (beliebige), alle":
You can come any time you like. (Du kannst jederzeit kommen.) – Any suggestions are welcome. (Jeder Vorschlag ist willkommen.)
Im Zusammenhang mit *without*, **hardly/scarcely/barely**, *seldom*, **never** steht *any* statt *some*.
We solved the problem without any difficulties. – Paul never mentions any details of his private life. – There are hardly any famous English writers Sheila does not know.
In *if*-Sätzen ist *some* oder *any* möglich; *some* wird bevorzugt, wenn die angegebene Voraussetzung **wahrscheinlich** ist, *any* dagegen, wenn sie **ungewiß** erscheint.
If you want some/any information, turn to Bob. – If you need some practice in English, you can attend a refresher course. – If you have any questions, please ask Fred.
Statt *not ... any* kann *no* verwendet werden.
I don't have any money left. = I have no money left.
any vor Komparativen bleibt unübersetzt.
We needn't wait any longer. – Dick doesn't smoke any more.

15.6.1.1. *some* und *any* können in folgenden Zusammensetzungen stehen:
somebody/someone (irgend) jemand; *something* (irgend) etwas; *anybody/anyone* (irgend) jemand, jeder (beliebige), alle; *not ... anybody* niemand; *anything* (irgend) etwas, alles, ganz gleich was; *not ... anything* nichts.
Die Anwendung entspricht den unter 15.6.1. genannten Regeln.
'I think someone/somebody has rung the bell. Has anyone/anybody looked who it is?' – 'We haven't heard anybody/anyone ring.'
'I would like to know something about Roy's research work. Do you know anything about it?' – 'No, I don't know anything definite about it.' Would you like something to drink?
'Can somebody help me?' – 'Of course, we can.'
I think anybody might answer this question. – I can hardly tell you anything about Jim's intentions. – If anything/something happens, please inform me.
Statt *not ... anybody* kann *nobody*, statt *not ... anything* kann *nothing* stehen, im Subjektfall muß *nobody* bzw. *nothing* stehen.
I don't know anybody in this house. = I know nobody in this house. I can't tell you anything about it. = I can tell you nothing about it.
Some und *any* kommen auch in Zusammensetzungen mit adverbialem Charakter vor: *somehow* (verstärkt: *somehow or other*) irgendwie; *sometimes* manchmal; *somewhat* etwas; *somewhere* irgendwo; *anyhow* ohnehin; *anywhere* irgendwo; *not ... anywhere* nirgends.
We should try to reach an agreement somehow (or other). – This is somewhat difficult to explain. – The book must be somewhere on the desk. – I'll talk to Tom anyhow. – I have been looking for my glasses, I can't find them anywhere.

15.6.2. much – many

much (Bezugswort immer im Singular) = viel
many[4] (Bezugswort immer im Plural) = viele
kommen vorzugsweise in verneinten und Fragesätzen vor.[5] In bejahenden Sätzen steht meist *a lot of*, umgangssprachlich auch *lots of/plenty of*. In etwas formalerem Stil findet sich auch *a large/great number of* (+ Substantiv und Verb im Plural), *a great/good deal of* (+ Substantiv und Verb im Singular), formal außerdem *a great/good many* (+ Substantiv und Verb im Plural).
Clare hasn't got many dresses but a lot of sweaters and skirts.
'Do you have much trouble with your new dish-washer?' – 'Quite a lot.'
'Are there many trees in your garden?' – 'Yes, there are plenty.'
A great number of tests were necessary to confirm the hypothesis. – A great deal of time has been spent on problems of organization. – Lake Baikal is fed by a great many rivers.

Much und *a lot* kommen auch als Adverb vor, dt. "sehr, viel".
I like Rita very much. – *Businessmen travel a lot.*
Much, *a lot* und *many* können Komparative verstärken.
The problem was much more complicated than we had thought. – I feel a lot better today. – Many more students attended the lecture than we had expected.

15.6.3. little – few

little (+ Substantiv im Singular) = wenig
few (+ Substantiv im Plural) = wenige
a little = ein wenig; *a few* (= some) = einige

little und *few* werden umgangssprachlich häufig durch *not much*, *not many* ersetzt.
Fred takes little interest in sports. (= Fred doesn't take much interest in sports.) – Only few people attended the performance. (= Not many people attended ...) – Leo speaks only a little English. – I'm feeling a little better today. – You should tell me a few details on the situation.

Beachten Sie: *little by little* nach und nach, allmählich; *some few* einige wenige; *quite a few* ziemlich viele; *every few days* alle paar Tage.

15.6.4. all / all of

All (of) Cliff's friends are very intelligent. – All (of) these books are useful for me. – I didn't read all (of) the articles you gave me. – All of us enjoyed the trip.

all + **Substantiv ohne Artikel** bezieht sich auf eine Gruppe von Personen oder Sa-

---

[4] "many a" (meist literarisch) = manch(-e, -er, -es), viele: Like many a woman Joan spends a lot of time on her make-up. (Wie viele Frauen verwendet Joan viel Zeit für ihr Make-up.)

[5] In formalerem Stil kommen "much" und "many" auch in bejahenden Sätzen vor: Much work has been done recently in biogenetics.
"much" and "many" stehen immer nach "too, so, as, very":
Bob should not drink so much. – Peggy has read too many detective stories. – You can eat as many biscuits as you like. – There is very much time left.

L 15.6.5.

chen in der Gesamtheit. Wird auf eine begrenzte Anzahl bzw. Menge verwiesen, so steht oft *all the*.
All scientists should be able to understand two languages. – All the scientists who co-operated in the project were awarded a prize.

all kann auch dem Pronomen oder Substantiv folgen. Es steht dann unmittelbar nach dem Subjekt, wenn ein Vollverb folgt, bzw. nach dem ersten Hilfsverb oder nach einer Form von *be* im *Present* oder *Past Tense*.
We all (= all of us) agree. – You should all have read this book. = All of you should have read this book. – We are all satisfied. = All of us are satisfied.

all kann ohne Bezugswort stehen (= alles).
All that glitters is not gold. – That's all I can tell you.

all (the) ist oft mit *whole* austauschbar:
all (the) afternoon = *the whole* afternoon; all the world = *the whole* world; all my life = my *whole* life.[6]

Beachten Sie Wendungen wie: *with all my heart* von ganzem Herzen; *be all ears* ganz Ohr sein; *all in good time* alles zu seiner Zeit; *that's all the better* das ist umso besser.

15.6.5.   each – every

every bezeichnet eine Gesamtheit von Personen oder Sachen und betont das kollektive Moment; *each* verweist mehr auf die einzelnen Personen oder Sachen und betont das individuelle Moment. Doch werden beide Pronomen auch ohne Bedeutungsunterschied verwendet. Nach *almost, nearly, practically* steht *every*.
each of hebt einzelne Personen oder Sachen aus einer Gesamtheit heraus; zuweilen findet sich auch *every one of.*
Every student at a technical college must take courses in mathematics. – Each season has its attractions. – Every conductor must be able to play at least two instruments. – Each great conductor has a different style of interpretation. – I'm interested in every/each detail. – Each/every time I see Helen I'm impressed by her beauty. – Gary told me almost/nearly/practically every detail. – Each of these books is worth reading. – Each of us has made a mistake. – Each of the seats (= every one of the seats) was taken.

each kann auch dem Subjekt, einem indirekten Objekt oder dem Prädikatsnomen folgen. Bei Bezug auf das Subjekt steht es vor dem Vollverb bzw. nach dem (ersten) Hilfsverb.
We each have a different opinion about this topic. (= Each of us has a ...) – My friends have each attended college. (Each of my friends has ...) – I gave the girls each a piece of chocolate. (= I gave each of the girls ...) – These books are ten marks each. (= Each of these books is ten marks.)

---

[6] Bei Bezugswort im Plural haben "all" und "whole" unterschiedliche Bedeutung: All villages within 20 kilometres were destroyed by the eruption of the volcano. (Alle Dörfer ...) – (aber:) Whole villages were destroyed within 20 kilometres ... (Ganze Dörfer ...)

L 15.6.5.1.

Zusammensetzungen mit *every*: *everybody/everyone* jede(-r, -s), alle; *everything* alles; *everywhere* überall
Everyone who goes to Leningrad should visit the Hermitage. – The train is coming, everybody should take care of their luggage. (s. 15.6.5.1.) – Everything is ready for the test. – We looked for Tom everywhere.

Beachten Sie Wendungen wie: *every two days/every second day* alle zwei Tage; *every now and then* gelegentlich; *have every reason* wirklich Grund haben; *his every word* jedes seiner Worte.
Tom is every inch a gentleman. (Tom ist durch und durch Gentleman.)

15.6.5.1. Nach *everybody, everyone, each (of)*, sowie nach *somebody, someone, anybody, anyone, nobody* steht ein dazugehöriges Possessivpronomen oder Personalpronomen häufig im Plural.
Everybody was doing *their*/his best to make the party a success. – Each of the girls thought *their*/her dress was the most beautiful one. – If somebody/anybody comes, tell *them* (him) I'm not at home. – Someone has forgotten *their*/his briefcase in the office.

15.6.6. both (of)

both steht vor dem Substantiv, *both* und *both of* vor Substantiv in Verbindung mit Artikel, Possessiv- und Demonstrativpronomen, nur *both of* vor Personalpronomen.

Both
Both (of) the ⎫
       my ⎬ sisters are very attractive.
       these ⎭
Both of them are very attractive.

Vor allem bei Subjektbezug kann *both* auch nachgestellt werden; es steht dann vor dem Vollverb, nach *be* im *Present* bzw. *Past Tense* oder bei mehreren Hilfsverben nach dem 1. Hilfsverb.
We both/Both of us talked to Bob. – They are both/Both of them are older than I. – They have both been asked/Both of them have been asked. – I met them both/both of them.

both kann auch substantivisch verwendet werden.
I have seen these two films, both are interesting.

Beachten Sie: *both ... and* sowohl ... als auch: We are both hungry and thirsty. (= We are hungry as well as thirsty.)

15.6.7. either – neither

either jede(-r, -s) von beiden, beide, einer von beiden.
There are meadows on either side of the river. (= ... on both sides of the river.) – You can visit me on Saturday or Sunday, *either* day *is* all right. (= ... *both* days *are* all right.) – Either of my brothers is younger than me. (= Both my brothers are ...) Has either of your grandfathers been a teacher? (= Has one of your grandfathers ...) – (aber:) Have both (of) your grandfathers been teachers?

either wird in **verneinten** Sätzen, häufig in verneinenden Kurzantworten, verwendet und steht jeweils am Satzende (= auch nicht). 'I don't know Eric.' – 'We don't, either.' (= 'Nor do we / Neither do we.') (s. 12.3.) – Diana dislikes detective stories, and she doesn't enjoy science fiction, either.

neither keine(-r, -s) von beiden. Bei *neither of* (+ Substantiv im Plural) steht das Verb im Singular, umgangssprachlich auch im Plural.
Neither solution is correct. = Neither of these solutions is / are correct. – Neither of my parents has / have ever been abroad. (= Both of my parents have never been abroad.) – Neither of them knows / know the answer. (= Both of them don't know, the answer.) – I like neither of these books. (= I don't like either of these books.) (Aber nur: Neither of these books is interesting.)

neither wird in verneinenden Kurzantworten und bei Gegenüberstellungen verwendet (= auch nicht).
'I don't like this novel.' – 'Neither do I / Nor do I.' (= 'I don't, either.') (s. 12.3.)
I didn't support the proposal (and) neither did my colleagues.

Beachten Sie: either ... or entweder ... oder; **neither ... nor** weder ... noch:
Either you or I must do it. – They can either stay with us or pass the night in a hotel. – Neither my sister nor my brother is / are married.

15.6.8. *other / another*

other andere(-r, -s); *(the) others* (die) anderen; *another* noch eine(-r, -s), ein anderer.
Please show me the other photos. – I don't like this shirt, please show me some others. – Do you want another bottle of beer? (= one more bottle of beer.) – Our hot water heater is often out of order, we'll buy another (one). – They want to stay another two weeks. (= two more weeks.)

Unterscheiden Sie: Can I have *another* glass of wine? (= ... one more glass of wine.) – (aber:) This wine is too sweet, let's order a *different* sort. (= not another bottle of the same sort.)

Beachten Sie: *the other day* neulich; *on the other hand* andererseits; *other than* außer; *otherwise* sonst.

15.6.9. *one*

one ist
– **Indefinitpronomen** (dt.: man): One can say ...
– oder **substitute word** (Ersatzwort), um die Wiederholung eines Substantivs zu vermeiden – in Verbindung mit dem bestimmten bzw. unbestimmten Artikel + Adjektiv, nur mit dem bestimmten Artikel oder nach **which** als Fragewort.

Lucy has got some green and blue dresses, now she would like to have a red one. 'Which of these blouses do you want to buy?' – 'The green one.'

'I'd like to try on one of these coats.' – 'Which one?' – 'The one over there.'
'Which of these sweaters do you like best?' – 'This one.'[7]

Beachten Sie: *one Mr Miller* ein gewisser Herr Miller; *one by one* einer nach dem anderen; *one and the same* ein und derselbe.

15.6.10. no – none

no steht vor Substantiven (= not ... any).
There were no tickets left. / There weren't any tickets left. – We had no/We didn't have any opportunity to talk to Mr King.

no findet sich auch vor Komparativen: There were no more than forty people present. – Ellen is forty, but she looks no older than thirty. (= ... she doesn't look older than thirty.)

Zusammensetzungen: *nobody/no-one* (= *not ... anybody/anyone*) niemand, keiner; *nothing* (= *not ... anything*) nichts; *nowhere* (= *not ... anywhere*) nirgends.
Nobody/No-one saw Fred leave. – I met nobody/I didn't meet anybody whom I could ask. – I know nothing/I don't know anything about it. – Roy was nowhere to be seen. / Roy was not to be seen anywhere.

Beachten Sie: *nothing but* nichts als; *nobody/no-one but* niemand außer.

none (of) bezieht sich auf ein Substantiv oder Pronomen. Bei Pluralbezug kann das folgende Verb im Plural oder Singular stehen.
None of my friends were/was at home. (stärker betont: Not one of my friends was .../Not a single one of my ...) – We have seen none of these films. = We haven't seen any of these films. – I have met none of them. – I wanted to buy French cognac but there was none to be had.

Beachten Sie: 'Any problems?' – 'None whatsoever/None at all.' (Überhaupt keine.) – It's none of your business. (Das geht dich nichts an.) – Your translation is second to none. (... unübertroffen.)

15.7. The Relative Pronouns – Die Relativpronomen

Es gibt zwei Arten von Relativsätzen:
– den bestimmenden Relativsatz *(Defining Relative Clause)*
– den erläuternden Relativsatz *(Non-Defining Relative Clause)*.

Bestimmende Relativsätze sind unentbehrlich, um den Satz in seiner Gesamtheit zu verstehen; sie werden ohne Komma angeschlossen.
Do you know the author who wrote this book? (Kennst du den Autor, der dieses Buch schrieb?)

---

[7] "one" findet sich oft nach "this, that"; es ist möglich nach Superlativen und nach "each, every, either, neither". Es steht verhältnismäßig selten bei Ordnungszahlen, nie bei nichtzählbaren Substantiven und nach "own".
I have three brothers, Peter is the youngest (one). – I read some detective stories during my holidays, each (one) was very good. – There are several versions of this play, the third (one) is the most interesting (one). – Thermal energy can be converted into electrical energy. – I didn't borrow the book, it's my own.

Erläuternde Relativsätze enthalten eine ergänzende Information zum Bezugswort, die für das Verständnis des Satzes in seiner Gesamtheit nicht erforderlich ist; sie werden durch Komma vom Hauptsatz abgetrennt.
Gary's articles, which appear in several newspapers, are widely read. (Garys Artikel, die in mehreren Zeitungen erscheinen, werden viel gelesen.)
In der Umgangssprache werden statt dessen meist zwei Hauptsätze gebildet: Gary's articles are widely read. They appear in several newspapers.
Relativpronomen sind:

Subjekt	Objekt	
who	who(m)	bezogen auf Personen
which	which	bezogen auf Sachen
that	that	

that – nur in bestimmenden Relativsätzen, bezogen auf Sachen und Personen; häufig nach Superlativen sowie nach: *all, something, anything, everything, nothing, little, much, few, only.*

15.7.1. Defining Relative Clauses – Bestimmende Relativsätze

Relativpronomen als **Subjekt** des Relativsatzes:
What's the name of the professor who/that examined you? – Botany is the science which/that deals with plants. – Shakespeare was one of the greatest dramatists that/who ever lived. – I don't believe everything that has been said. – The only books that interest Rose are love stories.

Relativpronomen als **Objekt** des Relativsatzes:
Als Objekt eines bestimmenden Relativsatzes wird das Relativpronomen sehr oft weggelassen; das ist besonders typisch für die Umgangssprache. Wird ein Relativpronomen verwendet, dann findet sich
- bei **Personen** *that* häufiger als *who*; *whom* kommt nur im formalen Stil vor, dann aber immer, wenn eine Präposition vorausgeht.
- bei **Sachbezug** *which* oder *that, which* kaum nach *all, something,* etc.

The girl we met at the theatre was my niece.
The girl that/who (oder: whom) we met at the theatre was my niece.
The book you gave me is very interesting.
The book which/that you gave me is very interesting.
You have told me something (that) I know already. – Is there anything (that) I can do for you?
Bei **Verb + Präposition** oder **Adjektiv + Präposition** folgt im modernen Englisch die Präposition sehr oft dem Verb oder Adjektiv, auf das sie sich bezieht; das gilt besonders für die Umgangssprache und immer wenn *that/who* Relativpronomen ist.
Do you know the man I was talking to?
Do you know the man that/who I was talking to?
Do you know the man to whom I was talking?

This is a subject Lucy knows a lot about.
This is a subject which/that Lucy knows a lot about.
This is a subject about which Lucy knows a lot.[8]
Mr Green has got a daughter (that) he can be proud of. − This is a solution I am not very happy about.

15.7.2. Non-Defining Relative Clauses − Erläuternde Relativsätze

Erläuternde Relativsätze kommen umgangssprachlich relativ wenig vor. Das Relativpronomen kann nicht entfallen. *that* ist als Relativpronomen nicht möglich; auf Personen bezogen steht im Objektfall *whom*. Präpositionen stehen oft vor dem Relativpronomen. Der erläuternde Relativsatz wird durch ein Komma abgetrennt.
Mr Brown, who is an engineer, has gone to Ethiopia for two years. − Professor Smith, whom we all know, is a cybernetician of international reputation. − This book, which every student of mathematics should read, deals with problems of computer engineering. − Amundsen was a famous Norwegian explorer, about whom many books have been written. − The plenary session, at which three papers will be read, begins at 9 a.m.

15.7.2.1. *of whom* (bei Personen), *of which* (bei Sachen) stehen im formalen Stil nach Ausdrücken, die eine Anzahl oder Menge bezeichnen − z. B. *some, several, many, most, few, both, all, a number of, a majority/minority of, none* − und nach Superlativen.
The conference was attended by scientists from different countries, many of whom came from Britain and the United States. (= ... many of them came ...) − Sinclair Lewis wrote more than 20 books, some of which have become best-sellers. (= ..., some of them ...)

15.7.3. *whose* ist ein Relativpronomen mit einer dem Possessivpronomen entsprechenden Funktion, das sich auf **Personen und Sachen** bezieht. Bei **Sachbezug** findet sich auch *of which*[9].
Graham Greene is an English writer whose books are known all over the world. − This is Jack, whose brother you know already. − We visited the Museum of National Literature in Prague, whose library contains a famous collection of old books. (= ..., the library of which ...)

15.7.4. *which* (dt.: was) kann sich auf die Aussage eines ganzen Satzes beziehen, von dem es durch Komma abgetrennt wird.
Mr King walks two hours a day, which is very good for a man of eighty.

---

[8] Die Präposition steht oft vor "which", wenn sie bedeutungsmäßig nicht unmittelbar zum Verb gehört: This is the street in which Eve lives = ... the street where Eve lives. (oder:) This is the street which/that Eve lives in. (oder:) ... the street Eve lives in.
[9] Bei nicht unmittelbar possessiver Funktion kann "of which" ohne Bezugswort im Relativsatz vorkommen: My diploma thesis, of which I have written about 100 pages, must be finished by the end of the year.

Auch **what** kann die Funktion eines Relativpronomens haben im Sinne von *the thing(s) that.*
What Eric told us was very instructive. – Do you believe what Jim told us? – I was very interested in what Liz told us.

who als Relativpronomen kann **nicht ohne vorausgehendes Bezugswort** stehen.
He who told you that is wrong. (= Those/The people who ..., nicht: Who told you that is wrong.)

whoever = wer auch immer; *whichever* = welche(-r, -s), wer auch immer; *whatever* = was auch immer.
Whoever comes will be welcome. – Here are some magazines, take whichever you like. – Do whatever you want.

Nach Zeitangaben wie *the day/month/year*, etc, oder *the time* kann *that* stehen oder der Nebensatz ohne Relativpronomen angeschlossen werden.
It was very cold the day (that) we arrived in Moscow. – Do you remember the time we fell in love with each other?

16. The Adjective – Das Adjektiv

Adjektive bleiben in Genus, Numerus und Kasus unverändert; sie können **attributiv** und **prädikativ** verwendet und durch ein Adverb näher bestimmt werden. (Zur Steigerung s. 18.)
(attributiv:) We had **bad** weather at the seaside.
(prädikativ:) The temperature was very **low**.

16.1. Einige Adjektive werden **nur prädikativ** verwendet, z. B.: *abroad, afraid, alive, alone, asleep, awake, aware* (bewußt), *content* (zufrieden), *well.*
They are abroad. – I'm not well today. – Is Eve asleep or awake?

16.2. Einige Adjektive kommen auf Grund ihrer Bedeutung bzw. in bestimmten Ausdrücken **nur attributiv** vor, z. B.: *the chief/main thing* die Hauptsache; *joint efforts* gemeinsame Bemühungen; *the prewar/postwar situation* die Vorkriegs-/Nachkriegssituation; *a heavy smoker* ein starker Raucher; *an early riser* ein Frühaufsteher.
Beachten Sie auch Wortverbindungen wie *the very opposite* das genaue Gegenteil; *the very idea* der bloße Gedanke; *the then president* der damalige Präsident; *a three-year-old boy*; *a five-pound note*; *a four-day visit*; *an iron stove*; *a silver coin*; *a gold medal* (aber übertragen: *the golden age*); *the Dresden University of Technology*; *the Edinburgh Festival*; *the deputy minister of trade*;
next Sunday (oder:) *(on) Sunday next*; *last Friday* (oder:) *(on) Friday last.*

16.3. Einige Adjektive weisen in **prädikativer** und **attributiver** Verbindung **unterschiedliche Bedeutung** auf:
present: How many people were present? (Wie viele waren anwesend?) – Those present agreed. (Die Anwesenden stimmten zu.)

the present situation die gegenwärtige Situation; *the present report* der vorliegende Bericht.
ill: Doris is ill. (Doris ist krank.) – Tom is in ill health. (Es geht Tom gesundheitlich schlecht.)
sick: *a sick person* ein Kranker – John was sick after two bars of chocolate. (John wurde übel nach zwei Tafeln Schokolade.) – (AE:) Jim is sick with pneumonia. (Jim ist an Lungenentzündung erkrankt.) = (BE:) Jim has been taken ill with pneumonia.
be sea/air-sick.

16.4. Bestimmte Adjektive können **substantivisch** verwendet werden. Einige Adjektive bilden **Singular und Plural**:
a black/the blacks; (ebenso:) *a white*; *an individual*; *a progressive*; *a reactionary*; *a native* ein Eingeborener; *a male/a female* eine männliche/weibliche Person; *a superior* ein Vorgesetzter.

Mit dem **bestimmten Artikel** und folgendem **Verb im Plural** bezeichnen einige Adjektive, auch Partizipien, eine **Gruppe** oder **Gesamtheit** von Personen:
the rich die Reichen (Singular: *a rich man* ein Reicher); (ebenso:) *the wealthy/the well-to-do* die Wohlhabenden; *the poor* die Armen; *the blind* die Blinden; *the deaf* die Tauben; *the mute* die Stummen; *the dead* die Toten;
the English/the French die Engländer/Franzosen (Singular: *an Englishman, an Englishwoman/a Frenchman, a Frenchwoman*);
the defeated die Besiegten; *the wounded* die Verwundeten; *the injured* die Verletzten; *the living* = die Lebenden; *the good* die Guten; *the bad* die Schlechten.

Einige Adjektive können mit dem **bestimmten Artikel** und **Verb im Singular** auch einen **abstrakten Begriff** bezeichnen:
the good das Gute; *the bad* das Schlechte; *the evil* das Böse; (ebenso:) *the rational, the irrational, the normal, the abnormal.*

16.5. Die wichtigsten **Suffixe** zur Bildung von Adjektiven sind:
-able: *considerable, remarkable, comparable, desirable*
-ible: *responsible, comprehensible, negligible, visible*
-ical[1]: *political, critical, physical, chemical*
-ic[1]: *scientific, (in)organic, artistic, atomic, psychic*
-al: *natural, structural, additional, educational, emotional*
-ful: *beautiful, useful, peaceful, successful, careful*
-less: *careless, hopeless, harmless, useless*
-ive: *expensive, constructive, creative, aggressive*
-y: *easy, sunny, rainy, sexy, hungry, thirsty, trendy*
-ial: *official, financial, territorial, controversial*

---
[1] Beide Suffixe sind möglich bei: electric(al), mechanic(al), psychologic(al), biologic(al), automatic(al).
Beachten Sie den Unterschied zwischen economic (wirtschaftlich) und economical (sparsam): The economic situation in France; (aber:) an economical housewife.

-*ate* [it]: *separate, passionate, considerate, approximate*
-*ist*: *Marxist, socialist, communist, capitalist*
-*ory*: *satisfactory, contradictory, compulsory*
-*ous*, -*eous*, -*ious*, -*uous*: *dangerous, analogous; spontaneous, gaseous; conscious, cautious; continuous, ambiguous*
-*ary*: *revolutionary, fragmentary, documentary*
-*an*, -*ian*: *American, African; Hungarian, Italian, Norwegian*
-*ese*: *Japanese, Chinese, Portuguese, Vietnamese*
-*ish*: *English, Spanish, Swedish; selfish, reddish, childish*
-*ly*: *friendly, daily, weekly, monthly*
-*like*: *ladylike, gentlemanlike, lifelike, warlike*
-*ative*: *qualitative, quantitative, talkative, illustrative*
-*fold*: *twofold, threefold; manyfold*
-*some*, -*most*: *troublesome, quarrelsome; uppermost, outermost*
-*en*, -*ed*: *wooden, woollen; gifted, talented*
-*ual*, -*uble*: *usual, habitual, sexual; (in)soluble*
-*ward*: *backward, forward, homeward, eastward*

Die wichtigsten **Präfixe** zur Verneinung sind:

un-: *unimportant, uncommon, unsatisfactory, unreasonable*
in-: *independent, inexpensive, insignificant, incalculable*
ir-: *irregular, irrelevant, irresponsible*
im-: *impossible, impolite, immobile*
il-: *illogical, illegal, illegible*
dis-: *dishonest, disloyal, disobedient*
non-: *non-essential, non-linear, non-aggressive*
anti-: *anti-imperialist, anti-communist, antibacterial*

17. The Adverb – Das Adverb

Adverbien erläutern Verben (a), Adjektive (b), Adverbien (c), ganze Sätze (d) oder Satzteile (e).
Tom always drives *carefully*. (a) – We finished the test in a *relatively* short time. (b) – Edith speaks English *fairly* well. (c) – *Obviously*, Tom's hypothesis is wrong. (d) – Jim lives *almost* in the centre of the town. (e)
Es gibt
- ursprüngliche Adverbien: *now, soon, here, there, fast, quite, rather, perhaps*, etc;
- abgeleitete Adverbien, die durch Anfügung von -*ly* an Adjektive, Partizipien oder Substantive gebildet werden: *slowly, surprisingly, excitedly, partly*, etc;
- und adverbiale Bestimmungen: *as usual, in time, in a hurry*, etc.

Ihrer Bedeutung nach lassen sich Adverbien einteilen in:
Zeitadverbien: *today, yesterday, tomorrow, in 1980, in March, on Sunday, at Christmas*, etc; *again, afterwards*, etc;
Ortsadverbien: *at home, in London, at/in the university, at the disco, in the street*, etc; *outside, upstairs, downstairs*, etc;

L 17.1.

Adverbien der Art und Weise: *quickly, fast, easily, well,* etc;
Häufigkeitsadverbien: *often/frequently, always, sometimes, never, ever, rarely/seldom, usually, occasionally,* etc;
Gradadverbien wie: *completely/totally/wholly, absolutely, very[1], much[1], very much, a lot; a little/a bit; almost/nearly, hardly/scarcely/barely; highly, greatly; largely* weitgehend; *fairly[2], quite[2], pretty[2], rather[2]*;
Satzadverbien wie: *probably, perhaps/maybe, of course, (un)fortunately/(un)luckily, really/actually, certainly, definitely; possibly, obviously, apparently, moreover/furthermore/besides, incidentally* (= *by the way), similarly.*

17.1. Abgeleitete Adverbien werden mit dem Suffix *-ly* gebildet: *quick → quickly; careful → carefully.*
In einigen Fällen treten dabei orthographische Veränderungen auf:
-y → -ily: easy → easily; heavy → heavily
-le → -ly: possible → possibly; (aber:) *whole → wholly*
-ue → -uly: true → truly; due → duly
-ic → -ically: automatic → automatically; systematic → systematically; (aber:) *public → publicly.*

Adjektive auf *-ly* wie *friendly, lively, lovely,* werden gewöhnlich Teil einer adverbialen Bestimmung *in a ... manner/way.*
Peter is a careful driver. He drives *carefully.* – The translation is easy. I can *easily* translate the text. – Sue is *friendly.* She welcomed us *in a very friendly way.*

17.2. Adjektive und Adverbien mit **gleicher Form** und **gleicher Bedeutung:**

early, hourly, daily, weekly, monthly, yearly; fast; hard; straight; twofold/threefold, etc; *much; little; far.*
Peter's daily walk to the office. – This paper is edited daily. – This is a very fast car. – Donald talks very fast.

17.2.1. Adjektiv und Adverb mit **gleicher Form** aber **unterschiedlicher Bedeutung**, z. B.:

	Adjektiv	Adverb		Adjektiv	Adverb
only	einzig	nur; erst	*(be) well*	wohl (fühlen)	gut
dead	tot	völlig	*(be) ill*	krank (sein)	schlecht

---

[1] "very" intensiviert Adjektive (a) und Adverbien (b), "(very) much" Verben (c), Adjektive und Adverbien im Komparativ (d), oft auch das Past Participle, wenn es eine Handlung zum Ausdruck bringt (e). The text was very difficult (a), but you have translated it very well (b). – I like her very much. (c) – I much regret not being able to help you. (c) – Tom is much taller than his brother. (d) – Mrs Turner drives much more carefully than her husband. (d) – Tom's new book is (very) much discussed. (e) – (aber:) I was very surprised.

[2] Diese Adverbien charakterisieren in der nachstehenden Reihenfolge eine Eigenschaft in zunehmendem Maße als positiv oder negativ: (not difficult) – fairly difficult – quite difficult – pretty difficult – rather difficult (– very difficult).

William is an only child. − It happened only last week.
Are you well today? − I know Monica well.
My grandparents are dead. − I'm dead sure I am right.
Jane is ill. − You are ill-advised.

17.3. Adverbien mit **zwei Formen** bei gleicher oder unterschiedlicher Bedeutung, z. B.:

	Adjektiv	Adverb ohne *-ly*	Adverb mit *-ly*
close	nahe, eng	nahe, dicht, fest	eng; genau
clear	klar, rein	klar, deutlich	deutlich, offensichtlich
fair	fair, gerecht; blond	fair	ziemlich; gerecht
hard	schwer, hart	schwer, hart	kaum
high	hoch	hoch	sehr, höchst
just	gerecht; richtig	nur	zu Recht
late	spät; (attributiv auch: verstorben)	spät	in letzter Zeit
most	das meiste, die meisten	sehr, höchst, am meisten	meist
near	nahe	nahe	fast
pretty	hübsch	ziemlich	hübsch, nett
right	richtig; rechte(-r, -s)	rechts; genau; unmittelbar	richtig, zu Recht
wide	breit, weit	weit; völlig	weit, weithin
wrong	falsch	falsch	falsch, zu Unrecht

They are close friends. − Fred walked close behind us. − The door isn't shut close. − They are closely related. − This term is not closely defined.
The situation is *clear*. − Please speak loud and *clear*. − We didn't see them *clearly*. − You *clearly* need to see a doctor.
It was a *fair* match. − Jane's hair is *fair*. − You should play *fair*. − The book is *fairly* interesting.
We had a *hard* winter last year. − I must work *hard*. − We *hardly* know William.
A *high* mountain. − Modern aircraft can fly very *high*. − A *highly* complicated problem.
A *just* decision. − *Just* try! − Bob was *justly* criticized.
Don't be *late*. − The *late* president. − Mary arrived *late*. − I haven't met John *lately*.
Most people watch television. − Mabel is a *most* charming girl. − What annoys me *most* is Tom's arrogance. − We *mostly* meet at the club.
The station is quite *near*. − Come a little *nearer*. − This is *nearly* impossible.
A *pretty* woman. − It's *pretty* cold today. − A *prettily* dressed girl.
My *right* arm hurts. − We must turn *right* now. − Peter left *right* after lunch. − Are you *rightly* informed?
A *wide* range of topics. − Wilfred left the door *wide* open. − A *widely* known author.
A *wrong* answer. − My watch goes *wrong*. − I've been *wrongly* informed. − Norman was *wrongly* suspected.

L 17.4.

17.4. Nach den Verben *look, feel, appear, taste, smell* steht das Adjektiv, wenn eine Eigenschaft des Substantivs beschrieben wird, das Adverb dagegen, wenn das Verb näher erläutert werden soll.
Sarah looked happy. – Joan looked happily at her baby.
I'm feeling bad today. – The doctor felt Lily's pulse carefully.
Anne appears/seems angry. – Bob appeared (= came) quite unexpectedly.
This perfume smells very good. – Arthur smelt the soup sceptically.
The soup tastes delicious. – Mary tasted the soup carefully.
Nach *seem, sound* steht nur das Adjektiv.
Norman's proposal sounds reasonable. – Their offer seems attractive.

17.5. Oft werden deutsche Adverbien im Englischen umschrieben, z. B.
I hope John will come. (Hoffentlich ...) – I'm sure/certain they will help us. (Sicher/Gewiß ...) – You're sure/certain to enjoy this film. (... sicher ...) – It is likely to rain. (... wahrscheinlich ...) – I think/believe/suppose Vera will accept our invitation. (Vermutlich ...) – I'm afraid I can't take part in the excursion. (Leider ...) – Do you happen/chance to know this abbreviation? (... zufällig ...) – Liz may be ill. (... vielleicht ...) – Go on translating. (8.7.2.) (Übersetzen Sie weiter!) – They kept talking. (9.4.) (Sie unterhielten sich immer weiter.)

17.6. Stellung des Adverbs

Es gibt drei Möglichkeiten für die Stellung des Adverbs: am Satzende, in der Mitte und am Anfang des Satzes, z. B.:
He went away suddenly. – He suddenly went away. – Suddenly he went away.
In Mittelstellung stehen Adverbien gewöhnlich
– vor dem Vollverb: I really like Theresa. – We often talk to Toby. – I usually get up at six.
– zwischen Hilfsverb und Vollverb[3]: Jane has just left.
– nach den Formen von *be* in Präsens und Präteritum: John is always a reliable partner. – Jane was probably in Berlin yesterday.
– unmittelbar vor einem Adjektiv oder Adverb, das sie näher bestimmen: The problem was extremely difficult. – This is an extraordinarily well written book.
Treffen mehrere Adverbien am Satzende zusammen, so ist die Wortfolge nach konventionellem Sprachgebrauch:
Adverb der Art und Weise, des Ortes und der Zeit (= **A – O – Z**).
Bei mehreren Zeitadverbien am Satzende steht die näher bestimmende Angabe meist vor der allgemeineren.
Our visitors arrived at ten last night. – The amateur players of our university performed very well at the festival last week. – Albert Einstein was born in Ulm on March 14, 1879 and died in Princeton on April 18, 1955.
Anmerkung: Setzen Sie Adverbien nicht zwischen Vollverb und Objekt.

---

[3] Bei mehr als einem Hilfsverb steht das Adverb oft nach dem ersten Hilfsverb: I would never have been able to translate this text without your help. – This innovation will soon be put into practice. – We could easily have solved the problem. (auch:) We could have easily solved the problem.

17.6.1. **Adverbien der Art und Weise** kommen vorzugsweise in Endstellung, doch auch in Mittelstellung vor. Bei Mittelstellung in Passivsätzen stehen sie meist unmittelbar vor dem *Past Participle.*
We walked slowly through the Park. – John has translated the text very carefully. – Peter readily answered our questions. – The dictionary has been completely revised.
Bei besonderer Betonung stehen Adverbien der Art und Weise manchmal am Satzanfang:
Cautiously the waiter opened the bottle of champagne.

17.6.2. **Orts- und Zeitadverbien** können in Anfangs- oder Endstellung vorkommen; am Satzanfang sind sie stärker betont. In Endstellung stehen Ortsbestimmungen gewöhnlich vor Zeitbestimmungen.
A group of British trade unionists arrived in Berlin yesterday. Today they will go to Dresden. – Now we won't wait any longer.
In Mittelstellung findet sich
– immer *just*: Fred has just come.
– meist *already*: Mary has already left.
– oft unbetontes *now, soon*: We'll now finish our discussion. – I'll soon be back.

17.6.3. **Häufigkeitsadverbien** haben gewöhnlich Mittelstellung:
Susan always talks about her boyfriends. – Have you ever been abroad? – John has never driven a car.
Occasionally, usually, sometimes finden sich auch am Anfang oder Ende des Satzes; *often* kann am Ende des Satzes stehen.
We sometimes visit an exhibition./Sometimes we visit.../We visit an exhibition sometimes. – Do you often see Mildred? (oder:) Do you see Mildred often?
Adverbiale Bestimmungen mit *every/each* oder *a/an* stehen am Ende oder am Anfang des Satzes:
They meet every week. – Once a month I go to the cinema.

17.6.4. **Gradadverbien** stehen vor dem Adjektiv, Adverb oder Verb, das sie näher bestimmen.
The problem is rather/pretty/quite difficult. – Frank plays chess very well. – We completely forgot to inform you. – I nearly missed the bus. – These two methods are largely different. – I hardly recognized them. (s. auch: 13.5.1.2.)

much/a lot; *a little/a bit*; *rather* (hier etwa: doch etwas) können vor einem Komparativ stehen:
Could you speak a little/a bit more slowly? – Jane is much/a lot prettier than her sister. – The problem is rather more difficult than I had thought.

very much/a lot; *a little/a bit* stehen am Satzende, wenn sie ein Verb näher beschreiben; *enough* steht hinter dem Adjektiv oder Adverb, auf das es sich bezieht.
John doesn't like operas very much. – Thank you very much. – Fred reads a lot. – The calculation was not exact enough.

17.6.5. **Satzadverbien** stehen oft am Satzanfang, kommen aber auch in Mittelstellung, viel seltener am Satzende vor.
Fortunately, it isn't raining today. – Of course, you are right. – Tom will probably come tomorrow. – Actually[4], I don't like the way Sophie dresses.

perhaps; *moreover/furthermore/besides*; *incidentally* (= *by the way*); *similarly* stehen in der Regel am Satzanfang.
Perhaps you are right. – Moreover, we can say that ... – Incidentally / By the way, where were you yesterday?

17.6.6. In **Endstellung** stehen die Adverbien *too/as well* auch; **hard** schwer, sehr; *fast* schnell; *either* auch (in verneinten Sätzen); *again*; *yet* schon (im Fragesatz); *at all*[5] überhaupt; sowie **well** und **badly**.
You should ask them, too. – Walter has a record-player and a cassette recorder as well. – We must work hard. – It's raining hard. – I didn't read the book either. – You are late again. – Do you know Percy at all? – They'll come today, if they come at all. – Joe has done the job well[6]. – They translated the text badly[6].

17.6.7. Im **verneinten Satz** kommen Adverbien häufig in Endstellung vor – vor allem Adverbien der Art und Weise (a); bei Betonung stehen Zeit-, Orts-, Häufigkeits- und Satzadverbien am Anfang (b). Adverbien in Mittelstellung stehen vor oder nach dem (ersten) Hilfsverb (c); das Adverb kann nie zwischen *do/does/did* und *not* stehen (d).
They did not check the results exactly. (a) – Tomorrow I shan't be in the office. (b) – We probably will not attend the conference. (c) (oder:) We will probably not attend the conference. (c) – (aber nur:) We probably won't attend the conference. – I usually do not go to bed before eleven. (d) – We do not often have a chance to see such a good film. (d)

Anmerkung: Je nach Stellung des Adverbs kann sich ein Bedeutungsunterschied ergeben.
I don't really know him. (etwa:) I don't know him very well. – (aber:) I really don't know him. (etwa:) I don't know him at all.

---

[4] "actually" hat nie die Bedeutung von "aktuell" (= current, topical: "current problems, topical information"). Es wird verwendet, um auszudrücken, daß jemand etwas richtig vermutet hat (a), zum anderen, um etwas richtigzustellen (b), oder um etwas schonend mitzuteilen (c). 'Did you enjoy the party?' – 'Very much, actually.' (a) (= very much, indeed.) 'Did you like the book?' – 'Well, actually, I haven't read it yet. (b) (= Well, as a matter of fact, I haven't read it yet.)
'I hope you apologized to her.' – 'No, actually, I didn't.' (b) (= To tell the truth, I didn't.) 'Where's the vase I gave you?' – 'Well, actually, I broke it.' (c) (= Frankly / Honestly, I broke it.)

[5] not at all kommt auch in Mittelstellung vor: My brother is not at all interested in pop music.
Beachten Sie: 'not at all', auch 'don't mention it' (vor allem BE), 'you're welcome' (vor allem AE) als höfliche Reaktion auf 'thank you.' (deutsch: Bitte sehr, keine Ursache.)

[6] Im Passivsatz stehen "well" und "badly" vor dem Past Participle: The book is well illustrated. – The film was badly synchronized.

17.6.8. Bei Verbindungen **Verb + Adverb** (= *Phrasal Verbs*), z.B.: ***put on*, *take off*,** etc (4.3.), kann das Adverb vor oder nach dem Objekt stehen, wenn dieses ein Substantiv ist. Ist das Objekt ein Pronomen, dann muß das Adverb nach diesem stehen.
Take your coat off. (oder:) Take off your coat. – (aber nur:) My coat is too warm, I'll take it off.

18. The Comparison of Adjectives and Adverbs – Die Steigerung von Adjektiven und Adverbien

18.1. Steigerung der Adjektive

	Positiv	Komparativ	Superlativ
Synthetische Steigerung	great	greater	greatest
Analytische Steigerung	beautiful	more beautiful	most beautiful

Es gibt bestimmte Regeln, ob ein Adjektiv synthetisch oder analytisch gesteigert wird, doch sind für die Wahl der Steigerungsart oft auch Gründe des Stils oder des Satzrhythmus wesentlich.

18.1.1. Synthetische Steigerung

Einsilbige Adjektive werden in der Regel synthetisch gesteigert.

tall   *tall*er   *tall*est
young [ŋ]   *young*er [ŋg]   *young*est [ŋg]
large[1]   *larg*er   *larg*est

Auch zweisilbige Adjektive, die auf *-y* enden, werden synthetisch gesteigert.

happy   *happier*   *happiest*

Bei der Bildung des Komparativs und Superlativs ergeben sich folgende orthographische Besonderheiten.

– stummes *-e* des Positivs entfällt:

fine   *finer*   *finest*

– nach kurzem, betontem Vokal wird der Endkonsonant verdoppelt:

big   *bigger*   *biggest*

– auslautendes *-y* **nach Konsonant** verwandelt sich in *-i*:

tidy   *tidier*   *tidiest*

Which of the boys is younger? – Maud is the prettiest girl I have ever seen. – London is one of the biggest towns of the world.

---

[1] Entscheidend für die Einsilbigkeit ist die Aussprache.

18.1.2. Analytische Steigerung

Drei- und mehrsilbige Adjektive sowie Partizipien werden analytisch, d. h. mit *more* und *most* gesteigert.

Die analytische Steigerung findet sich auch bei zweisilbigen Adjektiven, die nicht auf *-y* enden. Bei zweisilbigen Adjektiven, die auf *-er, -le, -ow* enden sowie bei *polite, quiet, common, handsome, pleasant, severe, sincere* ist neben der analytischen auch die synthetische Steigerung möglich.

Positiv	Komparativ	Superlativ
wonderful	more wonderful	most wonderful
incomprehensible	more incomprehensible	most incomprehensible
exciting	more exciting	most exciting
interested	more interested	most interested
famous	more famous	most famous
exact	more exact	most exact
clever	more clever / cleverer	most clever / cleverest
gentle	more gentle / gentler	most gentle / gentlest
narrow	more narrow / narrower	most narrow / narrowest
polite	more polite / politer	most polite / politest

You should be more accurate. – Leningrad is one of the most beautiful towns of the Soviet Union. – Flying is nowadays the most common / the commonest form of long-distance travel.

18.1.3. Unregelmäßige Steigerungsformen

much	= viel	more	most
many	= viele		
small, little	= klein	smaller	smallest
little	= wenig, gering	less (lesser[2])	least
good	= gut	better	best
well	= wohl (= gesund)		
bad	= schlecht	worse	worst
ill	= krank (nur prädikativ)		
	= schlecht (Adverb)		
near	= nahe	nearer	nearest / next
far	= weit	farther / further	farthest
late	= spät	later / latter	latest / last
old	= alt	older / elder	oldest / eldest

Erläuterungen:

– *small* und *little* beziehen sich auf Umfang und Größe; *little* wird meist nur attributiv verwendet und ist oft gefühlsbetont:
My friend lives in a small / little village. – Tom is very small for his age, he is the smallest in his class. – (aber:) Jane is a nice little girl, she is the smallest, the most intelligent and the least quarrelsome of all her friends.

---

[2] = weniger bedeutend: a lesser author.

- *well* nur prädikativ (nach *be, feel*): Fred's translation is good but Tom's is much better. – Yesterday I wasn't well, today I feel much better.
- Mary's dictation is bad but Joan's is much worse. – I felt ill yesterday but today I feel even worse.
- *nearest* = räumliche Entfernung; *next* = Reihenfolge: This is the nearest way to the station. – We must get off at the next stop.
- räumliche Entfernung = *farther/further* im BE, meist nur *farther* im AE; *further* außerdem im übertragenen Sinne "weiter(-e, -er, -es), zusätzliche (-r, -s)": Berlin is farther/further away from Dresden than Leipzig. – Do you have any further questions?
- *later/latest* = Zeitbezug; *latter* = letztere(-r, -s) (bezogen auf ein zuvor genanntes Substantiv oder Pronomen); *last* = Reihenfolge:
Peter came later than expected. – Of the two methods only the latter is applicable here.
'Have you read the latest number of "New Scientist"?' – 'No, the last I read was that of December last year.'
Beachten Sie: *the former ... the latter* = der erstere ... der letztere: There is a difference between mechanisation and automation, the former being a preliminary stage for the latter.
- *elder/eldest:* im BE bezogen auf Personen bei einem Verwandtschaftsverhältnis, nur attributiv und substantivisch verwendet.
My elder sister is a teacher. – Which is the elder of your daughters? – (aber:) My brother is older than my sister.
- *the* + *most* + Adjektiv = Superlativ; *(a) most* + Adjektiv = sehr, höchst: This is one of the most fascinating crime novels I have read lately. It has a most unusual plot and the characters are most plastic.

18.1.4.   Möglichkeiten des Vergleichs

as ... as so ... wie; *not so/as ... as* nicht so ... wie.
Sue is as pretty as Jane. – Tom is not so/as good at languages as his brother.
(better/more interesting) than (besser/interessanter) als:
Jane is nicer and more intelligent than Anne. – This book is less interesting than I had thought.
Umgangssprachlich steht nach *than, as ... as, not so ... as* ein Personalpronomen häufig im Objektfall. Oft wird beim Vergleich das Hilfsverb wiederholt, anstelle des Vollverbs die entsprechende Form von *do* ergänzt; ein vorausgehendes Personalpronomen steht dann natürlich im Subjektfall.
Fred is stronger than me. (umgangssprachlich) – (oder:) Fred is stronger than I (am). – Tom earns as much money as I (do). – (oder:) Tom earns as much money as me.
the ... the je ... desto: The sooner you come the better.
Komparativ + *and* + Komparativ = immer + Komparativ: It is getting darker and darker. – The problem is becoming more and more complicated.

18.1.4.1. Häufig werden *as*, *like* und *how* verwechselt; beachten Sie deren unterschiedliche Verwendung:
as steht, wenn ein Satz mit Subjekt und Verb folgt (a) oder in Wendungen mit Präpositionen (b) sowie nach *the same* (c); *like* wird verwendet, wenn ein Substantiv oder ein Pronomen folgt (d):[3]
Rose wants to become a famous actress as her grandmother was years ago. (a) – (aber:) Rose wants to become a famous actress like her grandmother. (d) – As in 1970; as in this case, etc (b) – My car has the same colour as yours. (c)

Beachten Sie: Tom works *as a* chemist in our plant. – Jim spoke *as an* expert (**als Experte**). – (aber:) Jim spoke *like* an expert (**wie ein Experte**).

how steht nur in direkten und indirekten Fragesätzen oder in Ausrufen: How did you repair the projector? – Tell me how you did it. – (aber:) I did it as you told me. – How smart you look today!

18.2. Steigerung der Adverbien

Steigerungsfähige Adverbien werden nach dem Muster von Adjektiven gesteigert (18.1.1. / 18.1.2. / 18.1.3.):
fast – faster – fastest;
early – earlier – earliest;
seldom – more seldom – most seldom;
carefully – more carefully – most carefully;
well – better – best:
They left earlier than usual. – Toby spoke faster and faster. – This work should be done most carefully. – Robots are being used more and more frequently in industry.

19. The Noun – Das Substantiv

In der Mehrzahl der Fälle ist das Geschlecht eines Substantivs im Englischen nicht an seiner Form zu erkennen, z. B.:
student Student(in): Roger / Sandra is a student.
Ebenso: writer, artist, painter, scientist, engineer, doctor, teacher, worker, secretary, dancer, etc.

Substantive, die Gegenstände oder abstrakte Begriffe bezeichnen, sind in der Regel sächlich. Das gilt auch für Tiere, nur Haustiere werden gelegentlich personifiziert.[1]
the table der Tisch: **It** is round. (**Er** ist rund.)
the lamp die Lampe: **It** is new. (**Sie** ist neu.)
the book das Buch: **It** is expensive. (**Es** ist teuer.)

---

[3] Vorzugsweise im AE steht "like" auch vor Substantiv / Personalpronomen + Verb: Nobody understands me like she does.

[1] (the bird:) It has laid five eggs in its nest. – (our cat:) She has just caught a mouse.

19.1. Wenn erforderlich, ist eine Differenzierung nach männlichem und weiblichem Geschlecht möglich durch:
- *woman/man* (Plural s. 19.3.6.1.): *woman teacher,* (ebenso: *woman engineer/ journalist/driver/worker/pilot/clerk); woman friend* (oder: *lady friend); woman doctor* (oder: *lady doctor)*[2]; (auch:) *woman student, man student; Englishman/Englishwoman; Frenchman/Frenchwoman; policeman/policewoman; postman/postwoman; salesman/saleswoman;* (aber: *milkman/milkmaid)*
- *male/female: male/female student; male nurse* Krankenpfleger; *male/female worker*
- *boy/girl: boy-friend/girl-friend; boy-cousin/girl-cousin; boy-scout/girl-scout* Pfadfinder; *salesgirl*
- *he/she: bear: he-bear/she-bear; wolf: he-wolf/she-wolf; goat: he-goat/she-goat*
- *-ess: actor/actress; waiter/waitress; steward/stewardess; host/hostess* Gastgeber(in); *manager/manageress; author/authoress; ambassador/ambassadress* Botschafter; *mayor/mayoress* Bürgermeister(in); *heir/heiress* Erbe/Erbin; *prince/princess; count/countess* Graf/Gräfin; *duke/duchess* Herzog(in); *emperor/empress* Kaiser(in); *god/goddess; lion/lioness; tiger/tigress.*

Beachten Sie: *hero/heroine; usher/usherette* Platzanweiser(in); *widower/widow* Witwer/Witwe; *fiancé/fiancée* Verlobter/Verlobte; *bridegroom/bride* Bräutigam/Braut.

19.2. Bei Ländernamen, Schiffen und Schiffsnamen steht das Personalpronomen oder Possessivpronomen oft in der weiblichen Form.
The lecture is to give a survey of present-day Britain and *her* economy. – The damaged ship was able to continue *her* voyage to a nearby port.

19.3. The Formation of the Plural – Die Pluralbildung

19.3.1. Regelmäßige Pluralbildung

-s: book → *books; boy* → *boys; flower* → *flowers*
-es nach Zischlauten: *bus* → *buses; glass* → *glasses; box* → *boxes; match* → *matches; wish* → *wishes*
-ies bei Singular auf Konsonant + *y: story* → *stories*

Aussprache:
- [s] nach stimmlosen Konsonanten: *books, lamps, cats*
- [z] nach stimmhaften Konsonanten und Vokalen: *friends, toys, windows*
- [iz] nach [s, z, ʃ, tʃ, dʒ]: *glasses, roses, wishes, matches, bridges.*

19.3.2. Eine Reihe von Substantiven auf *-o* hat *-oes* im Plural: *hero/heroes;* (ebenso:) *potato, tomato, volcano, mosquito, veto, tornado, cargo* (AE: cargos). Nur *-os* haben: *ratio/ratios* Verhältnis; (ebenso:) *radio, dynamo, zero, kilo, manifesto, scenario, piano, photo, studio, disco, motto, ghetto, buffalo.*

---
[2] We have a woman doctor working in our factory. – I really like our lady doctor.

19.3.3. *-f(e)* → *-ves* [vz]: *wife/wives*; (ebenso:) *knife, life, half, leaf, thief, shelf, wolf, loaf.*

Nur **s-Plural** haben: *proof/proofs*; (ebenso:) *roof, safe, handkerchief, chief, cliff,* etc.

19.3.4. Unregelmäßige Pluralbildung haben auch: *child/children*; *ox/oxen*; Würfel *die – dice*; (aber:) Matrize *die – dies.*

19.3.5. Einige Substantive bilden den Plural durch Änderung des Vokals: *man/men*; *gentleman/gentlemen*; *woman* ['wumən]/ *women* ['wimin]; *foot/feet*; *tooth/teeth*; *goose/geese*; *mouse/mice*; *louse/lice.*

19.3.6. Bei der Pluralbildung **zusammengesetzter Substantive** wird das *-s* in der Regel dem Grundwort hinzugefügt: *broadcasting stations, fathers-in-law, mothers-in-law,* etc. *lookers-on, passers-by, secretaries-general, commanders-in-chief.*

Bei substantivierten Ausdrücken ohne Substantiv wird *-s* meist dem letzten Bestandteil hinzugefügt:

grown-ups Erwachsene; *ten-year-olds*; *drive-ins* Autokinos; *sit-ins* Sitzstreiks; *have-nots* Besitzlose; *forget-me-nots* Vergißmeinnicht; *go-betweens* Vermittler; *good-for-nothings* Taugenichtse; *close-ups* Großaufnahmen; *lay-bys* Park- und Rastplätze.

19.3.6.1. Bei Zusammensetzungen mit *woman* und *man* (19.1.) stehen beide Substantive im Plural, z. B.: *women teachers/doctors/drivers/engineers*; *men students.*

19.3.7. Pluralbildung nach dem Lateinischen

– *-us* → *-i* [ai]: *nucleus/nuclei*; (ebenso:) *radius*; *stimulus*; *bacillus, fungus* Pilz; *alumnus* Hochschulabsolvent.

– *-us* → *-i* [ai]/*-uses*: *focus* → *foci/focuses*; (ebenso:) *syllabus* Lehrplan; *cactus.*

– *-us* → *-uses*: *bonus/bonuses* Prämie; (ebenso:) *prospectus*; *chorus*; *circus*; *campus* Universitätsgelände; *apparatus* (Plural selten: *apparatuses*).

– *-um* → *-a*: *quantum/quanta*; (ebenso:) *stratum, momentum, bacterium, erratum* Druckfehler.

Neben *-a* gelegentlich auch *-ums* bei: *maximum*; *minimum*; *optimum*; *vacuum*; *curriculum* Lehrplan; *auditorium*; *symposium*; *sanatorium*; *memorandum*; *referendum*; *millenium.*

Nur *-ums*: *museum, album, asylum, chrysanthemum, premium.*

– *-a* → *-ae* [i:]: *larva/larvae*; (ebenso:) *alga/algae* ['ældʒi:]; *nebula* Nebelfleck; *vertebra* Rückenwirbel.

– *-a* → *-ae/-as*: *formula* → *formulae/formulas*; (ebenso:) *retina* Netzhaut; *antenna* → *antennas* (technische) Antenne / *antennae* Insektenfühler.

– *-ix* → *-ices* [-isi:z]/*-ixes*: *matrix* → *matrices/matrixes*; (ebenso:) *appendix* Anhang, Blinddarm; *radix* Wurzel.

– *-ex* → *-ices/-exes*: *index* → *indices/indexes*; (ebenso:) *vortex* Wirbel; *apex* Scheitelpunkt, Höhepunkt.

19.3.8. Pluralbildung nach dem Griechischen

– *-is* → *-es* [iːz]: *analysis/analyses*; (ebenso:) *synthesis, thesis, hypothesis, basis, catalysis, crisis, axis, oasis, diagnosis, parenthesis, synopsis*.
– *-on* → *-a*: *phenomenon/phenomena*; (ebenso:) *criterion, automaton* → *automata/automatons*.

19.4. Besonderheiten bei der Verwendung von Singular und Plural

19.4.1. Die folgenden Substantive bilden auch bei Pluralbedeutung keinen Plural, das dazugehörige Verb steht im Singular:
knowledge Kenntnis(se); (ebenso:) *information*; *progress*; *interest* Zinsen; *damage* Schaden; *news*[3]; *advice*[3]; *furniture*[3].
Walter's knowledge of English is very good. (Walters Englischkenntnisse sind sehr gut.) – Some more information is necessary to solve this problem. (Einige weitere Informationen sind erforderlich, um das Problem zu lösen.) – Here is the latest news. (Hier sind die neuesten Nachrichten.)

19.4.2. Auf *-ics* auslautende Wissenschaftsbezeichnungen werden als Singular behandelt, z. B.: *mathematics, physics, mechanics, electronics, cybernetics, linguistics, genetics, robotics*, etc.
Robotics, a term introduced in 1939 by Isaac Asimov, writer of science fiction, *covers* the design and application of robot devices.

19.4.3. Die folgenden Substantive haben im Singular und Plural dieselbe Form:
means Mittel; *series* Serie(n); *species* Art(en); *crossroads* Straßenkreuzung(en), (aber: *a crossroad* eine Querstraße); *headquarters* Zentrale(n), Hauptquartier(e); *barracks* Kaserne(n); Baracke(n);
aircraft Flugzeug(e); *spacecraft* Raumschiff(e); *hovercraft* Luftkissenfahrzeug(e); *Japanese, Chinese, Portuguese, Vietnamese*; *Swiss*.
In the first decades of the twentieth century the aeroplane was becoming a new means of transport. – Nowadays, audio-visual means of instruction are being widely used.
Auch einige zoologische Bezeichnungen haben im Singular und Plural dieselbe Form: *sheep* Schaf(e); (ebenso:) *carp, trout* und andere Fischnamen, z. B.: *mackerel* Makrele(n); *halibut* Heilbutt(e); *tunny* Thunfisch(e); *pike* Hecht(e); *salmon* Lachs(e); *plaice* Scholle(n); *perch* Barsch(e).
Mr Green keeps a sheep/two sheep in his garden. – There are plenty of trout in this brook. – How many carp did you catch yesterday?

19.4.4. Einige Substantive kommen **nur im Plural** vor; das dazugehörige **Verb** steht **im Plural**, z. B.: *surroundings/environs* Umgebung; *outskirts* Stadtrand; *premises* Grundstück, Gelände; *credentials* Beglaubigungsschreiben; *earnings* Einkommen;

---
[3] Bei diesen Substantiven kann der Singular mit "a piece of" bezeichnet werden: This is an interesting piece of news.

data Angaben, Daten; *particulars* Einzelheiten; *thanks* Dank; *clothes* Kleidung (aber: *an article of clothing*); *lungs* (aber: *the left/right lung*).
Bei einigen Substantiven können Einzelstücke mit *a pair of* ausgedrückt werden: *glasses/spectacles* – *a pair of glasses/spectacles* Brille; (ebenso:) *trousers*; *jeans*; *pyjamas*; *tights*; *shorts*; *braces* (AE: *suspenders*) Hosenträger; *scissors*; *tongs* Zange.
The surroundings of the town are very beautiful. – Tom's clothes look rather shabby. – Taking photos is not allowed on the premises of the research centre. – Peter's earnings are smaller than mine. – Where are my glasses? – You should buy a new pair of trousers.

19.4.5. Einige Substantive haben **Pluralform**, das dazugehörige **Verb** steht **im Singular**, z. B.:
the United States/the USA; *the United Nations/the UN*;
billiards; *draughts/chequers* Damespiel; *darts* Pfeilwurfspiel; *dominoes*; *marbles* Murmelspiel;
measles Masern; *mumps* Ziegenpeter; *shingles* Gürtelrose.
The United States is the leading capitalist country. – *Billiards is* a popular game. – *Shingles is* rather a serious disease.

Beachten Sie: *works* Werk, Fabrik, z. B.: *steel/gas works*;
(aber:) Our professor's *work* in the field of microprocessors has attracted international attention. (Die *Arbeiten* unseres Professors ... finden weite Anerkennung.) – Shakespeare's works are known all over the world. (Shakespeares Werke sind in der ganzen Welt bekannt.)

19.4.6. Einige Substantive haben **keine Pluralform**, das dazugehörige **Verb** steht jedoch **im Plural**:
people[4]; *the police*; *the rest/the remainder* die übrigen;
(ebenso:) *cattle* Vieh (*three head of cattle* 3 Stück Vieh);
deer Rotwild (*a head of deer*, auch: *a deer/many deer*).
A lot of people *were* queuing up for tickets. – The police *have* arrested the thief. – Some thirty (head of) cattle *are* grazing in the meadow.

19.4.7. Einige Substantive haben im Plural eine zusätzliche Bedeutung: *custom(s)* Sitte(n) – *customs* Zoll; *arm(s)* Arm(e) – *arms* Waffen; *minute(s)* Minute(n) – *minutes* Protokoll; *pain(s)* Schmerz(en) – *pains* Mühe; *picture(s)* Bild(er) – *go to the pictures* ins Kino gehen; *scale* Maßstab, Skala – *scales* Waage; *spirit* Geist, Esprit – *spirits* Spirituosen – *be in good/bad spirits* guter/schlechter Laune sein; *content* Gehalt, Menge – *contents* (of a novel, etc) Inhalt.
We were ten minutes late. – The official records of a meeting are called the minutes. – The students had to determine the content of aluminium in the alloy. – The contents of this novel is/are very interesting. – Great pains were taken to settle the problem.

---
[4] "peoples" = Völker.

19.4.8. Bei **Kollektivbegriffen**, die auf Personen bezogen sind, steht das dazugehörige Verb häufig im **Plural**, wenn an die einzelnen Angehörigen der Gruppe gedacht wird. Das Personalpronomen ist dann *they*, das entsprechende Relativpronomen *who*. Solche Substantive sind u. a.:
family, government; committee; council; commission; group; team; club; firm; administration; the audience Zuhörer; *the staff/personnel* das Personal; *the public* die Öffentlichkeit; *the crew; the orchestra; the press; the youth; the clergy* Geistlichkeit; sowie Länder- und Ortsnamen, wenn sie für Sportmannschaften von Ländern oder Orten stehen. My friend's family were very kind to me when I visited them. – The Swedish government have repeatedly proposed an atom-free zone in Central Europe. – The audience were fascinated by the performance. – All the staff have gone to the meeting. – Manchester United, who have won several matches in succession, are now taking the leading position in England's first division. They defeated Liverpool 2:1 last Saturday.
Wird die **Gruppe als Ganzes** gesehen, so kann das **Verb im Singular** stehen, das Pronomen ist dann *it*, das Relativpronomen *which*. Das trifft immer zu nach *this/ that; each/every*.
The family is the smallest social unit. – The Dresden Philharmonic is an orchestra which has a world-wide reputation. – This crew is well trained.

19.4.9. Verschiedene Substantive bezeichnen im **Singular** einen **Kollektivbegriff**, im **Plural Einzelstücke**, z. B.: *fruit, hair, coal, fish.*
The trees in our garden bear a lot of fruit. – Mary likes whipped cream with fruits. – Our teacher's hair has turned grey. – There are some hairs on your coat. – Don't split hairs. – We eat a lot of fish. – There are ten fishes in my aquarium.
Einige **nichtzählbare Substantive** können bei Bestellungen oder Sortenangaben im **Plural** verwendet werden:
'Two teas and three coffees, please.' – We've bought different wines and cheeses.

19.4.10. Bei **zählbaren Substantiven** steht das **Verb im Plural** nach *a (great) number of, a group of, a lot of, lots of, part of, plenty of, one third/quarter/fifth*, etc *of*.
A great number of scientists *are* working on this problem. – Part of the listeners *were* not satisfied with the lecture. – A lot of books *have* been published on this subject. – (aber:) A lot/good deal of money *has* been spent on the restoration of the castle.

19.4.11. Bei Angaben von **Mengen, Entfernungen** oder **Zeitabschnitten im Plural**, die als Einheit betrachtet werden, steht das dazugehörige Verb im Singular. Das gilt auch bei *more than*.
Ten marks is all I have on me. – The last three months has been a time of hard work for us. – More than two thirds of our planet is covered with water.

19.5. **Bildung des Genitivs**

Es bestehen zwei Möglichkeiten, den Genitiv zu bilden:

of + **Substantiv** und *s*-**Genitiv**.

L 19.5.

Die *of*-Fügung wird vor allem bei Sachbezug verwendet: the results of the test, the length of the bridge, the history of modern literature, the extent of automation, the making of steel.

Der *s*-Genitiv wird vorzugsweise bei Lebewesen verwendet; er wird gebildet
- im Singular durch Hinzufügung von Apostroph + *s*: the girl's name, my aunt's address, St James's [dʒeimziz] Park;
- im Plural durch Hinzufügen von Apostroph an Plural-*s*, bei unregelmäßigem Plural von *'s*: the boys' father, the children's toys.

Die *of*-Fügung wird auch bei Lebewesen verwendet, vor allem
- wenn die Person besonders hervorgehoben werden soll oder durch ein längeres Attribut näher bestimmt wird:
It was the paper of Professor Martin that attracted the greatest attention at the conference. – I always enjoy listening to the reports of foreign correspondents stationed in different parts of the world.
- bei Personen in der Pluralform – vor allem im gesprochenen Englisch –, wenn im Falle des *s*-Genitivs eine Verwechslung mit dem Singular möglich wäre: the examination of the students.

Beachten Sie: His girl-friend's photos are very good. (= the photos taken by his girl-friend.) – (aber:) The photos of his girl-friend are very good. (= The photos in which his girl-friend is to be seen are very good.)

Der *s*-Genitiv kann auch stehen
- bei Organisationen und Institutionen, Länder- und Städtenamen, geographischen Bezeichnungen wie **town, country, lake, earth, moon, sun,** etc: *the company's president* (oder:) *the president of the company*; (ebenso:) *the university's teaching staff*; *Britain's export and import*; *London's famous museums*; *the town's traffic problems*; *the earth's surface*;
- in der Schriftsprache gelegentlich bei Verkehrsmitteln, Maschinen oder anderen Sachobjekten: *the generator's capacity, the reactor's dimensions, the play's conflict*;
- bei Zeitbestimmungen wie **today, tomorrow, yesterday, last week,** etc: *today's newspapers, this month's issue of "Chemical Analysis"* und Zeitangaben wie: *a two hours' flight* (= *a flight of two hours / a two-hour flight*); (ebenso:) *a fifteen minutes' break*; *a three hours' walk*; (aber nur: *a five-day week*)
- in bestimmten Wendungen wie: *a stone's throw* ein Katzensprung; *be at one's wit's end* mit seiner Weisheit am Ende sein

Der *s*-Genitiv kann ohne Bezugswort stehen
- um die Wiederholung eines bereits erwähnten Substantivs zu vermeiden: I need this dictionary, you can take my friend's.
- wenn ein dazugehöriges Substantiv wie **shop, house, home** aus dem Zusammenhang erschließbar ist: There's a baker's round the corner. – My wife is at the butcher's. – Were you at the hairdresser's / greengrocer's / tailor's, etc?
Beachten Sie: I spent the weekend at my aunt's. (= at my aunt's home) – I spent the weekend with my aunt. (= I was together with my aunt over the weekend.)
- am Anfang des Satzes bei Bezug auf ein folgendes Substantiv: My friend's was the best design. (= The design of my friend was the best.)

Bei Personen findet sich auch die Kombination von *of* + **Substantiv** im s-Genitiv:
- vor allem mit unbestimmtem Artikel sowie mit *some, several, any, every*: Ben Jonson was a famous contemporary of Shakespeare's. – Among the highlights of the exhibition there are some early paintings of Picasso's.
- nach Demonstrativpronomen + Substantiv, um Verwunderung oder eine negative Reaktion zum Ausdruck zu bringen: I simply don't like that dress of Anne's.

Wird bei zwei oder mehreren Personen eine Partnerschaft zum Ausdruck gebracht, so erscheint der s-Genitiv nur beim letzten Wort: Rodgers and Hammerstein's musicals, (aber:) Mozart's and Beethoven's symphonies.

20. The Article – Der Artikel

20.1. The Definite Article – Der bestimmte Artikel

Der bestimmte Artikel *the* ist seiner Form nach unveränderlich, hat aber unterschiedliche Aussprache:
- [ðə] vor konsonantisch anlautenden Wörtern: *the door, the doors, the university* [juni'və:siti]
- [ði] vor vokalisch anlautenden Wörtern: *the apple, the apples, the hour* ['auə]
- [ði:] wenn betont: That's *the* problem. (Das ist *das* Problem.)

Wann der bestimmte Artikel verwendet wird, läßt sich nicht immer eindeutig festlegen; oft spielen dabei stilistische Erwägungen eine Rolle. Im folgenden werden generelle Hinweise gegeben.

20.1.1. Der bestimmte Artikel steht, wenn ein Substantiv durch eine folgende Genitiv-Fügung mit *of*, einen bestimmenden Relativsatz oder eine Partizipialkonstruktion näher definiert wird: *the history of art, the age of the earth, the heating of steel, the chemistry of hydrogen, the Dresden of today.*
The information you gave me is very interesting. – The data obtained are important.

20.1.2. Wird ein Substantiv durch eine präpositionale Fügung oder ein Adjektiv – oft im Superlativ – näher definiert, dann steht in der Regel der bestimmte Artikel, bei allgemeinen Definitionen dagegen meist nicht.
The furniture in this room is very expensive. – Do you know anything about the latest progress in genetics?
The action of Shakespeare's 'Hamlet' takes place in Denmark/in 16th century Denmark./(aber:) in the Denmark of the 16th century. – One of Karel Čapek's famous plays is entitled 'The Life of the Insects'. – Human life should never be threatened by war again.

20.1.3. Mit dem bestimmten Artikel stehen:
- Bezeichnungen von technischen Geräten und Musikinstrumenten: *the telephone, the radio, the piano,* etc.

L 20.1.4.

Do you play the piano? – I didn't see Jane, I spoke to her on the telephone. – (aber: We got the information by telephone.) – We heard the news on the radio. – (aber: The Cup Final will be broadcast by radio.) – We need somebody to repair the television. – (aber: Last night there was an interesting panel discussion on television.)

– geographische Begriffe wie Namen von Flüssen, Ozeanen, Kanälen, Gebirgen, nicht-englischen Bergen, Inselgruppen sowie bei einigen Länderbezeichnungen und Namen von Hotels, Theatern, Kinos, außerdem bei den Himmelsrichtungen:
the Thames, the Rhine; the Mediterranean, the Atlantic Ocean, the Baltic, the Black Sea; the Suez Canal; the Alps, the Rocky Mountains, the Caucasus; the Matterhorn; the Falklands, the West-Indies; the United Kingdom, the United States, the Soviet Union/the USSR, the German Democratic Republic, the Federal Republic of Germany, the People's Republic of China, the Netherlands, the Sudan; the Royal Theatre; the Odeon (Cinema); the Palace Hotel; in the east/west/south/north (aber: *from north to south*);

– Eigennamen im Plural: the Smiths, the Millers;

– *double*[1]: double the sum;

– Wendungen wie: *in the presence/absence of; with the help/aid of; in the case of; on the one/the other hand* einerseits/andererseits; *on the part of* seitens; *on the occasion of* anläßlich; *on the contrary* im Gegenteil; *at the latest/earliest* spätestens/frühestens; *at the worst* schlimmstenfalls; (aber:) *at best* bestenfalls; *at most* höchstens.

20.1.4. Der bestimmte Artikel entfällt:

– bei nichtzählbaren Substantiven, wenn sie nicht durch eine Genitiv-Fügung mit *of,* einen bestimmenden Relativsatz oder eine Partizipialkonstruktion näher bestimmt werden. Dazu gehören:
abstrakte Begriffe, z. B.: *science, technology, industry, education, higher education* Hoch- und Fachschulwesen, *automation, society, art, literature, traffic, transport, history, theory, practice, youth, age, old age* das hohe Alter, *labour/manpower* Arbeitskräfte, *business, man/mankind, wealth, poverty, life, love, hatred, nature, peace, war, money, socialism, communism, capitalism, imperialism;*
(aber:) *the public, the proletariat, the bourgeoisie;*
Stoff- und Gattungsbezeichnungen, z. B.: *matter* Materie, *energy/power, iron, steel, coal, wood, silk;* außerdem: *meat, butter, cheese,* etc;[2]
Namen wissenschaftlicher Fachrichtungen, z. B.: *mathematics, chemistry, electrical engineering, cybernetics, psychology,* etc.
Abkürzungen von Organisationen, wenn sie als ein Wort gesprochen werden: *UNESCO, UNO, NATO;* (aber:) *the EEC:*

---

[1] Zu "both" und "all" s. 15.6.6. + 15.6.4.
[2] Bei Angaben einer bestimmten Menge steht der Artikel: The cheese is in the fridge. – (aber: Cheese is made of milk.)

Nowadays automation is used almost everywhere in industry. – Lots of things are easier in theory than in practice. – It is very interesting to see how the literature of the 20th century reacts to the developments of modern science. – Chemistry is the science which deals with the composition of matter.;
- bei Substantiven wie *school, hospital, church, prison/jail, court*, wenn die Institution gemeint ist; ist das Gebäude gemeint, so steht der Artikel:
Peter is at school now. – (aber:) The school is over there. – Jane was in hospital some days. – (aber:) The hospital is quite a new building.;
- bei den Namen der Monate, Wochentage, Festtage und Mahlzeiten, sowie Jahreszeiten[3], z. B.: *January, in January; Monday, on Monday, next Monday, on Monday next, last Friday, on Friday last; Christmas/Easter/Whitsun(tide), at Christmas*, etc.; *breakfast/lunch/dinner, at breakfast*, etc.
We'll meet again at Christmas. – Lunch is ready. – Autumn is the season I like best.;
- bei Verkehrsmitteln in Verbindung mit *by*, z. B.: *(go) by train/tram/plane/bus/car/boat/underground/bicycle*:
Did you go by train? – (aber:) I met John on the train.
- bei Namen von Ländern, Seen und Bergen (vor allem in Verbindung mit *Lake* bzw. *Mount*), sowie Bezeichnungen von Straßen, Gebäuden, Plätzen, Parks und Brücken:
Great Britain, Switzerland, Turkey, etc; *Lake Michigan; Mount Everest, Mont Blanc; Downing Street; Westminster Abbey,* (aber: *the Tower); Trafalgar Square; Hyde Park; Tower Bridge;*
- vor *most*; bei *last* und *next* in Zeitbestimmungen, z. B.:
most people, most of the time, most of us, in most cases; *last week/month*, etc; *next Tuesday*, etc, *next week/month/year*;[4]
- in einigen feststehenden Verbindungen, z. B.: *go to town, go on foot/horseback, shake hands, lose courage, lose sight/track of* aus den Augen verlieren, *keep in mind, take into consideration/account, at first sight, from hand to mouth, be in/come into power* an der Macht sein/an die Macht kommen.

20.2. The Indefinite Article – Der unbestimmte Artikel

Der unbestimmte Artikel hat zwei Formen:
- *a* [ə] vor konsonantisch anlautenden Wörtern: *a table, a chair, a helicopter, a useful* ['juːsful] *talk, a European* [juərə'piːən];
- *an* [ən|æn] vor vokalisch anlautenden Wörtern: *an office, an hour* ['auər][5], *an MP* (*Member of Parliament*).

---

[3] In Verbindung mit "in" ist der Artikel möglich: in (the) winter.
[4] Der bestimmte Artikel steht bei Angaben von Zeitabschnitten, die bis heute dauern oder heute beginnen: The last week has been very busy (= the seven days until today). – (aber:) I was ill last week (= the week before this one). – Susan is coming next week (= the week after this one). – (aber:) I'll be away for the next week (= the seven days from today on).
[5] Ebenso: *an* vor honour, honorary, honourable, honest, honesty, heir(ess).

20.2.1. Der unbestimmte Artikel steht:

- um Zugehörigkeit zu einem Beruf, einer Nationalität, Partei oder Religion auszudrücken:
  Jane is a teacher. – I want to be an engineer. – Is Pedro a Spaniard or a Mexican? (aber auch: Is Pedro Spanish or Mexican?) – Our English friend is a socialist. – Mary is a Protestant. – Susan works as a stewardess.;
- bei Zeit-, Maß- und Mengenangaben (Im Sinne von "pro, je"):
  John earns 120 pounds a week. – I go to the theatre once a month. – This wine costs 3 pounds a bottle. – Jack's car does eighty miles an hour.;
- vor den Zahlbegriffen *hundred, thousand, million, dozen*:
  About a thousand people had come to see the match.[6];
- nach *quite* und *rather*, wenn ein Substantiv unmittelbar folgt:[7] It was quite/rather a disappointment that you didn't come.;
- nach *such* vor Substantiv oder Adjektiv + Substantiv:[8] You shouldn't do such a thing again. – We haven't seen such a good film for a long time.;
- im formalen Stil nach *so, too* (= zu), *how* + **Adjektiv** vor dem folgenden Substantiv:
  This is too small a room for two people to live in. = The room is too small for... – How pretty a girl Paula has become. = What a pretty girl...;
- in bestimmten Wendungen, z. B.: *be in a hurry, take a seat, have a mind/half a mind to do sth* Lust haben/fast Lust haben, *it is a pity/shame, make a noise, make it a rule/a condition/a duty* es sich zur Regel/Bedingung/Pflicht machen, *as a rule* gewöhnlich, *come/bring to an end/a close* zu Ende gehen/bringen, *have/run a temperature* Fieber haben, *have a headache*[9]/*a sore throat* Kopfschmerzen/Halsschmerzen haben.

20.3. Der Artikel steht nach *half* und *twice*, d. h. je nach Kontext der bestimmte oder unbestimmte Artikel:
half an hour, twice a week, half the amount, twice the sum (= *double the sum*).

Unterscheiden Sie: We spent half a day translating the text. (= today, yesterday or some other day)
(aber:) We spent half the day ... (= the day under discussion).

Beachten Sie: vor *part of* und *plenty of* steht **kein** Artikel: John told us only part of the story. – We have plenty of time.

---

[6] Bei besonderer Betonung steht *one* statt *a*: More than one thousand people ...
[7] Folgt ein Adjektiv, so kann der unbestimmte Artikel vor **oder** nach *quite* und *rather* stehen: That is rather a good idea/a rather good idea.
[8] Bei nichtzählbaren Substantiven entfällt der unbestimmte Artikel: Don't say such nonsense.
[9] I've got a headache today. (aber:) I often have headaches.

Übungen

Die Ziffern des Übungsteils verweisen auf die im Schlüssel gegebenen Lösungen.

1.1.1.
A. Geben Sie die Fragen deutsch wieder, und versuchen Sie zu antworten:
1. Who is your favourite author?   2. What is Joan's address?   3. How many of your friends live in a students' hostel?   4. Whose camera is this?   5. What's the date today?   6. What dictionary is this?   7. Who wants to ask a question?   8. What type of car is this?   9. Which of your friends wants to become an interpreter?   10. Which beverages contain alcohol?   11. What kind of disease is hepatitis?   12. Which materials conduct electricity?

B. Fragen Sie,

wer Peters Englischlehrer ist,[1] wie er heißt (was sein Name ist); wessen Auto das ist; wie viele Familien in diesem Haus wohnen;[2] was für Pflanzen im Botanischen Garten (botanical garden) der Universität wachsen; wer dieses englische Wort kennt; welche Vorlesungen (lectures) am Nachmittag stattfinden; welcher von Johns Brüdern Chemie studiert;[3] wer den Text übersetzen kann; wer die Frage beantworten will; wer von den ausländischen Touristen deutsch spricht.

1.1.2.
A. Geben Sie deutsch wieder, und antworten Sie:
1. How old are your parents?   2. How is your wife?   3. Is Dr. Smith an architect or a civil engineer?   4. Where can I meet you tomorrow?   5. How much is this TV set?   6. Whose shopping bag may I take?   7. How far is the congress centre from the station?   8. What would you like to drink?

B. Fragen Sie,

ob Jack zu Hause ist;[4] ob Herr Schmidt Physiker oder Chemiker ist; wo die neuen Zeitschriften sind; wo die nächste Bushaltestelle ist; wieviel dieser Plattenspieler (record player) kostet;[5] ob Sie jetzt mit dem Direktor sprechen können oder ob er sehr beschäftigt ist (busy);[6] wen Sie in dieser Angelegenheit (matter) fragen können; ob Sie eine Frage stellen dürfen (ask a question); ob Susan sich für Sport interessiert;[7] wie es Helens Mutter geht.

Ü 1.

1.1.3.
A. Geben Sie deutsch wieder, und antworten Sie (bei *yes/no*-Antworten L 1.2.2.):
1. Do you go to work by bus or by tram? 2. What do you do in your spare time? 3. Do you often watch television? 4. How often do you go to the cinema? 5. Did your girl-friend like the film? 6. Do you like to go to the theatre? 7. Who(m) do you want to visit over the weekend? 8. When do you want to go on holiday this year? 9. How long does it take to go from Berlin to Havana by plane? 10. When does the lecture begin? 11. Does Peter speak French? 12. Which do you prefer, beer or lemonade? 13. What did Mary suggest? 14. Do you agree with her? 15. How long does Mike intend to stay in Dresden? 16. What do the abbreviations e.g. and i.e. mean? 17. How long does it usually take you to write such an article?

B. Stellen Sie Ihrem Gesprächspartner Fragen, und lassen Sie ihn antworten (bei *yes/no*-Antworten L12.2.).*
Erkundigen Sie sich,

wo er arbeitet;[8] wo er studiert hat;[9] ob er Physik oder Chemie studiert hat;[10] ob er in der Forschung arbeitet (do research work); was für Untersuchungen er durchführt (make investigations); ob sein Betrieb mit ausländischen Firmen zusammenarbeitet (cooperate); ob er manchmal ins Ausland fährt; wie oft er sich im Ausland aufhält (stay); ob er Russisch und Englisch spricht; ob seine Frau in demselben Werk arbeitet; ob sie auch studiert hat; ob seine Kinder schon zur Schule gehen; ob er in der Nähe (near) seiner Arbeitsstelle (dem Ort, wo er arbeitet) wohnt;[11] wie er dorthin kommt (get); was er in seiner Freizeit tut (spare time); ob er gern ins Konzert geht;[12] was für Stücke er am liebsten sieht (like best); ob er seinen Urlaub dieses Jahr an der See verbringen will (at the seaside); ob er manchmal mit seiner Frau ins Kino geht; ob er gern fotografiert (take photos).

1.1.4.
Sie treffen während des Urlaubs einen Bekannten und erkundigen sich,

ob er irgendwelche Probleme mit seiner Unterkunft (accommodation) hat;[13] ob er ein Zimmer in einem Hotel hat; ob er einen Fernseher in seinem Zimmer hat; ob das Zimmer eine Klimaanlage hat (air-conditioning); ob seine Kinder ein eigenes (separate) Zimmer haben; ob er im Hotel frühstückt;[14] wo er zu Mittag ißt; ob er sich das neue Hotel am Strand angesehen hat (on the beach);[15] ob er in seinem Zimmer zu Abend ißt; ob er manchmal Ärger mit dem Service hat; ob er sich manchmal mit ausländischen Touristen im Hotel unterhalten hat;[16] ob er Gelegenheit hatte, eine Fahrt (trip) mit dem neuen Tragflächenboot (hydrofoil) zu machen.

---

*Die Sätze im Perfekt sind mit dem Präteritum wiederzugeben.

Ü 1.

1.1.5.
A. Übersetzen Sie, und geben Sie Antworten:
1. What did you talk about?   2. What does this article deal with?   3. Who are these books for?   4. What is the film about?   5. What do these photos remind you of?   6. Who can I turn to in this matter?   7. What job did you apply for?   8. Who do you think Bob knows these details from?   9. What do you want to talk to me about?   10. Who did you discuss the topic with?   11. What date do you think we can agree on?   12. What did your colleague complain about?   13. What did Susan speak to you about on the phone?   14. What does your decision depend on?   15. What does Fred need the money for?   16. What does an atom consist of?   17. What do these diagrams refer to?   18. What does the difference between mechanization and automation consist in?

B. Fragen Sie einen ausländischen Assistenten,

aus welchem Land er kommt[17]; auf welchem Wissenschaftsgebiet er arbeitet;[18] womit er sich in seiner Dissertation (doctoral thesis) beschäftigt; an wen er sich wendet (turn to), wenn er irgendwelche Probleme hat;[19] mit welchen Professoren er zusammenarbeitet (cooperate); über welches Thema er Vorlesungen hält (give lectures on a subject); um was für eine Stelle (job) er sich bewerben will, wenn er in seine Heimat (= nach Hause) zurückkehrt.[20]

C. Stellen Sie Fragen, und lassen Sie Ihren Gesprächspartner antworten:

1. Wovon handelt dieser Film?[21]   2. Auf wen wartest du (2.1.2.)?[22]   3. Womit beschäftigt sich Tom in seiner Diplomarbeit (diploma thesis)?   4. Über welches Thema will Herr Müller in seinem Vortrag sprechen?   5. In welcher Straße wohnst du?   6. Woher kommt das Telegramm?   7. Mit wem wollen Sie über diese Angelegenheit sprechen?[23]   8. Worüber hast du dich mit Susan unterhalten?   9. Von wo hat Bob angerufen?   10. Woraus besteht diese chemische Verbindung (compound)?

1.2.1.
A. Korrigieren Sie die folgenden Feststellungen mit den in Klammern angegebenen Wörtern:

Beispiel: *I'm hungry (thirsty)* → *I am not hungry, I'm thirsty.*
1. Mary is good at languages (mathematics).   2. Bill lives in London (Bristol).   3. Joe and Jack speak Spanish (French).   4. Fred can play the piano (the violin).   5. Mrs Smith is a typist (shop assistant).   6. We have tea at four (at five).   7. The Turners have got a house of their own (a big flat).   8. Peter knows English (Russian).   9. Anne has a day off every two weeks (once a month).   10. My girlfriend likes to read science fiction (detective stories).   11. Joan told me a lot about her country (only a little).   12. We had an English lesson yesterday (a French lesson).   13. I had toothache (a headache).   14. Jim grows potatoes in his garden (tomatoes).

Ü 1.

B. Verneinen Sie,

daß Sie Französisch sprechen;[24] daß Sie gut in Physik sind;[25] daß Sie wissen, wie ein Computer arbeitet; daß Sie Ingenieur werden wollen;[26] daß Sie sich für Sport interessieren; daß Sie Fußball spielen; daß Sie moderne Musik mögen; daß Sie viel Freizeit haben;[27] daß Sie ein Auto haben;
daß Mike oft ins Kino geht;[28] daß er gern Filme sieht;[29] daß er heute abend mit uns ausgehen will; daß er jeden Abend fernsieht; daß er jedes Wochenende tanzen geht (go dancing), weil er ein guter Tänzer ist (dancer);
daß Anne und Peggy viel Geld ausgeben (spend); daß sie oft einkaufen gehen[30]; daß sie teure Sachen (things) kaufen; daß sie sich schminken (put on make-up); daß sie rauchen; daß sie Alkohol mögen; daß sie mehr als einmal im Monat (once a month) mit ihren Freunden ausgehen;[31] daß sie ihren Urlaub dieses Jahr im Ausland verbringen wollen.

1.2.2.
Sie stellen Ihrem Gesprächspartner Fragen und lassen ihn antworten. (Bei *yes/no*-Antworten L 12.2.)

1. Arbeitet John nicht in deiner Abteilung (department)?[32]   2. Wer von euch kann den Text nicht übersetzen?[33]   3. Wer von deinen Freunden will nicht an dem Ausflug teilnehmen?   4. Ist Helen nicht eine sehr gute Hausfrau (housewife)?   5. Warum kommst du nicht mit? (= mit uns).   6. Hat Tom nicht Physik studiert?   7. Können Sie nicht ein paar Minuten warten?   8. Warum hast du heute morgen nicht gefrühstückt?   9. Ist das (= dies) nicht ein interessantes Buch?   10. Wolltest du gestern nicht ins Theater gehen?[34]   11. Warum seid ihr nicht mit dem Taxi gefahren?   12. Warum hast du mich nicht gefragt?   13. Wem von euch hat der Film nicht gefallen?   14. Warum sind Sie nicht mit Ihrem Hotelzimmer zufrieden (satisfied)?

1.2.3.
A. Übersetzen Sie:

1. Don't translate word for word.   2. Don't worry.   3. Don't be afraid of the exams.   4. Please write your address clearly.   5. Don't forget your promise.   6. Take off your coat.   7. Take a seat, please.   8. Turn off the radio.   9. Have a good time.   10. Don't drop the vase.   11. Have another glass of wine.   12. Hurry up!   13. Be quiet.   14. Don't make a fool of yourself.   15. Let's have a break.   16. Don't let's wait any longer.   17. Help yourself.   18. Make yourself comfortable.   19. Take your time.   20. Keep off the grass.

B. Geben Sie englisch wieder:

1. Bitte störe mich jetzt nicht (disturb).[35]   2. Warten Sie eine Minute.   3. Vergeßt nicht, uns zu informieren.   4. Setzen Sie sich bitte.   5. Sei nicht so unhöflich (impolite).[36]   6. Bitte sprechen Sie nicht so schnell (fast).   7. Fragen Sie nicht so viel.   8. Geben Sie bitte eine Zusammenfassung des Textes (summary).   9. Ruf mich morgen an.   10. Lassen (leave) Sie nicht das Fenster offen.

1.1./1.2.
Komplexübungen zu Frage und Verneinung
A. Sie haben etwas nicht verstanden und fragen zurück.
Beispiel: *We want to meet Fred at the club. Who do you want to meet at the club? – Where do you want to meet Fred?*
1. I like *Joan*. 2. *Mary* didn't come to the party. 3. *Pete* phones me twice a week. 4. We saw *Sue* at the grocer's. 5. *Jim* says he is ill. 6. Bob wants to tell about *his* trip. 7. I discussed the matter with *Jack*. 8. We must wait for *Allan*. 9. I want to speak to *Mr Mack*. 10. Joe deals with *cybernetics*. 11. John doesn't *shave* any more. 12. We agreed on *Maud's* plan.

B. Geben Sie englisch wieder (bei *yes/no*-Antworten s. L 12.2.):*
1. Wann will Jane uns besuchen? 2. Wer von Ihnen kennt dieses Buch? 3. Wir hoffen, daß Jim nicht krank ist. 4. Habt ihr ein Auto? 5. Von wem ist dieser Brief? 6. Hattet ihr eine interessante Unterhaltung? 7. Wie viele Fehler hast du in deiner Übersetzung gemacht? 8. Seien Sie nicht böse (angry). 9. Warum denkst du, daß John uns nicht helfen kann? 10. Was für einen Fernseher habt ihr? 11. Warum habt ihr nicht im Restaurant gegessen? 12. Woher kennst du Brian? 13. Ich glaube, Susan ist nicht zu Hause (s. Fußnote L 1.2.1., 9). 14. Bitte erzählen Sie mir einige Einzelheiten. 15. Ich habe nicht viel Freizeit. 16. Iß nicht so viel. 17. Warum haben Sie mich nicht informiert? 18. Worüber habt ihr euch mit den ausländischen Touristen unterhalten? 19. Hatten Sie eine angenehme (pleasant) Reise? 20. Wer von Ihnen hat gestern nicht an dem Ausflug teilgenommen (take part in)? 21. Ich vermute, daß dein Freund nicht recht hat (s. L 1.2.1., 9, Fußnote). 22. Worüber wollen Sie sich beschweren? (complain about). 23. Hat es lange gedauert (take), das Problem zu lösen? 24. Hast du Harry gefragt, wie er mit seinem neuen Chef auskommt (get on with)? – Ja, aber er wollte nicht darüber sprechen. 25. Hat dir das Konzert gefallen (enjoy)? – Nein. – Warum hat es dir nicht gefallen (like)? – Mir gefällt moderne Musik nicht. 26. Kennst du Peggy? – Ja. – Weißt du, wo sie wohnt? – Nein. Ist sie nicht Lehrerin? (L 20.2.1.) – Ich glaube nicht (L 12.2.1.), ich denke, sie ist Dolmetscherin. – Was für Sprachen hat sie studiert? – Englisch und Russisch, soviel (as far as) ich weiß. – Wo arbeitet sie? – Ich weiß (es) nicht. 27. Wieviel kostet dieser Fotoapparat (camera)? – Ich glaube, er ist nicht sehr teuer (s. Fußnote L 1.2.1.,9). – Was verstehst du unter (by) nicht sehr teuer? – Ich glaube, er kostet etwa (about) 300 Mark. 28. Woher kommt (be) Gus? Ist er nicht Engländer (English)? – Ich weiß (es) nicht. Ich glaube nicht, daß er Engländer ist. Jedenfalls (at any rate) lebt er nicht in England.

2.1.1.
A. Setzen Sie dem Kontext entsprechend die folgenden Verben ein:
study – teach – go – do – buy – sell – fly – have – live.
We ... lunch at twelve. – Peter often ... to Moscow. – A butcher ... meat. – Sue often ... new shoes. – Joan always ... her shopping at the supermarket. – Bill still ...

---
*Die Sätze im Perfekt sind mit dem Präteritum wiederzugeben.

Ü 2.

to school. – Mr Turner ... at an elementary school. – John ... medicine. – My parents ... in the country. – Fred often ... trouble with his car.

B. Bilden Sie Sätze, und ordnen Sie dabei den Berufen die richtigen Tätigkeiten zu:

pilot[37] (drive a taxi) – postman (type letters) – secretary (sell food) – grocer (build houses) – author (deliver the mail) – charwoman (analyse substances) – chemist (clean the rooms) – architect (write symphonies) – composer (fly planes) – taxi driver (write books).

C. Geben Sie mit den folgenden Ausdrücken Ihren Tagesablauf wieder. Beginnen Sie: *Ich bin Sekretärin.*

5.30 Uhr aufstehen; 6.00 Uhr frühstücken; 6.25 Uhr von zu Hause weggehen (leave home); mit der Straßenbahn ins Büro fahren; zwanzig Minuten brauchen (take), um zur Arbeitsstelle zu gelangen (= Stelle, wo ich arbeite); 7.00 Uhr Arbeitsbeginn (start work); jeden Tag viel mit der Maschine schreiben (do a lot of typing); oft Protokolle schreiben auf Konferenzen (take the minutes); 9.30 Uhr eine Kaffeepause (coffee break) haben; 12.00–12.30 Uhr zu Mittag essen; manchmal ausländische Besucher empfangen (receive); etwas Englisch sprechen; 16.15 Uhr Arbeit beenden; Hausaufgaben der Kinder überprüfen (check homework); Abendessen vorbereiten; fernsehen; gewöhnlich gegen (about) 22.00 Uhr zu Bett gehen.

Geben Sie diesen Tagesablauf in der dritten Person wieder. Beginnen Sie: *Mary ist Sekretärin...*

D. Geben Sie englisch wieder:

Anne ist 21 Jahre alt. Sie ist Studentin an der Technischen Universität Dresden und studiert Chemie. Ihre Eltern wohnen nicht in Dresden, deshalb (that's why) hat sie ein Zimmer in einem Wohnheim zusammen mit zwei anderen Studentinnen. Von Montag bis Freitag steht sie um 6.00 Uhr auf. Die Vorlesungen (lectures) beginnen 7.30 Uhr. Anne frühstückt im Wohnheim, aber zu Mittag ißt sie in der Mensa der Universität (refectory). Nachmittags arbeitet sie oft in einer Bücherei (library). Manchmal hat sie nicht sehr viel zu arbeiten. Dann geht sie gern spazieren (go for a walk). Wenn (if) sie das Wochenende nicht in Dresden verbringen will, besucht sie ihre Eltern. Sie geht nicht gern ins Kino. Wenn (when) sie ihren Freund trifft, geht sie meist (mostly) mit ihm tanzen.

2.1.2.
A. Übersetzen Sie ins Deutsche:

1. Where are you going? – I'm going home.
2. What are you talking about? – We are talking about how to spend the weekend.
3. What is going on here? – We're moving the furniture, the paperhanger is coming tomorrow.
4. Why are you dressing up? – I'm going to a concert tonight.
5. Father is eating out as long as mother is in hospital.
6. Fred stays at home most of the time, he is preparing for his exams.

B. Geben Sie englisch wieder:

1. Ich fahre heute nach Prag (leave for). 2. Bob hat wenig Zeit, weil er ein Haus baut. 3. Vergiß deinen Schirm nicht, es fängt an zu regnen. 4. Fred kann heute nicht kommen, er geht mit seiner Frau ins Theater. 5. Auf wen wartest du? – Ich warte auf meine Freundin. 6. Mit wem spricht Joan am Telefon (on the phone)? – Ich glaube, sie spricht mit Kitty. 7. Kommt Anne heute abend? – Ich weiß nicht, wir erwarten eine Nachricht von ihr (message). 8. John, wo bist du? – Ich bin im Arbeitszimmer (study). – Was machst du da?[38] – Ich schreibe einen Brief.[39] – Wem schreibst du? – Ich schreibe an (to) Betty, die (who) ihren Urlaub im Ausland verbringt.

2.1.1. / 2.1.2.
A. Entscheiden Sie, ob *Present Simple* oder *Present Continuous* einzusetzen ist:

Liz: What a noise! What (you, do)?
Jim: I (work).
L.: What (you, make)?
J.: I (make) a bookshelf. And what (you, do)?
L.: I (wait) for the water to boil, because I (want) to make tea.
J.: Can't you help me a little?
L.: Of course, I can. (You, look) for something?
J.: Yes, I (look) for the screw-driver. Can you see it somewhere?
L.: You (sit) on it.
J.: Give me the hammer, please.
L.: Wait a moment, the telephone (ring).

Liz (go) to the telephone and (pick up) the receiver. Her friend Susan (be) on the phone.

L.: Where (you, ring) from?
S.: I (be) in London now.
L.: Where (you, stay)?
S.: I (stay) at the Imperial.
L.: Sorry, I can't hear you. Jim (make) a lot of noise, he (hammer).
S.: What (he, do)?
L.: He (try) to make a bookshelf. He often (make) things for our new flat. When he (come) home from the office in the evening, he (not sit down) and (read) a book or (watch) television, but he (spend) a lot of time in his workshop.
S.: That's marvellous. My husband (not like) to do such things. He usually (watch TV) or (go) to a pub after work.
L.: So you (stay) at a hotel. What (you, do) here in London?
S.: I (take part) in a conference.
L.: Would you like to come to dinner on Sunday?
S.: I'd love to.
L.: Good. We (expect) you on Sunday at 6 p.m.

Ü 2.

B. Unterscheiden Sie im folgenden genau zwischen *Present Simple* und *Present Continuous*:

1. Wir verbringen unseren Urlaub gewöhnlich im Gebirge (mountains), aber dieses Jahr fahren wir an die Ostsee (the Baltic).[40]
2. Diesen Monat regnet es sehr oft, heute regnet es wieder.
3. Wir frühstücken meist (usually) halb sieben, aber heute frühstücken wir halb acht.
4. Ich lerne jetzt Englisch; ich kenne schon viele Wörter.
5. Ich treffe Peggy nicht sehr oft, aber ich sehe sie heute nachmittag.[41]
6. Susan hat ein neues Kleid, ihre Freundin schaut es sich gerade an (have a look at).[42]
7. Sie sprechen zu schnell (fast), ich verstehe Sie nicht!
8. Bob liest gern Kriminalromane (detective novels). Aber jetzt liest er nur wissenschaftliche Literatur, weil er sich auf eine Prüfung vorbereitet.
9. Jane trägt gewöhnlich Jeans, aber heute hat sie ein Kleid an (zweimal: wear).
10. Mein Freund schreibt Romane. Er schreibt zur Zeit seinen dritten.
11. John kann heute nicht kommen, er hat einen Tag frei (a day off).
12. Ich kann dich diese Woche nicht besuchen, ich schreibe einen Artikel für eine Zeitschrift.
13. Unsere Nachbarn haben schon zwei Autos, jetzt kaufen sie (sich) einen Wohnwagen (caravan).
14. Anne hat einen neuen Freund, sie hat gerade eine Verabredung (date) mit ihm.
15. Ich koste gerade die Suppe, sie schmeckt sehr gut (zweimal: taste; s. L 17.4.).
16. Wo arbeitet Mary? – In einem Krankenhaus. Aber zur Zeit arbeitet sie in einer Poliklinik (outpatient department).
17. In welchem Hotel wohnen (stay) Sie gewöhnlich, wenn Sie eine Konferenz in Berlin besuchen? – Im Hotel Berlin. Aber dieses Mal wohne ich im Hotel Berolina.
18. Wann gehst du gewöhnlich zur Arbeit? – Um sechs. Ich fange um sieben zu arbeiten an. Aber heute gehe ich um neun, weil ich um zehn anfange.
19. Meine Eltern sehen jeden Abend fern, aber heute gehen sie ins Kino.
20. Dies ist ein interessantes Buch, es beschreibt (describe) die Entwicklung der Weltraumforschung (space research).

C. Geben Sie den folgenden Dialog englisch wieder:

A: Wie geht es dir?
B: Danke, gut (fine).
A: Wohnst du immer noch in der Nähe des Bahnhofs?
B: Ja, aber ich ziehe nächsten Monat in eine größere Wohnung (move into). Ich habe eine große Familie.
A: Wie viele Kinder hast du?
B: Ich habe drei Kinder, zwei Jungen und ein Mädchen.
A: Wie alt sind sie?
B: Mary geht in den Kindergarten, sie ist drei Jahre alt. Peter ist sechs, er fängt im September mit der Schule an (start school). Mein anderer Sohn besucht

(attend) eine Spezialschule, wo er drei Sprachen lernt. Er will Dolmetscher (interpreter) werden.
A: Wo arbeitet deine Frau?
B: Sie ist Laborantin (lab assistant). Zur Zeit (at present) arbeitet sie in einem Chemiebetrieb; aber da ihr die (ihre) Arbeit dort nicht sehr gefällt, hat sie jetzt vor (plan), ihre Arbeitsstelle (job) zu wechseln.

2.2.1.
A. Antworten Sie:
1. Where did you learn English? 2. How long did John stay abroad? 3. How much did Susan pay for her new dress? 4. Where were you yesterday? 5. Which colour did Bob choose for his car? 6. Where did you buy this camera? 7. How long did it take you to translate the text? 8. Where did John take his visitors? 9. Where did you spend the weekend? 10. What did Susan wear at the party? 11. What did you have for lunch? 12. When did you get up this morning? 13. When did you tell Fred about our plan? 14. Why did you go to bed so late last night?

B. Sagen Sie, was Sie gestern, vorgestern, vor 3 Tagen, voriges Wochenende, am Sonntag oder am Anfang der Woche tun wollten, aber nicht getan haben, und was Sie statt dessen getan haben.

Beispiel: *go dancing/go to a concert → I wanted to go dancing, but I didn't, I went to a concert.*

complete a translation/hear a concert on the radio;
tidy up the flat/fall asleep;
clean the windows/wash the car;
make a bookshelf/break the screw-driver;
watch television/see a film in the cinema;
eat out/have lunch at home.

C. Ordnen Sie den im folgenden gegebenen Ausdrücken die richtigen Namen zu; verwenden Sie dabei das *Past Simple*:

Einstein – Martin Luther King – Alfred Nobel – Newton – Louis Armstrong – Vasco da Gama – Hemingway – van Gogh – Rutherford – Shakespeare

write 'Hamlet' – do pioneering work in nuclear physics – be a famous 19th century painter – get the Nobel Prize for literature in 1954 – find the sea-route to India in 1497/98 – blow the trumpet and sing jazz – discover the laws of gravity – invent dynamite – fight against racism – develop the theory of relativity

D. Bilden Sie Fragen, und antworten Sie mit den Angaben in Klammern.

Beispiel: *Hannibal – invade Britain (invade Italy) → Did Hannibal invade Britain? No, he didn't; he invaded Italy.*

Balzac – be the author of 'Oliver Twist' (write 'Father Goriot'); Otto Hahn – deal with psychoanalysis (split the nucleus of uranium in 1938); Marco Polo – discover

Ü 2.

America (travel to China); The American War of Independence – start in 1865 (begin in 1775); Hamlet – say the words: 'Against stupidity the gods themselves struggle in vain' (say: 'To be or not to be – that is the question').

E. Bilden Sie Fragen, und geben Sie Antworten nach folgendem Muster:
Who ... 'King Lear'? (Dostoyevsky) → Who wrote 'King Lear'? Did Dostoyevsky write 'King Lear'? – No, he didn't; it was Shakespeare who wrote 'King Lear'.
Verwenden Sie dem Kontext entsprechend die Verben
make, invent, paint, win, reign, become known, produce, fall, create.
(Natürlich sollten dabei die absurd zugeordneten Namen bzw. Sachverhalte im richtigen Zusammenhang erscheinen.)
Who ... 'Mona Lisa'? (Newton)
Who ... himself a name as a famous detective? (Elvis Presley)
Who ... an international reputation as a pop star? (Agatha Christie)
Which British monarch ... from 1558 to 1603? (Romeo)
Who ... the differential calculus and the integral calculus? (Leonardo)
Who ... as Britain's 'Queen of Crime'? (Elizabeth I)
What ... Einstein ...? (the film 'The Battleship Potemkin')
Who ... Juliet ... in love with? (Sherlock Holmes)
What ... Sergey Eisenstein ...? (the theory of relativity)

F. Sie haben etwas nicht verstanden und stellen Rückfragen nach den hervorgehobenen Satzteilen:
Beispiel: *Galileo* discovered the law of *the pendulum*. → Who discovered the law of the pendulum? – Which law did Galileo discover?
1. *Dürrenmatt* wrote the famous play *'The Physicists'*.
2. *Picasso* painted the well-known picture *'Guernica'*.
3. *Washington* became the first president of the USA *in 1789*.
4. *Knobelsdorff* built *the Sans Souci Palace*.
5. *Wat Tyler* led the English Peasants' Revolt in the year *1381*.
6. *Lindbergh* made the first flight across the Atlantic Ocean *in 1927*.
7. *G. B. Shaw* wrote *some fifty* plays.
8. *Freud* dealt with *psychoanalysis*.
9. *Bulwer-Lytton* wrote about the *destruction of Pompeii*.
10. *N. Wiener* founded the science of *cybernetics in 1947*.
11. *'The Communist Manifesto'* appeared *in 1848*.
12. *Descartes* coined the phrase *'I think, therefore I am'*.

G. Sagen Sie, was Sie vorige Woche abends getan haben:
Briefe an einige Verwandte schreiben; einkaufen gehen; einen Freund treffen; einen kleinen Spaziergang durch das Stadtzentrum machen (take a stroll); ein Buch lesen; ein Radio kaufen; einen Vortrag halten (give a lecture).

H. Geben Sie die Fragen englisch wieder, und antworten Sie:

1. Wo hast du Shirley kennengelernt?[43] 2. Was für einen Film habt ihr gestern gesehen? 3. Wann hat Manfred geheiratet? 4. Wann hast du zu studieren begonnen? 5. Wo habt ihr euch getroffen? 6. Wolltest du uns nicht Einzelheiten erzählen?[44] 7. Warum seid ihr zu spät gekommen (be late)? 8. Wann hast du das Buch gelesen? 9. Worüber habt ihr euch unterhalten?[45] 10. Mit wem hast du über die Angelegenheit gesprochen? 11. Wie lange hat die Konferenz gedauert (last)? 12. Wann ist Fred im Ausland gewesen? 13. Wo haben Sie diesen schönen Ring gekauft? 14. Wann habt ihr unser Telegramm bekommen? 15. Wie lange war Anne krank? 16. Hat dir das Buch gefallen? 17. Wann ist das Flugzeug gestartet (take off)? 18. Wann seid ihr angekommen? 19. Wann ist Jack abgereist (leave)? 20. Wo hat das Symposium stattgefunden? 21. Worüber hat Professor Black in seinem Vortrag gesprochen? 22. Warum hast du unsere Einladung nicht angenommen (accept)? 23. Wie lange habt ihr gebraucht, das Zimmer zu tapezieren (paper a room)?[46] 24. Warum ist Mary nicht mitgekommen?

I. Übersetzen Sie die Fragen Ihres Gesprächspartners, und antworten Sie:

Wo hast du voriges Jahr deinen Urlaub verbracht? In welchem Monat bist du gefahren? Mit wem bist du gefahren? Wo hast du gewohnt? Hattest du ein schönes Zimmer? Wie hast du die Abende verbracht? Was für Wetter (sort of weather) hast du gehabt? Wem hast du während deiner Ferien geschrieben? Wieviel hat der Urlaub gekostet (cost)? Bist du oft schwimmen gegangen (go swimming)? Was hast du gemacht, wenn es regnete?

J. Geben Sie englisch wieder:

1. Wir sind gestern im Theater gewesen.[47] 2. Ich habe Henry vorige Woche getroffen. 3. Jim hat vor 5 Jahren geheiratet.[48] 4. Voriges Jahr bin ich mehrere Wochen im Krankenhaus gewesen. 5. Es gab viele falsche Antworten auf diese Frage.[49] 6. Ich habe vor einigen Tagen mit meinem Direktor gesprochen. 7. Wir haben Anne nach (about) ihren Problemen gefragt, aber sie wollte nicht darüber sprechen. 8. Jack ist vor 10 Minuten gegangen. 9. Bob hat das Labor vor einer Viertelstunde verlassen. 10. Die französische Delegation ist am Freitag nach Paris zurückgekehrt. 11. Das Flugzeug aus Prag ist vor einer halben Stunde gelandet. 12. Fred hat mich vor einigen Minuten angerufen. 13. Mein Freund ist vor mehreren Jahren nach Berlin gezogen. 14. Ich habe diesen Roman vor vielen Jahren gelesen. 15. Wir haben dieses Problem ausführlich (in detail) auf unserer letzten Konferenz behandelt. 16. Ich habe 'Romeo und Julia' in der Schule gelesen.

2.2.2.
Übersetzen Sie:

1. They were talking all afternoon. 2. John was reading while Susan was writing a letter. 3. When we came to the station, the train was just arriving. 4. Who was the pretty girl that you were talking to when I saw you yesterday? 5. Yesterday

Ü 2.

evening, as usual, mother was solving a crossword puzzle, my brother was watching TV, my sister was knitting, and father was dozing in an armchair.

2.2.1. / 2.2.2.
A. Entscheiden Sie bei den folgenden Sätzen, wo *Simple Past* bzw. *Past Continuous* zu verwenden ist:

Beispiel: *The sun (rise) when we (leave) home.* → *The sun was rising when we left home.*

1. Bob (stand) in a queue outside the theatre when I (see) him.   2. We (have) lunch when you (ring).   3. Joan (peel) potatoes when she (cut) her finger.   4. Pete (do) his homework when I (come).   5. It (begin) to rain when we (leave).   6. I (look) for you at the conference all morning, where (you, sit)?   7. I (sleep) soundly when a noise (wake) me up. I (know) somebody (come) because the dog (bark) furiously.   8. What (you, do) when I (try) to phone you last night? I (ring) several times, but you (not answer) the telephone.
9. We (wait) for the bus when a car (come) round the corner. It was my neighbour who (drive) home. When he (see) us, he (stop) and (offer) us a lift. So we (get) home very quickly.
10. At the pub last night some of the guests (drink) together, when an argument (break out). As the men (begin) to fight the innkeeper (call) the police. The situation (become) rather uncomfortable when a policeman (arrive) and (restore) order.

B. Setzen Sie die Verben in die dem Kontext entsprechende Form:[50]

Yesterday Bob (go window-shopping) with his girl-friend Peggy. They (walk) down the street when she suddenly (stop) outside a jeweller's shop. While they (look) at the things on display Peggy suddenly (get excited). There (be) a ring in the shop-window which she (like) very much. They (go) into the shop and (tell) the jeweller, who (stand) behind a big showcase, that they (want) to see the ring. He (show) it to them. While Peggy (have) a close look at the ring, Bob desperately (count) the money in his purse. He (know) how fond Peggy (be) of jewels. And, indeed, she (find) the ring very beautiful. It (be) rather expensive, and Bob (not have) enough money on him. When they (leave) the shop he (notice) that she (look) a little depressed. So he (promise) he would buy her the ring as soon as possible.

C. Setzen Sie in dem folgenden Dialog die richtigen Verbformen ein:

When (you, go) to Weimar? – We (go) there last weekend.
(You, go) by train or by car? – We (want) to go by train, but since we (not get) a taxi we (miss) the train. So Susan (take) us there in her car. We (be) very glad that she (have) time to do so. But it (be) rather a long trip. We (drive) on the motorway at a high speed, when the car (begin) to skid. At first we (not know) what (be) wrong. Susan (drive) to the next lay-by (Autobahnparkplatz) and (get out). She (notice) at once that one of the tires (be) flat. It (take) her about half an hour to change it. Lots of cars (pass by), but only some of the drivers (stop) and (offer) to help her. But she (not need) any help. Later on, there (be) another delay. When we (approach) Weimar, there (be) a diversion. The bypass (have) plenty of potholes and all the cars (move) very slowly. It was late in the afternoon when we (get) to Weimar.

D. Geben Sie englisch wieder:

1. Wir frühstückten gerade, als das Telegramm kam.[51]   2. Der Zug fuhr gerade ab, als wir zum Bahnhof kamen.   3. Als Peter anrief, sah ich mir gerade einen Film im Fernsehen an.[52]   4. Ich habe gestern meine Schlüssel verloren, als ich einen Spaziergang machte (have a walk).   5. Fred rasierte sich gerade (shave), als ich kam.   6. Gestern habe ich den ganzen Abend gelesen.   7. Mit wem hast du dich unterhalten, als ich dich traf?   8. Auf wen hast du gewartet, als ich dich gestern sah?   9. Susan wohnte bei ihrer Freundin (stay with), als ihre Eltern im Ausland waren.   10. Wir standen an der Bushaltestelle, als der Unfall passierte.

E. Schildern Sie die folgende Situation in Englisch:[53]

Am Sonntagmorgen war meine Familie sehr beschäftigt. Mutter putzte (clean) die Fenster, Vater reparierte das Auto. Mein kleiner Bruder machte seine Hausaufgaben (do one's homework). Meine Schwester Ellen las eine Modenzeitung (fashion journal). Plötzlich klingelte das Telefon. Ellen legte ihre Zeitung hin (put down), ging ins Wohnzimmer und nahm den Hörer ab (pick up the receiver). Es war ihr Freund, der sie besuchen wollte. Während Ellen mit ihrem Freund telephonierte (talk on the phone), klingelte jemand (ring the bell). Es war der Postbote (postman), der (who) ein Telegramm brachte.

Als Mutter das Mittagessen kochte (cook lunch), kam Frau Müller und erzählte ihr von der Hochzeit (wedding) ihrer Tochter. Sie unterhielten sich fast eine Stunde. Inzwischen (meanwhile) wartete Ellen auf ihren Freund. Als er kam, luden wir ihn zum Mittagessen ein.

2.3.1.

A. Verwenden Sie bei den folgenden Aussagen die in Klammern stehenden Verben im *Present Perfect*:

1. Can you tell me what the book is about? – No, I (not read)[54] it yet.   2. You can stop looking for my glasses; I just (find) them.   3. We don't know Mrs Martin; we never (meet) her before.   4. I can't show you the photos, I (not bring) them with me. I (forget) them.   5. I hear you are leaving us. – Yes, I (make up one's mind) to change my job.   6. I can't answer your question, I (not deal) with this problem so far.   7. Where have you been? I (not see) you all day.   8. We can't send John a letter, we (lose) his address.   9. Why do you ask me again, I often (tell) you what I think about it.   10. I'm not sure if I like olives, I never (eat) any before.   11. We (begin) a new series of tests this week. So far we (make) five experiments.   12. Have a look at these papers; I (not go) through them yet.   13. Where can Jack be? He (not come) until now.   14. I haven't been out this afternoon, I (write) some letters.

B. Bilden Sie Fragen, und geben Sie Antworten:

1. What films (you, see)[55] lately?   2. How often (you, be) abroad?   3. What novels by Hemingway (you, read)?   4. How much money (Peggy, spend) today?   5. (You, have) breakfast yet?   6. How many cigarettes (you, smoke) today?   7. What lectures (you, attend) since Monday?   8. What (the weather, be like) here these days?

Ü 2.

C. Verwenden Sie die gegebenen Ausdrücke, um zu sagen, was Sie heute getan haben, oder was Ihr Freund getan hat:

einkaufen (be shopping)[56]; eine Menge Geld ausgeben; Gardinen (curtains) für die neue Wohnung kaufen[57]; einige Freunde treffen; im Theater sein; ein interessantes Stück sehen; eine Ausstellung besuchen (exhibition); einige ausländische Kollegen durch die Stadt führen (take); viel im Haushalt arbeiten (do a lot of housework); das Wohnzimmer neu tapezieren (repaper); ein Bücherregal bauen (make a bookshelf); eine Bluse nähen; einen Schal stricken (shawl); eine Medaille (medal) in einem Schwimmwettbewerb gewinnen; eine Verabredung (date) mit Mary haben; sich in Mary verlieben.

2.3.2./2.3.3.
A. Übersetzen Sie:

1. I'm sorry, I haven't written for such a long time, but I have been very busy lately. 2. The symposium has been going on for two days. 3. John has been abroad for some months. 4. We haven't met for ages. 5. How long have you been working on your doctoral thesis? 6. This topic has been under discussion time and again. 7. We have known each other for years. 8. Mike has wanted to visit us for a long time. 9. Our friends from Czechoslovakia have been staying with us for a fortnight. 10. Can anyone tell me what has been going on here? Fred and Henry have been quarrelling 11. Mr. Mitchell has been head of our sales department for many years. 12. Lately I've been having trouble with my television over and over again. 13. Peter has been working in our office as long as he has lived in Berlin. 14. How long have you had your new car? 15. It's easy to get in touch with Helen. She has been on the phone since January. 16. The two secretaries have been talking on the phone for half an hour. 17. Since the introduction of penicillin in 1928 there has been a constant search for new antibacterial drugs. 18. It has been known since the second half of the 19th century that viruses are responsible for a large variety of diseases. 19. Nuclear transmutations have been known since the discovery of the unstable elements radium and polonium in 1898 by Pierre and Marie Curie. 20. Records have enjoyed ever-increasing popularity since they became commercially available after the invention of the gramophone with its wax-coated zinc plate by E. Berliner in 1887.

B. Setzen Sie die in Klammern angegebenen Verben in das *Present Perfect*. Beachten Sie, daß in einigen Fällen das *Present Perfect Continuous* nicht möglich ist, in anderen Fällen dagegen stehen sollte.

1. Why are you so late? I (wait)[58] for you for more than an hour. 2. Peter knows English quite well. He (learn) it for five years. 3. I need a break now. I (type)[59] all morning. 4. We are not at all satisfied with the new typewriter, we (have)[60] nothing but trouble with it since we bought it. 5. I'm glad you (come) at last. I (expect) you since 3 o'clock.[61] 6. How long (you, learn) Russian? I (have) Russian lessons for 8 years. 7. How long (you, have)[62] this washing machine? – I (have) it for five years. 8. (John, go)[63] abroad? I (not meet)[64] him for a long time. 9. Go out and get some fresh air; you (sit) over your books too long. 10. Harry likes Susan, he

(see)⁶⁵ her regularly for some time.   11. I'm not surprised that Anne (decide) to marry Allan. I always (think) it probable, because they (like) each other for a long time.   12. Jack and Jill are not twins, but they always (look) alike.   13. Roy never drinks alcohol, he always (be) a teetotaller.   14. How long (the Millers, live) in this flat? – As far as I know they (live) here for some ten years.   15. John (resemble) his father since he was a little boy.   16. We (try) to get in touch with Bob for weeks, but we (not meet) him yet.   17. I must see a doctor, I (not feel) well lately.   18. The streets are slippery; it (rain) all day.   19. Your friend (not ring); I (be) at home all the time.   20. We (discuss) the different proposals, but we must carry on because we (not reach) an agreement.   21. What (you, do)⁶⁶ this afternoon? – I (translate)⁶⁷ all the time. I (translate)⁶⁸ a long text.   22. Peter wants to leave today, he (stay) with us for two weeks.   23. I (trust)⁶⁹ Henry as long as I (know)⁷⁰ him.   24. John (teach) physics at a vocational school since he graduated from the university.   25. Mary and Joan (gossip) for hours, and there is no end in sight.   26. Peter looks angry; he (quarrel) with his wife.

C. Entscheiden Sie, ob das in Klammern angegebene Verb im *Present Perfect Simple* oder *Continuous* stehen sollte:

1. I must go to the post-office, I (write)⁷¹ three letters.   2. The interpreter needs a rest, he (interpret)⁷² for the past two hours.   3. Haven't you finished the book yet? You (read) it for more than a week.   4. I'm sorry, we are late; (you, wait) long?   5. You look hot; (you, run)?   6. My car is very reliable, I never (have) a breakdown until now.   7. We (live) in this house as long as we (be) in Dresden.   8. I wonder why Harry (not phone); I (expect) him to ring me for the past three hours.   9. I can't drive now, I (drink) three glasses of beer.   10. You must not drive now, you (drink).   11. Paula is a nice girl; I (like) her since we first met.   12. Little wonder that our fridge doesn't work anymore; we (have) it for more than ten years.

D. Ziehen Sie Schlußfolgerungen aus den beschriebenen Situationen. Verwenden Sie *for* und/oder *since*.

Beispiel: *Susan is fifteen now. She began to learn English when she was ten. Now she is still learning English.* → *Susan has been learning English since she was ten/for 5 years.*

1. I am translating a text. I began to translate at 11 a.m. Now it's 2 p.m.⁷³
2. My friend is a physicist in a research centre. He left the university in 1982.⁷⁴
3. We are waiting for Mike. He had told us he would come at ten. Now it's 11.
4. Fred began to collect stamps when he was a little boy. He is still collecting stamps.
5. Mary became a teacher in 1980. She is still teaching.
6. John is watching TV. He turned on the TV-set at 8 p.m. Now it's eleven p.m.
7. Mr Clark became head of department five years ago.
8. Jack and Susan are married. They got married two years ago.
9. I know Kate. I got to know her seven years ago.
10. Bob is studying. He came to the university four years ago.
11. Our secretary is typing letters. The first letter was dictated to her at 7 a.m. Now it's 10 a.m.

Ü 2.

12. Tom had his first French lesson when he was forteen. He is eighteen now and he is still having French lessons.
13. Fred is working on his doctoral thesis. He got the topic one year ago.
14. I last went to the theatre in March. Now it's August.[75]
15. The beginnings of football in Britain were in the Middle Ages. The game is still very popular there.
16. The last time I saw Mary was in mid-May. Now it's the middle of November.
17. Mr Birch fell ill when he came back from a business trip four weeks ago.
18. When we last met Paul, he was 25. Now he's 33.
19. It was two months ago that the negotiations began, and they are still going on.
20. I last went on holiday in May last year. That was one year and a half ago.[76]

2.3.1./2.3.2./2.3.3.
Geben Sie englisch wieder:

1. Ich kann meine Schlüssel nicht finden; ich habe sie wahrscheinlich (probably) verloren.   2. Fred und Susan sind sehr glücklich; sie haben gerade geheiratet (get married)[77].   3. John kennt unseren Plan; ich habe ihn schon informiert.   4. Warum kommst du so spät? Ich bin (schon) seit einer Stunde hier.   5. Mr. Swan ist ein erfahrener (experienced) Lehrer; er unterrichtet schon seit 15 Jahren[78].   6. Anne ist gerade gekommen; sie will mit dir sprechen.   7. Hast du den Film schon gesehen?[79] – Ja./Nein.   8. Nora kommt heute nicht (L 2.1.2.); sie ist krank geworden (fall ill).   9. Wie lange hast du schon dein Auto? Ich habe es seit über 10 Jahren[80].   10. Jack fühlt sich nicht wohl; deshalb ist er heute nicht im Institut gewesen.   11. Ich bin müde; ich bin die ganze Strecke (distance) zu Fuß gegangen[81].   12. John hat sich (schon) immer für das Theater interessiert; deshalb ist er Schauspieler geworden.   13. Ich habe noch nicht mit Jim darüber gesprochen; ich habe ihn lange nicht gesehen.   14. Wir können den Versuch nicht fortsetzen (continue), ehe wir den Fehler gefunden haben.   15. Ich kenne Janet schon lange; aber in letzter Zeit habe ich sie nicht gesehen.   16. Adam und Eve sind befreundet (be friends), seit sie sich vor drei Jahren trafen.   17. Es tut mir leid, daß ich zu spät komme; wartest du schon lange?   18. Wir wissen nicht, wo Sam ist; er ist gerade weggegangen (leave).   19. Es ist kalt geworden, die Temperaturen sind unter (below) Null gefallen (drop).   20. Wir sind heute nicht spazieren gegangen, weil es seit gestern abend regnet.   21. Mein Freund Mischa wohnt in Leningrad. Er will mich schon seit zwei Jahren besuchen[82].   22. Wir kennen uns (L 15.5.), wir sind uns schon früher begegnet.   23. Gehen wir in den Warteraum; der Zug ist gerade abgefahren.   24. Ich hatte bisher keine Gelegenheit, mich mit John über Einzelheiten seiner Reise zu unterhalten; er hat ferngesehen, seit er nach Hause kam.   25. Susan freut sich auf (look forward to) ihre Reise in die Sowjetunion; sie ist (noch) nie im Ausland gewesen.   26. Jim und Jill kennen sich (15.5.) seit zwei Jahren, seit einem Jahr sind sie verlobt (be engaged).   27. Peter arbeitet an der Technischen Universität Dresden, er ist seit 3 Jahren Assistent in der Sektion (department) Chemie.   28. Ich mag Evelyn, seitdem ich sie kenne.[83]   29. Seit über 200 Jahren beruht (be based on) die industrielle Entwicklung in erster Linie (pri-

marily) auf der Ausnutzung (utilization) von Kohle als Energiequelle. 30. Seit Anfang der 60er Jahre hat es in der Weltraumforschung (space research) eine sehr rasche Entwicklung gegeben.

2.3.4.
A. Entscheiden Sie, ob *Past* oder *Present Perfect* zu verwenden ist:
1. I (not attend) the conference yesterday, because I (not feel) well. 2. The Turners have a nice flat in a villa. They (live) there since last year. 3. We can't come with you; we (not finish) the translation yet. 4. We (meet) two years ago, but we (not meet) since.[84] 5. Peter (send) me a letter last week but I (not answer) it yet. 6. Last year my sister (be) still rather short, she (grow) a lot in the meantime. 7. I'm hungry, I (not eat) anything since breakfast. 8. We can recommend you this exhibition, we (be) there yesterday. 9. Bob and I (have) an argument the day before yesterday. We (not speak) to each other since then. 10. My friends (move) into their new flat last week. They already (settle down). 11. I (not meet) Alice since we (leave) school. 12. We (have) a small bungalow for several years; we (buy) it when I (get) my new job. 13. I know this place, I (be) here before[85]. 14. We (not see) John for months; he (go) abroad early this year.[86]

B. Geben Sie englisch wieder, unterscheiden Sie dabei zwischen *Past* und *Present Perfect*:
1. Peter ist seit einigen Jahren Assistent an der Humboldt-Universität zu Berlin; er hat vor drei Jahren angefangen, dort zu arbeiten (start work).[87] 2. Warst du diese Woche im Kino? – Ja, ich habe gestern abend einen interessanten Film gesehen.[88] 3. Wie lange lernen Sie schon Französisch? – Ich habe vor zwei Jahren angefangen. Zuerst fand ich es sehr schwierig, und mein Lehrer war nicht sehr zufrieden mit mir. Aber seit einiger Zeit mache ich Fortschritte (make progress). 4. John ist gerade aus Österreich zurückgekehrt. Er ist einige Tage in Wien gewesen, wo er an einer Konferenz teilgenommen hat. 5. Hast du Mary in letzter Zeit gesehen? – Ich habe sie das letzte Mal (last) vor einigen Monaten gesehen. Vorige Woche wollte ich sie besuchen, aber sie ist seit einiger Zeit verreist (be away on a journey).[89] 6. Habt ihr schon die Ergebnisse der Versuche analysiert? – Nein, wir haben noch nicht die Zeit (dafür) gehabt; wir haben die Versuche erst (only) gestern abgeschlossen. 7. Spielen Sie gern Volleyball? – Als ich jung war, habe ich (es) oft getan, aber vor etwa 20 Jahren hatte ich einen Unfall, und seitdem spiele ich nicht mehr. 8. Peter interessiert sich seit seiner Kindheit für Musik. Er wollte Dirigent (conductor) werden, aber da er die Aufnahmeprüfung (admission test) an der Musikhochschule (academy of music) nicht bestanden (pass) hat, ist er Musiklehrer geworden. Er unterrichtet seit einigen Jahren an einer Erweiterten Oberschule (extended secondary school). 9. Ich möchte (would like to) Ihnen Mr Smith vorstellen. – Das ist nicht nötig. Wir kennen uns (L 15.5.) schon seit einigen Jahren. Wir haben uns auf einer Konferenz in Berlin kennengelernt (get to know). 10. Fotografieren Sie gern (take photos)? – Ja, aber ich habe erst vor 5 Jahren während einer Auslandsreise (trip abroad) (damit) begonnen; seitdem habe ich viele schöne Aufnahmen gemacht (take pictures).[90]

Ü 2.

2.4.
A. Antworten Sie, und verwenden Sie dabei das *Past Perfect*.
Beispiel: *Why didn't Jane come? (fall ill)* → *Jane didn't come because she had fallen ill.*
1. Why didn't Peter take part in the meeting? (fly to Moscow the evening before). 2. Why couldn't you ask John? (go away). 3. Why did Joe come back? (forget one's wallet) (s. L 15.3.1.). 4. Why didn't you discuss the problem yesterday? (talk about it the day before). 5. Why did you stay away from the sports lesson yesterday? (hurt one's ankle). 6. Why did you have a stomach ache? (eat too much icecream).

B. Verwenden Sie in den folgenden Sätzen *Past Tense* und *Past Perfect*:
Beispiel: *When I (get) to the club, Mary already (leave)* → *When I got to the club, Mary had already left.*
1. Fred (want) to visit Leningrad, because he never (be) there before. 2. When I (come), the meeting already (begin). 3. Anne (be delighted) because Arthur (give) her a very beautiful birthday present. 4. We hardly (recognize) each other, because we (not meet) for many years. 5. Peter (not come), because he (fall ill). 6. I (call) at the office to talk to Sue, but I (discover) I just (miss) her. 7. A search party (set out) for the climbers, who (leave) the hotel early in the morning but who not yet (come back) late in the evening. 8. Tom's marks last term (be) better than he (expect). 9. Suddenly we (see) a solution to the problem that we (deal with) for a long time. 10. I (have) to get a new passport, because my old one (expire). 11. Once we (find) the mistake, it (be) easy to finish the calculation. 12. As soon as they (reach) an agreement they (draw up) the contract.

C. Geben Sie englisch wieder:
1. Peter kam nicht, obwohl wir ihn eingeladen hatten.[91] 2. Niemand hatte den Fehler bemerkt (notice). 3. Der Bus war schon abgefahren, als wir kamen. 4. Niemand wußte genau (L 17.1.), was geschehen war. 5. Mary hatte gerade angefangen, den Tisch zu decken (lay the table), als die ersten Gäste erschienen (turn up). 6. Wir waren etwa eine Stunde gefahren, als wir merkten, daß wir kein Benzin mehr hatten (be out of petrol).[92] 7. Nachdem der Assistent gekommen war, analysierten wir die Ergebnisse. 8. John war schon weggegangen, als ich anrief.

2.2. / 2.4.
A. Geben Sie englisch wieder. Unterscheiden Sie dabei zwischen *Simple Tense* und *Continuous Tense*.

1. Mary ging gerade weg, als Peter anrief. – Mary war schon gegangen, als Peter anrief.[93]
2. Das Flugzeug landete gerade, als wir zum Flughafen kamen. – Das Flugzeug war schon gelandet, als wir zum Flughafen kamen.
3. Als wir ins Kino kamen, hatte der Film schon angefangen. – Als wir ins Kino kamen, fing der Film gerade an.
4. Susan kochte (make) schon Kaffee, als wir kamen. – Als wir kamen, machte Susan Kaffee für uns.[94]

B. Geben Sie die folgende Situation englisch wieder. Beachten Sie wieder die Verwendung von *Past Simple/Continuous* und *Past Perfect Simple/Continuous*:

Mr und Mrs Miller hatten gestern abend einen Verkehrsunfall (traffic accident), als sie mit dem Auto ins Theater fuhren. Mr Miller saß am Steuer (drive). Er war müde, weil er länger als gewöhnlich gearbeitet hatte. Es hatte den ganzen Tag geregnet, und die Straßen waren noch naß. An einer Kreuzung (crossroads) beachtete (notice) Mr Miller nicht, daß ein anderer Wagen die Vorfahrt (right of way) hatte. Obwohl der Fahrer sofort bremste (pull the brakes), gab es einen Zusammenstoß (collision), und beide Wagen wurden beschädigt (get damaged). Zwei Polizisten, die gerade die Straße herunterkamen, sahen den Unfall aus einer Entfernung (distance) von etwa hundert Metern. Beide Fahrer beschrieben ihnen (L 11.4.), wie es zu dem Zusammenstoß gekommen war (happen). Eine Alkoholprobe (breathalyser test) zeigte, daß Mr Miller keinen Alkohol getrunken hatte. Tatsächlich (in fact) hatte er den ganzen Tag nur einige Glas Milch getrunken (have some glasses ...)

Komplexübungen zu *Present, Past, Present Perfect, Past Perfect*.

A. Ermitteln Sie im folgenden die richtige Form:

1. I know him since 1980. – I am knowing him since 1980. – I have known him since 1980.
2. Know he you? – Knows he you? – Does he know you?
3. I don't know where does he work. – I don't know where he works. – I don't know where works he.
4. How long do you work in this plant? – How long have you been working in this plant? – How long have you yet worked in this plant?
5. What about are you talking? – What are you talking about? – What about do you talking?
6. Carol is a student since September. – Carol is being a student since September. – Carol has been a student since September.
7. He has just come. – He is just come. – He has just been coming.
8. She has been abroad for two months. – She is being abroad for two months. – She has been abroad since two months.
9. What did he told you yesterday? – What he told you yesterday? – What did he tell you yesterday?
10. I met him at the theatre for some days. – I have met him at the theatre some days ago. – I met him at the theatre some days ago.
11. We have lived here since three years. – We have been living here for 3 years. – We lived here for three years ago.
12. They are gone ten minutes ago. – They went ten minutes ago. – They have been going ten minutes ago.
13. He was arrived before we came. – He had arrived before we came. – He had been arriving before we came.
14. She has been ill before she went abroad. – She was been ill before she went abroad. – She had been ill before she went abroad.

Ü 2.

B. Verwenden Sie dem Kontext entsprechend *Present, Past, Present Perfect, Past Perfect*:

Fred and Mary

Fred: We (not meet) for ages.
Mary: I think, I (see) you at the theatre some weeks ago; but you (not see) me, you (talk) to a friend.
F.: (You, still work) at the university?
M.: No, I (change) my job. I now (work) as head of department in a design office.
F.: (You, finish) your doctoral thesis yet?
M.: Yes, I ..., I (finish) it last year.
F.: How long (you, work) in this design office?
M.: I (begin) to work there after I (take) my doctoral degree.
F.: I hear you (be married). When (you, get married)?
M.: I (get married) four years ago.
F.: (You, have got) children?
M.: Yes, I ... a boy and a girl. My daughter (be born) in 1985, my son (be) now one year old.
F.: (You, still live) in the flat you (have) when you (be) an assistant at the department of architecture?
M.: No, one year after I (get married) we (move) into a new flat. It (be) in the centre of the town and (have) four rooms. And where (you, work) now?
F.: I still (work) at the university. I (not finish) my doctoral thesis yet, but I (plan) to finish it this year.

2.5.
Übersetzen Sie ins Deutsche:

1. I'm not going to repeat this mistake.   2. We shan't leave before we have reached an agreement.   3. You won't be late, I'll give you a lift.   4. What are we going to have for dinner today?   5. You look tired, I'll make you a cup of coffee.   6. I'm not going to put up with Peter's arrogant behaviour.   7. These flats will be ready for occupancy next month.   8. When are you going to finish your diploma thesis?   9. Peter and Susan say they will be getting married soon.   10. We must hurry up, the plane will be taking off in a few minutes.   11. Don't worry, I'll repair the device for you.   12. Anne and Fred are having a housewarming party on Saturday. Are you going?   13. I'm afraid, our team won't be scoring any goals today.   14. You needn't write to Bob, I'm seeing him tomorrow.   15. We shall visit you tomorrow if we have time.   16. My girl-friend eats a lot of sweets, I'm afraid she is going to put on too much weight.   17. The play is a box-office success; it's going to be difficult to get tickets for it.   18. The fridge isn't working. – I'll see to it.
19. Excursion to Berlin on May, 21: The coach leaves at 7 a.m. sharp and arrives in Berlin at 9 a.m. approximately. Lunch is at 1.30 p.m. at the Hotel Berlin. The theatre performance starts at 7.00 p.m. The coach departs for home at 9.30 p.m.
20. The phone is ringing. – I'll answer it.

2.5.1.1.
Verwenden Sie in den folgenden Sätzen sowohl *will/shall*-Futur als auch *going to*:

1. I am writing a letter; Mary (post) it tomorrow morning. 2. We (have) a cup of coffee after the conference. 3. Susan (clean) the windows. 4. I think it (be) not tomorrow. 5. You (not see) Peter until next week. 6. We (think) about your proposal. 7. I (not repeat) this mistake. 8. The weather forecast says it (not rain) tomorrow. 9. What you (do) about this matter? 10. Bob has promised he (not make) this mistake again. 11. Which team do you think (win) the match? 12. I (give) you the book as soon as I have finished it.

2.5.1.2.
Reagieren Sie auf die angegebenen Situationen.

Beispiel: *This problem is very difficult for me. (help)* → *I'll help you.*

1. I am hungry. (make you a sandwich)
2. It's getting dark. (switch on the light)
3. Mary has forgotten to clean the window. (do)
4. I've lost my pencil. (look for)
5. Jane's trunk is very heavy. (carry)
6. My friend is short of money. (lend him some)

2.5.1.3.
Verwenden Sie im folgenden die Kombination *Past Simple* bzw. *Present Perfect* + *going to*:

1. Ich habe meinen Regenschirm verloren, morgen werde ich (mir) einen neuen kaufen (15.6.9.).[95]
2. Fred hat das Buch voriges Jahr gelesen, und es hat ihm sehr gefallen; deshalb will er es noch einmal lesen.[96]
3. Ich wollte den Brief heute vormittag schreiben, aber ich hatte keine Zeit. Ich werde ihn heute abend schreiben.
4. Gestern hat es geregnet, und heute wird es wieder regnen, glaube ich.
5. Ich habe die englischen Vokabeln (words) noch nicht gelernt, ich werde sie heute nachmittag lernen.
6. Bob hat sich vor einiger Zeit scheiden lassen (get a divorce), aber er wird wieder heiraten.
7. Wir sind vorgestern im Kino gewesen, und morgen werden wir uns wieder einen Film ansehen (see another film).
8. Ich war am Mittwoch beim Zahnarzt (at the dentist's), und übermorgen werde ich zu einem Internisten gehen (see an internist).
9. Jack hat sich mit seiner Freundin überworfen (fall out with), aber am Wochenende will er sich wieder mit ihr treffen.
10. Wann werdet ihr den Versuch wiederholen? – Wir haben es schon getan.

Ü 2.

2.5.1.
Entscheiden Sie, ob *going to* oder/und *will/shall* verwendet werden sollte:

1. Peter has told us he (be) 30 next month.[97] 2. There's no wine left, I ... go and get a bottle.[98] 3. I've lost my ring. ... you help me to look for it?[99] 4. Mary has told me she ... buy a new dress.[100] 5. Listen to my arguments, then you ... understand me.[101] 6. John has bought some tins of paint, he ... paint the fence over the weekend. 7. Wait a minute, I ... be with you right away. 8. Somebody is ringing, I ... go and answer the bell. 9. We don't have enough money on us, ... you accept a cheque? 10. Do you know when you (be) back? – I'm afraid, I (not be)[102] back until Friday. 11. Fetch me the hose, I ... water the garden. 12. We must save a lot of money because we ... buy a new car. 13. I think they ... be satisfied with our work. 14. Look at all these clouds, it (rain).[103] 15. I think Joe (be) able to pass the driving test. 16. When Jane (have) her baby?[104] 17. Wait a moment I (come) with you. 18. Next Monday (be) the first of May. 19. Where you (spend) your holidays this year? 20. This time next week we (be) at the Black Sea. 21. If we don't hurry up, we (miss) the train. 22. I'm afraid, you (not like) this wine. 23. Their wish probably (come true). 24. I (not make) a decision until I have thought the matter over. 25. Wait a moment, I (see) what I can do for you. 26. I (give) Jane the letter as soon as I see her. 27. Our dog (have) puppies soon, our neighbour's cat (have) kittens at about the same time. 28. We (wait) until you come. 29. I borrowed 100 marks from Bob. I (pay) him back next month. 30. You (get used) to the new method, when you have worked with it a little longer.

2.5.1.5. / 2.5.1.3.
Beachten Sie bei der Übersetzung den Unterschied von *going to* im *Präsens* und *Präteritum*:

1. What are you going to do over the weekend? / What were you going to do when we came?
2. I think it's going to snow tonight. / I didn't think it was going to snow.
3. I don't know what he's going to say. / What were you going to say when I interrupted you?
4. When is Bob going to start work on his diploma thesis? / When I last saw Bob he was going to start work on his diploma thesis.

2.5.2.
Fragen Sie Ihren Gesprächspartner, was er nächste Woche von Dienstag bis Sonntag abends tun wird, und lassen Sie ihn mit den folgenden Wendungen im *Present Continuous* antworten.

Beispiel: *What are you doing on Monday evening? – (ins Kino gehen)* → *I'm going to the pictures.*

Meinen Geburtstag feiern; lange (late) im Büro arbeiten; einkaufen gehen; eine Verabredung (date) mit meiner Freundin haben; zu Hause fernsehen; meinen Onkel treffen.

2.5.2. / 2.5.1.2.
Verwenden Sie in den folgenden Sätzen *Present Continuous* und *will/ shall*-Futur:
1. Ich sehe Helen heute abend; ich werde ihr die Fotos geben.[105]
2. Wir gehen morgen in einen Buchladen; wir werden versuchen, ein schönes Buch für deinen Freund zu bekommen.
3. Ich schreibe Alice heute abend; ich werde sie von dir grüßen (give s.b. one's kindest regards).
4. Bob ruft Joan heute abend an; er wird sie zu unserer Party einladen.
5. Wir gehen heute nachmittag aus; wir werden deinen Brief einwerfen (post).
6. Ich habe morgen eine Verabredung (appointment) mit unseren Kollegen aus Berlin. Ich werde ihnen sagen, daß du auch mit ihnen sprechen willst.

2.5.3. / 2.5.1.2.
Entscheiden Sie, ob *will/shall*-Futur oder/und *Future Continuous* zu verwenden ist:

1. When we arrive in Berlin Anne (wait) for us at the station. We (recognize) her very easily, she (wear) a red dress and white shoes.[106] 2. What do you think you (do) this time tomorrow? – I think I (have) a bottle of wine with my friends.[107] 3. I (not get) home till about nine today, because I (work) late at the office. 4. You should go to see Joan tomorrow, she (expect) you. 5. We can't work this afternoon, I (have) visitors. 6. Will you (come) to the club this evening? If so, we (meet) you there.

2.5.3.
Ergänzen Sie die Sätze mit dem *Future Continuous*:

1. Don't ring us tonight, we (visit) friends. 2. I haven't seen Tom for a long time, but I (see) him some time next week. 3. Mike is in Hungary now, he (come) back in May. 4. Can I have your typewriter tomorrow, or (you, use) it yourself? 5. Mr Smith already (read) his paper when we get to the conference hall. 6. Peter has stayed at home; I think he (watch TV) all evening.

2.5.6.
A. Übersetzen Sie:
1. Hurry up, we are about to leave. 2. I was about to go to bed when your telegram arrived. 3. Don't worry, Susan is sure to come. 4. Professor Baker's latest article is likely to attract a lot of attention. 5. Scotland Yard arrested the wanted criminal in Liverpool, where he was on the point of embarking for America. 6. Bob is not likely to accept such an offer. 7. A depression over Iceland is likely to cause wet weather in Britain tomorrow.

Ü 2.

B. Bilden Sie die folgenden Sätze je nach Aussage mit *likely* oder *unlikely/not likely* bzw. *certain/sure* um:
1. You will certainly enjoy this book.[108]   2. Jane will probably be very busy tomorrow.[109]   3. I am sure you will like Susan.   4. Probably Bill won't change his mind.   5. It is improbable that they will come to an agreement at once.   6. The device will probably cost a lot of money.   7. You will certainly be impressed by the exhibition.   8. It will probably take us a lot of time to solve this problem.

Komplexübungen zum Futur (2.5.)

A. Geben Sie englisch wieder. Beachten Sie, daß oft mehrere Möglichkeiten bestehen.

1. Ich werde heute nachmittag mein Fahrrad reparieren.   2. Mary hat viel (a lot of) Wolle gekauft. Sie will (= wird) einen Pullover stricken (knit).[110]   3. Erzähle John, was dich bedrückt (worry); er wird dich verstehen.[111]   4. Wo wird die Versammlung stattfinden?[112]   5. Janet heiratet zu Ostern.[113]   6. Wir fliegen übermorgen nach Moskau.   7. Ein Mechaniker (mechanic) kommt heute abend, er wird den Durchlauferhitzer (heating boiler) reparieren.[114]   8. Du hast vergessen, den Wagen zu waschen. – Entschuldige, ich werde es jetzt tun.   9. Was macht Susan heute abend? – Frage ihre Schwester, sie wird es wissen.[115]   10. Ich denke, Peter wird unserem Plan zustimmen.   11. Wir werden die Sache mit ihnen besprechen.   12. Paul wird seine Garage vermieten (sublet), weil er einige Jahre in Berlin arbeiten wird.   13. Gehst du am Sonnabend zu Rogers Party?   14. Wenn ich John heute abend zum Bahnhof bringe (take), werde ich zwei Flaschen Wein kaufen (get).   15. Wirst du an der Konferenz teilnehmen?   16. Einen Moment bitte, ich schreibe deine Telefonnummer auf, ehe ich sie vergesse.   17. Wann werdet ihr euch treffen?   18. Wann fährst du nach Prag?   19. Wann zieht ihr in eure neue Wohnung (move into)?   20. Man (they) wird uns nicht mehr bedienen (any more), das Restaurant schließt in einigen Minuten.
21. Kannst du mir sagen, wann das 21. Jahrhundert beginnt? – Ich denke, es beginnt am 1. Januar des Jahres 2000. – Nein, das ist nicht richtig, es beginnt am 1. Januar 2001.
22. Im Jahre 2005 werde ich 40 Jahre alt sein. – Meine Eltern werden 65 sein. – Ich glaube nicht, daß meine Großmutter dann noch leben wird (be alive). – Wenn sie noch lebt, wird sie fast 100 sein.

B. Geben Sie die beiden folgenden Dialoge englisch wieder, und entscheiden Sie, welche Form des Futurs jeweils anzuwenden ist, bzw. ob es mehrere Möglichkeiten gibt:

John und Fred
John: Gehst du heute abend zu Peters Geburtstagsfeier?
Fred: Ja, er hat mich eingeladen.
J.: Jane kommt auch. Sie hat ein Taxi bestellt, sie wird mich am Bahnhof mitnehmen (pick up). Wir werden dort Punkt 7.00 Uhr (at seven sharp) auf dich warten, wenn du nicht mit der Straßenbahn fahren willst.

F.: In Ordnung.
J.: Ich denke, es wird ein netter Abend werden (be). Wir werden uns gut amüsieren (have a good time). Peter wird uns ein gutes (substantial) Abendessen vorsetzen (serve). Später wird er Punsch machen (punch). Wir werden den ganzen Abend Schallplatten hören (listen to) und tanzen.

Mr Carter und Mr Baker
Mr Carter: Wo werden Sie Ihren Urlaub verbringen?
Mr Baker: Wir werden dieses Jahr nach Bulgarien reisen. Wir haben gerade von Freunden in Varna eine Einladung bekommen.
Mr C.: Wann wollen (werden) Sie fahren (leave)?
Mr B.: Wir fahren (go) Ende August.
Mr C.: Werden Sie fliegen oder mit der Bahn fahren?
Mr B.: Wir werden versuchen, (noch) einen Flug zu buchen. Aber ich fürchte, es wird schwierig sein. Deshalb fahren wir wahrscheinlich mit dem Zug.
Mr C.: Werden Sie die ganze Zeit in Varna bleiben?
Mr B.: Wir werden eine Woche dort sein. Dann werden uns unsere Freunde noch einige andere Orte (places) am Schwarzen Meer zeigen.

2.6.
A. Übersetzen Sie:

1. I think we shall have settled the matter before you come back.   2. We hope you will have realized by now that you have made a mistake.   3. I am sure our secretary will have prepared the documents by 2 p.m.   4. Mr Hunter is a dyed-in-the-wool pedagogue; by the end of the year he will have been teaching for a quarter of a century.

B. Verwenden Sie in den folgenden Sätzen *Past Tense* bzw. *Present Perfect* und *Future Perfect*:

1. I (begin) to put by money regularly 10 years ago, by the end of this year I (save) enough to buy a car.[116]   2. John not yet (inform) us whether he (return) by Friday.   3. Our friends (leave) two hours ago, they (get home) by now.   4. They (check) the calculations for the past three hours, I am sure they (find) the error by now.   5. Peter (tell) me repeatedly he hopes he (take) his doctoral degree by this time next year.   6. You (realize) in the meantime that Jack (be) reliable as long as we (know) him.

Komplexübungen zu Kapitel 2

A. Stellen Sie sich vor, Sie haben etwas nicht genau verstanden, und Sie fragen zurück.

Beispiel: *I talked to George about our project.* → *Who did you talk about our project to?* – *What did you talk to George about?*

1. I saw *Joan* yesterday.   2. Paolo is from *Sicily*.   3. I've parked my car *near the Zwinger*.   4. Jack's sister studies *chemistry*.   5. *Our head of department* wrote the

Ü 2.

letter.   6. Susan has been studying medicine *for three terms*.   7. We are going to plant some *peach* trees in my garden.   8. We are meeting *Rose at a jam session tonight*.   9. I want to talk to *Garret* about this matter.   10. I'm going to wait *for another 10 minutes*.   11. This book deals with *robotics*.   12. Paul and Paula have been married since *Whitsun*.   13. I was standing *at the bus stop* when the accident happened.   14. We are going *to the Baltic on Saturday*.   15. We asked our boss for *a day off*.   16. Tomorrow they'll show the film *'Limelight'* on TV.   17. Sue looks like a *beautician*.   18. I booked tickets for a *ballet*.   19. Jane kept us waiting *for two hours*.   20. I tried to look up the word *'hijacker'* in the dictionary.   21. Mother is looking for *her keys*.   22. My wife is afraid of *mice*.   23. One could take *Liz* for a pop star.   24. We ran into *Arthur* last night.   25. Mark has been ill *for a fortnight*.   26. We spoke to Jack *only a couple of minutes ago*.   27. We shall be having lunch *at the Palace Hotel tomorrow*.   28. Peter is going to dictate his manuscript to *Jill*.   29. I shall borrow *Ted's* dictionary.   30. I'm going to turn my shed into *a garage*.

B. Setzen Sie die in Klammern angegebenen Verben in die richtige Zeitform. Beachten Sie dabei den Unterschied zwischen *Simple Tenses* und *Continuous Tenses*:

It was 8 o'clock yesterday morning. I (drive) from Dresden to Potsdam. The roads (be) slippery, because it (rain) several hours the night before. That's why most of the cars (move) rather slowly. Though I (concentrate) completely on the road, I suddenly (see) a young girl standing at the roadside, who obviously (wait) for someone to give her a lift. Already from a distance she (strike) me as rather attractive. A heavy bag (stand) beside her. I (stop) the car and (ask) her, if she (want) a lift.
She (say): 'Yes, please, if you (go) to Potsdam. I (miss) the train this morning, and I (not want/wait) four hours until the next train (leave).'
'You are lucky, that's exactly where I (go).'
'I'm so glad. I (wait) for more than half an hour and lots of cars (pass by). I (be) afraid nobody (be going to) stop.'
The girl (get in) and (sit down) beside me. 'How long (you, think) it (take) us to get to Potsdam?' she asked.
'I (not know) exactly, because I (not go) this route before, I think we (be) there at about 11 o'clock.'
After a few minutes I realized I (begin) to like her, so I (try) to get some more information out of her. This (be) no problem because she (turn out) to be rather talkative.
'What (you, do) in Potsdam?'
'I (visit) a friend of mine who (teach) at a school there. We (know) each other for some years. We (make friends) while we (study) at a college of education. I (not see) her since we (take) our exams two years ago. She (get married) recently. Now she (expect) a baby. I (arrange) to stay a few days with her. And of course, I also want to know what kind of man she (be married) to. We (exchange) letters these two years, but she (not tell) me much about him.'
'And what about you? (You, be married), too?'
'No, I'm not. I (make up one's mind) not to get married so soon. I (travel) a lot since I (leave) college. Of course, I've got a boy-friend but I'm not sure yet if I

(marry) him. He (have) a car for some time, and we often (go) for a drive over the weekend.' 'I see. I (be going to) suggest that we meet again, but I'm afraid you (not like) the idea, if you go steady with someone.'
'Well, why shouldn't we meet again. As I (say), it's nothing final. Moreover, my boy-friend never (be) jealous so far, and I have always liked to talk to interesting people.'

3.1.
A. Übersetzen Sie:

1. How long do you think it would take you to translate this text? – I'm afraid it's rather difficult, it would take some days.   2. I would be glad to see you again next year.   3. Would you tell me what time it is?   4. Would it be possible to visit the testing ground?   5. I would never have guessed that Paula is a teacher.   6. Would it be convenient for you to call on us tomorrow?   7. Jean was rather tired last night; I suppose she would have preferred not to entertain guests.   8. Why didn't you invite Peter; I think he would have liked to come with us.   9. It would have taken too much time to walk all the distance.   10. It would have been easier to perform these calculations with the help of a computer.   11. Compulsory road education for cyclists and pedestrians would reduce traffic accidents considerably.   12. Who would have thought of manned space flight fifty years ago?

B. Geben Sie englisch wieder:

1. Ich würde die Angelegenheit sofort klären (settle).   2. Würden Sie mir einen Gefallen tun (favour)?   3. Ich hätte dein Angebot angenommen.[117]   4. Wäre es möglich, den Ausflug zu verschieben (postpone)?   5. Nora sagt, sie wäre gern Tänzerin geworden.[118]   6. Ich wollte Anne von meinen Problemen erzählen; aber ich glaube, sie hätte mich nicht verstanden. (s. Kap. 1, Fußnote 9)[119]   7. Jane hat sich sehr (a lot) verändert; ich glaube nicht, daß du sie wiedererkannt hättest (recognize).   8. Wärst du bereit, uns zu helfen?   9. John wird nicht wissen, daß wir auf ihn warten. Wäre es nicht besser gewesen, ihn vorher anzurufen?   10. Wir sind mit der Straßenbahn gefahren; es hätte zu lange gedauert zu laufen (walk).[120]   11. Was hättest du an meiner Stelle getan (in my place)?   12. Wieviel würde es kosten, die Uhr zu reparieren? – Es wäre ziemlich teuer. Ich würde Ihnen empfehlen (recommend), eine neue (L 15.6.9.) zu kaufen.

3.2.
Übersetzen Sie:

1. We won't arrive on time, if we don't hurry up.   2. If I knew his address I would write him a letter.   3. We'll be back by 8 o'clock unless the train is late.   4. Wouldn't it be better if you told us the truth?   5. If I were you I would buy this stereo-recorder.   6. What would you have said if John had asked you?   7. We would be glad if you stayed over the weekend.   8. I won't phone unless I'm prevented.   9. We shall sign the contract provided (that) the terms are favourable.   10. I'll come even if I don't feel well.   11. We wouldn't have disturbed you if we

Ü 3.

had known you were so busy.   12. I'll give the keys to my neighbour in case the plumber is coming while I'm away.   13. Peter hasn't worked much recently, I shouldn't be surprised if he failed the exam.   14. I shouldn't have been late if my watch hadn't run down.   15. They will print your article in the next issue of the journal on condition that you submit it this week.   16. If it wasn't for the fact that I have to drive I would drink another glass of wine.   17. I don't know what would have happened if the brakes had failed, when the lorry suddenly came round the corner.   18. Sue and Liz wouldn't have stopped talking if their husbands hadn't shouted for lunch.

3.2.1.
A. Was wird geschehen, wenn ...?

Beispiele: *(I) see Jane/ask her* → *If I see Jane, I'll ask her.* – *(You) not work hard/not pass the examination* → *If you don't work hard/Unless you work hard, you won't pass the examination.*

1. (I) have time/come on Sunday.   2. (They) not take a taxi/be late.   3. (I) meet Oliver/inform him.   4. (We) get tickets/phone you.   5. (You) not eat less/put on too much weight.   6. (We) want to go to the theatre/have to organize a baby-sitter.   7. (You) not pay for the damage/get into trouble   8. (I) not too busy/go to the pictures tomorrow.

B. Bilden Sie Sätze mit *if not/unless* nach folgendem Muster:

Either you apologize or Fred will be angry. → *If you don't apologize/Unless you apologize Fred will be angry.*

1. Either we wait or we won't meet Susan until next week.   2. Either you marry Janet or she will leave you.   3. Either we turn down the radio or the neighbours will complain.   4. Either you do physical exercises or you won't keep fit.   5. Either I do the work now or I'll never do it.

3.2.2.
A. Was würde geschehen, wenn ...?

Beispiel: *If we (leave) now, we just (catch) the train.* → *If we left now, we'd just catch the train.*

1. If we (have) Jack's address we (send) him a note.   2. If I (know) John's telephone number, I (give) him a ring.   3. If the weather (be) better, we (make) a trip today.[121]   4. Peter (be) very disappointed, if you (not invite) him.[122]   5. I (go) swimming every day, if we (have) a swimming pool.   6. What (you, do), if you (win) a large sum on the pools?   7. If I (be) you, I (install) gas-heating.   8. What (you, say), if I (not be able) to pay back the money as agreed upon?   9. Wendy (be) unhappy, if William (not take) her out tonight.   10. How (you, feel) if you (become) head of department?   11. Which dictionary (you, use), if you (have to) translate an article about civil engineering?   12. How (you, behave), if your wife (fall) in love with another man?/... if your husband (fall) in love with another woman?

B. Was wäre, wenn ...?

Beispiel: *We (be) glad/you (visit) us soon.* → *We would be glad if you visited us soon.*
1. Bob (get married)/he (find) the right girl.   2. You (know) Peggy better/you (understand) her.[123]   3. We (save) a lot of time/we (go by car).   4. I (not be) so busy/ I (go) to the theatre more frequently.   5. The room (look) better/you (repaper) it.   6. I (have) enough time/I (type) the manuscript.   7. It (be) less expensive/we (buy) a second-hand car.   8. We (be) glad/you (visit) us at Christmas.

C. Fragen Sie, was geschehen könnte, wenn ..., und geben Sie nach eigenem Ermessen Antworten:

1. Where (you, go) for a holiday if (you, have) plenty of money?   2. What places of interest (you, want) to visit if you (go) to Leningrad?   3. What (you, do) if (your car, break down)?   4. (You, prefer) to live in the country or in a big town if (you, have) the choice?   5. Where (you, go) if (you, lose) your umbrella?   6. How do you think (your wife, react) if (you, forget) your wedding day?   7. What (you, do) if you (go) to an expensive restaurant and the waiter (be) rather impolite?   8. How (you, feel) if your girl-friend (let) you down?   9. What famous film star (you, like) to meet if (you, have) the chance?   10. What (you, do) if your neighbour (be blowing) the trumpet all night?   11. What (you, say) if one of your guests (come) to your wedding party in shorts?   12. What first name (you, choose) for yourself if you (have) a chance to change it?

D. Sie sagen einem Freund, der an Kreislaufbeschwerden leidet, was Sie an seiner Stelle tun würden, und beginnen jeweils mit *If I were you* ....

zeitig zu Bett gehen; nicht so lange fernsehen; früh nicht so spät aufstehen; rechtzeitig die Wohnung verlassen; nicht zur Straßenbahnhaltestelle rennen; sich nicht mit Kollegen streiten (quarrel); nicht so viel Kaffee während der Arbeit trinken; das Rauchen einschränken (cut down on smoking); nach der Arbeit spazierengehen; mehrmals in der Woche Gymnastik treiben (do physical exercises).

3.2.3.
A. Was wäre geschehen, wenn ...?

Beispiel: *If you (come) earlier you (meet) Jane.* → *If you had come earlier you would have met Jane.*
1. If I (see) John, I (inform) him.   2. If we (not book) a room we (not know) where to stay overnight.   3. I (oversleep) if I (not set) the alarm-clock.   4. If you (not be driving) so fast the policeman (not stop) you and you (not be fined).[124]   5. I (try) to get tickets if there (not be) such a long queue.   6. If George (not be late) for work so often he (not be dismissed).   7. If Bob (not hold me up) I (catch) the train.   8. If we (know) the service was so slow we (go) to a self-service café.

B. Fragen Sie, was geschehen wäre, wenn ..., und geben Sie Antworten:

1. Do you think (Susan, be) very angry if (we, forget) her birthday?[125]   2. What (happen) if Tom (not stop) at the stop sign?   3. How (you, feel) if they (make) you

Ü 3.

our new boss? 4. What (you, do) if your girl-friend (go) on holiday with Peter?
5. How do you think (Fred, react) if Jane (ask) him to marry her? 6. What (your wife, say) if you (not come) home last night?

C. Boy Meets Girl
Verbinden Sie die folgenden Feststellungen miteinander. Beginnen Sie jeweils mit *If ... hadn't.*

Mike went to Jack's party. He saw Maud.[126] He asked Jack to introduce him to her. He enjoyed the party very much. He stayed until midnight. He danced with Maud very often. The two of them fell in love with each other. They got engaged.

D. Verknüpfen Sie die in der folgenden Erzählung hervorgehobenen Feststellungen durch Bedingungssätze:

Beispiel: *Last Sunday we made a trip to the mountains. Lots of things happened that we had not foreseen. **It was raining most of the morning, so we got wet through.***
Sagen Sie also: *If it had not been raining most of the morning we wouldn't have got wet through.*
We had not listened to the weather forecast; therefore we didn't take our raincoats with us.[127] But there were other unpleasant things as well. *We lost our way because we had left the map at home.*[128] After some hours we felt hungry. Finally we came to a restaurant. *But since it was already a quarter past two they didn't serve lunch any more.*[129] In the afternoon *it began to rain again, and we got soaked a second time.*[130] So we decided to return home. On the way to the bus stop *I stumbled and sprained my ankle, and so I was not able to walk fast.*[131] *We got to the bus stop so late that the bus had already gone.*[132] *We had to wait two hours until the next bus came*; that's why *it was late in the evening when we got home.*[133]

3.2.1. / 3.2.2. / 3.2.3.
A. Setzen Sie die vorgegebenen Verben in die richtige Form:

1. If you (not put on) a coat today you will probably catch a cold. 2. Mrs Mason (be) very glad if her husband gave up smoking. 3. I would have enjoyed the party more if Jane (come). 4. If I (be) you I would accept the offer. 5. We (be) late for the theatre unless we go by car. 6. If you had taken my advice you (not make) this mistake. 7. I would be disappointed if there (be) no chance to have another talk before you leave. 8. If you (read) this book a second time you would perhaps have understood it. 9. What (we, do) if we miss the train? 10. If these shoes were my size I (buy) them. 11. It (be) a nice crossing if the sea hadn't been so rough. 12. I would not buy the painting even if it (be) cheaper. 13. If you play the piano late at night, the neighbours (bang, continuous form) on the wall. 14. We (go) without you if you hadn't come. 15. I am sure Sue will lose weight if she (go) on a diet. 16. If the weather had changed we (go) for an outing. 17. How do you think Susan (react) if I invited her? 18. If you had set your alarm-clock you (not oversleep).

B. Geben Sie englisch wieder:

1. In unserem Kino läuft ein interessanter Film (be on at our cinema). Wenn ich Zeit habe, werde ich ihn mir am Wochenende ansehen (go and see).
2. Peter ist selten pünktlich. Ich würde mich nicht wundern (be surprised), wenn er wieder zu spät käme (be late).[134]
3. Der Unfall hätte sich nicht ereignet, wenn sich die beiden Fahrer an die Geschwindigkeitsgrenze gehalten hätten (keep within the speed limit).[135]
4. Susan kommt am Sonntag nach Rostock. Sie würde sich freuen, wenn du sie am Bahnhof abholst (meet).[136]
5. Beeile dich, wir werden den Bus nicht erreichen, wenn wir nicht sofort gehen (leave).
6. Du siehst gut aus (17.4.) in diesem Anzug, an deiner Stelle würde ich ihn kaufen.[137]
7. Warum bist du weggegangen? Du hättest Mary getroffen, wenn du noch (another) 10 Minuten gewartet hättest.
8. Falls es am Sonnabend nicht regnet, werden wir im Garten grillen (have a barbecue).
9. Der Flug hätte sich nicht verzögert (be delayed), wenn nicht Nebel (fog) am Flughafen gewesen wäre.[138]
10. Das Warenhaus schließt um 19.00 Uhr. Wir werden nicht rechtzeitig hinkommen (get), wenn wir so langsam gehen (17.1.).
11. Wenn der Zug pünktlich gewesen wäre, hätten wir den Anschluß (connection) nicht verpaßt.
12. Ich mag die Kriminalromane von Agatha Christie. Wenn ich besser Englisch könnte (know), würde ich sie in Englisch lesen.
13. Was wärst du gern geworden, wenn du nicht Chemiker geworden wärst?[139]
14. Wenn ich im Lotto oder Toto gewinnen würde (have a win on the pools), würde ich zuerst (first of all) alle meine Freunde einladen und mit ihnen ein paar Flaschen Sekt trinken. Dann würde ich eine Kreuzfahrt (cruise) auf dem Schwarzen Meer machen. Wenn ich eine große Summe gewinnen würde, würde ich ein Haus mit einem Garten kaufen.
15. Wenn ich voriges Wochenende eine große Summe im Lotto oder Toto gewonnen hätte, hätte ich sofort eine Reise nach Samarkand gebucht (book a journey).

3.3.1. / 3.3.2. / 3.3.4. / 3.3.5. Komplexübungen

Setzen Sie die Verben in die richtige Form, und ergänzen Sie, wo erforderlich, das fehlende Hilfsverb:

1. If you multiply 11 by 11 you (get) 121. 2. If you (lose) your cheque-book you ... tell the bank.[140] 3. Take your umbrella with you in case it ... rain this afternoon.[141] 4. If you mix black and white you (get) grey. 5. John ... read the book provided I (get) it back next Friday. 6. My wife (not want) another fur coat if our neighbour (not buy) a new one. (3.3.4.)[142] 7. If you ... wait a few minutes I ... try to find the book. (3.3.2.)[143] 8. If Mary ... come tell her I (be) a bit late.[144]

Ü 4.

9. ... Tom arrive early ask him to wait.[145] 10. If uncle Richard (be) hard of hearing he ... wear a hearing-aid.[146] 11. You ... make an omelette if you (not have) eggs. 12. If you ... cook the dinner I (do) the washing-up afterwards. (3.3.2.)[147] 13. If I ... be late don't wait for me. 14. If you (take) my advice you (not be) in a difficult position now. (3.3.4.) 15. If they (build) a cinema in the vicinity we (go) to the pictures more frequently. (3.3.4.) 16. If they (install) a lift in the building we (not have) to walk up so many stairs. (3.3.4.) 17. If you ... need to consult me again you ... contact me at the office this afternoon.[148] 18. If only Jim (listen) to reason, he (not be) in trouble now. (3.3.4.)

4.1./4.2.
A. Übersetzen Sie:

1. The new shopping centre will be opened next month. 2. John can't use my typewriter, it hasn't been repaired yet. 3. We have been told that Peter is ill. 4. If I am offered this job, I shall accept it. 5. Have you been given an interesting topic for your diploma thesis? 6. The Japanese visitors will be shown the sights of our town. 7. My mother-in-law does not like to be contradicted. 8. We were told that the castle had been restored the year before. 9. The students will be given half an hour to summarize this article. 10. We have been granted a long-term credit. 11. If you had followed my advice you would have been spared a lot of inconvenience. 12. It is a fact that safe driving is adversely affected even by very small amounts of alcohol.
13. Last year we visited Venus, a Romanian seaside resort, which was designed entirely by women architects. 14. Yesterday's lecture on town planning was followed by a heated debate. 15. Dresden's famous Christmas Cakes, called 'Stollen', have been baked since approximately 1400. 16. The results of the tests remain to be checked. 17. On April 12, 1961, the first manned space vehicle was launched by Soviet scientists. 18. Plastics have been used for more than half a century. 19. The famous Soviet writer Mikhail Sholokhov was awarded the Nobel Prize for literature in 1965. 20. Penicillin has been used as an antibiotic since it was discovered by Alexander Fleming in 1928. 21. It is common knowledge that some of our natural resources will have been exhausted by the middle of the 21st century. 22. For about 30 years the terms 'laser' and 'maser' have been applied. 23. Hundreds of houses have been destroyed by an earthquake in Jugoslavia. Twelve people were killed, some eighty injured. 24. For many centuries atoms were considered the smallest particles of nature. It was not until the discovery of electrons that this assumption came to be refuted.
25. The geocentric conception of the universe which had been formulated by Ptolemy about 140 A.D. continued to be taken for granted until the 16th century. It was called in question by Copernicus and later disproved by Galileo. In 1633, one of the most famous trials in the history of science took place when Galilei was accused of heresy by the Inquisition and forced to revoke his theory.
26. Historical descriptions of viral diseases may be traced back as far as the 10th century BC. From the 18th century the virus that causes cowpox was used in vaccines to prevent smallpox. Since Louis Pasteur developed a weakened rabies vi-

rus (Tollwutvirus) for therapeutic use in 1884, viruses have been increasingly applied in medicine. But it was not until the independent discovery of viruses that infect bacteria by the two bacteriologists Twort and d'Hérelle in 1915 and 1917, respectively, that modern virology came to be established.

B. Verwandeln Sie die folgenden Sätze in Passivsätze, wobei die eingeklammerten Wörter nicht mehr erscheinen.

1. (They) opened a new youth club last week.[149]   2. Several thousand people attended the performances of the film festival.   3. (You) must finish the translation by eight o'clock today.   4. I don't think (anyone) can solve this problem today.   5. (We) ought to discuss this matter at once.   6. (They) have to repeat the test.   7. (You) should tidy up the room.   8. I think (one) could find a better solution.   9. How much did (they) pay you for your old car?   10. Our director will sign the contract tomorrow.   11. (Someone) should tell us what to do.   12. Did (they) give Fred a bonus?   13. Has (someone) made the necessary arrangements?   14. (Someone) must teach Peter a lesson.[150]   15. Do you know why (they) haven't offered Jim the job?   16. Didn't (they) promise you a reward?   17. (Someone) should adjust the brakes.   18. (I) have to change the tyres.   19. (Somebody) must replace the spark-plug.   20. (They) ought to repair the left mudguard.   21. (We) have to check the battery.   22. N. A. Otto developed the four-stroke internal-combustion engine in 1876.   23. Where can (one) use robots in modern industry?   24. In 1643, Torricelli invented the barometer by which (one) can measure the atmospheric pressure.   25. (Somebody) has stolen Bob's car. (They) didn't find out until after some hours that (somebody) had stolen it. (They) finally discovered that (someone) had abandoned the car in a side-street and stripped it of most of his fittings (Zubehör). The police arrested the car thief after they had tracked him down in his flat.

C. Bilden Sie Mini-Dialoge nach folgendem Muster:

Beispiel: *bring back the book*: *Has the book been brought back yet? – No, it hasn't. – Can you tell me when it will be brought back?*

repair the car; open the exhibition; hold the conference; carry out the experiment; check the results; publish the article; give the slide-lecture on Tanzania; show the film on TV; make the analysis

D. Vervollständigen Sie die folgenden Sätze mit den vorgegebenen Verben:

1. In Scotland, kilts (wear) by men and women.[151]   2. English (speak) in many countries of the world.   3. Visitors (request) not to touch the exhibits.   4. The negotiations (resume) last week.   5. The mistake (not find) yet.   6. In this experiment the temperature must (keep) constant.[152]   7. These goods should (handle) with great care.   8. This problem (discuss) at our next meeting.   9. We just (tell) that John is abroad.[153]   10. Take some of these cherries, they just (pick).   11. You (meet) at the station when you come to Berlin.[154]   12. Bob (give) a serum yesterday, because he (bite) by a snake.[155]   13. Cotton (grow) in Egypt.   14. These medicaments should (keep) out of the reach of children.   15. Esperanto (teach) in

special courses only.   16. A great deal of research (do) into the development of new computers during the past decades.

E. Beantworten Sie folgende Fragen:

1. What foreign languages were you taught at school?   2. How much are you paid a month?   3. What is a patient given when he has severe pains?   4. In an examination at a university – who is asked what by whom?   5. Which is a student granted – a scholarship or a fee?   6. Which syllable is stressed in the word 'catastrophe'?   7. How is the capital of Austria spelled and pronounced?   8. Who was the novel 'David Copperfield' written by?

F. Beantworten Sie folgende Fragen; verwenden Sie dabei das Passiv:

1. When did they build the Eiffel Tower? (in 1889)[156]   2. Who wrote the novel 'War and Peace'? (Tolstoy)   3. Who appoints the British Prime Minister? (the King or Queen)   4. Where and when did they build the first railway line? (between Stockton and Darlington in Britain in 1825)   5. Who discovered radioactivity? (Becquerel)

G. Bilden Sie selbst Fragen im Aktiv wie in den Sätzen der Übung F und antworten Sie im Passiv:

introduce coffee in Europe (in the 16th century);[157] develop the atomic model (Niels Bohr);[158] hold the first Olympic Games (776 BC); launch the first artificial satellite (in 1957); reopen the Dresden Semper Opera (13th February, 1985); write the play 'The Marriage of Figaro' (Beaumarchais).

H. Geben Sie bei den folgenden Fragen die richtige Antwort, und verwenden Sie dabei das Passiv:

1. Do they speak French in Chile? (Spanish)[159]   2. Do they grow rice in Sweden and Denmark? (India and China)   3. Do physicists treat patients? (physicians)   4. Do physicians deal with physics? (physicists)   5. Do plumbers sell plums? (greengrocers)   6. Do technicians do research work in technology? (scientists)   7. Do cows catch mice? (cats)   8. Do carpenters make carpets? (weavers)   9. Do motorists design motors? (engineers)   10. Can one grow wine in the Antarctic? (for example in ...).

I. Bilden Sie Fragen im Aktiv, antworten Sie im Passiv, und korrigieren Sie dabei die absurden Angaben:

Beispiel: *find the sea-route to India (Columbus)* → *Did Columbus find the sea-route to India? – No, he didn't. The sea-route to India was found by Vasco da Gama.*

cross the North Pole in an airship (Galileo)
build the Dresden Zwinger (Semper)
invent the telephone (Leonardo da Vinci)
write Don Carlos (Karl May)
make the first parachute (Philipp Reis)
beat the Spanish Armada in 1588 (Argentina)

develop the Periodic Table of the Elements (Röntgen)
design the Dresden Opera House (Pöppelmann)
develop the law of falling bodies (Amundsen)
win the Football World Championship in 1986 (Britain)
write 'The Treasure in the Silver Lake'(Schiller)
discover the X-rays (Mendeleyev).

J. Geben Sie englisch wieder:

1. Jedes Jahr werden Tausende von Menschen in Verkehrsunfällen getötet oder verletzt (injure). 2. Was stellt man in diesem Betrieb her?[160] 3. Der Versuch ist soeben beendet worden.[161] 4. Diese Richtlinien (instructions) müssen genau befolgt werden.[162] 5. Ist der Vertrag schon unterzeichnet worden? 6. Dieser Vorschlag ist sehr gut, man sollte ihn unterstützen. 7. In welchem Stadtteil wird man das neue Motel bauen? 8. Die Friedenskundgebung (peace rally) wurde von mehr als tausend Menschen besucht. 9. Wissen Sie, ob dieser Artikel schon übersetzt worden ist? 10. Die Ausstellung wird morgen vom Präsidenten der Geographischen Gesellschaft eröffnet werden. 11. Hat man Ihnen (schon) gesagt, wann die Delegation ankommt?[163] – Man wird uns die genaue Zeit morgen mitteilen. 12. Peter übertreibt (exaggerate) oft, man kann seinen Geschichten nicht immer glauben. 13. Ist Ihnen ein günstiger Preis (a fair price) für den Bungalow angeboten worden? 14. Wenn man uns gesagt hätte, daß einige Teilnehmer verhindert sind, hätten wir die Besprechung verschoben (postpone).[164] 15. Die Versuchsreihe muß fortgesetzt werden, sobald die Zwischenergebnisse (intermediate results) ausgewertet worden sind (evaluate).[165] 16. Ich hoffe, man wird uns die Versuchsanlage (pilot plant) zeigen, die vor einiger Zeit fertiggestellt wurde. 17. Der Brand konnte erst unter Kontrolle gebracht werden (get under control), nachdem beträchtlicher Sachschaden (material damage) verursacht worden war.[166] 18. Das neue Wasserkraftwerk (hydroelectric power station) wird nächsten Monat in Betrieb genommen (put into operation). 19. Die Buchdruckerkunst (printing) wurde 1450 von Gutenberg erfunden und 1476 von Caxton in England eingeführt. 20. Radioaktive Isotope werden seit einigen Jahrzehnten in der Industrie verwendet. 21. Shakespeares Stücke werden überall in der Welt aufgeführt. 22. Die USA (L 19.4.5.) wurden 1776 gegründet. 23. Die Romane von Mark Twain sind in viele Sprachen übersetzt worden. 24. Die Sixtinische (Sistine) Madonna wurde von Raffael gemalt. 25. 1964 wurde Martin Luther King der Friedensnobelpreis verliehen.

4.3.
A. Übersetzen Sie:

1. We have some very old trees in our garden that are going to be cut down next month. 2. The manuscript should be looked through before it is handed in. 3. Such useless quarrels ought to be put a stop to once for all. 4. Some details of the contract still have to be dealt with before an agreement can be arrived at. 5. This is an opportunity that should be taken advantage of. 6. The negotiations will fail unless a compromise is agreed on. 7. I'm afraid your request

Ü 4. 160

can't be complied with.   8. The proposals that have been put forward should be gone into very carefully.   9. The twentieth century is often referred to as the age of the atom.   10. The various possible causes of cancer have not yet been fully accounted for.   11. Pop singers and rock groups are usually made a great fuss of by their fans.   12. Present-day computers may be thought of as counterparts of the human brain.   13. Apartheid cannot be simply reformed, it must be done away with completely.   14. Throughout G. B. Shaw's plays the British way of life is made fun of.   15. There is increasing agreement on an international scale that the danger of environmental pollution must be provided against by all possible means.

B. Vervollständigen Sie die folgenden Sätze:

1. The new words must (look up) in a dictionary.[167]   2. The agreement (draw up) next week.   3. I hope my request (not turn down) when it (talk about) tomorrow.[168]   4. The verbs 'raise' and 'rise' often (mix up).   5. While the Bakers were on holiday their flat (break into).   6. Joan seems to be seriously ill; why a doctor (not send for) yet?[169]   7. I just (tell) that the conference must (put off).   8. This problem not yet (deal with).[170]   9. The questionnaire has to (fill in) quite exactly; this is a formality that can't (dispense with).[171]   10. The matter not yet (look into).   11. The jet plane (lose sight of) shortly after it had taken off.   12. The truth has to (face up to).   13. A new series of tests (carry out) next week.   14. How can the necessary changes (bring about)?   15. These questions should (bring up) at our next meeting.   16. This place looks as if it (not live in) for a long time.

C. Vervollständigen Sie die folgenden Sätze mit dem jeweils passenden Verb. Verwenden Sie jedes Verb nur einmal:

break into – call off – go through – insist on – look after – look up to – look upon as – make out – make up of – make up for – object to – put up with – rely on – step up – sum up – switch on – talk about – take up

1. Somebody must have come; the light ... just ....[172]   2. Our garage ... some days ago.   3. The match may have to ..., the ground is too slippery.   4. Are you sure that these data can ...?   5. At yesterday's jazz festival the audience ... largely ... teenage fans.   6. Mary is rather unhappy these days, she should ....[173]   7. I am afraid our project might ... by the committee.   8. Prescriptions ... by doctors.   9. This idea is very good, it should ....   10. The calculations must ....   11. There are always things that must ....   12. Dr Martin ... a brilliant surgeon.   13. Let's think about how the loss of time can ....[174]   14. A resumption of the talks should ....[175]   15. Professor Smith is a scientist who ... by all his colleagues.[176]   16. The details of the plan must ... very carefully.   17. For purposes of documentation the article must ... on one page.   18. As a result of several innovations, production ... considerably ... in our plant within the past two years.

D. Geben Sie englisch wieder; verwenden Sie dem Kontext entsprechend die folgenden Verben:

agree on – agree to – carry out – deal with – fill in – hand in – look into – look through – lose sight of – make fun of – make use of – put forward – put off – refer to – size up – speak about – talk about – think over

Ü 4.

1. Die Versammlung muß verschoben werden. 2. Über dieses Thema ist noch nicht gesprochen worden.[177] 3. Vergessen Sie nicht, den Fragebogen (questionnaire) auszufüllen; er muß heute abgegeben werden. 4. Die Angelegenheit sollte sorgfältig überprüft werden.[178] 5. Wissen Sie, was für Themen man auf der Konferenz behandeln wird? 6. Ist die Übersetzung schon durchgesehen worden? 7. Auf Einzelheiten wird im nächsten Kapitel verwiesen. 8. Das Problem sollte noch einmal überdacht werden, ehe eine Entscheidung getroffen wird (make/take a decision). 9. Ich verstehe nicht, warum über dieses Problem noch nicht gesprochen worden ist. 10. Wir hoffen, man wird unserem Vorschlag zustimmen. 11. Ich mag es nicht, wenn man sich über mich lustig macht (L 8.7.1.).[179] 12. Man sollte diese Sache nicht aus den Augen verlieren.[180] 13. Zunächst muß man sich auf die Tagesordnung (agenda) einigen. 14. Die Situation wurde von den Rednern unterschiedlich (differently) eingeschätzt. 15. Einige Berechnungen sind noch durchzuführen (remain + passivischer Infinitiv), ehe endgültige (final) Ergebnisse vorgetragen werden können.[181] 16. CAD/CAM-Verfahren werden in vielen Industriezweigen angewandt.

4.4.
Bilden Sie Passivsätze mit *it*, wobei die eingeklammerten Wörter nicht mehr erscheinen.

1. (They) hope that a solution will soon be found.[182] 2. (We) fear that the committee will not approve of our project. 3. (They) believe that the fire was caused by carelessness.[183] 4. (They) have decided to continue the negotiations.[184] 5. (They) claim that the drug produces no undesirable side-effects. 6. (They) have proved that the hypothesis is correct. 7. (Somebody) suggested that the talks should be postponed. 8. (They) have announced that the plane will be delayed by an hour. 9. (They) have planned that the new residential area will be completed by August next year. 10. There are estimates that the costs for the project will amount to 300,000 marks.[185] 11. There have been reports that new oil deposits have been discovered in the North Sea. 12. (One) should remember that new inventions and discoveries have often met with indifference or even opposition.

4.5./4.6.1.
A. Beachten Sie bei der Übersetzung die unterschiedliche Bedeutung der Passivformen:

1. A new department store is being built in the centre of our town. 2. You can have the results in a few minutes; the calculations are just being checked. 3. When we passed the theatre the performance was already finished and the lights were just being turned out. 4. The test was being started the moment we came into the laboratory, and it was not yet finished when we left. 5. You can't have the film today, it isn't developed yet. – You can have the film tomorrow, it is being developed right now. 6. A medical examination revealed that the patient's spine was seriously injured. – The driver was seriously injured in the accident.

Ü 4.

7. We couldn't enter the park because the gate was locked. – When we came to the park the gate was being locked. – The door has been locked all day. – Our front door is locked at ten every day.
8. The letter is typed, you can sign it. – The letter is being typed, you can sign it in half an hour. – Business letters are usually signed by our head of department. – The letters can't be mailed yet, they aren't signed.
9. My car is usually repaired by a very reliable mechanic; that's why I was astonished that it was not repaired the day before yesterday when I wanted to get it back. At my request it was repaired yesterday. I am glad that it is repaired now because I shall need it badly tomorrow.
10. We couldn't buy anything to drink, because the shops were already closed. – When we came to the shopping arcade the shops were just being closed. – The restaurant has been closed for several years. I wonder if it will ever be reopened. – Some weeks ago the restaurant was closed for one year. – The restaurant was closed one year for purposes of renovation, yesterday it was reopened. – The restaurant is closed for some months. – The restaurant will be closed until the end of the year.

B. Entscheiden Sie, ob die einfache Form oder die Verlaufsform des Passivs zu verwenden ist:

1. I must go by train today; my car (repair).[186]   2. The shop at the corner (close)[187] all day yesterday.   3. When we visited the exhibition hall, an interesting experiment (demonstrate).[188]   4. Mary always well (prepare) for her examinations. 5. Many old houses now (pull down) in our town to make way for new buildings. – The old theatre (pull down) two years ago, now a modern one (erect) at the same place.   6. Last week my flat (do up). – I stayed with a friend last week because my flat (do up).   7. Jane's sitting-room (redecorate) every three years. – Jane doesn't receive visitors these days, her sitting-room (redecorate).   8. The letter still (type) when I wanted to sign it. – The letter (type), but it (not sign) yet by the manager. – Wait a minute, the letter just (type).

C. Geben Sie englisch wieder:

1. Unsere Koffer sind gepackt.[189] – Unsere Koffer werden gerade von meiner Frau gepackt.[190]   2. Die Konferenz war gut vorbereitet. – Die Konferenz wird zur Zeit von einigen unserer Assistenten vorbereitet.   3. Im Süden unserer Stadt entsteht (build) ein neues Wohngebiet (residential area). Jeden Monat werden etwa 100 Wohnungen fertiggestellt (complete).   4. Wir kommen zu spät, das Geschäft ist schon geschlossen. – Mehrere Geschäfte wurden geschlossen, weil die Gebäude baufällig sind (in disrepair). – Das Geschäft an der Ecke ist seit mehreren Monaten geschlossen, es wird nächsten Monat wieder eröffnet werden. – Als wir um die Ecke kamen (turn the corner), wurde das Geschäft gerade geschlossen.

4.6.2. / 4.6.3.
A. Übersetzen Sie:

1. Jim's trousers got torn when he climbed over the fence.   2. Do you know why Mike didn't get invited to the party?   3. Our carpet got damaged when we moved

out. 4. Mary is a shy girl; she gets confused each time a boy wants to embrace her. 5. Are you dressed for going out? – No, I'm just getting dressed. 6. My beautiful vase is broken; I wonder how it got smashed. 7. John has been interested in chess for many years. After he got married he also became interested in classical music. 8. Fontane had been known as a journalist for many years before he became known as a novelist.

B. Bilden Sie Sätze im Passiv mit *be* bzw. *get/become*, wobei zu beachten ist, daß in einigen Fällen beide Formen möglich sind:

1. When (this church, built)?[191] 2. Lots of houses (destroyed)[192] during the thunderstorm. 3. How (the pane, broken)?[193] 4. John (caught)[194] by the police exceeding the speed limit. 5. (you, acquainted) with Mary? – Yes, I ... – When (you, acquainted)[195] with her? 6. Walking down the street I nearly (hit)[196] by a brick that fell from the roof. 7. When (Jane, engaged)[197]? 8. How long (you, married)?[198] 9. Mike and Marion (divorced)[199] last year, she never (used)[200] to his stinginess. 10. Have you (used)[201] to the American pronunciation of English?

4.7.
Übersetzen Sie:

1. This material is rather cheap, but it does not wash. 2. Our front door doesn't lock easily. 3. This type of car drives very easily. 4. Rice digests well. 5. Susan bought this dress five years ago, it has worn well. 6. Your situation does not compare with mine. 7. Such spots won't wash off well. 8. Shaw's plays act better than those of T. S. Eliot.

Komplexübungen zum Passiv

A. Übersetzen Sie, wobei Sie die Verben in die zutreffende Form bringen:

Among the first fossil fuels that (exploit) were wood, coal, and gas. About 1000 BC natural gas already (make use of) in China for lighting, heating and cooking, but for many centuries wood (employ) as the most important fuel for these and other purposes. The wind as an energy source for ship propulsion (use) by man for thousands of years. Wind mills probably (invent) in China and first (build) in Europe during the 12th century. With the development of steam power in the 18th century energy exploitation came (revolutionize).

Energy can (change) in form, but the total amount of energy, in an isolated system, cannot (change). Thus, energy can neither (create) nor (destroy).

According to the theory of relativity which (put forward) by Einstein in 1905, the mass of the body increases in proportion to its kinetic energy. Thus, mass and energy (say) to be equivalent, and one can (convert) into the other. It may (show) that this relationship between mass and kinetic energy applies to all other forms of energy as well.

Ü 4.

B. Geben Sie englisch wieder:

1. Gestern wurde berichtet,[202] daß mehrere Dörfer in den Schweizer Alpen durch heftige Schneestürme von der Außenwelt (outside world) abgeschnitten worden sind.[203] Es wird vermutet,[204] daß viele Menschen obdachlos geworden sind (become homeless). Man befürchtet,[205] daß der Sachschaden (material damage) beträchtlich ist. Durch Flugzeuge wird die Bevölkerung zur Zeit mit Nahrungsmitteln und Medikamenten versorgt (supply)[206]. Auch Ärzte werden in das Katastrophengebiet (stricken area) eingeflogen (fly into)[207]. Man hofft, daß die Verbindung mit der Außenwelt bald wiederhergestellt werden wird.[208]

2. Zwischen 600 und 400 v. u. Z. (BC) war Britannien von den Kelten in Besitz genommen worden (take possession of). In den Jahren 55 und 54 v. u. Z. wurde von Julius Cäsar der Versuch unternommen (make an attempt), die Britannier (Britons) zu unterwerfen (subdue), aber die eigentliche Eroberung (actual conquest) großer Teile des Landes wurde erst unter dem römischen Kaiser (emperor) Claudius im Jahre 43 unserer Zeitrechnung begonnen und etwa im Jahre 70 vollendet. Die Truppen der britischen Königin Boadicea, die einen Aufstand gegen die Römer angeführt hatte (lead a revolt), wurden im Jahre 60 besiegt (defeat). Britannien war etwa 400 Jahre von den Römern besetzt. Es ist bekannt, daß die Römer die ersten großen Straßen im Lande bauten. Wahrscheinlich wurde auch die erste Kirche von ihnen errichtet. Im Jahre 410 wurden die letzten Legionen (legion) aus Britannien zurückgezogen (withdraw). Drei Jahrzehnte später begannen germanische Stämme (tribe), vor allem Angeln und Sachsen (Angles and Saxons), das Land zu besiedeln (settle). Die meisten keltischen (Celtic) Einwohner wurden entweder getötet oder nach Wales und Schottland vertrieben (drive).

In der folgenden Zeit war England in mehrere Königreiche (kingdom) aufgeteilt. Im 9. Jahrhundert drangen Skandinavier in das Land ein (invade sth, Passiv). Im Jahre 878 wurden die Dänen von Alfred dem Großen besiegt. 1066 wurde die Armee des englischen Königs Harold von den Truppen des normannischen Herzogs (Norman duke) William, dem von Eduard dem Bekenner (Edward the Confessor) der englische Thron versprochen worden war, in der Schlacht von Hastings geschlagen. Nach der normannischen Eroberung vollzogen sich (bring about, Passiv) grundlegende politische und kulturelle Umwandlungen (change). Auch die englische Sprache wurde durch den Einfluß des Französischen wesentlich verändert.

3. Der Nobelpreis ist 1895 von dem schwedischen Chemiker Alfred Nobel gestiftet worden (found), dessen Name mit der Erfindung des Dynamits verbunden ist (associate). Dieser Preis wird seit 1901 jedes Jahr für hervorragende Leistungen in den Naturwissenschaften (the natural sciences), in Medizin und Literatur sowie zur Förderung (promotion) des Weltfriedens verliehen. 1969 wurde außerdem ein Preis für Ökonomie gestiftet (set up an award). Vielen berühmten Wissenschaftlern und Schriftstellern ist dieser Preis bisher verliehen worden. Den ersten Nobelpreis auf dem Gebiet der Physik erhielt (give) Röntgen im Jahre 1901.

Ü 5.

5.1.–5.6.
Übersetzen Sie:

1. We'd rather stay at home tonight. 2. The streets are slippery, you'd better not drive to the office. 3. We could visit Tom, but I would as soon go to bed early today. 4. Henry is a brilliant orator, one cannot but admire his eloquence. 5. We'd better leave now in order not to be late for the theatre. 6. Would you rather have tea or coffee? 7. It's never too late to fall in love. 8. Why spend so much money at a posh hotel, we can have lunch at a pub. 9. The director is very busy this morning, I'd rather not disturb him. 10. If the method is not efficient enough why not try another one? 11. There's a draught, would you be kind enough to close the door? 12. Be so kind as to inform me at your earliest convenience. 13. We left the car on a parking lot outside the centre so as to avoid the traffic jams. 14. How dare you talk to me like that? 15. Mary and I don't always agree on domestic affairs, but I wouldn't dare to contradict her in this respect. 16. Don't be so unreasonable as to reject this offer. 17. We have booked tickets for the performance in order not to have to queue a long time. 18. You should choose your words carefully so as not to be misunderstood.
19. You needn't come with us if you don't want to. 20. I would prefer not to go on a business trip on Friday, but I am afraid I'll have to. 21. We can't take part in the excursion though we'd like to. 22. Susan doesn't go dancing often, but she used to when she was a student.
23. It is essential to fully investigate this problem. 24. I would like to really understand the theory of relativity.
25. There is nothing to be said against this argument. 26. You are to be congratulated on your brilliant paper. 27. I've been looking for my passport all morning, but it's nowhere to be found. 28. It was to be expected that Roger would fail the exam. 29. Several questions remain to be answered. 30. The book I need is not to be had anywhere. 31. It is to be feared that there will be another cold spell next week. 32. It remains to be seen if our plan will work. 33. Dresden is a nice town to live in. 34. Do you have anybody to converse with in English? 35. I need a corkscrew to open the bottle with. 36. This is no problem to quarrel about. 37. We are now preparing the symposium to be held at our institute next month. 38. Have you agreed on the items to be included in the agenda? 39. Some of the papers on environmental protection to be read at our symposium today will be presented by foreign scientists. 40. We have discussed further measures to be taken for improving working conditions in our plant. 41. Penicillin was the first antibiotic to be introduced into clinical practice. 42. 'Chemical Engineering' is one of the most important journals to appear in the field of chemistry. 43. The first play by a negro authoress to be produced on Broadway was Lorraine Hansberry's 'A Raisin in the Sun' in 1959.
44. Please show me how to handle this device. 45. Didn't they tell you when to come? 46. I didn't know whether to accept the proposal. 47. Mary is never at a loss what to do when her car breaks down. 48. We haven't found out yet how to tackle this problem. 49. Can you tell me who to see about this matter? 50. We missed the beginning of the performance because Mary couldn't make up her mind which dress to put on.

Ü 5.

5.1.1.
Ergänzen Sie dem Sinn entsprechend die Sätze mit *so as (not) to, in order (not) to* und den Ausdrücken in Klammern:

1. It's raining, I'll stay indoors (catch a cold).[209] 2. Mary dresses loudly (make people look at her).[210] 3. You had better turn the radio down (disturb father). 4. I've written down Jim's address (forget it). 5. I must work hard (finish the article by Saturday). 6. I am going to ring Mary (explain why I didn't come) 7. There was so much noise that we had to shout (understand). 8. We left early (avoid the rush-hours). 9. We should break the news gently to Peter (shock him). 10. We had to look up some words in the dictionary (make any spelling mistakes). 11. Fred does a lot of jogging (keep fit). 12. We took a stroll through the town (while away the time). 13. John drove slowly (cause an accident). 14. Susan wore a very low-cut blouse (attract attention). 15. I was very quiet when I came home (hear, by anybody).[211]

5.2.
A. Formen Sie die folgenden Sätze dem Kontext entsprechend mit *(I) had better, (I) would rather, why not, why* um:

1. You should discuss the matter with one of your colleagues.[212] 2. John said he would prefer to go to the theatre rather than watch TV.[213] 3. I think we should cancel the appointment. 4. Couldn't we have a break now?[214] 5. Why shouldn't we try to settle our dispute. 6. I think there is a bus to Weimar at 9.30, but you should make sure. 7. Susan would prefer to buy a black dress rather than a blue one. 8. I advise you not to use this old device any longer.[215] 9. Oughtn't we to alter the programme?[216] 10. Why should we spend a lot of time arguing? 11. Thank you, I don't like beer, I'd prefer to have a glass of wine. 12. We ought to read the minutes of the last session. 13. Why should we bring up the topic again? 14. This wine is not very good, shouldn't we order a different sort?

B. Verwenden Sie dem Kontext entsprechend *(you) had better*; *(I) would rather*:

1. Es wäre besser, wenn du anrufst, ehe du kommst.[217] 2. Tom würde lieber ein Haus als ein Auto kaufen.[218] 3. Du hast Fieber (a temperature), du solltest zum Arzt gehen (see a doctor). 4. Ich mag Kuchen nicht, ich würde lieber ein Sandwich haben. 5. Tom sollte selbst eine Entscheidung treffen, ich mische mich lieber nicht ein (interfere). 6. Die Straßen sind heute vereist (icy), wir sollten das Auto lieber zu Hause lassen.

5.4. / 5.4.1.
A. Entscheiden Sie, ob Infinitiv des Passivs oder Infinitiv des Aktivs zu setzen ist:

1. John was nowhere (see).[219] 2. Whether Jack is right or wrong is hard (say). 3. It is (hope)[220] that a solution will soon be found. 4. The test is easy (prepare). 5. I think Jim's proposal is (take) seriously. 6. You must take your shoes (mend).[221] 7. The journal I am looking for is not (have)[222] in our library. 8. We

must talk about the next steps (take). 9. Is there anything (add)? 10. The situation is difficult (describe). 11. My friend will take part in the swimming contest (hold)[223] at our college next week. 12. We've got a lot of things (attend to)[224] today. 13. Some of the data remain (check).[225] 14. Your English translation leaves a lot (desire). 15. The advantages (gain) from this technique are obvious. 16. The measurements (make) require very sensitive instruments.

B. Geben Sie englisch wieder:

1. Die Frage ist schwer zu beantworten. 2. Wir haben heute einige komplizierte Themen zu behandeln. 3. Das Wörterbuch, das ich brauche, ist nirgends zu haben. 4. Das Problem war leicht zu lösen. 5. Es sind noch einige Briefe zu tippen. 6. Dieses Medikament ist dreimal täglich (L 20.2.1.) zu nehmen. 7. Wir haben uns auf die Maßnahmen geeinigt, die zu treffen sind.[226] 8. Es bleibt abzuwarten (see),[227] wie John auf unseren Vorschlag reagieren wird. 9. Die Qualität meines Kassettenrecorders läßt viel zu wünschen übrig. 10. Die meisten (L 20.1.4.) Referate (paper), die auf der heutigen Sitzung gehalten (present) werden sollen, werden in Englisch vorgetragen (read).

5.5.
A. Bilden Sie Sätze mit Fragewort + Infinitiv.

Beispiel: *Where can I contact Mary? (I don't know ...)* → *I don't know where to contact Mary.*

1. What shall I tell him? (I don't know ...) 2. How do we get to the station? (Can you tell me ...) 3. What shall I do now? (Tell me ...) 4. How do you spell this word? (I don't know ...) 5. Where could I get the book? (I've no idea ...) 6. How can we solve this problem? (Will you explain to us ...) 7. Where shall we spend our holidays? (We haven't decided yet ...)[228] 8. Shall I accept Fred's invitation? (I'm not sure ...)[229] 9. Where shall we put the luggage? (Ask them ...) 10. When is he to come? (Did you tell him ...) 11. How is this device used? (Can you show us ...) 12. Should we consult Professor Smith? (We are not sure ...) 13. Who can I invite to the party? (I wonder ...)[230] 14. How shall I get in touch with Mr Ward? (I've not the slightest idea ...)

B. Geben Sie englisch wieder:

1. Ich wußte nicht, was ich sagen sollte.[231] 2. Sage mir, wann ich dich anrufen soll.[232] 3. Wir haben uns noch nicht entschieden, wann wir unseren Urlaub nehmen. 4. Das Wort Psyche gibt es auch im Englischen; wissen Sie, wie man es ausspricht? 5. Das ist eine schwierige Frage, ich weiß nicht, wie ich sie beantworten soll. 6. Ich bin (mir) nicht sicher, ob ich Martin fragen soll. 7. Jane konnte sich nicht entscheiden, mit wem sie ausgehen sollte.[233] 8. Können Sie mir erklären (L 11.4.), wie man diese Maschine bedient (operate)?

5.6.
Verkürzen bzw. verbinden Sie die folgenden Sätze mit dem Infinitiv.

Beispiele: *Do you know anybody to whom I could turn for further information?* → *Do you know anybody to turn to for further information?*

Ü 5.

Where is the spade with which I can dig the garden? → *Where is the spade to dig the garden with?*

1. I need a knife because I want to cut the bread.[234]   2. Arthur is not the sort of man who can move mountains.   3. Tom has only a couch on which he sleeps.   4. I don't know anybody with whom I can talk this matter over.[235]   5. Have you got a sheet of paper on which I can write the address?   6. This is not a problem about which one need worry.   7. I can't open the bottle because I haven't got a corkscrew.[236]   8. It is a good thing always to have something pleasant that one can look forward to.   9. I need thread and a needle because I want to sew on a button.   10. Eve is not the kind of girl that one can trifle with.   11. We are glad that we have several friends we can rely on when we need help.   12. I'm sorry I have only wine glasses out of which we can drink the champagne.[237]   13. Jane has never told a lie, I would be the last who doesn't believe her.   14. Everybody knows that Soviet scientists were the first who launched a manned space vehicle.

5.1. / 5.1.1. / 5.6.
Geben Sie englisch wieder:

1. Es ist zu spät, um (noch) ins Theater zu gehen.   2. Sei so nett und leihe mir dein Fahrrad.[238]   3. Wir müssen uns beeilen, um nicht zu spät zu kommen.[239]   4. Sei so gut und decke den Tisch (lay the table).   5. Leider kann ich nicht kommen, obwohl ich (es) gern möchte.[240]   6. Würden Sie so freundlich sein, Bescheid zu hinterlassen (leave word), wann ich Sie sprechen kann?   7. Ich werde ein Taxi nehmen, um den Zug nicht zu verpassen.   8. Es ist zu früh, etwas Genaues (definite) zu sagen.   9. Ich habe meinem Freund geraten, den Vertrag zu unterschreiben, aber er wollte es nicht.   10. Mein Kollege schließt sich oft ein (lock the door), während er arbeitet, um nicht gestört zu werden.[241]   11. Ich werde einen Konversationskurs in Englisch besuchen, um mich auf Konferenzen mit englisch sprechenden Wissenschaftlern verständigen (communicate) zu können.   12. Alcock und Brown waren die ersten, die den Atlantik in einem Motorflugzeug (powered aeroplane) überflogen.

5.7.1. – 5.7.3.
Übersetzen Sie:

1. We didn't hear you come home last night. – 2. I think John is still in the office, I didn't see him leave.   3. Fred doesn't like to work in the kitchen, but he likes to watch his wife cook.   4. We heard them talk but we didn't hear what they were speaking about.   5. John had a nice girlfriend, I can't imagine what made him break with her.   6. I don't like Arthur's jokes, they hardly make anybody laugh.   7. Don't play up the problem, it is less complicated than you make it appear.   8. An economical wife knows how to make a little money go a long way.   9. Last week Mr Brown was ready to support our project, I wonder what may have made him change his mind.   10. Do to others as you would have them do to you.   11. I am very busy, have somebody else look into the matter.   12. Don't let yourself be talked into doing anything you might regret some day.   13. I failed the admission test, but I won't let myself be discouraged, I'm going to try again.

14. Do you want me to give a detailed report? 15. Our director wants us to call on him at ten sharp. 16. Why don't you want us to help you? 17. I want you to check these data immediately, the professor expects us to have the results available this afternoon. 18. Would you like me to show you some of the photos I took while I was in Cuba? 19. John didn't want to talk about the matter; at least he didn't want it to be discussed in public. 20. We'd like you to let us know your decision until tomorrow. 21. I don't like people beating about the bush; I want you to speak out what you think. 22. Susan wants to become a screen star, she imagines herself well suited for this job. 23. We expect you to be punctual. 24. Bob was rather rude, you should tell him to apologize. 25. If Tom interferes again, tell him to mind his own business. 26. Recently I read in the newspaper that a bee caused a bus to collide with a car when it stung the bus driver near his eye. 27. We were shown through the whole factory, they even allowed us to see the pilot plant. 28. Ben has been fined for exceeding the speed limit, I have repeatedly warned him not to be so careless. Yesterday I warned him again to drive more carefully. 29. Let us assume this hypothesis to be correct. 30. The management expects labour productivity to be raised considerably by the introduction of computer aided design and manufacturing. 31. The results obtained allow the following conclusions to be drawn. 32. Sensitive measuring instruments allow minute traces of radioactivity to be detected. 33. Automation enables entire manufacturing processes to be supervised by a minimum of operators. 34. The extensive application of cybernetics requires many modern achievements of technology, e. g. electronic computing machines and communication equipment to be made use of. 35. The fusion process requires extremely high temperatures to be produced, several hundred million degrees centigrade. 36. Democritus and other Greek and Roman philosophers assumed atoms to be indivisible and indestructible. 37. The Greek philosopher Plato considered material objects to be merely images or reflections of ideas. 38. Faraday's discoveries in electromagnetism allowed significant progress to be made in the fields of electric power, transport, communications and even automatic control.

5.7.2./5.7.2.1.
A. Bringen Sie einen Wunsch zum Ausdruck.
Beispiel: *I ... (you, listen very carefully)* → *I want you to listen very carefully.*

1. We'll give John our telephone number. We ... (he, get in touch with us as soon as possible). 2. The boss ... (I, take the minutes). 3. I'll leave the letter on the table; I ... (Tom, see it at once when he comes). 4. The two girls talked in undertones; they ... (not want, we overhear their conversation). 5. This matter is very important for Jane. Her parents ... (she, consider it very carefully) 6. Mary said she ... (not want, I think she was angry).[242]

B. Formen Sie die Sätze nach dem folgenden Muster mit Objekt + Infinitiv um.
Beispiel: *We must be on time. (Fred has told ...)* → *Fred has told us to be on time.*
1. Jane can go dancing once a week. (Mother allows ...)[243] 2. I am to read this

Ü 5.

book. (Mary wants ...)²⁴⁴ 3. Peter should not smoke so much. (The doctor told ...) 4. We should apologize. (They expect ...) 5. We had to submit a summary of our paper. (The chairman made ...)²⁴⁵ 6. John said I could use his car. (John allowed ...) 7. I have to finish my doctoral thesis this year. (Professor Lewis expects ...) 8. She should be informed about this matter. (I want ...)²⁴⁶ 9. We had to wait a long time at the dentist's. (The dentist had ...) 10. Your article will be printed. (The chief editor will cause ...)²⁴⁷ 11. We are not to pass on this information. (Our director does not want ...) 12. My friends are not to be kept waiting. (I don't want ...)

C. Geben Sie die folgenden Aussagen mit Objekt + Infinitiv wieder, und verwenden Sie dabei die Verben in Klammern.

Beispiel: *Peter said we should wait. (tell)* → *Peter told us to wait.*

1. I'm rather certain he will come. (expect)²⁴⁸ 2. Nora said we should lay the table. (tell) 3. When am I to come? (want)²⁴⁹ 4. You should see to it that the test is repeated. (cause)²⁵⁰ 5. Jim said I shouldn't worry. (tell) 6. I do hope that they will keep me up to date. (expect) 7. What are we to do now? (want) 8. John said I could use his slide projector. (allow) 9. Our head of department said we should give a detailed report on the conference. (make, tell, have) 10. This technique makes it possible to step up production. (enable)²⁵¹ 11. I believe Paula is a good teacher. (consider) 12. They suppose that the hypothesis is correct. (assume) 13. Evidence revealed that the suspect's alibi was beyond doubt. (show) – 14. At a very early age Mozart showed that he was a virtuoso pianist. (show oneself)²⁵²

5.7.1.–5.7.2.
Geben Sie englisch wieder, wobei Sie entscheiden, ob der Infinitiv mit oder ohne to zu verwenden ist:

1. Jane ist nicht zu Hause, ich habe sie vor zehn Minuten weggehen sehen.²⁵³ 2. Hast du gehört, ob Mike gekommen ist? 3. Roger ist immer optimistisch; ich habe nie gehört, daß er sich beklagt (complain). 4. Wir wissen nicht, was Peter veranlaßt hat, plötzlich abzureisen.²⁵⁴ 5. Du solltest Peggy veranlassen, sich die Sache noch einmal zu überlegen (think over). 6. Wollen Sie, daß ich mich sofort entscheide?²⁵⁵ 7. Wir erwarten, daß alle Kollegen an der Versammlung teilnehmen. 8. Es ist schon spät, willst du, daß ich dich nach Hause fahre? 9. Wir möchten, daß unser Vorschlag auf der Versammlung besprochen wird.²⁵⁶ 10. Willst du, daß ich dir Einzelheiten erzähle? 11. Mutter ist sehr müde, sie möchte nicht, daß sie jetzt gestört wird. 12. Warum wollt ihr nicht, daß wir euch helfen? 13. Ich hätte nicht erwartet, daß dieser Roman ein Bestseller wird. 14. Warum wolltest du nicht, daß wir Mary zu unserer Party einladen? 15. Der Arzt hat mir gesagt, ich soll im Bett bleiben. 16. Hast du Harry gesagt, daß er um zehn Uhr hier sein soll? 17. Du solltest Fred veranlassen, sich zu entschuldigen (mehrere Möglichkeiten).²⁵⁷ 18. Der Assistent hat veranlaßt, daß der Versuch wiederholt wird (s. L 5.7.2.) 19. Sag ihm, er soll vorsichtig mit der Schreibmaschine umgehen.²⁵⁸ 20. Vielleicht könnten wir Mary veranlassen, ihre Meinung zu ändern (mehrere Möglichkeiten!). 21. Bill hat gesagt, er sei bereit, auf der Konfe-

renz zu dolmetschen; wir erwarten, daß er sein Versprechen hält. 22. Ich möchte, daß das Manuskript sofort fotokopiert wird (copy). 23. Heute sind viele Probleme zu besprechen; du kannst nicht erwarten, daß alle (von ihnen) geklärt werden (settle). 24. Wir hatten nicht erwartet, daß der Vortrag so gut besucht ist. 25. Hast du Peter erlaubt, dein Auto zu benutzen? 26. Ich halte (L 5.7.2.1.) es für falsch, das Gespräch zu verschieben. 27. Wir setzen die Temperatur bei diesem Versuch als konstant voraus. 28. Ich nehme an, daß die Daten schon überprüft worden sind.[259]

5.7.4.
A. Übersetzen Sie:

1. Jane is rather fidgety, she is waiting for her boy-friend to take her out. 2. It's high time for you to get married. 3. We have arranged for them to meet Bob at five. 4. It is unusual for Mary to drink beer. 5. It is advisable for you to consult your wife before you decide what to do. 6. The performance was booked up, and lots of people were waiting for tickets to be returned. 7. We have a flat which is too small for guests to be put up. 8. Hundreds of fans were waiting at the airport for the pop star to arrive. 9. It is necessary for every student of technology to take courses in mathematics. 10. The negotiations were too complicated for the two sides to come to an immediate agreement. 11. The organizing committee will arrange for all the participants in the conference to be accommodated at a hotel. 12. For reliable results to be obtained some more experiments will have to be made.

B. Bilden Sie Sätze mit *for* + Infinitiv:
Beispiel: *I can't believe this. (It's hard ...)* → *It's hard for me to believe this.*

1. We don't understand him. (It's impossible ...)[260] 2. Mary doesn't smoke as a rule. (It is quite unusual ...) 3. You'll have to wait until they come. (It will be necessary ...) 4. We have made it possible that the Millers can stay at the holiday home of our plant over the weekend. (We have arranged ...)[261] 5. We ought to know all the details. (It is essential ...) 6. They should be informed about our plan right away. (It is vital ...)[262] 7. We needn't postpone the decision. (There isn't any reason ...) 8. She ought to be told all the particulars of our arrangement. (It is important ...)

C. Geben Sie englisch wieder:

1. Ist es nötig, daß ich komme, oder genügt es anzurufen?[263] 2. Der Text ist zu schwierig, als daß wir ihn ohne Wörterbuch übersetzen könnten.[264] 3. Würde es dir passen, uns morgen zu besuchen?[265] 4. Es ist ungewöhnlich, daß unsere Sekretärin zu spät kommt. 5. Das Problem ist schon mehrmals erörtert worden; es ist höchste Zeit, daß wir zu einer Einigung kommen.[266] 6. Es ist uns leider nicht möglich, die Verabredung (appointment) einzuhalten. 7. Lassen Sie mich (nach)denken; die Frage ist zu kompliziert, als daß ich sie sofort beantworten könnte. 8. Ich habe die heutige Zeitung noch nicht gelesen; ich warte darauf, daß der Briefträger (postman) sie bringt. 9. Wir haben arrangiert, daß Professor White an der Besprechung teilnimmt.[267] 10. Wenn ich einen Vortrag auf dem Symposium halten soll (L 6.5.3.1.), ist es wichtig, daß ich rechtzeitig informiert werde.

5.8.
A. Übersetzen Sie:

1. Tom hasn't visited us for some weeks; he is supposed to be abroad.   2. The thief can't have got far, he has just been seen to leave the shop and run down the street.   3. I have been told to revise my article.   4. This information is strictly confidential, you are not supposed to pass it on.   5. Mike is spending most of the weekends at the institute, he is said to be working on a project which has to be finished by the end of the month.   6. The hypothesis is generally assumed to be wrong.   7. Some thirty people are reported to have been injured in the train accident, twelve of them were stated to have been taken to hospital while the others were allowed to continue their journey after first-aid treatment.   8. The negotiations are reported to have been successful.   9. The new hydroelectric power station is planned to be put into service next year.
10. The famous American actor Buster Keaton was nicknamed 'The Great Stone Face', because he was never seen to smile in any of his films.   11. Ernest Rutherford, the reputed British physicist, was reported to have believed that no physical theory was of much value if it could not be explained to a barmaid.   12. The famous conductor Arturo Toscanini was said to be able to visualize an entire musical score in his mind's eye whenever he wanted. People with such capabilities are said to have photographic memories (L 6.5.3.3.).   13. The aboriginals of Australia are believed to have occupied the continent via a land bridge from Indonesia in prehistoric times.   14. Britain's offshore natural gas resources are expected to be sufficient to meet the country's major requirements into the next century.   15. Leibniz is usually said to have been the last of the polyhistors.   16. The first psychological laboratory is known to have been established by Wilhelm Wundt at the university of Leipzig in 1879.   17. The first recorded observation about electricity is supposed to have been made by the Greek philosopher Thales.   18. The terms 'electric' and 'electrified', derived from the Greek word 'elektron' for amber, are said to have been coined by Sir William Gilbert, physician to Queen Elizabeth I, after experiments made by him had proved many substances to behave as amber does, when they are rubbed.   19. Power today is known to be based on three major sources: the burning of fossil fuel, water, and nuclear energy.   20. All heavier atoms are thought to be built up of protons, electrons and neutrons.   21. The electron, the lightest stable subatomic particle known, is considered to be the basic charge of electricity.   22. A proton is any of a group of stable subatomic particles that has been found to have a mass 1,836 times that of an electron.   23. Photons, which travel at the speed of light, are believed to be the carriers of the electromagnetic field.   24. Quarks are subatomic particles which are thought to be among the fundamental constituents of matter. Protons und neutrons which make up atomic nuclei, are believed to consist of quarks, a term introduced by the American physicist Murray Gell-Mann, who adopted it from a passage in James Joyce's novel 'Finnegans Wake'.   25. The term cybernetics is known to have been introduced by the American mathematician Norbert Wiener in 1947. Nowadays cybernetics is understood to be applicable to the solution of control problems in many fields of science and technology, even in meteorology, where it is expected by experts to influence the weather and the climate.

B. Geben Sie die folgenden Aussagen in Sätzen mit Subjekt + Infinitiv wieder, und verwenden Sie dabei die Verben in Klammern.
Beispiel: *They want us to be punctual. (expect)* → *We are expected to be punctual.*
1. People say Dr Peters is an excellent surgeon. (know)[268]   2. They want me to give a slide lecture on Bulgaria. (expect)   3. You must not smoke here. (suppose)[269]   4. Somebody has told me that this play is very good. (say)   5. Children may see this film. (allow)   6. Somebody watched the thief drive off on a motorbike. (see)   7. They think that the calculations are wrong. (assume)   8. Everybody is of the opinion that Barbara is a beautiful girl.   9. Don't park your car here. (suppose)   10. May you take a day off tomorrow? (permit)   11. They want us to meet the deadline at any rate. (expect)   12. Shall I clean the car alone? (suppose)[270]   13. They said we shouldn't disturb the director. (tell)   14. Shall we finish the translation today? (suppose)   15. People say that Mrs Tailor is a very good actress. (repute)   16. John ought to be back by ten. (expect)   17. We are to submit the manuscript by the end of the month. (expect)   18. You should be working now. (suppose)

C. Geben Sie die folgende Schilderung eines Banküberfalls so wieder, wie sie sich häufig im Stile der Massenmedien findet, d. h. mit Passiv + Infinitiv, wobei die kursiv gedruckten Wörter nicht mehr erscheinen.

Ein Bankangestellter berichtet:
When the bank robbers came in *they* forced everybody except me to lie down[271] and told them not to move.[272] *The gunmen* didn't allow us to talk.[273] Then *they* ordered me to open the safe.[274] Next *they* compelled me to put all the bank notes on the counter.[275] *They* warned me not to ring the alarm[276] and had me lie down like the others.[277] Some minutes after the gangsters had escaped by car, the police arrived and made us tell them[278] what had been going on. *We* told them they couldn't expect us to describe the robbers in detail[279] because they had been masked.

D. Geben Sie englisch wieder:
1. Ich kann das Buch nicht länger behalten, man hat mir vorige Woche in der Bibliothek gesagt, daß ich es zurückgeben soll.[280]   2. Susan kommt heute abend nicht, sie soll krank sein.   3. Hat man dir gesagt, daß du den Fragebogen sofort ausfüllen sollst?   4. Dr. Baker gilt als ausgezeichneter Chirurg.[281]   5. Die Wände in unserem Haus sind sehr dünn, man kann oft hören, wie sich die Nachbarn streiten.   6. Wir werden uns die neue Inszenierung (production) des 'Galilei' im Berliner Ensemble ansehen, die sehr gut sein soll.   7. Man stellte fest, daß das neuentwickelte Medikament sehr wirksam ist (efficacious)[282].   8. Man erwartet, daß ich den Bericht heute abgebe (hand in).   9. Das neue Hotel im Stadtzentrum soll 600 Gästen Unterkunft gewähren (accommodate).[283]   10. Die sowjetischen Konferenzteilnehmer sind schon in Dresden; sie sollen gestern abend angekommen sein.   11. Der englische Konversationskursus soll zwei Semester dauern.[284]   12. Berichten zufolge sollen durch das Erdbeben in Japan Tausende von Häusern zerstört worden sein.[285]   13. Diese Vorlesungsreihe soll einen Überblick über Anwendungsmöglichkeiten von Robotern in der Industrie geben   14. Es wird

Ü 6. 174

vorausgesetzt, daß A < B ist. 15. Die Waldbrände (forest fire) in Südfrankreich haben Schäden verursacht, die sich schätzungsweise auf 1 bis 2 Milliarden Francs belaufen (amount to)[286] 16. Es wird erwartet, daß die Verhandlungen bald wieder aufgenommen werden (resume). 17. Arthur Miller, der Autor von 'Death of a Salesman' und 'The Crucible', ist bekanntlich einer der führenden Vertreter (representative) des sozialkritischen (sociocritical) amerikanischen Theaters. 18. Es ist bekannt, daß die Sonnenstrahlung (solar radiation) die größte Energiequelle ist. 19. Es wird als sicher angenommen, daß das erste Rundfunkprogramm am Weihnachtsabend 1906 von einer Versuchsstation (experimental station) in Massachusetts ausgestrahlt wurde (broadcast).[287] 20. Bekanntlich beruht die Rundfunkübertragung (radio transmission) wesentlich auf der Erfindung der drahtlosen (wireless) Telegraphie durch Marconi im Jahre 1896.

Komplexübung: Setzen Sie dem Kontext entsprechende Formen des Infinitivs ein.

Peter has had a road accident. It was an accident that ought not (happen)[288] because the driver who caused it was found (drink)[289] several bottles of beer before. Peter appears (injure)[290] rather badly, since it was necessary for him (take)[291] to hospital. And he even had (operate on).[292] At first the doctors didn't want anybody (visit)[293] him, but within the past days his health seems (improve)[294] steadily. We have been told that he is likely (discharge)[295] at the end of this week. He hopes (allow/work)[296] again before long.

6.1.–6.4.
A. Übersetzen Sie:

1. Can you answer the question? 2. Mike can't speak English. 3. Sometimes Amanda can be very arrogant. 4. We shall be at home all day, we can drop in any time you like. 5. Can I have a glass of beer? 6. I could be wrong. 7. Could you tell me where Mr Brown works? 8. Couldn't we go to the movies tonight? 9. Could I leave now, I have an appointment at three. 10. I think Mary could help us to wash the dishes. 11. My father was good at athletics, he could run a hundred metres in 11.5 seconds. 12. Peter's ex-wife could be very unpleasant when he didn't humour her. 13. Do you think you will be able to do simultaneous interpreting at the conference? 14. We haven't been able to solve this problem until now. 15. Ask John he might be able to give a hint. 16. I think I would have been able to translate the text myself if I·had had enough time. 17. A scientist who fails to keep up with the latest developments in his special field will soon be unable to do effective work. 18. The human body is capable of converting excess carbohydrates into fat. 19. Frank's point of view is rather controversial; I wonder whether he will manage to hold his ground in the debate tomorrow.
20. I don't know what Roger thinks of our proposal because I haven't had an opportunity to talk to him as yet.
21. Mr Thomson may be in his late forties. 22. This hypothesis may be right. – This hypothesis cannot be right. – This hypothesis may not be right. 23. Don't fall in love with Barbara, she might be your daughter. 24. May I ask another

question? 25. Might we ask you a favour? 26. The head of the laboratory told us that we might be present at the test. 27. In a museum you must not touch any of the exhibits. 28. Were you allowed to talk to the patient? 29. The nouns 'fabric' and 'factory' must not be mixed up.
30. Will you have another cup of coffee? 31. Would somebody shut the door please? 32. Won't you take a seat? 33. I can't drive you to the supermarket, the car won't start. 34. You will have heard that Susan has got a divorce.
35. Who do you want to talk to? 36. Fred is busy, he doesn't want to be disturbed. 37. I could help John if he wants me to. 38. Anne came quite unexpectedly, she may have wanted to surprise us. 39. I'd like to have a word with you. 40. Would anybody like to make a suggestion? 41. We intend to discuss this matter tomorrow. 42. Don't misunderstand me, I didn't mean to insult you. 43. Our secretary refused to be transferred to another department. 44. Iron will melt at a temperature of 1539°C. 45. Peter and Anne would go dancing every weekend before they got married. 46. Why are you such a football fan; did you use to play yourself when you were young? 47. The launching of a spacecraft is no longer the sensation it used to be in the sixties. 48. In antiquity and throughout the Middle Ages it used to be taken for granted that the sun and all the other planets revolve round the earth.

B. Formen Sie die folgenden Sätze mit *may, might/could, may not, can't* um (s. L 6.2.).

Beispiel: *It is possible that Frank is on holiday.* → *Frank may be on holiday.* – *It is not impossible that Frank is on holiday.* → *Frank might/could be on holiday.*

1. The weather will possibly change. 2. Perhaps John is right. 3. It's possible that I'm wrong. 4. It is possible that Harry will not be interested in our project.[297] 5. It's possible that my uncle will be visiting us tomorrow.[298] 6. It is possible that you won't like this book.[299] 7. Perhaps this isn't true. 8. It is possible that Anne is getting married soon. 9. It is not impossible that John knows more about this matter.[300] 10. It is impossible that Mary is in the office.[301] 11. It is not impossible that Arthur will phone you this afternoon. 12. Perhaps my sister will come with us. 13. It is impossible that Susan is in love with Henry. 14. It is not impossible that Jack will change his mind. 15. It is possible that we won't get hotel accommodation because we haven't booked rooms.[302] 16. Don't let's wait any longer, it's possible that my friend won't be coming tonight. 17. Owing to the fog there will possibly be train delays. 18. Perhaps our neighbour will be able to repair the radio. 19. It's not quite impossible that you will find the book in the library. 20. Wait a minute, perhaps my brother wants to come with us.[303] 21. Perhaps my parents are going to the seaside this summer. 22. It is impossible that this theory is correct. 23. It is not impossible that the negotiators will reach an agreement at the last moment.

C. Setzen Sie *could* und/oder die entsprechende Form von *be able to* ein. (s. L 6.1.2.)

1. Peter told us he ... (not come)[304] today, but that he might come tomorrow.
2. When I first talked to an Englishman I found I ... (understand)[305] English better

Ü 6.

than I had thought. 3. In the hotel we stayed at we ... (overhear)[306] every word our neighbours said. 4. If I had tools I would ... (repair)[307] the shelf. 5. You ought ... (solve)[308] this problem yourself. 6. We had to walk because we ... (not get)[309] the car to start. 7. I'd like ... (speak)[310] French fluently. 8. If the traffic weren't so heavy we ... (drive)[311] faster.

D. Setzen Sie in den folgenden Sätzen *can, cannot, may, may not, must not* ein und verwenden Sie jede Form nur zweimal.

1. Ask somebody else, I ... answer this question. 2. This is a bad mistake; you ... make it again. 3. We'll visit John tomorrow; he ... be at home today. 4. Mike is in hospital; he ... come tonight. 5. This information is confidential; you ... pass it on. 6. Let's wait for Janette; she ... want to accompany us. 7. Give me your English text, you ... be able to translate it, but I ... translate it. 8. My colleague ... be able to help you; he ... speak Spanish.

E. Verwenden Sie *can/could* mit den in Klammern gegebenen Wendungen, um eine Eigenschaft auszudrücken (L 6.1.1.; L 6.1.2.).

Beispiel: Sue doesn't always remember things. (quite forgetful) → *Sue can be quite forgetful.*

1. John is not always impolite. (quite polite) 2. Autumn isn't by any means a bad time for taking a holiday. (a good time) 3. Harry was not always unpleasant when we asked him a favour. (occasionally quite obliging) 4. The English method of numbering houses is not always clear for a stranger. (rather confusing) 5. When I was at college the lectures were not always very interesting. (sometimes very boring)

F. Bilden Sie die folgenden Sätze mit der entsprechenden Form von *be able to* um (L 6.1.1.).

1. It has been impossible for me to contact the manager so far.[312] 2. In a week's time the doctors will be in a position to give you the results of the check-up. 3. Peter is going to take a crash course in English because he wants to be in a position to speak it well when he goes on business to Ethiopia. 4. If we don't work over the weekend it won't be possible for us to finish the manuscript by Monday.

G. Bilden Sie die folgenden Sätze mit *might* um (L 6.2.1.).

1. Perhaps you would let me know your answer tomorrow.[313] 2. Perhaps we should ask Peter if he wants to come with us.[314] 3. We are annoyed that you don't try to help us.[315] 4. I'm irritated that Roy isn't more considerate.[316]

H. (L 6.3.) Setzen Sie dem Kontext gemäß *may, might, must not, (not) be allowed/permitted to* ein. (Beachten Sie, daß in einigen Fällen may bzw. might oder die entsprechende Form von be allowed/permitted to möglich ist.)

1. ... I borrow your pen? 2. The manager is back in his office, you ... (see) him now. 3. We ... (park) the car in front of the theatre, but we ... (park) it at the rear of the building. 4. Peter is very busy, you ... (disturb) him now. 5. John's health has been improving steadily since his operation, I think we ... (visit) him on

Ü 6.

Sunday. 6. I told Mary she ... (use) our typewriter if she wanted to. 7. ... I smoke here? – No, you ...; smoking ... in this restaurant during lunch hours. 8. Yesterday evening there were some funny cartoon films shown on TV, so the children asked if they ... (stay up) a little longer. 9. If you had finished your work on time you ... (come) with us now (L 3.3.4.). 10. The symposium in Berlin will probably be very interesting, we hope to ... (attend) it. 11. When Anne asked her mother if she ... (go) to the movies she was told she ... to because she hadn't cleaned her room yet. 12. Arthur has often been late for work recently; I'm afraid he ... (keep) his job unless he realizes he ... (be) so careless.

I. Drücken Sie in den folgenden Sätzen die Wahrscheinlichkeit mit *will* aus (L 6.4.5.).

1. It's no use ringing my parents now, they are probably at the theatre.[317] 2. I'm rather sure Bob knows that we are expecting him. 3. Anne has probably come back by now.[318] 4. Don't let's disturb Peter, he is probably taking a nap.[319] 5. Harry probably doesn't know me, I haven't met him before.

J. Drücken Sie in den folgenden Sätzen die Gewohnheit oder typische Eigenschaft mit *will, would, used to* aus (L 6.4.4.).

1. Joan's husband loves watching TV, he sits[320] for hours at the goggle-box without talking to anyone. 2. When we still lived in our old flat the water pipes often froze[321] in winter. 3. Mr Brown was[322] a teacher at a school, for three years he has been teaching at the university. 4. Wasn't there[323] a park where the new high-rise complex has been built? 5. When I was a student I drank[324] a lot of beer, now I prefer wine. 6. William is very absent-minded, he often mislays things where he can't find them. 7. Jack didn't smoke until recently; now he smokes a pipe from time to time. 8. Didn't you have a dog when you lived in the country?

K. Bringen Sie in den folgenden Sätzen den Wunsch mit *want to, would like to*, – die Weigerung mit *not want to, refuse to*, die Funktionsunfähigkeit mit *won't* bzw. *wouldn't* zum Ausdruck (L 6.4.2.; 6.4.3.).

1. My parents are coming tomorrow, that's why I ... (take) a day off. 2. I ... (go) with you, but I have some letters to write. 3. We invited Susan to the barbecue, but she ... (come). 4. Why ... (you, not tell)[325] us the story yesterday? 5. The door ... (lock). 6. ... (you, play) a game of chess with me? 7. Peter is learning French because he ... (be able) to read French authors in the original. 8. We repeatedly attempted to win Roger for our project, but each time he flatly ... (cooperate).[326] 9. Harry wouldn't have been able to help us even if he ...[327] 10. I had to go on foot because the car ... (start).

L. Geben Sie englisch wieder:

1. Ich kann die Frage beantworten. 2. Kannst du tanzen? 3. Könnten Sie mir den Weg zum Bahnhof zeigen? 4. Wir haben den Fehler noch nicht finden können.[328] 5. Ich glaube, ich werde das Auto selbst reparieren können. 6. Mary

Ü 6.

behauptet, fließend Englisch und Russisch sprechen zu können.[329]   7. Konntest du alle Prüfungsfragen beantworten?[330]   8. Wir hatten gehofft, du würdest uns helfen können.   9. Die Probleme, die gestern nicht gelöst werden konnten, müssen morgen besprochen werden.   10. Ich kann mich irren.[331]   11. Was Peter uns gestern erzählt hat, kann nicht stimmen (be true).   12. Diese Themen können heute nicht behandelt werden.   13. Susan kommt vielleicht mit dem Taxi.[332]   14. Darf ich Ihnen Mr Grey vorstellen?   15. Anne hat uns nicht geschrieben, vielleicht kennt sie unsere Adresse nicht (L 6.2.2.).   16. Dürfte ich Sie um ein Glas Wasser bitten (trouble for)?[333]   17. John ist nicht gekommen, er ist vielleicht krank.   18. Wir dürfen diesen Fehler nicht (noch) einmal machen.   19. Es ist noch nicht sicher (certain), ob Robert an dem Schwimmwettkampf teilnehmen darf (Futur).   20. Wir durften die Versuchsanlage (pilot plant) nicht besichtigen, weil gerade ein neuer Maschinentyp erprobt wurde (L 4.5.).   21. Die Montagehalle (assembly shop) darf nicht ohne Sondergenehmigung betreten werden.   22. Wir fragten unsere Zimmervermieterin (landlady), ob wir nächstes Jahr wiederkommen dürften.   23. Harry ist sehr beschäftigt, er will nicht gestört werden.   24. Ich würde gern einige Fragen stellen.   25. Möchten Sie zum Mittagessen bleiben?   26. Wir wollten die Ausstellung gestern besuchen, aber sie war nicht geöffnet.   27. Ich hätte den Film gern gesehen.[334]   28. Wen möchten Sie sprechen?   29. Fred will seine Meinung nicht ändern (change one's mind), wir haben ihn nicht überreden (persuade) können, unserem Vorschlag zuzustimmen.   30. Wolltest du uns nicht vorige Woche besuchen?   31. Ich will schon lange mit Ihnen reden (L 2.3.3.).   32. Was wollten Sie gerade sagen (L 2.5.1.5.), als ich Sie unterbrach?   33. Als ich jung war, bin ich viel Ski gefahren (go skiing).[335]   34. Mein Freund wohnte früher in Berlin, jetzt wohnt er in Leipzig.   35. War hier nicht früher ein Kino?   36. Mary ist früher oft ins Theater gegangen, ehe sie Paul heiratete; jetzt verbringt sie die Abende gewöhnlich damit (L 9.2.6.) zu stricken oder fernzusehen.[336]

6.5. / 6.6.
Übersetzen Sie:

1. Your suitcase is rather heavy, shall I carry it?   2. Peter really should apologize to uncle Simon for keeping him waiting so long.   3. There is a good film showing at our cinema; shouldn't we try to get tickets?   4. Which topic do you think we should discuss next?   5. The windows in the living room are rather dirty, you ought to clean them.   6. The TV picture is rather fuzzy, the tubes ought to be replaced.   7. These tablets should be kept out of the reach of children.   8. More streets should be made into pedestrian zones.   9. You should try to get in touch with Mary as soon as possible.   10. Fred will want to know if he is to come, what shall I tell him?   11. The test has failed, we are to repeat it tomorrow.   12. John was to meet us at the station, but he didn't come.   13. The exhibition is to be prolonged for another month.   14. The following questions are to be answered in writing.   15. The lecture on Prevention of Coronary Thrombosis was to take place yesterday, but it had to be postponed because the physician who was to have given it had to perform an urgent operation.   16. When we took leave of our Japanese colleagues at the end of the conference, we thought we wouldn't see them again for

a long time; but, quite unexpectedly, we were to meet again at another symposium after just a few weeks.   17. Twenty people were injured in the train accident, three of them are said to be in a serious condition.   18. Peter graduated from college last year, he is said to be working in a design office.   19. I've already lost count of Anne's boyfriends, and now she is said to have fallen in love again.   20. There are pictures you can look at for hours without discovering what they are supposed to mean.   21. I wonder where Bill is hanging about, he is supposed to be in the office now.   22. Put out your cigarette, you are not supposed to be smoking here.   23. According to first investigations the train accident is supposed to have been due to human failure.   24. The new bridge is due to be opened to traffic tomorrow.   25. The autumn term is due to finish on January 28.   26. The new bypass is intended to relieve traffic in the narrow streets of the centre.   27. I think what Bob said was a joke; at any rate it was not meant to be taken quite seriously.   28. I can't decide this myself, I must ask somebody.   29. You needn't wait if you don't want to.   30. Do I need to explain all the details?   31. We have already made up our minds, they don't need to try to persuade us.   32. How many lectures do you have to attend a week?   33. We have to discuss this problem, it has got to be settled today.   34. Did you have to queue up long for tickets?   35. Let's make a reservation at the restaurant; if we don't, we might have to wait some time before we get a table.   36. Several old tenement houses had to be pulled down where the new residential area is being built.   37. The contract has been drawn up in broad outline, but a few items may have to be altered before it will be signed by our partners. 38. The in vivo tests will have to be continued for some time before the new medicament can be marketed.   39. We were afraid the project might meet with so much opposition that it would have to be abandoned, but our fears were groundless; finally, it didn't even have to be modified.   40. Once radioactivity had been discovered it became evident that it was bound to be of enormous importance in science and technology.

6.5.
A. Geben Sie einen Rat oder eine Empfehlung mit *should/ought to* **und den eingeklammerten Wendungen. (s. L 6.5.2.)**

1. You would enjoy this book. (read)[337]   2. Dorothy is running a temperature. (stay in bed today)   3. My wife has put on a lot of weight. (go on a diet)   4. It has begun to rain. (put on one's coat)   5. This is quite a crucial decision. (consider the pros and cons)   6. The train leaves in ten minutes. (hurry up)

B. Bringen Sie die Wahrscheinlichkeit mit *should/ought to* **zum Ausdruck. (s. L 6.5.2.)**

1. It is quite probable that Mary will be back by ten tonight.[338]   2. We expect to be able to settle the matter tomorrow.   3. Most probably it won't be difficult for Paul to repair the motorbike.   4. It is quite probable that they will be able to solve this problem.

Ü 6.

C. Setzen Sie dem Kontext entsprechend *be to* – wo möglich, auch *shall* –, *be supposed to* bzw. *be said to* ein. (s. L 6.5.3.)

1. ... I (order) a taxi for you?[339]   2. Don't dawdle, you ... (meet)[340] Harry in a quarter of an hour.   3. Fred shouldn't be playing table tennis now; he ... (be doing)[341] his homework.   4. The boss wants to speak to me, I ... (report) to him at ten.   5. John ... (be ill).[342]   6. Mary ... (have got engaged).   7. ... I (explain) the details to you?   8. We ... (not leave)[343] until Harry comes.   9. The negotiations ... (have been resumed).   10. ... we (give) you a lift?   11. You ... (repeat) your lecture this week.   12. Anne ... (study) in Moscow for one year.

D. Bringen Sie bei den folgenden Aussagen die Aufforderung oder Erwartung mit *be to* – wo möglich, auch *shall* – oder *be supposed to*, die Vermutung mit *be said to* zum Ausdruck. (Dabei wird nicht erwähnt, wer etwas von Ihnen erwartet, s. L 6.5.3.)

1. Do you want me to paint the fence?[344]   2. They say Anne has inherited a lot of money from her grandmother.[345]   3. Wait your turn, you shouldn't interrupt us all the time.[346]   4. They expect you to apologize for your rudeness.   5. I want to read this book; I have been told it is very good.   6. Do you want me to make tea?   7. Mary wants us to do the washing up today.   8. We should visit the exhibition, they say it is quite interesting.   9. We have told Peggy to be back before midnight.[347]   10. They told me to send in the questionnaire yesterday, but I forgot it.[348]

E. Entscheiden Sie, ob *was/were to* bzw. *should/ought to* einzusetzen ist. (s. L 6.5.3.1.2.)

1. You ...[349] consider the pros and cons before you make up your mind.   2. I ...[350] take off for Budapest at ten this morning, but the flight had to be cancelled due to dense fog.   3. You ... be very careful in handling this device.   4. The symposium which ... be held last week has been postponed until next month.   5. I wonder why Henry hasn't come yet, he ... be here one hour ago.   6. My sister just wanted to walk the dog for half an hour, she ... be back soon.   7. The programme ... be discussed in detail before it is put to the vote.   8. The meeting ... last half an hour, but it did last two hours.   9. The importance of this innovation ... not be underestimated.   10. A new American space shuttle ... be launched the day before yesterday, but it has been announced by NASA that there will be a considerable delay owing to technical problems.

6.6.

A. Verwenden Sie in den folgenden Sätzen *must, have (got) to, don't have to, needn't, don't need to, need.*

Beispiel: *It isn't necessary to tell Mike about it.* → *(You/...) needn't/don't have to tell Mike about it.*

1. It's necessary for us to hurry up.[351]   2. Is it necessary that you take the 7.30 train?[352]   3. It isn't necessary that Walter comes to our meeting.[353]   4. It isn't necessary that you wait any longer.   5. It is necessary to discuss this problem in

detail.³⁵⁴   6. The performance doesn't start till eight, it isn't necessary for us to leave right away.   7. It will be necessary to check the results once again.³⁵⁵   8. You are not obliged to take a decision immediately.   9. It will be necessary for us to keep this appointment.   10. Is it necessary that I take part in the consultation?   11. The professor wants to know why it had been necessary to interrupt the test.³⁵⁶   12. The advantage of hire purchase is that you are not obliged to pay the full amount at once.   13. You are not obliged to believe everything people tell you, are you?³⁵⁷   14. If Jack were more helpful it wouldn't be necessary for his wife to do all the housework herself.   15. It is hardly necessary for me to say how grateful I am for your assistance.³⁵⁸   16. If we talk the matter over now, we shan't be obliged to meet again tomorrow.   17. Barbara didn't know what to do when her car broke down; she had never been obliged to deal with such a situation before.   18. Our director speaks English and Russian very well, it isn't necessary for him to have an interpreter when he conducts negotiations abroad.   19. Since the main road was under repair, it was necessary for us to take an alternative route.   20. If John had more initiative it wouldn't be necessary always to tell him what to do.³⁵⁹

B. Setzen Sie *must, have to, needn't, don't have to, must not* ein:

1. You ... (come)³⁶⁰ if you don't want to.   2. We ... (make) a detour because there was an accident on the main road.   3. I'm sorry to ... (tell) you that you ... (repeat) the examination.   4. I ... (be off) now.   5. Very few people like ... (work)³⁶¹ on Sundays.   6. When we have finished this project, we ... (work) quite so hard for some time.   7. You ... (do) such a thing again.   8. I hope I ... (operate on).³⁶²   9. The negotiating parties have made a lot of progress, but we ... (forget) that several major issues ... (settle) before agreement is in sight.   10. Why ... the test ... (repeat)³⁶³ yesterday?   11. Fortunately, I've a key on me, otherwise I might ... (wait) outside until my mother comes back.   12. Arthur is pampered by his wife, he ... never ... (work)³⁶⁴ in the household as long as I have known him.

C. Drücken Sie in den folgenden Sätzen mit den in Klammern gegebenen Wendungen eine Wahrscheinlichkeit aus; verneinen Sie dann die Wahrscheinlichkeit. (L 6.6.3.)

Beispiel: Peter's girl-friend writes to him very often. (like very much) → *She must like him very much. – Peter's girl-friend doesn't write to him very often.* → *She can't like him very much.*

1. Jack answered the phone. (be at home now)   2. Mr Miller is an old man. (be seventy)   3. Harry meets Janet frequently. (know very well)   4. Bob always wears glasses. (his eyesight, bad)   5. Anne hasn't forgiven me. (be very angry)

6.5./6.6.
Geben Sie englisch wieder:

1. Wann sollen wir kommen?³⁶⁵   2. Was soll ich Peter sagen, wenn er mich fragt?   3. Wir sollten die Angelegenheit morgen noch einmal besprechen.   4. Tom müßte wissen, daß wir ihn erwarten.   5. Ich soll morgen einen Vortrag im Klub halten.³⁶⁶   6. Du solltest sorgfältiger arbeiten.   7. Soll ich das Fenster öffnen?   8. Wir sollen

Ü 6.

Susan heute abend anrufen.[367]   9. Bob sollte uns begleiten, aber er wollte nicht.[368]   10. Das neue Geschäftszentrum soll diesen Sommer eröffnet werden.[369]   11. Ich soll einen Weiterbildungskursus (refresher course) in Englisch besuchen.   12. Die Verhandlungen sollten gestern wieder aufgenommen werden (resume).   13. Ich weiß nicht, wo John ist; er sollte schon vor zwei Stunden zurück sein.   14. Sie sollten sich (eigentlich) bei Mrs Miller entschuldigen.   15. Es müßte möglich sein, eine Einigung zu erzielen.   16. Wieso ist Tom jetzt auf dem Sportplatz (sports field), er soll doch jetzt in der Schule sein.[370]   17. Jane muß in der Küche sein, sie soll das Geschirr abwaschen (wash the dishes).   18. Die Premiere (première) sollte gestern stattfinden, aber sie mußte auf nächste Woche verschoben werden, weil einige Schauspieler erkrankt sind.   19. Anne soll sich verlobt haben.[371]   20. Ich will mir die Neuinszenierung von 'What You Will' ansehen, sie soll sehr gut sein.   21. Mein Freund mußte vor einigen Tagen ins Krankenhaus gebracht werden, aber sein Zustand (condition) soll sich inzwischen gebessert haben.   22. Das Buch soll einen Überblick über die neuesten Entwicklungstendenzen (most recent trends) der Rechentechnik (computer engineering) geben.[372]   23. Können Sie sich vorstellen, was dieses Bild bedeuten soll?[373]   24. Marys Besuch soll eine Überraschung sein, ich soll niemandem davon erzählen.
25. Ich kann nicht lange warten, ich muß um 10 Uhr im Büro sein.   26. Wann mußt du das Buch zurückgeben (return)?   27. Wo muß ich aussteigen (get off)?   28. Der Vertrag sollte schon vorigen Monat in Kraft treten (come into effect), aber einige Punkte mußten geändert werden, ehe er unterzeichnet werden konnte.   29. Mußtest du lange warten?[374]   30. Mrs Martin kann nicht 30 sein, sie sieht jünger aus als sie ist (not look one's age), sie muß etwa 40 sein.   31. Wir werden die Einzelheiten des Plans noch einmal besprechen müssen.   32. Warum mußte der Versuch abgebrochen werden (break off)?   33. Wenn sich Peters Zustand verschlechtert (get worse), werden wir einen Arzt holen (send for) müssen.   34. In diesen Berechnungen muß ein Fehler sein, man wird sie noch einmal überprüfen müssen.

6.7.

A. Übersetzen Sie:

1. We didn't hear you last night, it must have been very late when you came home.   2. I forgot to post the letter, you should have reminded me.   3. Peter could have won the contest, he ought not to have given up.   4. Anne isn't at home, she may have gone dancing.   5. I'm quite all right again, you needn't have worried.   6. Jane hasn't come yet, she must have been detained by somebody.   7. We could have explained the problem to you if you had asked us.   8. I can't find my watch, where can I have put it?   9. It was wrong of Susan to hitchhike, she might have got into trouble.   10. The performance has already begun, we ought to have hailed a taxi.   11. The slide lecture was not very well attended last week, it needn't have been repeated this week.   12. Aunt Mary is a bit hard of hearing; I'm afraid she may not have caught what we have said, we should have been talking a little louder.   13. I can't understand why Mike didn't advise you, he ought to have been able to give you some hints.   14. The medical check-up was rather unpleasant, but it

might have been worse.   15. Some of the papers read at the symposium were too long; the speaking time should have been limited to 30 minutes.   16. This accident might have been prevented, if adequate precautions had been taken.   17. This church is Romanesque in style, it may have been built in the 12th century. 18. Polly is always curious, she might have been trying to eavesdrop, but we were talking at such a low voice that she can't have overheard what we were saying.

B. **Unterscheiden Sie die unterschiedliche Bedeutung von** *should* **bzw.** *might* **bei der Übersetzung.**

1. I should have worked last night instead of going to the pictures. – I should have worked last night if I hadn't been so tired.
2. We should have helped Michael if he had asked us. – We should have helped Michael in this difficult situation.
3. I think we can eat in a few minutes; Jane should have prepared lunch by now. – Jane should have prepared lunch rather than chat with her friend.
4. Anne might have come if you had invited her. – Anne might have come while we were out, but she didn't leave a message.
5. We might have put you up for the night, if you hadn't got hotel accommodation. – Harry didn't come home yesterday evening; his friends have a guest-room, they might have put him up for the night.

C. **Formen Sie die folgenden Sätze dem Kontext entsprechend mit Hilfsverb + Infinitiv Perfekt um.**

Beispiel: *It is almost certain that John missed the bus.* → *John must have missed the bus.*

1. It's possible that my colleague has already left.[375]   2. Mark was looking in the other direction, it's impossible that he saw us.[376]   3. Your sweater was still good; it was wrong to throw it away.[377]   4. All seats are taken; it would have been necessary for us to book tickets last week.   5. This vase is too expensive; it was a mistake that you bought it.   6. It was wrong to tell Anne about your affair.   7. It would have been impossible for us to walk all the distance.[378]   8. It is impossible that Harry stole the bicycle.   9. It was wrong of Peter not to invite Jane.   10. It is most probable that something unforeseen has happened.[379]   11. Wouldn't it have been better to send your parents a telegram?   12. It wasn't necessary to go into all these details.[380]   13. Frank was told to come but he didn't.   14. The door is open, it is possible that grandmother forgot to lock it.   15. Anne apologized but it wasn't necessary.   16. It was wrong of you not to marry Barbara.   17. It is rather hot, it wouldn't have been necessary for us to take coats.   18. It would have been impossible for me to help them.   19. It was wrong of the director not to inform us in time. 20. It's possible that Jerry has solved the problem in the meantime.   21. It was a mistake that I lent Maggie so much money.   22. It's not quite impossible that Jack tried to phone us while we were away.[381]   23. I'm sure it would have been possible for you to catch the train.   24. You can rely on Peter, it was quite unnecessary for you to have been so distrustful.   25. The light has been on all night; it was most careless of you not to turn it off before you went to bed.

Ü 6.

D. Ergänzen Sie die folgenden Aussagen dem Sinn entsprechend mit *must, needn't, should/ought to, may not, cannot* + Infinitiv Perfekt.

Beispiel: *Nobody answered the phone. (the Smiths, go out)* → *The Smiths must have gone out.*
1. Tom didn't keep our appointment. (he, forget)[382]   2. Why didn't you walk this short distance? (you, take a taxi)[383]   3. Your letter arrived too late. (you, send a telegram)   4. It's quite obvious how the thief got into the flat. (he, use a skeleton key)   5. Lots of people are waiting on the platform. (the train, leave, yet)[384]   6. I wonder why Richard didn't address us at the theatre. (he, see us)   7. I forgot to set the alarm last night. (you, wake me up)   8. I would have been able to translate the text myself. (you, help me)   9. I could have told you what to do in this situation. (you, ask me)   10. I think I know why Mary hasn't come yet. (she, keep in the office)   11. We talked very softly. (our conversation, not overhear)[385]   12. I forgot to add the post code on the letter. (it, misdirect)[386]   13. Your article is too long. (some details, include)   14. I could imagine why Ted didn't want to go to the mountains with us. (he, like the idea to stay in a hut)[387]

E. Vervollständigen Sie die folgenden Sätze mit einem unvollständigen Hilfsverb + Infinitiv Perfekt:
1. I have plenty of food at home, you (buy) any more.   2. You (phone) us when you realized you would be late.   3. Peter is always polite, he (say) a thing like that.   4. You (turn off) the radio before you went away.   5. We've run out of petrol, we (refill) before we left.   6. I would think John (arrive) by now.   7. They (leave) yet, the lights are still on.   8. I'm afraid I (offend) aunt Agatha.   9. You (ski) down this steep hill, you (hurt oneself).   10. Harry hasn't turned up yet, what (happen)?

F. Geben Sie englisch wieder:
1. Jane und Tom sind noch nicht gekommen, sie müssen den Zug verpaßt haben.
2. John hat nicht geschrieben, vielleicht hat er meine Adresse vergessen.[388]   3. Barbara ist nicht zu Hause, sie ist vielleicht ins Theater gegangen.   4. Ich hätte wissen müssen,[389] daß ich mich auf Peter verlassen kann.   5. Die Prüfungsergebnisse hätten besser sein können.   6. Ihr hättet eine Nachricht hinterlassen (leave a message) sollen.   7. Dieses Mißverständnis hätte vermieden werden können.[390]   8. Ich habe den Brief heute morgen eingeworfen (post), Mrs Smith kann ihn noch nicht erhalten haben.   9. Walter kann sein Scheckheft (cheque book) nicht finden, er muß es verloren haben.   10. Du hättest nicht auf mich zu warten brauchen.[391]   11. Der Fernseher ist noch an (on), John muß eingeschlafen sein, als er fernsah.   12. Du hättest in der Lage sein müssen, selbst eine Entscheidung zu treffen (take a decision)[392]   13. Edward sollte uns heute Bescheid geben (inform); er könnte angerufen haben, als wir einkaufen waren.[393]   14. Die Sache war klar; man hätte nicht stundenlang darüber zu sprechen brauchen.[394]   15. Gestern habe ich einen Brief von Jean erhalten, den ich beantworten wollte; aber er ist nirgends zu finden, ich muß ihn verlegt haben (mislay).   16. Als mein Kollege erfuhr (tell, Passiv), daß er in eine andere Abteilung versetzt (transfer) würde, war er nicht überrascht; er muß vorher informiert worden sein.   17. Peter hätte nicht in einem Hotel zu übernach-

ten brauchen (pass the night), er hätte bei uns wohnen (stay with) können, wenn er es gewollt hätte.[395] 18. Mein Freund hat seine Dissertation zurückbekommen, er muß sie überarbeiten (rework); sein Professor sagte ihm, die neuesten Forschungsergebnisse müßten (noch) einbezogen werden (take into consideration).

Komplexübungen zu den unvollständigen Hilfsverben

A. Setzen Sie dem Kontext entsprechend unvollständige Hilfsverben oder, wo erforderlich, deren Äquivalentformen ein:

1. I'm not sure if I ... come tonight.   2. Peggy is eating a lot today, she ... be very hungry.   3. There's plenty of time, we ... hurry up.   4. A shop-assistant ... always be polite to his customers.   5. You ... smoke in a hospital.   6. You ... smoke if you want to.   7. Janet isn't back yet, she ... have to wait at the butcher's.   8. Half an hour ago I left my bicycle outside the shop, somebody ... (steal) it.   9. You ... take your umbrella, it ... be raining this afternoon.   10. Arthur ... bring a doctor's certificate because he didn't come to work for two days.   11. Peggy is very tired, she ... (be working hard) all day.   12. My gloves are nowhere to be seen; where ... I ... (put) them.   13. The method ... (be) old, but it is still effective.   14. John is very happy because his first book ... (publish)[396] soon.   15. When I met Susan for the first time I didn't know that I ... (marry)[397] her.   16. The train is overdue, it ... (arrive)[398] half an hour ago.   17. Things that are forbidden ... (do).   18. Animals in a zoo ... (feed).   19. The restaurant ... be expensive, but the cuisine is excellent.   20. The production of 'Othello' was very good, you ... (go and see) it.   21. In an art gallery you ... touch the paintings but you ... copy them.   22. Mary felt rather excited because she ... (go) by plane for the first time the following day.   23. The writing table I bought last week ... (deliver) yesterday, but it hasn't come yet.   24. You ... tell Kate the story, she ... get angry.   25. Bill knows the facts, he ... (inform) by someone.   26. It was 15 kilometres to the beach from where we lived, we ... (walk)[399] all the distance two times a day.   27. The concert I ... (go to) ... (take place) yesterday, but it ... (cancel) because the soloist had fallen ill.   28. Why don't you switch on the light? – I can't, the fuse ... (blow).   29. The bell is ringing, that ... be Susan. – No, it ... be Susan, she is still in hospital.   30. I don't know where my keys are. I ... (leave) them at home because I remember locking the door. As I missed them when I arrived at the office, I ... (lose) them on the way there. I ... (drop) them when I pulled out my purse at the newsstand.

B. Setzen Sie in dem folgenden Gespräch dem Sinn entsprechende unvollständige Hilfsverben bzw. deren Äquivalentformen ein:

Tom and Jane meet outside a bookshop.
Tom: What are you doing here? – *Jane:* I ... (buy) a book. They ... (say; have; L 6.5.3.3.) a good choice of guide-books here. ... you come with me? – *Tom:* What guide-book ... you ... (buy)? – *Jane:* One about Romania.
They go into the bookshop.
Shop-assistant: ... I help you? – *Jane:* I ... (have) a guide-book about Romania.
The shop-assistant shows her three guide-books.

Ü 7.

Jane (to Tom): Which one ... I take? – *Tom:* You ... take this one with the beautiful photographs. – *Jane (to the shop-assistant):* ... you wrap it up, please? Where ... I ... (pay)? – *Shop-assistant:* At the counter over there.
Tom and Jane leave the shop.
Jane: ... we have a cup of coffee? There ... (be) a café round the corner. – *Tom:* All right, but I ... (write) a postcard.
Tom (to the waitress): ... we have two cups of coffee please?
Tom ... (write) his postcard, but Jane is talking all the time.
Tom: ... you please be quiet for a minute, I ... (concentrate).
She goes on talking.
Tom: ... I just finish my card? – *Jane:* Just one question. What are you doing tonight? ... we go to a concert? – *Tom:* Yes, we ..., that's an excellent idea.

C. Setzen Sie dem Kontext entsprechend *must, have to, should, may, might, can't* ein:

Jane: Why are you stopping? – *Joe:* Something ... be wrong with the engine. It isn't going properly. – *Jane:* We ... be out of petrol. – *Joe:* That ... be possible; I refilled before we left. – *Jane:* You ... have a look at the carburettor. – *Joe:* I'm afraid I ... find out what is wrong. We ... wait until someone comes who ... help us. – *Jane:* But that ... take rather long. There is a call-box over there, we ... try to telephone a repair shop.

D. Vervollständigen Sie den folgenden Bericht mit *be said to, might, may, ought to, could, be supposed to, must*:

The fur shop at the corner was broken into last night. Fur coats to the value of several thousand pounds ... (steal). There are different possibilities of how it ... (happen). The thief ... (get in) through the shop window. But in this case the burglar alarm ... (start). The shop assistants ... (take) the missing objects, but they ... (be) very reliable and furthermore, their alibis have been checked. At any rate, the thief ... (use) a skeleton key, because the lock had not been tampered with.

E. Übersetzen Sie:

Peter: Weißt du, wo Barbara ist? – *Walter:* Sie kann ins Kino gegangen sein.[400] Gestern hat sie mir gesagt, daß sie sich einen englischen Kriminalfilm ansehen will, der sehr gut sein soll.[401] – *Peter:* Das hätte sie mir sagen können;[402] sie müßte wissen, daß ich Krimis auch mag. Ich wäre gern mitgegangen.[403] – *Walter:* Sie muß aber nicht (unbedingt) ins Kino gegangen sein,[404] vielleicht macht sie auch einen Spaziergang mit ihrer Freundin.[405] Eigentlich sollte sie jetzt arbeiten.[406] Sie muß morgen eine Prüfung ablegen (take).[407]

7.1./7.2.
Übersetzen Sie:

1. I know that Jill isn't at home, I think she has gone to the cinema. 2. We suppose that Tom will help us. 3. John writes in his letter that he got married three months ago. 4. Do you think it's going to rain? 5. Mike has told me that Anne is

ill. 6. Fred will tell you that he can't come. 7. Michael has said that he won't accept our offer. 8. It is hoped that the treaty will be signed before long. 9. I have been told that the conference has been postponed.
10. I thought you were ill.
11. Mark said he didn't know Anne but he would like to make her acquaintance.
12. Susan told me last week she was going to get engaged. 13. I had thought that Bill was more reliable. 14. The interpreter told me the British delegation was staying at the Hotel Bellevue. 15. Mary said she had no mind to go dancing tonight.
16. The accused admitted he had committed the burglary. 17. Jane said she didn't want to go to the theatre with us, she would prefer to stay at home and listen to some records. 18. We had hoped they would be able to reach an agreement.
19. Anne said she was very happy that she had passed the examination because she had been afraid she would have to repeat it. 20. The editor said the article would have to be reworked before it could be published. 21. Tom told me that he had to put off his holidays because he was to take part in a conference. 22. Bob said he was going to spend his holidays in Sotshi this year. He told us he had already wanted to go there last July but had been forced to give up his plan because he had fallen ill. 23. The heart specialist pointed out in his lecture that a new type of pacemaker, which had been developed recently, was being tested successfully and would soon be produced in series.
24. The doctor told the patient he didn't have to be hospitalized. – The doctor told the patient he wouldn't have to be hospitalized unless his condition deteriorated. – The doctor told the patient he hadn't had to be hospitalized because his condition had been improving recently. – The doctor told the patient he wouldn't have had to be hospitalized if he had followed his advice.

7.1./7.1.1.
Geben Sie die folgenden Feststellungen in der indirekten Rede wieder:

1. Jane says, 'I like ice cream.'[408] – 2. Anne and Bob say, 'We shall get married soon.' – 3. The accused has repeatedly declared, 'I am innocent.' – 4. Peter says, 'I have been studying chemistry for three years.' – 5. Jack and Norman say, 'We have just finished our experiment.' – 6. Sheila says, 'I got to know my boy-friend half a year ago.'

7.2.1.
Gehen Sie von der Vergangenheit aus, und geben Sie die folgenden Feststellungen in der direkten und der indirekten Rede wieder.

Beispiele:
a) *Mark is tired.* → *Mark said, 'I'm tired.'* → *Mark said he was tired.*
b) *John likes our offer.* → *John said, 'I like your offer.'* → *John said (that) he liked our offer.*

1. Sue is busy. 2. Harry is not informed about the details. 3. Peter is studying mathematics. 4. Joan doesn't have a boy-friend. 5. Fred can't translate the

Ü 7.

text.[409] 6. Susan doesn't know our teacher. 7. Peggy is going to give up her job as a typist. 8. Harold doesn't agree to our proposal. 9. Anne doesn't like crime novels. 10. Liz can't ring us today. 11. Agnes is going to the theatre tonight. 12. James and Jane are looking forward to our visit. 13. Jim may be wrong (L 6.2.1.) 14. Tom has to prepare for a difficult test paper. 15. Bob is able to repair the washing-machine himself. 16. Mike is to give a talk this week. 17. Denise may meet Norman at the weekend (6.2.1.). 18. Alice mustn't watch TV every evening (L 6.3.).[410]

7.2.2.
Geben Sie die folgenden Feststellungen in der indirekten Rede wieder, und verwenden Sie dabei *say* oder *tell sb.*

Beispiel: *Joe was ill.* → *Joe said/told me (that) he had been ill.*

1. Bob saw Gary at the theatre. 2. Charles met Shirley in Berlin on Sunday. 3. Albert was abroad several times. 4. Roger has been informed by a colleague of ours. 5. Brian and James agreed to co-operate in the project. 6. Bill was working all day.[411] 7. I had no opportunity to see this film. 8. Henry was trying in vain to get tickets for the theatre. 9. Anne has been writing letters all afternoon. 10. I know that I've made a mistake.[412] 11. Fred thinks Mary hasn't gone away yet. 12. Arthur says the meeting has been postponed. 13. Liz is afraid Ronald might miss the train (6.7.).[413] 14. The test was successful. (It was announced ...) 15. My uncle's health has been improving during the last weeks. (My uncle said ...) 16. It is generally believed that the talks have been very useful. (The reporters agreed ...)

7.2.3.
Gehen Sie von der Vergangenheit aus, und geben Sie die folgenden Feststellungen in der indirekten Rede wieder.

Beispiel: *Bob will go to Berlin on Friday.* → *Bob said he would go to Berlin on Friday.*

1. Kitty will send me a picture-postcard from Bulgaria. 2. My brother will answer your letter right away. 3. Fred will be delighted to meet Marilyn. 4. John will have to ask his wife.[414] 5. Joe and Jim will be waiting for us at the station. 6. Mark will try to find Anne's address. 7. The remaining problems will be dealt with tomorrow. (The chairman announced ...) 8. I'm sure Harry will be able to solve the problem.

7.3.
A. Übersetzen Sie:

1. We don't know where Mr Hilton lives. 2. Can you tell me why Susan wants to break with her boy-friend? 3. I wonder why Bob didn't come yesterday. 4. Bill asked Alice where she had been. 5. Peter asked Eve if she would go to the pictures with him. 6. Tom didn't tell me whether he had booked rooms for us at a hotel. 7. I asked how long I would have to wait. 8. We enquired if we might come a little later. 9. The police tried to find out when and how the murder had been

committed. 10. We wonder why John and Jill didn't want to tell us what they had been talking about.

B. Setzen Sie die folgenden Fragen in die indirekte Rede:

1. Where is the hotel situated? (I don't know ...)   2. Did your parents spend their holidays abroad? (I asked Susan ...)[415]   3. What is the film about? (I can't tell you ...)   4. What time will Anne come? (Peter couldn't say ...)[416]   5. Is Mary at home? (Jane asked me ...)   6. How long was John ill? (The teacher wanted to know ...)   7. What did Janet buy at the department store? (Harry asked Janet ...)   8. Will Dorothy come to Frank's party? (I'm not sure ...)   9. Can I help you? (Bob asked me ...)   10. How did the accident happen? (The policeman enquired ...)   11. Is your husband on a business-trip? (I asked Liz ...)   12. When did the boss leave the office? (Nobody could tell me exactly ...)   13. Can you recommend this film? (Fred asked me ...)   14. Who did Mark get this information from? (We enquired ...)   15. What are Joe and Jill talking about all the time? (I wonder ...)   16. What hotel will you be staying at? (Tom asked me ...)[417]   17. Are you able to operate this device? (Arthur wanted to know from his colleague ...)   18. How long were you working on your diploma thesis? (I asked Bill ...)   19. Do I have to make up my mind at once? (Alice wanted to know ...)[418]   20. What did the customers complain about? (The manager enquired ...)

7.2./7.3.
A. Gehen Sie bei den folgenden Feststellungen von der Vergangenheit aus, und finden Sie dem Kontext entsprechend die richtige Zeitform für die indirekte Rede.

Beispiele: *I think Harry is at home.* → *I thought Harry was at home.*
We know they will help us. → *We knew they would help us.*
Sue wants to know if Fred went to the party. → *Sue wanted to know if Fred had gone to the party.*

1. I think Anne will come.   2. Bob admits that he was impolite.   3. The professor wants to know if we have finished the manuscript.   4. Joan denies that she was in love with Jack.   5. I suppose Mike was abroad.   6. Peter often promises that he will visit us.   7. We assume that the solution is correct.   8. The nurse often asks me how I feel.   9. I can't remember who I gave the book to.   10. John wants to know if he may accompany us (L 6.3.).

B. Stellen Sie die folgenden Aussagen in der indirekten Rede dar:

1. John has bought a new car. (John said ...)[419]   2. My aunt will soon visit me. (My aunt told me ...)[420]   3. What did you tell them? (Anne asked me ...)[421]   4. Mike was waiting for the bus half an hour. (Mike said ...)   5. Is Susan married? (Bob wanted to know ...)   6. Have the results been checked? (I don't know ...)   7. Has your mother been a teacher? (Jack asked me ...)   8. Our flat is being redecorated. (My parents-in-law told me ...)   9. The next symposium will be held in Vienna. (It was agreed ...)   10. Frank is late because he has missed the train. (Frank explained ...)[422]   11. Why didn't you buy this nice dress? (Bill asked Eve ...)

Ü 7.

12. Have the guests arrived yet? (I asked Peter ...)[423]   13. Our fridge will be repaired next week. (We were told ...)   14. A colleague of mine was doing a lot of overtime last week. (A colleague of mine informed the director ...)   15. Shall we wait a little longer? (We were not sure ..., 6.5.2.)   16. These letters will have to be typed at once. (The manager told our secretary ...)   17. The test is just being carried out. (The lab assistant informed us ...)   18. Will Mark be given a bonus? (I enquired ...)   19. What are Helen and Jim quarrelling about? (I didn't know ...)   20. What was the weather like at the seaside? (We asked our neighbours ...)   21. I hope we shall be informed in time. (Tom said ...)[424]   22. Who did you talk about the matter to? (I asked Fred ...)[425]

C. Setzen Sie die folgenden Feststellungen und Fragen in die indirekte Rede, und beginnen Sie mit *I/John/Joan – said/told sb/ wanted to know/asked*

1. Fred has moved into a new flat.[426]   2. I am busy.[427]   3. Will you go to Berlin next week?   4. Bob has bought a new suit.   5. Do you know anything about computers?   6. When did Harry graduate from college?   7. Mary has fallen ill.   8. Do you know French?   9. Susan hasn't finished her doctoral thesis yet.   10. Have you come by car?   11. Peggy is trying to solve the problem by herself.   12. He'll phone us tomorrow.   13. May I smoke here? (L 6.3.)   14. Why are you in a hurry?   15. Have you met Michael before?   16. We are planning to sell our garage.   17. When did you meet Paul?   18. I am going to queue up for tickets.   19. Does Mark have to repeat his test paper?   20. Do you think the test was successful?   21. What does John's girl-friend look like? – 22. Who is the girl that you talked to?

Komplexübungen zu 7.1./7.2./7.3.

A. Geben Sie englisch wieder, was Ihnen ein Bekannter erzählt. Beginnen Sie mit *My schoolfriend says ...* (L 7.1.)

er sei verheiratet; er sei seit 6 Jahren verheiratet; er habe 2 Kinder; er arbeite in einem Rechenzentrum; seine Arbeit gefalle ihm; er werde nächsten Monat zum Abteilungsleiter ernannt (L 11.2.); er müsse jedes Jahr an Weiterbildungskursen (postgraduate courses) auf seinem Gebiet teilnehmen; seine Frau sei Stenotypistin (shorthand typist); sie arbeitet zur Zeit nicht, weil sie wieder ein (= another) Baby erwartet; sie werde im Sommer nächsten Jahres ihre Arbeit wieder aufnehmen (resume).

B. Geben Sie englisch wieder, was Ihnen ein Bekannter erzählt hat. Beginnen Sie mit *My schoolfriend told me ...* (L 7.2.)

er sei Arzt; er habe vor 4 Jahren sein Studium abgeschlossen (graduate from the university); er arbeite in einer Poliklinik (outpatient department); er schreibe jetzt seine Dissertation (write one's doctoral thesis), er hoffe, sie in 3 Jahren beenden zu können (L 6.1.1.); er sei verheiratet; seine Frau sei Schwester (nurse) in einem Krankenhaus; sie hätten zwei Kinder.

C. Berichten Sie, was Sie einen Bekannten gefragt haben, und beginnen Sie mit *I/we asked (him)/wanted to know/enquired...*
Sie haben sich erkundigt:
warum Sie ihn solange nicht gesehen haben; ob er krank gewesen sei; ob er eine Dienstreise gemacht habe (be on a business trip); ob er im Ausland gewesen sei; ob er an dem Symposium über Strahlenschutz (radiation protection) in Wien (Vienna) teilgenommen habe; ob er dort einen Vortrag gehalten habe (read a paper); ob der Vortrag auf dem Symposium übersetzt worden sei, oder ob er selbst englisch gesprochen habe; ob er für seine Gespräche mit ausländischen Kollegen einen Dolmetscher gebraucht habe; wann er zurückgekommen sei; ob ihm der Aufenthalt gefallen habe; ob er mit den Ergebnissen der Konferenz zufrieden sei; ob sein Vortrag schon gedruckt vorläge (be available in print); wann die nächste Konferenz zu diesem Thema stattfinden würde; wo sie durchgeführt würde (hold); ob er daran teilnehmen würde; ob er bereit sei, wieder einen Vortrag zu halten, wenn man ihn darum bäte (L 5.1.2.)

D. Jane gibt ein Gespräch wieder, das sie mit ihrer Mutter hatte, als sie neulich spät nach Hause kam. – Zur Einleitung der indirekten Rede verwendet sie dabei die folgenden Verben an den gekennzeichneten Stellen, jeweils mit *mother* bzw. *I*:
ask (1); *say* (2) *and add* (3); *want to know* (4); *answer* (5); *tell* (6); *reply* (7); *say* (8); *enquire* (9); *say* (10); *want to know* (11); *explain* (12); *ask* (13); *answer* (14); *add* (15); *promise* (16).
Beginnen Sie also mit: *Mother asked if I realized...*

Mother: Do you realize what time it is? (1)
Jane: I think it's about midnight (2), I'm very tired (3).
Mother: What have you been doing all the evening? (4)
Jane: I've been having a good time. (5) First I went to the theatre, then we had some bottles of wine at a restaurant. (6)
Mother: That can't have taken so long. (7)
Jane: Afterwards we went dancing in a night club. (8)
Mother: Who did you spend the evening with? (9)
Jane: I met some fellow students at the theatre. (10)
Mother: Were these fellow students of yours boys or girls? (11)
Jane: We were three girls and three boys. (12)
Mother: Why didn't you phone us? (13)
Jane: I didn't think it necessary. (14) It's not the first time I have been out late. (15) But next time I'll ring you up so that you won't be worried. (16)

8.1.–8.5.
A. Übersetzen Sie:
1. Jogging has been very popular for some years. 2. Trying to 'turn the clock back' never works. 3. Informing, entertaining, and educating are key functions of television. 4. The compulsory wearing of seat belts has considerably reduced road accidents. 5. The signing of the contract took place yesterday. 6. Learning foreign languages is always useful. 7. Keeping the flat tidy, washing and mending

Ü 8.

clothes will continue to be a problem for the working woman.   8. The proof of the pudding is in the eating.
9. Excuse me for being late.   10. Aunt Margaret often complains about being lonely.   11. We have decided against postponing the meeting.   12. Unfortunately I am prevented from taking part in the conference.   13. My brother-in-law has a heart disease, the doctor has told him to abstain from smoking and drinking.
14. We are thinking of spending our holidays in Hungary this summer.   15. The speaker confined himself to pointing out the main aspects of the problem.   16. I must apologize for having forgotten our appointment.   17. For some time Peter has been thinking of changing his job.   18. Mr Turner didn't agree to what was being said, but he refrained from making any comment.   19. Susan is dreaming of marrying a football star.   20. Like all her friends Mary is intent upon losing weight.
21. Harry dislikes watching TV, but he is keen on seeing films at the cinema.
22. Jane enjoys spending her spare time reading detective stories, she is particularly fond of reading novels by Raymond Chandler.   23. I like watching people play table tennis, though I am rather bad at playing it myself.   24. A policeman saved our neighbour's son from being run over by a lorry yesterday.   25. We have repeatedly talked about building a garage behind our house, but putting the plan into practice is, among others things, a matter of getting somebody to help us.   26. I don't like this project, that's why I won't let myself be talked into supporting it.
27. Tom can be proud of having been awarded three medals in the swimming contest.   28. I'm tired of having to tell you the same things over and over again.
29. My wife takes pleasure in making dresses for herself.   30. You had better think carefully about what you are going to say now in order not to run the risk of being misunderstood.   31. The climbers were on the point of leaving the mountain cabin, when they heard the avalanches coming down.   32. Do you have any experience in handling a pocket computer?   33. Arthur is rather pig-headed; when he has an idea, however odd it may be, it is very difficult to talk him out of following it.
34. Mrs Smith makes a point of nagging at her husband in the presence of other people; I would object to being treated like that.   35. The manager of the department store is accused of having embezzled a large sum of money; two shop-assistants are suspected of being implicated in the affair.   36. Lots of people consider the end of the year an occasion for pondering upon the past and proposing to do better in the future.   37. The negotiating parties are still far from reaching an agreement.   38. A good detective story provides the key to solving the crime from the very beginning without making it easy for the reader to identify the culprit.
39. The chairman said he thought he was justified in calling the conference a success.   40. There is little point in bringing up this topic again.   41. Putting off doing a thing is putting off the satisfaction of having done it.
42. Don't forget to sign the customs declaration before checking in.   43. I only managed to catch the plane by taking a taxi.   44. You should come to the point instead of beating about the bush.   45. Don't leave without saying goodbye to grandfather.   46. John was stopped by a policeman this morning for driving too fast.   47. After taking a stroll along Nevsky Prospekt we went to the famous Pushkin Theatre.   48. Dr Frazer began his lecture on automation by giving a short survey of the history of automata.

Ü 8.

49. Would you mind shutting the door? 50. Do you mind taking the key to my flat, the plumber is coming this afternoon while I'm out. 51. I don't mind being criticized if the criticism is justified. 52. Would you mind waiting a few minutes, I just want to finish typing this letter. 53. We don't mind coming a little earlier tomorrow. 54. You should avoid making such a mistake again. 55. I dislike being kept waiting. 56. Joan and Fred consider getting married, but they haven't fixed the date yet. 57. Bob may resent not having been invited to our party. 58. I wonder why John has given up collecting stamps. 59. We narrowly escaped missing the last train. 60. Barbara enjoys being told that she is pretty, but she detests being soft-soaped. 61. Father has fallen ill, so we have to postpone redecorating our flat. 62. I suggest having a coffee-break before we discuss the next item. 63. Handing over the project at the appointed date will involve doing a lot of overtime. 64. I am looking forward to meeting Susan again, I remember meeting her when she was a little girl. 65. You risk losing a lot of money if you buy a second-hand car without having it thoroughly checked beforehand. 66. I am pretty absent-minded these days, I keep mislaying things. 67. The two accomplices were convicted of being involved in the murder though they denied having been present on the scene of crime. 68. What about dining out today? 69. How about having a drink at the snackbar over there? 70. I'm keen on buying this book, I've been told repeatedly that it is worth reading. 71. A job worth doing is a job worth doing well. 72. I'm afraid it's no use talking the matter over again. 73. We know the flight is booked up, it is no use telephoning the travel agency. 74. Anne is quite egocentric, but I can't help liking her. 75. You were talking so loud that we couldn't help overhearing what you said. 76. I'm rather tired, I don't feel like going for a walk now. 77. Bob says he doesn't feel up to discussing the book before he has read it a second time. 78. We'll take the tram today because our car needs servicing. 79. My trousers are baggy, they require pressing. 80. Don't put on these shoes, they want mending. 81. Apart from finding interesting topics teachers of foreign languages need a lot of skill in trying to make their pupils talk. 82. At conferences Martin often has difficulty in communicating with English speaking participants, like many of his colleagues he is used to reading scientific literature in his field but he is not accustomed to talking or being talked to in English. 83. The Soviet Union has repeatedly pointed out that there is no alternative to abolishing all nuclear weapons if the danger of an atomic war is to be banished for good. 84. Today everybody should contribute in his place to preventing the world from being plunged into a nuclear disaster. 85. A scientist needs imagination in creating new hypotheses as well as ingenuity and skill in devising experiments to test them and critical judgment in evaluating the results. 86. There is no denying the fact that in modernist art there is often a lack of consensus between the artist and the broad public. 87. A lot of measures remain to be taken at our institute with a view to promoting research. 88. Brecht's plays are convincing examples of how works of art can educate the audience as well as entertaining it. 89. An ancient myth tells us that Atlas was allotted the task of carrying the universe on his shoulders. 90. Edison's kinetoscope was one of the first devices capable of being used as a film projector. 91. The modern system of classification and nomenclature of plants and animals

Ü 8.

was developed by Linné in the 18th century, who succeeded in classifying every known animal and plant and assigning it to a position in his system. 92. When radio waves travel round the globe they do so by being reflected between the earth and the atmosphere. 93. The discovery of the process for making celluloid by Hyatt in 1870 was an essential prerequisite to producing films. 94. A substance that increases the rate of a chemical reaction without being used up in it is called a catalyst. 95. One of the main objectives of cybernetics is to increase the efficiency of human labour by controlling and governing processes in nature, technology and human society.

B. Verwenden Sie in den folgenden Sätzen das Gerundium; ergänzen Sie, wo erforderlich, die Präposition:

1. There are a lot of difficulties involved (solve)[428] this problem. 2. You should avoid (repeat) this mistake. 3. Harry doesn't take any interest (go) to concerts. 4. I'm very fond (listen) to records. 5. Who is responsible (leave)[429] the door unlocked last night? 6. I'm sure Susan would never think (marry) Simon. 7. John boasts (speak) four languages. 8. We are looking forward (meet) you soon. 9. Are you accustomed (stay)[430] up late? 10. I don't mind (wait) a few minutes. 11. What I dislike about Bob is that he will never admit (make)[431] a mistake. 12. Excuse me (be) late again. 13. Helen enjoys (knit) sweaters. 14. The factory has specialized (produce)[432] high-precision instruments. 15. I don't feel up to (go) out today. 16. Mike says he isn't used (speak)[433] in public. 17. I am sorry (keep) you (wait)[434]. 18. We are tired (listen to) Henry's complaints. 19. I am afraid Susan has little hope (pass)[435] the driving test tomorrow. 20. Many colleagues are glad you succeeded (settle) the issue. 21. I must apologize (not finish) the manuscript in time. 22. You can count (receive)[436] hospitably by our Czech friends. 23. Peter hates (call) a pusher. 24. We shall make up for lost time (get up)[437] very early tomorrow. 25. Some of the workers in our factory complain (expose to) too much noise during the working process. 26. Your dress is crumpled, it needs (iron). 27. I've been busy (write) letters all afternoon. 28. Each year life guards save a lot of careless bathers (drown).[438] 29. The natural hydrological cycle is capable (endlessly evaporate) water from the seas into the atmosphere and (precipitate) it onto the land as rain or snow before (return) it into the oceans again. 30. Chadwick's discovery of neutrons provided a method (bombard) the nucleus of atoms without the disadvantage of the positively charged protons (repel).[439]

C. Formen Sie die folgenden Sätze um, und verwenden Sie die in Klammern gegebenen Ausdrücke + Gerundium, wobei Sie, wenn erforderlich, die passende Präposition einsetzen.

1. Peggy likes very much to read detective stories. (Peggy is fond ...)[440] 2. We hope to see you soon. (We look forward ...)[441] 3. John is rather irritable today, you'd better not get on his nerves and ask silly questions. (You should stop ... by ...)[442] 4. I intend to spend the weekend with friends. (I'm thinking ...) 5. We continued to talk another hour or so after you had left. (We went on ...) 6. The driver said he had not caused the accident. (The driver denied ...)[443] 7. Mary pretends to be able to speak Portuguese. (Mary boasts ...) 8. It was very nice to talk to you. (I

enjoyed ...)   9. My wife says that our living-room should be redecorated. (My wife suggests ...)⁴⁴⁴   10. Have you written the essay? (Have you finished ...?)   11. Do you often speak Russian? (Are you accustomed ...?)   12. Mary doesn't smoke any more. (Mary has given up ...)   13. One can solve such problems in different ways. (There are different ways ...)   14. Susan really wants to learn Spanish. (Susan is keen ...)   15. I wouldn't interfere in their controversy. (I don't like the idea ...)   16. Jane didn't hand in her test paper on time. (Jane was criticized ...)⁴⁴⁵   17. Peter wanted to talk about the new film. (Peter suggested ...)   18. Our team are playing rather badly today, they don't have much of a chance to win the match. (They are far ...)   19. I usually don't stay up late. (I am not used ...)   20. Did you manage to find the error in the calculations? (Did you succeed ...?)   21. It was very stormy yesterday; two times I was almost hit by falling bricks. (Two times I narrowly escaped ...)⁴⁴⁶   22. Harry doesn't seem to be in a mood to talk today. (Harry doesn't seem to feel ...)⁴⁴⁷   23. Peter says he would rather not discuss the matter with us. (Peter objects ...)⁴⁴⁸   24. John wasn't given a bonus. (John made a fuss ...)⁴⁴⁹   25. I think I daresay our talks have been successful. (I think I'm right ...)⁴⁵⁰   26. Why should we invite Bob; he always says he has no time to go to parties. (It's no use ...; he keeps ...)

D. **Verkürzen Sie die hervorgehobenen Satzteile durch *after*, *aside from*, *without*, *before*, *on*, *by*, wobei die eingeklammerten Wörter nicht mehr erscheinen.**

James Clark is head of the research centre in our chemical plant. ***He left school at 18***, (then) he studied chemistry at a college of technology.⁴⁵¹ ***He took lessons in French and German*** (and) also learnt a little Japanese⁴⁵², but ***he did not finish the course.***⁴⁵³ James decided to take a doctoral degree (and then) ***to accept a job in industry.***⁴⁵⁴ ***When he started work in our plant***⁴⁵⁵ he was (at once) given the task to reorganize the research centre. Meanwhile his team has contributed to a considerable increase in productivity ***because they introduced several important innovations.***⁴⁵⁶

E. **Verkürzen Sie die folgenden Sätze mit dem Gerundium:**

1. We suggest that we tackle the problem at once.⁴⁵⁷   2. I remember that I was rather bad at mathematics at school.⁴⁵⁸   3. Peter says he regrets that he has told us an untruth.   4. I'm surprised that the door is open, I remember that I had locked it before I left.   5. Mary denies that she has fallen in love with Jack.   6. Do you recall that you have talked to Bob about my suggestion?   7. Fred is very dependable; we can't imagine that we might ever be left in the lurch by him.⁴⁵⁹   8. The accused admitted that he had robbed the shop.   9. The watchmaker said he didn't recollect that he had promised to repair your watch until yesterday.   10. Can you imagine that you would grow a beard?⁴⁶⁰   11. I can't remember that I have said any such thing.   12. We would have liked to take part in the excursion; we regret that we were informed too late.

F. **Verbinden Sie die folgenden Feststellungen mit dem Gerundium:**

1. John will get the job. He is sure of it.⁴⁶¹   2. I shall tell my boss that I have made a mistake. I don't mind it.⁴⁶²   3. Richard was so angry that he left and didn't say

goodbye.⁴⁶³ 4. Joan didn't do her homework. Instead, she went dancing.⁴⁶⁴ 5. We want to start the new project tomorrow. We are considering it. 6. I haven't booked tickets in advance. I have missed it. 7. Dr Graves completed his examination of the patient. Then he wrote out a prescription. 8. Harry's wife always has to spend a lot of time on housework. She dislikes it.⁴⁶⁵ 9. I tried in vain to reach Janet on the telephone yesterday. Then I sent her a telegram.⁴⁶⁶ 10. Glen will receive his salary today. Then he will be able to pay the next instalment for his colour TV set. 11. The head of department opened the meeting. Before, he had asked the secretary to take the minutes. 12. We can't discuss this topic today. We shall defer it. 13. Dr Brown presented a review of the literature in this field. He began his lecture in this way.⁴⁶⁷ 14. The chairman thanked the speaker for his paper. Then he said the topic was open to discussion.

G. Stellen Sie sich vor, Sie seien Schauspieler. Sagen Sie, was Sie in Ihrem Beruf gern tun und was Sie nicht mögen. Verwenden Sie dabei dem Kontext entsprechend die folgenden Ausdrücke jeweils einmal: *detest, dislike, dream of, enjoy, be fond of, be not so keen on, look forward to, don't mind.*
Sagen Sie, daß Sie gern auf der Bühne arbeiten, und beginnen Sie mit *I am fond of ....* Sagen Sie dann,

daß Sie nicht so gern in Filmen mitwirken (perform) – daß Sie, wie die meisten Schauspieler, davon träumen, eines Tages Hamlet darzustellen (do Hamlet) – daß Sie es nicht mögen, romantische Helden zu verkörpern (impersonate) – daß Sie sehr gern in Kriminalstücken auftreten (appear) – daß Sie nichts dagegen haben, von Zeit zu Zeit eine Rolle in einem Musical zu übernehmen (take) – daß Sie es überhaupt nicht mögen, in trivialen Komödien zu spielen (act) – daß Sie sich jetzt darauf freuen, die Hauptrolle (leading part) in einem Stück von Arthur Miller zu spielen.

8.6./8.6.1.
Übersetzen Sie:

1. Excuse me disturbing you. 2. Do you mind my asking you a favour? 3. Would you mind me turning on the radio? 4. Do you mind us bringing a few friends to our get-together? 5. I haven't seen Jane for a long time, but I remember her being quite a pretty girl. 6. We are surprised at Henry (Henry's) forgetting to ring us up. 7. I don't mind you keeping the book another few days. 8. Nothing can stop Peter talking once he has touched upon his favourite topic, which is collecting stamps. 9. Jean is rather capricious, I can't understand her changing her mind time and again. 10. I'm annoyed about Jack always waiting for me to pay when we go to a restaurant. 11. Mary's parents-in-law are very formal; I dislike them always standing on ceremony. 12. We wouldn't mind you not repairing the washing-machine today, if you promise to do it tomorrow. 13. My daughter Susan is 18 now and still very obstinate; I can't bear her behaving like a little child each time she is refused a request. 14. Does anybody object to the remaining items being dealt with tomorrow? 15. Helen is an acknowledged scientist, but I can also imagine her be-

ing a good housewife.   16. Three days after the shipwreck there is little hope of any more survivors being rescued.   17. Before the representatives of the Japanese firm agreed to sign the contract, they insisted on some items being worded more precisely in English.   18. The introduction of automation has led to the human element being eliminated increasingly in modern industry.   19. Leonardo da Vinci is credited with having designed the first parachute, there is, however, no evidence of it having been tested.   20. The discovery of the electron by J. J. Thomson in 1897 resulted in new concepts of the composition of matter being developed.

8.6./8.6.1.
Bilden Sie Sätze mit dem Gerundium, und verwenden Sie dabei die in Klammern stehenden Satzanfänge, wobei Sie, wenn erforderlich, die Präposition ergänzen.

1. May I open the window? (Do you mind ...?)[468]
2. Henry goes to the pub twice a week. (Anne dislikes ...)[469]
3. Jack won't reject our invitation. (I can't imagine ...)
4. Sue is planning to sing in a jazzband. (Her parents can't prevent ...)[470]
5. I'll answer your letter by return of post. (You can count ...)
6. Tom was quite insistent that we should come. (Tom insisted ...)[471]
7. It would be very kind of you to let us have an early answer. (We would appreciate ...)
8. Jean dislikes ballet. (I don't understand ...)
9. Could we come a little later tomorrow? (Do you mind ...?)
10. Why should Arthur spend all his holidays fishing? (I can't imagine ...)
11. John and Maggie intend to get divorced. (We are surprised ...)[472]
12. Mark says that we can leave now. (Mark doesn't mind ...)
13. It's not like you to be so tactless. (I can't understand ...)
14. We don't want Harry to think that we are angry with him. (We want to avoid ...)
15. It's impossible to persuade Peter not to join a rugby team. (We can't stop ...)[473]
16. I'm confident you will take care of this matter. (I shall rely ...)
17. It's not necessary that you invite Henry. (We wouldn't mind ...)[474]
18. I wish Anne and Glen didn't quarrel so much. (I dislike ...)

8.7.1./8.7.2./8.7.3.
Entscheiden Sie, ob Infinitiv oder Gerundium stehen muß:

1. I prefer (go) to the cinema to (watch TV).[475] I would prefer (go) to the cinema tonight rather than (watch TV).[476] Peter prefers (walk) to (go) by tram. Peter says he would prefer (walk) to the station rather than (go) by tram.
2. I remember (give)[477] John the book. I must remember (give)[478] John the book. Remember (lock) the door when you leave. I don't remember (lock) the door. Do you remember Susan (phone) us last week? Did you remember (phone) Susan?
3. I like (go) to concerts. I would like (go) to a concert tonight. Anne likes (go out), I think she would have liked (come) to our party.

Ü 8.

4. Have you ever tried (ride) a horse? The cowboy tried (ride) the wild horse, but he was thrown off.
5. I regret (tell)[479] you something wrong. I regret (tell)[480] you that you have failed the exam. I regret (cause) you an inconvenience because I didn't inform you.
6. Some time ago Peter stopped (smoke) cigarettes; now, while at work, he stops occasionally (smoke) a pipe.
7. If we don't stop them they will go on (talk) for hours. The chairman welcomed the participants in the conference and then went on (introduce) the first speaker.
8. If you had not reminded me I would have forgotten (give) uncle Fred the birthday present I had bought for him because I had actually forgotten (buy) it.
9. Jack is interested (learn) Japanese. I was interested (hear) that Jack was learning Japanese.
10. If you are hungry I propose (have) lunch now. I usually have lunch at home, but today I propose (dine out).
11. I think Bob didn't mean (be) impolite. To refuse our manager's invitation would mean (be) impolite.
12. The word 'forsooth' has ceased (be) in current use. At the age of 20, Mary ceased (go) to the disco.
13. There are snow-drifts on the road, I wouldn't advise (take) the car. I would advise you (take) the car instead of relying on the train.
14. It was beginning (rain) when we left. It began (rain) at about eight this morning. It was when Jane threatened to leave me that I began (understand) how much I liked her.

Komplexübungen zum Gerundium

A. Sagen Sie Ihrem Gesprächspartner,

– daß es sich lohnt, die Ausstellung zu besuchen[481]/sich den Film anzusehen/eine Reise (trip) nach Samarkand zu buchen/die Romane von Graham Greene zu lesen/zum Dresdner Dixieland-Festival zu gehen
– daß es keinen Zweck hat, sich nach Karten anzustellen[482]/zu versuchen, den Zug (noch) zu erreichen/den Versuch zu wiederholen/Susan zu bewegen (make, 5.7.1.), ihre Meinung zu ändern
– daß Sie damit beschäftigt sind, sich auf die Prüfung vorzubereiten[483]/das Zimmer aufzuräumen (tidy up)/einen Artikel für eine wissenschaftliche Zeitschrift zu schreiben/einen englischen Text ins Deutsche zu übersetzen
– daß Sie daran interessiert sind, Italienisch zu lernen[484]/sich an dem Preisausschreiben (prize competition) zu beteiligen/dem Jazzklub beizutreten (join)/eine Reise nach Jalta zu machen/einen Abendkurs über moderne Malerei zu besuchen (take)
– was Sie mögen bzw. nicht mögen (Entscheiden Sie bei den folgenden Angaben selbst, und verwenden Sie *be fond of, enjoy* bzw. *dislike*): ins Theater gehen/fernsehen/utopische Romane lesen/tanzen gehen/Kartoffeln schälen (peel)/Strümpfe stopfen (darn)/einkaufen gehen/Schallplatten hören/Museen besuchen

Fragen Sie Ihren Gesprächspartner,
ob er etwas dagegen hat, daß Sie eine Zigarette rauchen[485] / daß Sie das Fenster öffnen / daß Sie das Radio leise stellen (turn down) / daß Ihr Freund ihn in einer wichtigen Angelegenheit um Rat fragt (consult).

Entschuldigen Sie sich bei Ihrem Gesprächspartner,
daß Sie ihn stören[486] / daß Sie ihn unterbrechen / daß Sie ihn nicht rechtzeitig informiert haben.

B. Geben Sie englisch wieder:

1. Würden Sie bitte die Tür schließen[487] / Ihre Frage wiederholen / ein wenig lauter sprechen / mich um 5 Uhr abholen (pick up) / mir den Weg zum Bahnhof zeigen / mir sagen, wann die Vorstellung beginnt.
2. Wie wäre es, wenn wir heute abend in ein gutes Restaurant gehen[488] / über das Wochenende in die Berge fahren / Fred fragten, ob er mitkommt / einige Freunde zum Essen einladen.
3. Ich habe nichts dagegen, einige Minuten zu warten[489] / daß Sie etwas früher gehen / daß Peter seine Freundin mitbringt.
4. Vielen Dank, daß Sie uns geholfen haben. 5. Nachdem wir den Artikel gelesen hatten, mußten wir eine kurze Zusammenfassung (summary) geben. – 6. Ist es Ihnen gelungen, das Problem zu lösen? 7. Ehe ich gehe, muß ich (noch) mit Herrn Martin sprechen. 8. Du solltest nicht gehen, ohne dich zu entschuldigen. 9. Ich freue mich darauf, Sie nächstes Jahr in Berlin wiederzusehen (meet again). 10. Hast Du vor (think of), dir ein neues Auto zu kaufen? 11. Ich muß mich entschuldigen, daß ich Ihren Brief so spät beantworte.[490] 12. Nach Beendigung des Versuchs müssen wir die Ergebnisse analysieren. 13. Du kannst dich darauf verlassen, daß ich dich rechtzeitig informiere.[491] 14. Peggy ist nicht daran gewöhnt, selbst zu kochen. 15. Ich kann mich nicht erinnern, Herrn Martin schon einmal getroffen zu haben. 16. Wir schlagen vor, eine Pause zu machen. 17. Es gefällt uns nicht, daß Alfred so unzuverlässig ist.[492] 18. Susan ist sehr attraktiv, sie ist daran gewöhnt, von Männern bewundert zu werden.[493] 19. Ich kann mir nicht vorstellen, daß sich Michael für Fußball interessiert. 20. Wir sind nicht daran gewöhnt, in einem geheizten Zimmer zu schlafen. 21. Erinnerst du dich, daß John uns erzählt hat, daß er einige Jahre in Griechenland war? 22. Mike war sehr selbstgefällig (self-complacent), es dauerte lange, bis er sich daran gewöhnt hatte, kritisiert zu werden. 23. Wir bestehen darauf, daß die Angelegenheit überprüft wird. 24. Ich bedaure, Ihnen Unannehmlichkeiten bereitet zu haben (put sb to trouble).[494]

Komplexübungen: Gerundium oder Infinitiv?

A. Gerundium oder Infinitiv nach *to* (5.1., 6.4.4., 8.2.1./2.)

1. We are used to (eat) a lot of vegetables. 2. Peter used to (smoke) a lot of cigarettes a day when he was a student; now he has got accustomed to (smoke) a pipe from time to time. 3. Mary devotes a lot of time to (knit) sweaters. 4. I was in Leningrad three years ago, I am looking forward to (go) there again this summer.

Ü 9.

5. We don't object to (do) overtime this week. 6. While at college, Edward used to (rely) on the help of his friends, but now that he has started work in a design office he must get used to (work) independently. 7. It would be better to (discuss) the matter in English because our guests are not used to (speak) German. 8. Jane is very versatile, she plays the piano and writes poems, and now she has even taken to (paint) water-colours. 9. The judge told the witness to restrict himself to (mention) the relevant facts. 10. Aunt Agatha doesn't like town life, she is used to (live) in the country. 11. Mary enjoys being driven, but she is not used to (drive) herself. 12. Does anybody object to (alter) today's agenda? 13. We have not yet found a practical approach to (solve) this problem. 14. Nobody had an objection to (adjourn) the session.

B. Formen Sie die folgenden Sätze um, und verwenden Sie dabei die in Klammern gegebenen Ausdrücke:

1. Anne doesn't like flying (She is afraid of it).[495] 2. We have to finish this work today (Our boss expects it).[496] 3. I have seen this film before (I remember it). 4. You are expected to telephone Mary (You must remember it). 5. Bob can't take part in the conference (He is prevented).[497] 6. Edward doesn't work late at night (His doctor doesn't want it). 7. Tell her that she is pretty (She likes it).[498] 8. Tom has passed his exam quite successfully (He can be proud of it). 9. You may ask me some more questions (I don't mind it). 10. Go out with Jane (She expects it). 11. You should ask Fred (Don't forget it). 12. I'll close the window (Do you mind it?). 13. My wife says, 'Don't drink so much.' (My wife tells me ...). 14. Henry said to us, 'I'll be back in time.' (We can rely on ...). 15. Paula said that she would not talk to Paul again if he was not ready to apologize to her (Paula threatened ... if Paul objected to ...).

C. Entscheiden Sie, ob das Verb in der Form des Infinitivs oder des Gerundiums stehen muß. (Ergänzen Sie an den markierten Stellen die Präposition.) (5.1., 8.2.1., 8.3., 8.4., 8.6., 8.7.)

1. Jane enjoys (go) to the theatre. 2. Have you finished (read) the manuscript? 3. We are hoping (reach) an agreement soon. 4. Would you mind (show) me the sights of the town? 5. Are you used ... (speak) English? 6. I think I'll manage (solve) the problem by myself. 7. John has agreed (read) a paper at the symposium. 8. Jane doesn't mind (come) to the party. 9. I remember (meet) Mr Johnson before. 10. My wife detests (contradict). 11. We have arranged (stay) at a hotel. 12. The secretary objected ... (type) the manuscript a third time. 13. We would prefer (do) the work at once. 14. Anne says she prefers (go) by train to (fly). 15. Would you mind (leave) the door open? 16. Before (start) this work I expect (give) detailed instructions.[499] 17. Mike has been busy (write) letters all afternoon. 18. This play is worth (see). 19. We decided (let) the matter rest. 20. Can you afford (buy) such an expensive car? 21. Joe may resent (not invite).[500] 22. Peter hopes (offer) a good job. 23. I've made up my mind (learn) French. 24. Our boss dislikes (criticize). 25. Why did you refuse (sign) the contract? 26. On the way to the station we stopped (buy) a newspaper. 27. Why don't you stop (quarrel)? 28. I suggest (have) a drink somewhere. 29. Did you

apologize ... (break) the vase?   30. Our neighbours are proud ... (have) three very intelligent grandchildren.   31. I am not going (prevent) you (do) what you think is best for you.[501]   32. We're afraid we shan't succeed ... (check) all the data today.   33. Aren't you tired ... (watch TV) every evening?   34. I'm afraid I forgot (tell)[502] my wife that I'll come home late tonight.   35. I remember (inform) Susan about our arrangement but I am afraid I have forgotten (mention) something essential.   36. We shall try (paper) the flat ourselves, though we've never tried (do) such a thing before.[503]   37. Pedro and I wanted (have) a talk; I tried (speak) Spanish but without (manage/make) myself understood, and Pedro wasn't used ... (speak) German.[504]   38. I think Bob will remember (I, lend) him 100 marks; I hope he won't forget (pay me back) for he has a way ... (forget) things he doesn't like (remember).[505]   39. Mary dislikes (go) home late in the evening without somebody (accompany) her.   40. Fred is quite a bore, we should try (talk) Jane ... (invite) him to her birthday party.   41. Harry prides himself ... (know) a lot about modern art.[506]   42. Here is a photo of Petrodvorets, I think you'll remember (go) there with me some years ago.
43. 'Is Harry going (dig) the garden today?' – 'No, he has decided (not do) it today, he is thinking ... (do) it tomorrow.'
44. 'I remember (ask) you (get) a few stamps for me. I hope you didn't forget (go) to the post-office.' – 'I did go because I had some letters (post), but I am sorry (say) that I didn't remember (buy) stamps.'
45. 'Do you know if Susan expects me (put up) the shelf today?' – 'No, she wouldn't mind (you, not put it up) till tomorrow.'
46. 'I don't know where my wallet is, I seem (lose) it.' – 'Try (look) in the shopping bag, you may have forgotten (put) it there.'[507]

        A Talk
Jim: What are we going (do) tonight?
Liz: Didn't you say you wanted (finish/paint) the hall?
Jim: I'm quite ready (do) that but I thought you'd like (go out) with me.
Liz: Where do you suggest (go)?
Jim: We've promised (spend) an evening with the Millers, and I'd hate (disappoint) them.
Liz: I am sure they wouldn't mind (we, visit) them next Sunday, if you tell them we have no time (come) this evening.
Jim: Don't you think they might resent (put off) again? I can't help (think) the hall could wait another day.
Liz: I know you dislike (do) things like (paint), but I don't understand you always (put off) things that have got (do).
Jim: I'll telephone the Millers telling them (not expect) us tonight.

    9.1.–9.6.
    Übersetzen Sie:
        9.1.
1. Do you know the girl sitting next to Peter?   2. (A proverb:) A trouble shared is a trouble halved.   3. Today Professor Baker will talk about some of the problems

arising in connection with the large-scale industrial application of robots. 4. The speaker described the measures now being planned for the redevelopment of the old town centre. 5. There are still a great many problems involved in heart transplants. 6. The checks made show that some of the values obtained so far are inexact. 7. Details of the process referred to here will be discussed in the following section. 8. After two introductory chapters covering the history of high-speed calculators and the general principles underlying the way they operate the present book falls into two parts dealing with current types of electronic computers.

9.2.

9. Standing at the bus-stop this morning I met a friend I had not seen for some years. 10. Having studied the technical aspects of the new process, we must now consider the economic questions involved in putting it into practice. 11. (A proverb:) When in Rome, do as the Romans do. 12. Joe and Jane will spend the weekend hiking in the mountains. 13. Last night we had a lively lobby talk with some stage-managers and actors, discussing the highlights of the theatre season. 14. Being a specialist in the field of neurosurgery Dr Brown is often invited to present papers at medical congresses. 15. Peter told me that never having worked as a conference interpreter before he found it very difficult to keep up with the speed at which many of the papers were read. 16. While studying the phosphorescence of various materials in 1896, Henry Becquerel discovered radioactivity.
17. My friend told me the book was rather tedious; but having read it I found it quite interesting. 18. Having read a lot of British authors, Fred is considered an expert on English literature by his friends.
19. Though well produced and performed, the play seldom rose above average. 20. Copernicus rejected the Ptolemaic conception of the universe, placing the sun in its true position at the centre of the solar system. 21. Properly applied, the new measuring technique yields much more reliable results than methods previously used. 22. Bromine causes serious burns if allowed to touch the skin. 23. Geiger counters are available in different forms, depending on the type of radiation they are to measure and the kind of source emitting it. 24. There are forms of cancer in which there is a 50 to 70 per cent cure rate, provided they are recognized at an early stage. 25. Coal or petroleum, once burnt, is used up whereas solar energy is non-depletable. 26. With warmer air from the Atlantic spreading over Central Europe, temperatures will be rising markedly during the second half of this week. 27. With the test completed, we spent several hours analysing the results. 28. Three cars collided on the main road, thus causing a traffic congestion for more than two hours. 29. The authors of the book under review present an introduction to computer-aided engineering (CAE) which is relatively easy to understand, using as they do concepts familiar also to non-specialists.

9.3.–9.6.

30. Tom came hurrying to the station only to notice that the train had already gone. 31. The manuscript I was looking for lay buried under a pile of papers. 32. Some motorists who had seen the forest catching fire immediately informed the police. 33. Nobody likes to be kept waiting. 34. At the end of the meeting I was left won-

dering whether my arguments had convinced the audience.   35. The accused was repeatedly caught contradicting himself as he found himself being cornered by the prosecutor.   36. Anne strikes me as being a very intelligent girl.   37. Agatha Christie's plots are clever, her dialogues brisk and she keeps her readers guessing until the last page.   38. If copper is left exposed to the atmosphere it gradually becomes covered with verdigris.

9.1.
A. Setzen Sie die entsprechende Partizipform ein:

1. Who is the woman (talk) to John?   2. (On the phone:) This is Fred Brown (speak).   3. There's someone (knock) at the door, I think it's Tom.   4. The problems (talk about) in yesterday's panel discussion were quite topical.   5. Windsor Castle was one of a series of forts (build) around London after the Norman Conquest in 1066 to enable Norman legions to control the area (surround) the capital.   6. Edgar Allan Poe's short stories are among the most famous ever (write), some of his best tales are detective stories (illustrate) how cases of crime can be solved by force of intellect.   7. All the data (quote) in the present paper are based on results (obtain) from investigations (make) during the last two weeks.   8. Modern science can solve many problems previously (regard) as insoluble, e.g. problems (deal) with genetic engineering.

B. Verkürzen bzw. verbinden Sie die folgenden Sätze durch das entsprechende Partizip:

1. Chemistry is the science which deals with the composition of matter.[508]   2. The results which have been obtained are quite satisfactory.[509]   3. An electric cell is a device which converts chemical energy into electrical energy.   4. The agreement will come into effect next month. It was concluded yesterday.   5. The exhibition in the city hall consists of 1,500 archaeological finds. It was inaugurated by the mayor today. The finds were excavated in our town during the last twenty years.[510]   6. The Petri papyrus from Egypt (c. 1850 B.C.) is the oldest known medical text. It contains information on contraception.

C. Geben Sie englisch wieder. Verwenden Sie bei der Übersetzung zunächst Relativsätze (L 15.7.), verkürzen Sie diese dann durch ein Partizip.

1. Bekannte Wissenschaftler werden auf der Friedenskundgebung (peace rally) sprechen, die heute auf dem Russell Square (20.1.4.) in London stattfindet.[511]   2. Der von den Studenten übersetzte Text über Biogenetik war sehr schwierig.   3. Botanik (botany) ist die Wissenschaft, die sich mit Pflanzen beschäftigt.   4. Die in diesem Artikel behandelten Probleme sind für unsere Untersuchungen sehr wichtig.[512]   5. Die zur Zeit im Rathaus ausgestellten Modelle sind Entwürfe, die von bekannten Architekten für die Wiederbebauung (redevelopment) des Stadtzentrums eingereicht wurden.   6. Die vereinbarten (agree upon) Maßnahmen werden nächsten Monat in Kraft treten.   7. Alle Werte, auf die hier Bezug genommen wird (refer to), sind Untersuchungen entnommen worden, die von Smith und Mitarbei-

Ü 9.

tern (Smith et al.) kürzlich durchgeführt wurden. 8. Umweltverschmutzung (environmental pollution) ist eine der großen Gefahren, die die Menschheit heute bedrohen (threaten).[513] Der Schaden, welcher der Wirtschaft eines Landes durch die industrielle Verschmutzung zugefügt (to do) wird, ist unermeßlich.[514] Die Bemühungen, die Umweltverschmutzung zu verringern, die in den meisten Industrieländern unternommen werden (make efforts), erfordern riesige Geldsummen.[515] Die für nächstes Jahr von der UNESCO einberufene (convene) Konferenz zu diesem weltweiten Problem wird von Wissenschaftlern aus mehr als 50 Ländern, einschließlich einiger Entwicklungsländer (developing countries), besucht werden.[516]

D. Animal Quiz

Ordnen Sie die im folgenden genannten Tiere den Beschreibungen zu, und setzen Sie dabei das entsprechende Partizip ein: *lion, rabbit, squirrel, owl, hippopotamus, guinea-pig, monkey, falcon.*

1. ... is a small mammal of the hare family usually (live) in burrows.   2. ... is a small bird of prey sometimes (train) to hunt and kill other birds and small animals.   3. ... is a night-flying bird (have) large eyes, a hooked beak and (live) on small birds and animals, e.g. mice.   4. ... is a short-eared animal (belong) to the rodent family and often (keep) as pet or for research in biology.   5. ... is a small bushy-(tail) and tree-(climb) animal with red or brown fur (belong) to the rodent family.   6. ... is a large African mammal with short legs and thick skin, (inhabit) rivers.   7. ... is a member of the group of animals most closely (ally) to and (resemble) man.   8. ..., sometimes (call) the 'King of Beasts', is a large, strong, flesh-(eat) animal (find) in Africa and South Asia.

9.2.–9.2.8.
A. Bilden Sie Sätze unter Verwendung der entsprechenden Partizipform:

1. (Speak) French I often make mistakes.[517]   2. (Know) how fond his girl-friend is of music Jim sometimes buys her a record.   3. Last night John fell asleep (do one's homework).[518]   4. (Park one's car) in a side-street, we went for a walk through the centre of the town.[519]   – 5. (Invite too late), I could not attend the conference.   6. (Cross-examine) for more than an hour, the accused finally made a confession.[520]   7. (Complete one's practical) the students continued their studies at the university.   8. On our trip to the Saxon Alps we spent a day in Dresden (visit) the Green Vault and the Picture Gallery.   9. With more than 300 million people (speak) English as a first language, it is impossible to lay down a world standard for English pronunciation.   10. The old office (become) too small, the staff moved into another building.[521]   11. The potato, though (introduce) into England already in the 17th century, did not become a national staple food until the 19th century.   12. Milk is a complete meal in itself, (contain) as it does nearly all the ingredients our body needs.   13. (Give) the right treatment, some forms of cancer are curable.[522]   14. Ammonia will not burn in air unless (heat), but will burn in oxygen.   15. Sulphuric acid is the world's most important chemical, nearly 30 million tons of it (use) each year.[523]   16. Oxygen and silicon make up the major part of the composition of the earth's crust, both elements (occur) in chemical combina-

tion with others.   17. Many organic compounds such as fibres and plastics can be used for a great variety of purposes, (display) as they do a great many advantages.   18. The law of the conservation of energy states that no energy is lost or gained while (transform) from one form into another.⁵²⁴

B. Setzen Sie dem Kontext entsprechend die folgenden Wendungen an den markierten Stellen ein (L 9.2.8.): *supposing, provided (that), depending on, talking of, considering, judging from.*

1. ... no unforeseen delays occur, how long will it take you to finish this work?   2. ... it rains, what shall we do this afternoon?   3. ... what the critics say, the performance is worth seeing.   4. Mr Blake is very able-bodied ... his age.   5. ... holidays, what are you going to do this summer?   6. ... their composition, these alloys can be used for various purposes.

C. Verkürzen bzw. verbinden Sie die folgenden Sätze durch ein Partizip:

1. My girl-friend often knits while she is watching TV.   2. As Professor Baker was seriously ill, he had to cancel all his appointments.⁵²⁵   3. After we had talked to Tom we were convinced he would help us.⁵²⁶   4. As I was pressed for time, I could not wait any longer.⁵²⁷   5. The Smiths can't build a house of their own unless they are given financial support.   6. The letter could not be forwarded to Mr Brown because his address was unknown.⁵²⁸   7. A Japanese airliner crashed near Tokyo airport yesterday; all the crew and passengers were killed.⁵²⁹   8. After the necessary checks had been made, the analysis could be completed.⁵³⁰
9. Since copper is a good conductor of electricity, it is very often used for electrical wires.   10. After the alloy had been heated for several hours, it began to melt.
11. Though hormones are produced by the organism in minute quantities, they are capable of bringing about profound physiological effects.   12. As fission products from atomic reactors are highly radioactive, they must be handled with the utmost care.⁵³¹

D. Übersetzen Sie diesen Text, und entscheiden Sie, welches Partizip einzusetzen ist:

Tastefully (furnish) pubs are an attractive feature of Britain's countryside. Besides selling beer to their customers country pubs are now offering more and more delicious and relatively cheap food – at least (compare) with the high prices one has to pay when (eat) out at a posh restaurant. Many of these village pubs are very old, one of the oldest (be) the 'Royal Standard of England' near London, its name (go back) to Charles II, who sheltered there when (flee) to France after the battle of Worcester in 1651.
Carefully (restore), most of these old pubs are now excellent examples of modern comfort (combine) with architectural history. They usually offer a superb strong ale from recipes (hand) down from landlord to landlord and often (serve) in candle-lit lounges (decorate) with fascinating collections of curios from all over the world. Spending an evening in one of these village pubs (relish) some of the beers (offer) there will really make you feel at ease.

9.3.
Setzen Sie das entsprechende Partizip ein:

1. When I got home mother was sitting in an armchair (read) a detective story and father was lying on the couch (watch TV).   2. Fred came (run) round the corner (try, L 9.2.6.) to catch the bus.   3. Because of a traffic accident the motor way remained (block) for two hours.   4. During our holidays we often stood on the terrace of our hotel (watch) the sun go down behind the mountains.   5. London Bridge was sold to an American consortium; it now stands (reconstruct) in Arizona (span) a specially created lake.

9.4.
A. Entscheiden Sie, ob in den folgenden Sätzen *Present Participle* oder Infinitiv vorzuziehen ist:

1. I've seen many famous actors (play)[532] Hamlet.   2. We heard John (practise)[533] on the piano when we came.   3. Tom came home rather late last night; I heard him (open) the front-gate shortly after midnight.   4. Fred has found your penknife; I saw him (pick) it up.   5. Arthur must have left; I have just heard the door (slam).   6. Recently I happened to hear Ms Diamond (praise) as a versatile actress; I'd really like to see her (perform) in a musical.

B. Verwenden Sie in den folgenden Sätzen Passiv + Partizip, wo möglich auch Passiv + Infinitiv (s. Ende von 5.8.1.).

Beispiel: *They didn't see anybody entering the workshop.* → *Nobody was seen entering/to enter the workshop.*

1. They heard the chief engineer talking to the visitor in the office.   2. They left us waiting outside in the rain.[534]   3. They found the stolen car abandoned in a blind alley.   4. In Berlin one can see large numbers of foreigners doing the sights of the town all the year round.   5. People saw the motorist who had caused the accident driving on at top speed.   6. Today man can keep such organs as heart, lungs or liver going by artificial means.[535]

9.5.
A. Übersetzen Sie:

1. My watch always loses time, I'll have to have it repaired.   2. We are going to get our car overhauled completely, among other things we want to have it painted green.   3. Your manuscript contains a lot of errata, you ought to have it retyped.   4. Since Arthur is oversize and rather obese he has to have his suits and coats tailor-made if he wants to look smart.
5. The satellite that was launched last week had to have its trajectory corrected yesterday.   6. The crew of a Dutch trawler had their catch confiscated when they were caught fishing in Icelandic waters.   7. Several houses had their roofs blown off by the heavy storm last night.   8. We had the lock of our front-door broken open the other day, we'd better have it replaced by a safety lock.

B. Formen Sie die folgenden Sätze um unter Verwendung von *have/ get* **+ Objekt +** *Past Participle.* **Kommt ein Objekt im Ausgangssatz vor, so entfällt es** (Beispiel b).

Beispiele:
a) *The device has been tested by an expert (We)* → *We have had the device tested by an expert.*
b) *Jane asked her friend to make her a new dress.* → *Jane had a new dress made.*

1. I often have toothache; my teeth must be checked (I).[536]   2. The contract will be prolonged for another two years (The conductor of the Philharmonic Orchestra).   3. Mr Brown's appendix was removed last month (Mr Brown).   4. Enquiries are being made about the cause of the accident (The management).[537]   5. The last twenty issues of the magazine have been bound into one volume (The librarian).[538]   6. A new sport stadium is being built on the outskirts of the town (The town council).   7. I shall ask somebody to type my paper.[539]   8. The bridegroom instructed the photographer to take some photos of the wedding guests.   9. Jim should tell somebody to test the apparatus.   10. I can't get the car started; we'll have to ask somebody to tow it off.[540]

C. Vervollständigen Sie die Sätze nach folgendem Muster:
The brakes of the lorry are not working properly. (repair at once; repair before we started) → *You should/ought to have them repaired at once. – You should/ought to have had them repaired before we started.*

1. There are some mistakes in your English article. (look through before you hand it in; look through before you handed it in)   2. The apple tree is not bearing fruit any more. (cut down)[541]   3. Some of the data are not correct. (check immediately after the test)[542]   4. Your trousers are dirty. (clean)   5. John has sprained his left ankle. (X-ray)   6. The roof is leaky. (mend)   7. The text contained several misspellings. (retype; retype before it was posted)   8. One of my back teeth has been hurting for a long time. (treat long ago)

D. Die Wohnung, in die Sie eingezogen sind, muß renoviert werden. Sagen Sie, welche Veränderungen Sie vorhaben.
Beispiel: *install gas heating* → *I'll have gas heating installed.*
repaper the living-room; paint the kitchen; have to insert new window frames; install a shower; have to replace the old kitchen range by a new one; put in a telephone.

Setzen Sie das entsprechende Partizip ein (L 9.3.–9.6.):
1. Yesterday Peter's wife was caught (exceed)[543] the speed limit; if she goes on driving as recklessly as that she will have her licence (withdraw)[544] before long.   2. When I came to the meeting I found the participants (engage)[545] in a heated debate.   3. We've often heard it (say)[546] that Mike is the best player in his team.   4. 'I'll keep my fingers (cross) for you,' Paula said to her boyfriend before his final examination.   5. Mr Alexander, who is 63, had a pacemaker (fit) recently.   6. Old-age pensioners have got to have something that keeps them (occupy).   7. Two bridges near Los Angeles were reported (damage)[547] after an earthquake had hit

Ü 9.

Southern California yesterday. 8. In foreign language teaching the learners should always be kept (motivate). 9. A car came (race) down the street. Suddenly a wheel came off and remained (lie) in the middle of the road. It was a miracle that none of the pedestrians seeing the car (zigzag) towards them and (come) to a stop on the pavement, were hurt. 10. Speed is generally defined as (be) the time rate (require)[548] by a particle or body to move along its path.

Komplexübungen zum Partizip

A. Setzen Sie die entsprechende Partizipform ein:

1. Much of the information (present)[549] in this book is new and will not be found (publish)[550] elsewhere. 2. I have never heard the musical 'My Fair Lady' (sing)[551] in English. 3. Two of the climbers who had tried to reach the summit were found (freeze) to death at the foot of a glacier. 4. Some time ago the printing shop in the State prison in Columbia, South Carolina, was temporarily closed after a prisoner was found (make)[552] this own money. 5. Archimedes is said to have burnt Roman ships (besiege)[553] Syracuse in 212 B.C., (use)[554] the sun's rays (reflect)[555] and (concentrate) by the shields of hundreds of soldiers. 6. Over a hundred years ago the four great bronze lions (guard) the Nelson Monument in Trafalgar Square were unveiled. At that time the sculptures were described as badly (model) and badly (cast). Experts then said they found it (console) that they would probably last only a few years. But, a hundred years later, the lions are still there, (watch) the thousands of Londoners and tourists (crowd) the square. 7. Among the numerous inventions and discoveries (make) by Réaumur (1683–1757) were the thermometric scale (bear) his name and improvements (propose) for making steel. Moreover, he isolated gastric juice, (investigate) its role in the digestion of food, and wrote a famous book on insects, (entitle) 'The Natural History of Insects' and generally (consider) an early standard work in the field of entomology. 8. Carbohydrates are compounds (consist) of carbon, hydrogen and oxygen, the hydrogen and oxygen (be) usually in the same proportion as (find) in water.

B. Verkürzen Sie die folgenden Satzgefüge durch eine Partizipialkonstruktion:

1. If one judges from what the reviewers say this book is worth reading.[556] 2. As Peter had witnessed the traffic accident he was told to give evidence.[557] 3. I was very surprised when my car broke down because I had had it serviced shortly before.[558] 4. After the speaker had finished his lecture he was asked a lot of questions by the audience. 5. There are too many holiday-makers at this seaside resort in summer, we'd better go to some other place.[559] 6. I was ill for some time, therefore I couldn't finish the article last week. 7. When the Millers came home from their holidays they found that their garage had been broken into. 8. We had not received Susan's letter in time, so we did not know where to meet her. 9. Now that we have heard your arguments we can understand your decision. 10. Fred hasn't saved enough money, that's why he can't buy the car.

C. Setzen Sie das entsprechende Partizip ein:

Lake Baikal is the deepest continental body of water on earth, (have) a maximum depth of 1,620 m and (contain) about one-fifth of the fresh water on the earth's surface and four-fifths of that in the USSR. There are 336 rivers and streams (flow) into the lake. Baikal is also one of the biggest lakes, (cover) 31,500 sq km. Plant and animal life in the lake are rich and various with more than 1,200 animal species (find) at different depths and about 600 plant species (live) on or near the surface. Two thirds of the 1,800 animal and plant species (live) there are found nowhere else in the world. There are some 50 species of fish in the lake (belong) to seven families, the omul, the salmon of Lake Baikal, (be) the one (fish) in particularly large quantities.

Because of its remote situation Lake Baikal, sometimes (call) the pearl of Siberia, was safe from environmental pollution until this century, when industry began to develop in the region (surround) it. Wood felling close to the shores of the lake and the rivers (flow) into it caused severe soil erosion. Large amounts of timer (float) down the rivers and across the lake sank and were rotting away.

Comprehensive measures (take) by the Soviet government have helped to maintain the natural resources of the lake. For example, the floating of timber (mention) above has been replaced by road transport. Thus the number of the omul, a delicacy highly (appreciate) in Siberia, has also been increased.

D. Geben Sie englisch wieder. Verwenden Sie, wo vom Kontext her möglich, zunächst einen Relativsatz bzw. einen Adverbialsatz + Konjunktion, und verkürzen Sie dann durch die entsprechende Partizipform (L 9.1.–9.5.).

9.1.–9.4.

1. Die Fragen, die im Zusammenhang mit der Herstellung des neuen Gerätes entstehen (arise), können heute nicht im einzelnen erörtert werden.[560] 2. Die Erzeugnisse, die auf der Leipziger Messe ausgestellt werden, kommen aus allen Teilen der Welt.[561] 3. Während ich mich mit Herrn Green aus England unterhielt, bemerkte (notice) ich, daß er sehr gut deutsch spricht.[562] 4. Da wir voriges Jahr unseren Urlaub zu Hause verbracht haben, können wir uns dieses Jahr eine teure Auslandsreise leisten (afford).[563] 5. Peters älteste Tochter ist in Berlin und studiert Medizin.[564] 6. Die meisten in unserem Betrieb hergestellten Maschinen werden exportiert. 7. Wir haben das ganze Wochenende damit verbracht, unsere Wohnung zu tapezieren (paper).[565] 8. Nachdem ich meine Arbeit beendet hatte, ging ich ins Kino.[566] 9. Die erörterten Probleme waren sehr kompliziert.[567] 10. Donnerstag nachmittag sitzt Mike gewöhnlich in der Bibliothek und liest Fachzeitschriften (scientific journals). 11. Als wir die verschiedenen Berechnungen verglichen, fanden wir schließlich den Fehler. 12. Oft ist es für einen Gastgeber (host) schwer, die Konversation in Gang zu halten.[568] 13. Astronomie ist die Wissenschaft, die sich mit dem Studium der Himmelskörper (celestial body) beschäftigt. 14. Da ich den Wagen nicht reparieren kann, muß ich ihn in eine Werkstatt (repair shop) bringen.[569] 15. Der gestern unterzeichnete Vertrag wird nächstes Jahr in Kraft treten (come into effect/force). 16. Der Ingenieur zeigte uns die neue Maschine und erklärte uns ihre Arbeitsweise (mode of operation). 17. Jane kommt

heute nicht; sie will den Abend zu Hause verbringen und Briefe schreiben.
18. Die vorgeschlagene Resolution wurde von allen angenommen. 19. Gestern hat unser Assistent Peter wieder dabei ertappt, als er die Lösungen von seiner Freundin abschrieb.[570] 20. Als ich John besuchte, saß er wie jeden Sonnabend nachmittag auf der Couch und sah sich das Sportprogramm im Fernsehen an. 21. Wenn man alle Faktoren in Betracht zieht, kann man sagen, daß diese Entscheidung sehr vernünftig war.[571] 22. Obwohl Jack einige sehr spezielle Fragen gestellt wurden, bestand er die Prüfung.[572] 23. Wir haben uns gestern auf Mikes Geburtstagsparty gut amüsiert (have a good time), wir haben viel getanzt, uns Fotos angeschaut und uns über vergangene (old) Zeiten unterhalten.[573] 24. Mary konnte nicht an dem Ausflug teilnehmen, da der Arzt ihr gesagt hatte, sie solle im Bett bleiben (5.7.2.).[574] 25. Ich habe oft gehört, daß man Jim als guten Organisator bezeichnet (refer to as).[575] 26. Als Harry nach einigen Jahren in seine Heimatstadt zurückkehrte, stellte er fest, daß viele alte Gebäude abgerissen worden waren. 27. Obwohl sie oft englische Fachliteratur lesen, finden es viele Wissenschaftler schwierig, in Diskussionen auf Konferenzen englisch zu sprechen. 28. Nach dem zu urteilen, was ich gehört habe, war das Symposium sehr interessant.[576]
29. Nachdem der Techniker die defekten Sicherungen (fuse) ausgewechselt hatte, schaltete er die Versuchsanlage (pilot plant) wieder ein. 30. Falls das neue Verfahren in unserem Betrieb eingeführt wird, kann es zu einer beträchtlichen Produktionssteigerung (increase in production) führen.[577] 31. Die vorige Woche in unserem Institut durchgeführte Konferenz behandelte CAD/CAM-Probleme. 32. Die in den letzten Versuchen erhaltenen Daten sind möglicherweise (L 6.2.1.) nicht ganz zuverlässig; wenn sie nicht genau überprüft werden, sollte man sie nicht für weitere Messungen verwenden. 33. Da Wasserkraft eine unerschöpfliche Energiequelle ist, sollte sie genutzt werden (utilize), wo immer (es) möglich (ist).[578] 34. Die Atmosphäre enthält immer etwas Feuchtigkeit (humidity), wobei die Menge sich nicht nur von Tag zu Tag, sondern von Stunde zu Stunde ändert.

9.5.
1. Wir müssen unseren Fernseher reparieren lassen.[579] 2. Wie oft läßt du deinen Wagen waschen? 3. Susan ist zu Peggys Hochzeit eingeladen worden, deshalb läßt sie sich jetzt ein neues Kleid machen. 4. Johns Frau läßt sich das Haar (L 15.3.1.) färben (dye). 5. Wir wollen den Vortrag unseres amerikanischen Gastdozenten (visiting lecturer) auf Band sprechen (tape) lassen. 6. Der Abteilungsleiter wird die Angelegenheit überprüfen lassen. 7. Ich mußte mir voriges Jahr die Mandeln (tonsils) herausnehmen lassen.[580] 8. Du solltest die englische Fassung (version) deines Vortrages noch einmal durchsehen (look through) lassen, ehe du sie veröffentlichen läßt. 9. Lassen Sie bitte das Protokoll (the minutes) der letzten Sitzung mit der Maschine schreiben (type).[581] 10. Anne läßt sich nicht gern fotografieren.[582]

E. Geben Sie englisch wieder:
Die Galápagosinseln
Während seiner Teilnahme (L 9.2.1.) an der Reise des Vermessungsschiffes (surveying vessel) 'Beagle' um die Welt hatte Charles Darwin im Jahre 1835 Gelegenheit,

die Galápagosinseln zu besuchen. Er verbrachte dort viel Zeit dàmit, seltene Pflanzen zu sammeln und exotische Tiere zu beobachten (L 9.2.6.). Die auf diesen Inseln durchgeführten Beobachtungen trugen wesentlich zu seinem epochalen (epoch-making) Werk "On the Origin of Species" bei.

Die Galápagosinseln mit einer Gesamtfläche, die 3000 Quadratmeilen umfaßt und über etwa 23 000 Quadratmeilen Wasserfläche (ocean) verstreut ist (scatter), gehören zu Ekuador. Der Archipel (archipelago) ist berühmt für seine ungewöhnliche Tierwelt (animal life) und leitet seinen Namen von den riesigen Landschildkröten (land turtle) her (L 9.2.6.), die zu den Tieren mit der längsten Lebensdauer (life span) gehören (hier: Relativsatz) und ein Alter von 250 Jahren erreichen (L 9.2.6.). Zu den wichtigsten Erwerbszweigen (source of income) gehören (include) Landwirtschaft und Fischerei, wobei Barsch (grouper), Kaffee und Vieh die wichtigsten Exportartikel sind (L 9.2.7.1.).

Die im Jahre 1959 von der UNESCO und der 'International Union for the Conservation of Nature and Natural Resources' gegründete 'Charles-Darwin-Foundation' unternimmt alle Anstrengungen (make every effort), dieses Territorium zu schützen. Um die einzigartige (unique) Tier- und Pflanzenwelt zu erhalten (protect), wurden die Naturschutzgebiete (reservation) dieses Archipels 1969 von der UNESCO zum 'Erbe (heritage) der Menschheit' erklärt (L 11.2.).

Vor einigen Jahren brach ein heftiger Waldbrand (forest fire) auf La Isabela aus, der größten der Galápagosinseln, und verwüstete (devastate) über 20 000 Hektar des Naturschutzgebietes (L 9.2.6.) einschließlich einmaliger Vogelkulturen (bird culture). Die Riesenschildkröten und andere wertvolle Tiere im Norden der Insel wurden evakuiert, da sie auch von den Flammen bedroht waren.

10.1. / 10.2.
Übersetzen Sie:

1. I need the book Peter borrowed from me; I would ask that he return it at once. 2. Fred is often late; we insisted that he be punctual this time. 3. I suggested that John should read the article very carefully. 4. It is advisable that this medicine should be taken regularly. 5. Maggie has got a lot of money on her; I would recommend that she order another bottle of wine. 6. It's quite improbable that Bob should change his mind. 7. I've already had a lot of breakdowns with this second-hand car; I wish I hadn't bought it. 8. We wish we'd be able to help you. 9. It looks as if the matter were settled. 10. Susan is married; if only I had met her before. 11. You look as if you were ill. 12. Our boss sounds as if he were angry. 13. Mary doesn't like big towns; she wishes she lived in the country. 14. Suppose Mike hadn't helped you; what would you have done? 15. The majority of the committee urged that the item be put on the agenda. 16. The town council ordered that most of the old buildings be pulled down. 17. We missed the first part of the lecture, I wish we had been punctual. 18. The rapid increase of traffic casualties requires that close attention be given to road safety. 19. It is impossible that my friend should have forged the cheque. 20. The spokesman urged that an agreement not be delayed any more.

Ü 10.

10.1.
Bringen Sie mit *that*-Satz + Konjunktiv zum Ausdruck, was Sie vorschlagen oder fordern, bzw. was Sie für notwendig, wünschenswert oder wichtig halten. (Neben dem Konjunktiv ist natürlich auch *should* + Infinitiv, vor allem im Aktiv auch der Indikativ möglich.)
Beispiel: *Peter doesn't know where to stay (I suggest – stay at the Central Hotel).* → *I suggest that he (should) stay at the Central Hotel.*
1. Mary is ill (We recommend – see a doctor).   2. Susan can't make up her mind which dress to put on tonight (Her mother suggests – wear the blue one).   3. Walter doesn't know any foreign languages (His boss recommended – learn English).   4. Anne must be home by eight (It is advisable – leave now).   5. The text hasn't been translated yet (I suggest – translate, right away).[583]   6. These documents will be needed at the conference tomorrow (It is essential – type today).   7. The doctor can't see Mrs Mason today (He suggests – come tomorrow).   8. This topic couldn't be discussed yesterday (The chairman proposed – deal with today).   9. John's test paper is rather bad (The teacher insisted – repeat it).   10. We submitted our proposal to the committee (We requested – check it carefully).   11. The editor didn't accept my article (He demanded – shorten).   12. No agreement has been reached so far (The contracting parties insisted – hold another meeting as soon as possible).   13. This material is highly inflammable (It is imperative – not neglect adequate precautions).[584]   14. The working conditions in the lab are not good (The shop-steward urged – take immediate measures to improve them).

10.2. + Fußnote 3
A. Es wird bedauert, daß etwas nicht so ist, wie man es gern hätte. – Beginnen Sie mit *I/we/they wish ...; he/she wishes ...*
1. I don't have enough spare time (have more spare time).[585]   2. Bob isn't good at mathematics (be better at mathematics).[586]   3. Harry can't remember names and dates (be able to remember ...).   4. Mark hasn't got a colour television set (have).   5. Mary wants to be a ballet dancer, but she is too clumsy (not be so clumsy).   6. I have to type a lot (have a secretary).   7. Susan hasn't got a dish-washer (have a dish-washer).   8. I'm about to fall asleep, because the lecture is very boring (be more interesting).   9. Shirley is sorry that she is an only child (have a sister).   10. My girl-friend is always late (not always be late).   11. It's a pity that Mike and Mary don't like each other.[587]   12. Arthur is rather impolite.[588]   13. Mary dresses too loudly.[589]   14. It's a pity that we don't have enough money to go abroad every year.   15. I'm afraid Peter is driving too fast.[590]   16. Harry smokes too much.   17. It's a pity the pub is closed today.   18. Belinda falls in love too often.

B. Bringen Sie zum Ausdruck, daß ein Wunsch möglicherweise noch erfüllt werden kann: *wish + would.* Beginnen Sie wie bei A.
1. I am in a hurry but the bus doesn't come.[591]   2. We want to go for a walk but it is raining. (clear up)   3. Michael hasn't got a letter from Norma for a long time. (write soon)   4. My wife always wants to buy expensive things.[592]   5. Anne's parents don't like her latest boy-friend. (stop going out with him)   6. It's a pity you

can't stay a little longer. (be able to stay ...)   7. Susan can't get to sleep because her husband is snoring.   8. Mike is quite a problem child, he's getting on our nerves all the time.   9. I'm sorry, I must leave in a few minutes.[593] (have to go ...)   10. Margaret wants Bill to admire her new sweater, but he is watching TV.

C. Jemand bedauert, daß etwas geschehen bzw. nicht geschehen ist: wish + had. Beginnen Sie wie bei A.

1. The train is late again. (go by car)[594]   2. It is raining, and I've left my umbrella at home.   3. Peter was angry because we didn't ring him.[595]   4. I'm sorry I didn't visit the exhibition.   5. We spent our holidays at the seaside, and it was raining all the time.   6. The fish doesn't taste good. (choose a cutlet)   7. I walked out before the film was over because it was rather bad. (not be so bad)   8. Mary and John are quite incompatible. (never get married)[596]   9. The doctor told me to stay in bed a few days. (take his advice)   10. Alfred wore a pair of jeans to the wedding party, and all his friends were wearing suits. (put on a suit)   11. It's a pity Henry couldn't come. (be able to come)[597]   12. Fred's translation contained a lot of mistakes. (have it corrected by somebody, L 9.5.)[598]

D. Verwenden Sie dem Kontext entsprechend *wish* + *Präteritum*, *wish* + *Konditional*, *wish* + *Plusquamperfekt*. (Beginnen Sie wie bei A.)

1. Jim is rather careless.[599]   2. Peter has not kept the appointment.[600]   3. Anne talks too much.[601]   4. I was rude, but I didn't apologize.   5. We haven't finished our work.   6. John and Jane are always quarrelling.[602]   7. Jean won't visit us on Sunday.   8. David is sorry he didn't invite you.   9. I don't have time to attend the lecture.   10. John is sorry he didn't take part in the excursion.   11. I haven't seen Helen for a long time. (soon)   12. We are sorry we don't know their plans.   13. Unfortunately, the matter wasn't talked about yesterday.[603]   14. I'm sorry I haven't got anything to offer you.[604]   15. It's a pity Janet wasn't allowed to go dancing tonight.   16. I wanted to help my friend but I couldn't.[605]   17. It's a pity Sue is going steady with Harry.   18. Susan stayed at home yesterday because she had to work all day.[606]   19. It's a pity you must leave so soon.[607]   20. My wife is sorry she didn't have a new dress for the concert yesterday.[608]

E. Anne sagt, was sie sich wünscht; sie bedauert, daß etwas nicht so ist, wie sie es sich wünscht. Beginnen Sie mit: *I wish ...*

eine neue Wohnung bekommen[609]; einen Garten haben[610]; einen anderen Beruf gewählt haben[611]; Schauspielerin geworden sein; mehr gute Freunde haben; einen Arzt geheiratet haben; nicht so viele Probleme mit den Kindern haben; mehr Geld verdienen; mehr Schmuck (jewels) kaufen können; nicht so viel im Haushalt tun müssen.

Ü 11.

Komplexübungen zu Ergänzungen des Verbs (L 11.1. / 11.2. / 11.3.)

A. Übersetzen Sie:

1. Open the window, it's getting hot in here.   2. John's great-grandmother has gone blind.   3. It's getting late, I must be going.   4. Peter was dead-drunk last night; he behaved as if he had gone crazy.   5. Peggy turned green with envy when she saw Anne's new dress.   6. Your nose has gone blue with cold.   7. Fred went white with anger when Mary told him that she had fallen in love with another boy.   8. I'm sorry we can't drink this beer, it has gone flat.   9. I wouldn't eat this bread, it has gone stale.   10. Peter hasn't come, something seems to have gone wrong.   11. Mrs Turner doesn't look her age.   12. That looks like you.   13. What has happened? You sound rather excited.   14. There's a noise downstairs; it sounds like somebody trying to force the front door open.   15. Tom has turned out a brilliant pianist.   16. Harry seems to have become interested in science fiction.   17. The audience fell silent when the musicians stopped tuning their instruments.   18. Keep your temper!   19. I'm glad our calculations have proved correct.   20. Things have gone from bad to worse recently.   21. We shall keep early hours during our holidays.   22. I must look a dreadful sight, I've been walking in the rain without an umbrella.   23. They made the goal-keeper captain of the team.   24. Don't call Henry a liar if you can't prove it.   25. Who did they nominate successor of the late Vice-President of the Academy?   26. The jurors declared the defendant not guilty.   27. In 1703, Newton was elected President of the Royal Society.   28. In 1928, Pavlov was made an honorary member of the Royal College of Physicians in London.   29. In 1843, William Wordsworth, one of Britain's greatest poets, was designated Poet Laureate.   30. In 1958, an international jury of critics chose Eisenstein's 'The Battleship Potemkin' the best film ever made.

B. Für die folgende Übung, bei der Sie absurde Kombinationen in sinnvolle Aussagen verwandeln sollen, brauchen Sie etwas Humor:

1. The school ... has become a teacher.
2. My friend ... was crowned King of England.
3. The milk ... will turn bankrupt.
4. Fred's wife ... looks like a very old building.
5. Sheila ... turned out a falsification.
6. In 1625, Charles I ... was made captain of the football team.
7. I am afraid the firm ... has gone sour.
8. Susan ... tastes burnt.
9. The document ... sounds angry.
10. The pudding ... is getting fat.

C. Geben Sie englisch wieder:

1. Trinken Sie Ihren Tee, er wird kalt.[612]   2. Susan ist krank geworden.   3. Wir gingen nach Hause, als es begann, dunkel zu werden.[613]   4. Zieh deinen Mantel an, es ist kühl geworden.[614]   5. Der Broiler schmeckt gut.   6. Dein Anzug riecht nach Tabak.   7. Das Gebäude sieht wie ein Museum aus.   8. Deine Vermutung (supposition) hat sich als richtig erwiesen, Diana ist Schauspielerin geworden.[615]

9. Einige Probleme blieben in der Diskussion ungelöst. 10. John hat uns nicht informiert, etwas muß schief gegangen sein.[616] 11. Ich halte diesen Vorschlag für sehr vernünftig (reasonable). 12. Es hat sich herausgestellt, daß die Diagnose falsch war. 13. Wen hat man zum Sportler des Jahres gewählt?[617] 14. Dr. Martin ist als Professor für Mathematik berufen worden. 15. Mr Wilson ist zum britischen Botschafter (ambassador) in Brasilien ernannt worden. 16. Wer wurde zum Rektor (vice-chancellor) der Universität gewählt? 17. 1558 wurde Elizabeth I. Königin von England; 1952 wurde Elizabeth II. zur Königin von England gekrönt. 18. Wörter, die gleich (= alike) klingen, aber unterschiedliche Bedeutung haben, werden Homonyme genannt.

11.4.
Geben Sie englisch wieder:

1. Ich kann dir die Sache erklären.[618] 2. John hat uns die Methode genau beschrieben. 3. Bitte lies mir den Brief vor. 4. Ich werde Ihnen den Text diktieren. 5. Du brauchst die Angelegenheit Bill gegenüber nicht zu erwähnen. 6. Ich habe dir eine Tasse Tee gemacht. 7. Bitte erklären Sie mir das Problem noch einmal. 8. Ich werde dir die Theaterkarte bezahlen. 9. Hast du deiner Mutter schon ein Geschenk gekauft? 10. Wir werden die Angelegenheit dem Direktor unterbreiten.[619] 11. Wann mußt du das Manuskript dem Verlag vorlegen? 12. Wir haben den Diebstahl der Polizei gemeldet.

12.1.
A. Vergewissern Sie sich über die Richtigkeit einer Annahme, und verwenden Sie dabei *question tags*:

1. Joan's sister is a teacher, ...?[620] 2. Bob and Bill are mechanics, ...?[621] 3. John's grandfather is an actor, ...? 4. Paul is not English, ...?[622] 5. Mike is coming tonight, ...? 6. Helen wasn't at the office yesterday, ...? 7. Professor Brown speaks French, ...?[623] 8. Jack doesn't live here, ...?[624] 9. They know each other, ...? 10. You talked the matter over, ...?[625] 11. Peter didn't inform you, ...?[626] 12. Sue has given you the book, ...? 13. We haven't met before, ...? 14. The article hasn't been translated yet, ...? 15. Mother will visit us on Sunday, ...?[627] 16. You won't be late, ...?[628] 17. Jane would help us, ...? 18. You would have waited, ...? 19. Mary has got two brothers, ...?[629] 20. Shut the window, ...?[630] 21. I'm punctual, ...?[631] 22. Mary can translate this text, ...? 23. You can't stay, ...? 24. You couldn't have come earlier, ...? 25. This misunderstanding could have been avoided, ...?[632] 26. You had to queue up for tickets, ...?[633] 27. You didn't have to wait long, ...? 28. We should hurry up, ...? 29. Anne ought to give Fred another chance, ...? 30. They didn't invite you, ...? 31. You want to see this film, ...? 32. The agenda has been altered, ...? 33. The museum is closed today, ...? 34. Anne cooks well, ...? 35. Let's listen to some records, ...?[634] 36. You didn't see Sam at the meeting, ...? 37. Hurry up, ...? 38. Please phone me tonight, ...? 39. I'm wrong, ...? 40. Let's have a talk, ...? 41. I was rather impolite, ...? 42. Don't switch off the light, ...? 43. You love me, ...?

Ü 12.

44. Have a cup of coffee, ...?[635]   45. They haven't arrived yet, ...?   46. Turn down the radio, ...?   47. You have read this book, ...?   48. Let's wait some minutes, ...?   49. Don't lock the door, ...?   50. Peggy doesn't like beer, ...?   51. You won't forget to post the letter, ...?   52. We don't have to discuss all the details now, ...?   53. No one helped you, ...?[636]   54. Take a seat, ...?   55. Someone wanted to speak to me while I was away, ...?   56. Nobody found the mistake, ...?[637]   57. Let's have a break, ...?   58. Somebody told you the story, ...?   59. Everybody enjoyed the party, ...?   60. Nobody came, ...?

B. Geben Sie englisch wieder, und verwenden Sie *question tags*, um sich über die Richtigkeit der Aussage zu vergewissern:

Beispiel: *Jane ist krank.* → *Jane is ill, isn't she?*

1. John ist im Ausland.   2. Bob war nicht zu Hause.   3. Dein Bruder studiert Physik.[638]   4. Anne tanzt gern.[639]   5. Du hast ein Auto.   6. Harriet kann Maschine schreiben (type).[640]   7. Du kennst Harrys Adresse nicht.   8. Peter hat dir vor einiger Zeit geschrieben.   9. Arthur kann nicht Auto fahren.[641]   10. Susan wird uns bald besuchen.   11. Mary hat das Konzert nicht gefallen.   12. Deine Freundin hat einen Hund.[642]   13. Ihr seid gestern abend spät nach Hause gekommen.   14. Das Thema ist schon behandelt worden.   15. Ihr kennt euch (15.5.) seit vielen Jahren.   16. Die Theaterkasse (box-office) ist noch nicht geschlossen.   17. Ich bin immer fair.   18. Helen mußte die Prüfung wiederholen.[643]   19. Wir sollten ihn fragen, ehe wir eine Entscheidung treffen (make a decision).   20. Du wolltest mit John darüber sprechen.   21. Alle (everybody) sind mit dieser Lösung zufrieden.[644]   22. Du hättest den Zug erreichen können.   23. Kitty hat sich das Haar färben (dye) lassen (L 9.5.).[645]   24. Niemand hat angerufen.

12.2.

A. Vervollständigen Sie die Kurzantworten:

1. Are you interested in sports? – Yes, ...[646]   2. Is Mr Smith a psychologist? – Yes, ...   3. Are Jim and Wendy married? – No, ...[647]   4. Were you at home yesterday? – No, ...   5. Was the film good? – Yes, ...   6. Were your parents in Hungary last summer? – No, ...   7. Do you like red wine? – Yes, ...[648]   8. Does Peter speak Spanish? – No, ...[649]   9. Did John attend the conference? – Yes, ...   10. Are you going to the pictures tonight? – Yes, ...   11. Has Henry got a car? – Yes, ...[650]   12. Have you read 'Moll Flanders' by Defoe? – No, ...   13. Do you sometimes have trouble with your landlady? – No, ...[651]   14. Will Tom come tomorrow? – Yes, ...   15. Will you be back before ten? – No, ...   16. Would you like to come with us? – Yes, ...   17. Have you been working all day? – No, ...   18. Has your article been published yet? – Yes, ...   19. Would you have come if you had been invited? – Yes, ...[652]   20. Can I borrow your typewriter for an hour? – Yes, ...   21. Do I have to answer the question at once? – No, ...   22. Who wrote 'The Old Man and the Sea'? – ...[653]   23. Who discovered America? – ...   24. Which of these novelists wrote 'Gulliver's Travels': Fielding, Swift, H. G. Wells? – ...   25. 'Do you know Paul?' – 'Yes, ...' – 'Is he English?' – 'No, ...' – 'Does he come

from France?' – 'Yes, ...' – 'Is he from Paris?' – 'No, ...' – 'Is he a student?' – 'Yes, ...' – 'Does he study at the Medical Academy?' – 'Yes, ...' – 'Did you meet him there?' – 'Yes, ...'

    B. Reagieren Sie auf die folgenden Feststellungen mit Interesse, Verwunderung oder Besorgnis.

Beispiel: *'My girl-friend is going to buy a dog.' – 'Is she?'*
1. 'Peter is in love with Mary.' – '...?'[654]
2. 'My parents want to sell their caravan.' – '...?'[655]
3. 'We had a marvellous holiday.' – '...?'[656]
4. 'Peggy got engaged.' – '...?'
5. 'The play wasn't good.' – '...?'
6. 'Jack speaks Italian fluently.' – '...?'
7. 'Helen is going to get divorced.' – '...?'
8. 'Judith has slimmed down a lot.' – '...?'
9. 'Susan likes boxing matches.' – '...?'
10. 'I shall be fifty next month.' – '...?'

    12.3.
    A. Ergänzen Sie die folgenden Aussagen:

Beispiele:
a) *'Peter doesn't speak French.' (Bill)* → *'Peter doesn't speak French.' – 'Nor/Neither does Bill.' (oder: 'Bill doesn't, either.')*
b) *Mary is a lab assistant and ... (Jane).* → *Mary is a lab assistant and so is Jane.*

1. Harry is an engineer and ... (his two brothers).[657] 2. 'Dick doesn't play football.' (Jack)[658] 3. 'Maggie wasn't at John's party.' (we).[659] 4. John studies physics and ... (Mike). 5. 'Bob will go to Bulgaria this summer.' (we) 6. Anne has bought a new dress and ... (Joan). 7. 'I'm afraid we'll be late.' (I) 8. Anne can paint beautifully and ... (her brother). 9. My wife doesn't like brandy and ... (I). 10. 'John won't take part in the congress.' (I) 11. 'My grandfather will be eighty next year.' (mine) 12. 'Peter used to smoke a lot.' (I)[660]

    B. Geben Sie englisch wieder:

1. Mary ist Lehrerin, ihre Schwester auch.
2. "Peggy liebt Jazz." – "Ich auch."[661]
3. "Ich kann mich nicht an den Film erinnern." – "Ich auch nicht."
4. Donald hat kein Auto und John auch nicht.[662]
5. "Ich habe meinen Schirm vergessen." – "Ich auch."
6. Barbara kann nicht Englisch, ihre Freundin auch nicht.[663]
7. Meine Frau hat an der Humboldt-Universität studiert, ich auch.
8. "Ich bin nicht gut in Geographie." – "Ich auch nicht."
9. "Wir haben gestern den ganzen Abend ferngesehen." – "Wir auch."
10. Frank will nicht mitkommen, Harry auch nicht.
11. "Der Film hat uns nicht gefallen." – "Mir auch nicht."
12. "Wir mußten nicht lange warten." – "Ich auch nicht."

Ü 13.

Komplexübungen zu Möglichkeiten der Hervorhebung (13.)

A. Übersetzen Sie:

1. Do tell us the truth. 2. Do be reasonable. 3. The roads are slippery today, do be careful. 4. Do sit down. 5. Do have a glass of wine.
6. Anne's parents didn't want her to marry William, but she did marry him. 7. Do stop criticizing Janet, you are being unfair. 8. Peter will come any moment, do let's wait. 9. Don't think Mary doesn't want to have anything to do with you, she does like you. 10. What you say is quite wrong, who did tell you such nonsense?
11. 'Why aren't you listening?' – 'I am listening, I'm all ears.' 12. It's difficult to please aunt Margaret, she is always complaining about something. 13. My memory's rather poor, I am always forgetting names and dates. 14. If I were you I would be trying to make it up with him. 15. People don't like Fred very much, he is forever making trouble.
16. It was on Sunday that I met Jane. 17. It was Martin who discussed the matter with me. 18. It was not until his mid-fifties that Arthur got to know the woman who managed to make him marry her. 19. It was not until the turn of the century that the concept of the atom as the smallest particle was disproved. 20. What I dislike about John is his unreliability. 21. What matters is that we get exact instructions how to perform this task.
22. Hardly had I caught sight of Elizabeth when I began to like her, never before had I met such a beautiful girl. 23. My telephone rang six or seven times this morning; no sooner had I put down the receiver than there was another call.
24. So dense was the fog that we had to drive at snail's pace. 25. Not for one moment would I doubt Peter's honesty. 26. Under no circumstances can we accept these conditions. 27. Not until several days later was the stolen car discovered.
28. Only after repeated investigations did we succeed in solving the problem.
29. Only when the hijacker threatened to blow up the plane did the pilot agree to change his course. 30. Never again should mankind be threatened by the danger of mass destruction.

B. Heben Sie nacheinander die hervorgehobenen Satzteile hervor (L 13.3.):

1. *After a long period of research the Curies* managed to discover *polonium and radium in 1898.*
2. *In 1919, Alcock and Brown* made *the first transatlantic flight from Newfoundland to Ireland.*
3. *Two masked men* robbed *the jewelry shop at the corner last night.*
4. *Some drunken hooligans* threatened *an elderly lady with a knife in Soho yesterday.*

C. Geben Sie englisch wieder, und nutzen Sie dabei die Möglichkeiten der Hervorhebung:

1. Hören Sie doch auf zu streiten! 2. Du bist zu zerstreut (absent-minded), du vergißt (doch) immer etwas.[664] 3. Mary sieht heute wirklich elegant aus.[665] 4. Mike war gestern abend wirklich unhöflich,[666] als er mit uns sprach. 5. Nehmen Sie doch noch ein Stück Kuchen.[667] 6. Maggie ist immer aufrichtig gewesen (honest);

ich glaube schon, was sie mir erzählt hat.[668]   7. Konzentriere dich doch (bitte), du machst immer (wieder) denselben Fehler.   8. Sei doch (bitte) etwas geduldiger.[669]   9. Worauf es ankommt, ist, daß der Vertrag bis zum Ende der Woche unterschrieben wird.   10. Kaum war der Vortrag zu Ende, als eine heftige (heated) Diskussion begann.[670]   11. Erst nach einer Woche merkte ich (notice), daß ich meinen Paß verloren hatte.[671]   12. Du warst kaum gegangen, als Fred kam.   13. Erst als der Zollbeamte (customs officer) meine Zollerklärung sehen wollte, erinnerte ich mich, daß ich vergessen hatte, sie auszufüllen (fill in).   14. Kaum hatten wir das Problem gelöst, als neue Schwierigkeiten auftraten (arise).   15. Erst im 16. Jahrhundert wurde die Annahme, daß die Erde das Zentrum des Universums ist, durch Kopernikus und Galilei widerlegt (refute).[672]

Komplexübungen zu den Konjunktionen (L 14.)

A. Verbinden Sie die folgenden Sätze mit *because* oder *so, therefore, that's why*.

Beispiel: *We didn't like the play. We left.* → *We left because we didn't like the play.*
Oder:
We didn't like the play, therefore/that's why/so we left.

1. The train was late. We didn't arrive before ten p.m.
2. It is cold. I shall put on my coat.
3. I won't finish the book. I don't like it.
4. John is an excellent worker. He was given a bonus.
5. There was fog. The flight was delayed.
6. I hardly slept last night. There was a lot of noise in the street.
7. The film is very interesting. I decided to see it.
8. The beach was far from the hotel. It took us an hour to get there.

B. Verbinden Sie die zusammengehörigen Feststellungen zu einem Satz, und beachten Sie dabei den Unterschied zwischen *if* und *when*.

Beispiele: *Perhaps it will rain. We won't go for a walk then.* → *If it rains, we won't go for a walk.*
The clock will strike nine soon. Then I won't be here any more. → *When the clock strikes nine, I won't be here any more.*

1. Perhaps I'll meet Jack tomorrow. Then I'll give him the book.[673]
2. Perhaps the weather will get better. We'll make a trip to the mountains then.
3. We know we'll see Helen on Sunday. We'll tell her the news.[674]
4. Perhaps the performance will finish late. We won't go to a restaurant then.
5. The water will boil in a few minutes. I'll make tea then.
6. Perhaps Bob won't arrive until ten. I shan't be here any more.
7. Susan will be eighteen next month. She will get engaged then.
8. I'm sure Mary will come. I'll have a bottle of wine with her.
9. Perhaps Jack will propose to Susan. Then she'll say 'yes'.
10. We'll be on holiday in July. Mrs Miller will water the flowers.

Ü 14.

C. Setzen Sie dem Kontext entsprechend die folgenden Konjunktionen ein: *after; (al)though; because; before; both ... and; but; if; as if; even if; neither ... nor; no matter how/what/who; now that; otherwise; rather than; since; so that/in order that; unless; until; when; while.*

1. Fred couldn't come yesterday ... he had to attend a meeting. 2. I saw Peter ... I was at the seaside last year. 3. You needn't come ... you don't feel well. 4. ... the performance had ended, we went to a café. 5. ... the weather was rather bad, we decided not to postpone our excursion. 6. ... [675]it was the time of the summer vacation all the hotels were full. 7. I won't come ...[676] you phone me. 8. ... I visit a strange town I like to have a guide-book with me. 9. ... one judges by what the critics say the play is worth seeing. 10. ... the school has to be closed because of an influenza epidemic the children will have a week's holiday. 11. I shall wait ...[677] Susan comes, ...[678] she may not be back before midnight. 12. ... we hurry up we won't catch the bus. 13. ...[679] spring has come, the weather will perhaps change for the better. 14. I was very surprised ... my car broke down ... I had had it serviced only some days before. 15. My colleague knows ... English ... French. 16. I hope you won't forget me ... I am abroad. 17. We can't contact Jim ... he is on a business-trip. 18. I must think the matter over ... I take a decision. 19. ...[680] we had played better we would not have won the match. 20. You can depend on me ...[681] will happen. 21. Jane says she'd prefer to go dancing tonight ...[682] see a film. 22. Turn down the radio ...[683] the neighbours won't complain. 23. I haven't heard from Mary ... she went abroad. 24. John behaves ... he were annoyed. 25. Reading this book was ... instructive ... entertaining. 26. I'm very busy; I can't receive anybody today, ... comes. 27. You should inform Roger, ...[684] he will get angry. 28. You should settle the matter yourself ... rely on James. 29. I'm afraid we can't solve this problem by ourselves ... hard we try. 30. Our grandparents go for a one-hour walk every day, ... the weather is like. 31. It was not ... the 1950s that TV became available to the broad public. 32. The instructions are specified in detail ... there should be no misunderstanding.

D. Setzen Sie dem Kontext entsprechende Konjunktionen ein: *Should I Buy a Car?*

Today most people want to have a car, ...[685] cars are rather expensive. A car is ... fast ...[686] comfortable. ...[687] you have to go somewhere quickly, a car can be more reliable ... [688] the train ... [689] a means of transport ...[690] you don't depend on any timetable. ...[691] I have decided to buy a car even ...[692] it means ...[693] I must save a lot of money. The alternative is ... [694] to give up habits ...[695] travelling a lot ... [696] to do without a car.

A Visit to the Theatre

Last night I went to the theatre with Anne. We wanted to see the new production of Shakespeare's 'The Taming of the Shrew', ... our friends had told us we would miss something ... we didn't see it. Anne always takes a lot of time dressing up ... she goes out. ... we started rather late. ... we were waiting for the bus Anne suddenly noticed ... she had left the tickets at home. ... I was annoyed, especially ... she

keeps forgetting things, I said I would be waiting ... she came back even ... we would miss the beginning of the performance.
And indeed, the play had already begun a few minutes ... we arrived. ... we were looking for our seats, one of the actors was just speaking the lines, 'What's here? One dead or drunk?' – And the actor he was speaking to changed his text ... he saw us, answering, 'No, two late-comers.'

E. Geben Sie englisch wieder:
1. Als wir unsere Arbeit beendet hatten, gingen wir ins Theater. 2. Harry will uns helfen, obwohl er wenig Zeit hat. 3. Wir werden Sie informieren, sobald wir Einzelheiten wissen.[697] 4. Es sieht aus, als ob es regnen würde. (L 2.5.1.4.) 5. Wir werden nicht warten, wenn du nicht pünktlich bist.[698] 6. Mary will entweder Schauspielerin oder Tänzerin werden. 7. Bitte stören Sie unsere Sekretärin nicht, während sie das Gutachten abschreibt (type the expertise). 8. Jetzt, da ich deine Argumente kenne, verstehe ich dich besser. 9. Anne hat versprochen, uns am Sonnabend zu besuchen, selbst wenn sie sehr beschäftigt ist.[699] 10. Wir wissen nicht, wo Mike ist; er ist weder zu Hause noch im Büro. 11. Du solltest jemand um Rat fragen, ehe du dich entscheidest (make up one's mind). 12. Professor Meier kann nicht an der Konferenz teilnehmen, weil er krank ist. 13. Es wird lange dauern, bis wir uns wiedersehen (meet). 14. Wir werden warten bis du kommst, selbst wenn es spät wird. 15. Du kannst uns heute anrufen, ganz gleich wie spät es ist.[700] 16. Peter hat gesagt, er wolle kommen, selbst wenn er sich nicht wohl fühlt. 17. Jetzt, da der Fehler gefunden ist, können wir den Versuch fortsetzen. 18. Es sind drei Monate vergangen (pass), seit ich das letzte Mal mit Maggie gesprochen habe.[701] 19. Da noch keine Einigung erzielt worden ist, müssen die Verhandlungen nächste Woche fortgesetzt werden. 20. Mary will ihren Geburtstag mit ihrer Familie feiern und nicht viele Freunde einladen.[702]

15.2. / 15.3.
Ergänzen Sie die folgenden Sätze mit einem Possessiv- oder Demonstrativpronomen. (Beachten Sie, daß in einigen Fällen nicht das Possessivpronomen, sondern der bestimmte Artikel verwendet wird, L 15.3.1.)
1. I've got a sister, ... name is Betty. 2. Billy has got a brother, ... name is Bob. 3. John and Mike are brothers, ... family name is Smith. 4. Is ...[703] your dictionary? – No, it isn't, ...[704] is over there. 5. Have you got a house of ... own? 6. I haven't made up ... mind yet. 7. Jack has broken ...[705] right leg. 8. Don't forget ... umbrella. 9. Anne has cut ... finger. 10. Harry took me by ...[706] arm. 11. You should mind ... own business. 12. They seem to have lost ... way. 13. I dislike people slapping me on ... shoulder. 14. I have known Peter for a long time, he is a close friend of .... 15. You shouldn't always interfere in things which are no business of ....

Ü 15.

15.3./19.5.
Üben Sie die Possessivpronomen ein:

Beispiel: *car (you – Fred)* → *Whose car is this? Is it your car? – No, it isn't my car, it's Fred's, it's his car, it's his.*
coat (Jane – I); gloves (John – Joan); books (you – my parents); penknife (Glen – Fred); glasses (Susan – you); keys (your friend – we)

15.2./15.3.
Geben Sie englisch wieder:

1. Wie heißen Sie? 2. Liz hat ihre Meinung geändert. 3. Deine Übersetzung ist besser als meine. 4. Ein Freund von uns[707] besucht uns heute abend. 5. Ich habe mir den Knöchel (ankle) gebrochen.[708] 6. Hat Peter eine eigene Wohnung? 7. Johns Auto ist schneller als unseres. 8. Dein Vortrag war der interessanteste.[709] 9. Das ist nicht mein Schirm, er gehört meinem Bruder. (L 19.5.)[710]
10. Wessen Tasche ist das? Ist es deine? – Nein, es ist nicht meine, sie gehört meinen Eltern. (L 19.5.)
11. Ist Mike ein Freund von dir?[711] – Nein, er ist ein Freund meiner Schwester. (L 19.5.)[712]
12. Wessen Koffer (suitcase) sind das? Sind es Ihre? – Nein, meine sind es nicht. Ich glaube, sie gehören (L 19.5.) dem Reiseleiter (tour conductor).
13. Kann ich dein Wörterbuch benutzen? – Es ist nicht meins. Mary hat es mitgebracht (bring), es gehört ihr.
14. Sind das deine Bücher? – Nein, es sind nicht meine, sie gehören meinem Bruder (L 19.5.), er hat sie gerade gekauft.
15. Ist das meine Brille? – Nein, es ist die von Fred (L 19.5.), du hast deine auf der Nase.
16. Wessen Dias (slide) sind das? – Sie gehören Anne (L 19.5.).[713] Sie braucht sie für einen ihrer Lichtbildervorträge (slide lecture).

15.4./15.4.1.
A. Ergänzen Sie das entsprechende Reflexivpronomen:

1. We enjoyed ... at the party. 2. Joan often looks at ... in the mirror. 3. Did you find the mistake ...? 4. I did it all by ... 5. Susan likes to hear ... talk. 6. Behave ..., Bob! 7. I've typed the text .... 8. Help ... to another piece of cake. 9. Did your friend paint the room ...? 10. Do you think Anne can manage by ...? 11. Jack and Jim try to teach French to .... 12. Don't make a fool of ....

B. Entscheiden Sie, ob an den markierten Stellen ein Reflexivpronomen einzusetzen ist (L 15.4.):

1. Do you remember ... me? 2. We have informed ... about all the details. 3. You can rely ... on me. 4. She has changed ... a lot since I last saw her. 5. Please, apply ... to my colleague. 6. Did your friends manage to make ... understood in English when they were abroad? 7. Tom has behaved ... quite

correctly. 8. I'm glad you have recovered ... from your disease. 9. We have committed ... to perform this task. 10. I can't recollect ... talking to Mr Ward; I think we have never met ... before. 11. Harry often contradicts .... 12. Don't worry ...! 13. I hope you didn't hurt ... 14. Simon's wife completely devotes ... to the household. 15. You should concern ... with this affair as soon as possible. 16. I can't find little Peggy anywhere; I wonder where she is hiding ....

C. Geben Sie englisch wieder:

1. Du mußt dich beeilen. 2. Wir haben uns gestern abend im Theater getroffen. 3. Hast du den Text selbst übersetzt? 4. Erinnerst du dich an unsere erste Begegnung?[714] 5. Wir haben uns überzeugt, daß die Angaben (data) stimmen.[715] 6. John und Susan haben sich verlobt. 7. Wir freuen uns auf Ihren Besuch. 8. Ich habe mich heute nicht rasiert. 9. Ich hoffe, du wirst dich bald erholen.[716] 10. Wir haben uns über unsere Arbeit unterhalten. 11. Ich muß mich mit diesem Problem beschäftigen.[717] 12. Die Situation hat sich verändert. 13. Habt ihr euch auf einen Termin (date) geeinigt? 14. Ich kann mich auf meine Freunde verlassen. 15. Du solltest dich bei ihr entschuldigen. 16. Haben Sie sich über die Teilnahmegebühren (participation fees) informiert? 17. Setz dich und versuche, dich zu entspannen.[718] 18. Hast du dich daran gewöhnt (L 8.2.1.3.), in einem Hochhaus (high-rise building) zu wohnen? 19. Würden Sie sich bitte auf das Wesentliche (essential facts) beschränken? 20. Peter kennt meine Meinung; ich habe selbst mit ihm gesprochen. 21. Wir würden uns gern mit dem Direktor persönlich (= selbst) unterhalten.[719] 22. Ich kann mir nicht vorstellen, wie ich mich verhalten würde, wenn ich mich sofort entscheiden müßte.

15.4./15.5.

A. Entscheiden Sie, ob an den markierten Stellen ein Reflexivpronomen oder ein reziprokes Pronomen einzusetzen ist:

1. Bill and Mary have known ... for some years. 2. Janet cut ... peeling potatoes. 3. Peter and his mother-in-law often criticize .... 4. Our charwoman often talks to .... 5. I hope you will enjoy .... 6. They help ...[720] whenever they can. 7. It isn't always easy to make ...[721] understood in another language. 8. Take care of .... 9. John and Liz always want to sit next to ... 10. Help ...[722] to another piece of chocolate. 11. Susan and George seem to have quarrelled, they didn't talk to ... last night. 12. My friend denies ...[723] many pleasures, he devotes ...[724] almost exclusively to his scientific work. 13. Plastics lend ... to lots of things. 14. Positive electric charges repel ....

B. Geben Sie englisch wieder, wobei Sie zwischen Reflexivpronomen und reziprokem Pronomen unterscheiden:

1. John und Jane mögen sich. 2. Ich werde die Angelegenheit selbst erledigen (settle). 3. Wo habt ihr euch kennengelernt (get to know)? 4. Wir wissen, daß wir uns aufeinander verlassen können. 5. Wir haben uns gestern abend sehr amüsiert, als wir uns von unseren Ferienerlebnissen (= was wir in den Ferien erlebten) erzählt haben.[725] 6. Mary hört sich gern reden, am liebsten (what she likes most

Ü 15.

is ...) spricht sie über sich selbst. 7. Um sich zu verstehen, ist es wichtig, miteinander zu sprechen.[726] 8. Wir haben uns verpflichtet, die Arbeitsproduktivität (labour productivity) bis zum Ende des Jahres um 5 Prozent zu erhöhen.

C. Geben Sie englisch wieder:

Meine Freundin Ruth will abnehmen (lose weight). Sie bildet sich ein, sie sei zu dick (fat). Deshalb zwingt sie sich, so wenig wie möglich (L 18.1.4.) zu essen. Ich selbst sehe es anders (see things differently); ich fürchte, sie wird sich nur krank machen. Jeden zweiten Tag wiegt sie sich. Ihre Freundin Susan hat sich auch entschlossen abzunehmen. Beide kennen sich schon einige Jahre und unterhalten sich oft darüber, wie sie schnell schlank werden können (get slim). Für Susan ist es schwieriger, sie kann sich nicht beherrschen, wenn sie Süßigkeiten sieht. Jedes Mal, wenn (L 15.7.4.) beide (the two of them) sich treffen, erzählen sie sich, wieviel sie abgenommen haben. Sie sind sehr zufrieden mit sich, wenn sie Fortschritte gemacht haben. Ich habe mich schon gefragt, ob ich meine Freundin nicht dazu bringen könnte (L 5.7.1.), sich die Sache aus dem Kopf zu schlagen (get out of one's head). Aber dann sage ich mir, daß es sich nicht lohnt, darüber zu streiten (L 8.4.).

15.6.1.
A. Formen Sie die folgenden Fragen in bejahende und verneinende Aussagen um.

Beispiel: *Are there any fruit-trees in your garden?* → *There are some fruit-trees in our garden. There aren't any fruit-trees in our garden. There are no fruit-trees in our garden.*

1. Do you know any details about the project? 2. Is there anybody in the office now? 3. Has John told you anything about his trip to Cuba? 4. Have you got any books on 20th century French painting? 5. Did you consult anybody in the matter? 6. Did they hear anything new from him? 7. Did anybody phone? 8. Is there any beer left?

B. Setzen Sie dem Kontext entsprechend *any, anybody/anyone, anything, some, somebody/someone, something, somewhat, somehow, nobody/no-one, nothing, somewhere, anywhere, sometimes* ein:

1. Are there ...[727] questions? 2. Please give me ...[728] more bread. 3. I won't tell Fred ...[729] about the matter. 4. Does ...[730] remember the name of our former teacher? 5. When we returned, ...[731] was at home. 6. We saw ... of your fellow-students at the club. 7. There is ... tea left in the kettle. 8. My camera is very good, I've never had ...[732] problems with it. 9. There was ... to be done. 10. I haven't seen ... good films recently. 11. Would you mind buying ...[733] picture postcards for me? 12. We can't do ... for you. 13. May I offer you ... to eat? 14. We got a taxi without ... trouble. 15. Could you lend me ...[734] money? 16. ...[735] may have seen me when I came. 17. I haven't got ... time to talk to you now. 18. ... of us didn't like the play. 19. Does ... know the answer?

Ü 15.

20. Would you like ... tea? 21. Fred's grandmother didn't leave ... money, but she left ... valuables. 22. I can't see ...[736] now because I have ...[737] urgent work to do. 23. We wanted to buy ... food on Sunday, but there weren't ... shops open. 24. Do you know ... to discuss the problem with? 25. My mother needs ... sleep, please don't make ... noise. 26. There's hardly ...[738] bread left. 27. ... could answer my question. 28. I need ... cinnamon, have you got ...? 29. We shouldn't put off our talk ... longer. 30. Roger hasn't come, ...[739] must have gone wrong. 31. Do you have ... special requests? 32. Anne was ...[740] astonished when I invited her. 33. 'I've lost Peter's address, can ... remember it?' 34. The lecture-room was crowded, ...[741] 150 people had come. 35. Susan speaks French pretty well, and she knows ... Spanish, too. 36. You look rather depressed, is ... the matter with you? 37. I must be off now; I have ... errands to do. 38. Is there ... to be added? 39. Is ... of these ball-point pens yours? 40. Have ... more cake if you want to. 41. Peter sent me ... postcards ... weeks ago, but since then I haven't heard ... from him. 42. We always find ... to talk about. 43. Peggy lives at ...[742] place on the coast, but we have never been ...[743] around there. 44. I haven't got ... to eat at home, but I can offer you ... to drink. 45. Please get me ... stamps, I don't have ... left. 46. Can you spare me a moment, I have got to tell you ... important. 47. Open the door, there is ... outside. 48. I'm sorry I can't find the tickets .... 49. We must try to solve the problem. ...[744] 50. I don't like this restaurant, let's go ...[745] else. 51. Is there ... essential we've forgotten to mention? 52. I looked up the word in ... dictionaries, but I didn't find it .... 53. We needn't go shopping; there isn't ... cheese left, but we've got ... butter and ... slices of cold meat in the fridge. 54. I don't know ... about it. (= I know ... about it.) 55. We shall meet ...[746] time next week. 56. I must write ... letters today, I haven't written ... for ... weeks. 57. You can visit us ...[747] time you like. 58. I'm afraid the situation is ... complicated. 59. There must be ...[748] solution to the problem. 60. Mary lives ... in the vicinity. 61. We can't help you, ask ... else. 62. I didn't like ... of the records John played last night, a few others were rather good. 63. There is practically ... I don't like about her. 64. ... people left before the end of the performance. 65. 'Could you give me ... of these journals?' – 'You can have them all, I don't need ... of them.' 66. We should try to come to an agreement ... or other. 67. Do you know Billy Wilder's film '... like it hot'? 68. Weather forecast: It will be mainly dry with ... frost at night. 69. The symposium began yesterday with ... 50 scientists from non-socialist countries taking part. 70. Beginners are often inclined to believe for ... time that there isn't ... difficulty in learning English; but once they have acquired ... knowledge of English they realize that it is ... more difficult than they had thought. After ... years they feel ... that they know practically ... about the language.

C. Geben Sie englisch wieder:

1. Jemand wollte dich sprechen. 2. Ich habe Frank vor einigen Tagen im Theater gesehen. 3. Darf ich Ihnen etwas zu essen anbieten?[749] 4. Hat jemand angerufen, als ich nicht zu Hause war? 5. Nichts ist einfacher als andere zu kritisieren. 6. Ich habe keine weiteren Fragen.[750] 7. Jemand muß sich um die Sache kümmern (take care of). 8. Haben Sie irgendeinen Roman von Henry Fielding

Ü 15.

gelesen? 9. Niemand wußte, was geschehen war. 10. Komm her, Peter will uns etwas Interessantes erzählen. 11. Haben Sie irgend etwas zu verzollen (declare)? 12. Richard arbeitet nicht mehr in unserem Betrieb.[751] 13. Ich weiß fast nichts über Kybernetik. 14. "Möchtest du etwas trinken?" – "Ich hätte gern etwas Tee." 15. Wo sind meine Pantoffeln? Ich kann sie nirgends finden.[752] 16. Tom und Bill haben sich gestritten, sie sprechen nicht mehr miteinander. 17. Ich werde versuchen, dir irgendwie zu helfen, aber ich kann es nicht versprechen. 18. Ich habe mir die Adresse irgendwo aufgeschrieben, aber ich kann sie nirgends finden. 19. In unseren Berechnungen muß irgendein Fehler sein.[753] 20. Haben Sie irgendwelche Informationen (L 19.4.1.) für mich? 21. Hat dir irgend jemand etwas über das Ergebnis des Versuches erzählt? 22. Ich hoffe, wir werden uns irgendwann nächstes Jahr wiedersehen. 23. Das Museum muß irgendwo in der Nähe (= near) des Bahnhofs sein. 24. Ich mag Menschen nicht, die keinerlei Sinn für (sense of) Humor haben. 25. Wir sollten die Entscheidung nicht länger hinausschieben. 26. Ich glaube, irgend etwas ist nicht in Ordnung (wrong) mit diesem Gerät. 27. Die Konferenz hat vor etwa zwei Jahren stattgefunden. 28. Bewerber (applicants) für diese Stelle müssen einige Fremdsprachenkenntnisse (L 19.4.1.) haben. 29. Der Vortrag war sehr langweilig, kaum jemand hörte zu, und am Ende wollte niemand etwas in der Diskussion sagen.[754] 30. "Wissen Sie irgendwelche Einzelheiten über das Symposium nächste Woche?" – "Ich habe (noch) nichts Genaues (definite) erfahren (tell, Passiv). Ich weiß nur, daß etwa 10 Vorträge gehalten werden (read a paper). Aber ich habe noch keine Informationen (L 19.4.1.) über die Tagesordnung (agenda) erhalten."

31. "Ich brauche etwas zu lesen für meinen Urlaub. Hast du irgendwelche Krimis (crime stories), die du mir leihen könntest?" – "Im Augenblick habe ich keine, die du nicht schon kennst. Aber ich könnte dir einige utopische Romane geben."

32. "Mary geht jetzt einkaufen, brauchst du irgend etwas?"
"Ja, sag ihr, sie soll etwas Käse kaufen (L 5.7.2.), es ist keiner mehr da.[755] Ich brauche auch einige Brötchen (rolls)."
"Wie ist es mit Butter?" (How about ...)
"Nein, danke, ich brauche keine. Aber ich hätte gern etwas Obst."
"Hast du gestern nicht einige Kilo Pflaumen gekauft?"
"Nein, sie hatten keine."

15.6.2.
much oder *many*

1. How ... sandwiches do you want? 2. How ... beer did you drink last night? 3. How ... days did Fred stay in Berlin? 4. How ... people attended the meeting? 5. How ... time did it take you to repair the fence? 6. Tom is a busybody, I don't think ... of him. 7. We didn't spend ... money in our holidays. 8. I don't know ... of the words in this text.

15.6.3.
little oder *few*

1. Bob says he has only ... time to read novels.   2. ... people can speak more than one foreign language fluently.   3. This article is of ... use to me.   4. This time you have made only ... mistakes in your dictation.   5. Please, try to make as ... noise as possible.   6. John is a man of ... words.

15.6.2. / 15.6.3.
Setzen Sie dem Kontext entsprechend *much, many, a lot (of), few, fewer, little, less* ein:

1. Hurry up, I haven't got ...[756] time.   2. Tell me all about it, we've got ...[757] time.   3. Thank you very ... for your invitation.   4. Don't talk so ...   5. I have ...[758] spare time than you.   6. The streets are slippery, we've had ... rain today.   7. I've got ...[759] books, but I don't have ...[760] records.   8. John takes only ... interest in TV, that's why he reads ...   9. Jim doesn't earn as ... as his friends; that's why he can spend ... money on books and records than they.   10. Only ... people know old languages today.   11. We were quite busy today, we worked so ... that we had very ... time to talk.   12. It's ... use discussing the matter again.   13. Peter doesn't have ... friends, he is too ...[761] of an outsider.   14. The performance was attended by ... people than we had expected so that ... seats remained empty.   15. Jack cares ... about his health, he does ... swimming, he doesn't smoke ..., and he drinks very ... alcohol.   16. The air is very clean in our town, because there is only very ... industry here.   17. ... towns have so ... historical buildings as Rome.   18. There is only ... hope of the missing mountaineers being rescued.

15.6.5. / 15.6.10.
Setzen Sie dem Kontext entsprechend *each, every, everybody, everything, everywhere, no, nobody, nothing, none* ein:

1. The Millers take a walk ... day.   2. Three of my colleagues are going to attend the conference, and ...[762] of them will present a paper there.   3. Let's begin, ... is waiting.   4. The variety show was very well attended, ... of the seats were vacant.   5. I'm ready to tell you ... I know about this affair.   6. We spend our holidays abroad almost ... year.   7. There is ... time to discuss details now.   8. We've been looking for you ....   9. I've ... idea what you mean.   10. We meet ...[763] two weeks.   11. When I'm in Moscow, I'll be visiting ... of my Soviet friends.   12. Tom is happy ... time he sees Mary.   13. I've ... to add to what you've said.   14. John is very honest; we have ...[764] reason to believe him.   15. The two motorists were fined £5 ....[765]   16. It's ... use asking him again.   17. We've checked ... result of the test very carefully.   18. ... branch of science can contribute to other fields of science.   19. When we came to Mike's flat, ... answered the door bell, and ... was to be heard inside; obviously, ... had gone out.   20. There was ... agreement, ... of those present accepted the proposals made.

15.6.9.
Geben Sie englisch wieder:

Jim: Mein Mantel ist ziemlich schäbig (shabby), ich brauche einen neuen.[766]
Bob: Gestern habe ich einige modische (trendy)[767] im Kaufhaus (department store) gesehen.
Jim: Meinst du das[768] in der Nähe des Opernhauses?
Bob: Nein, das gegenüber dem Hauptbahnhof.
Jim: Gehen wir gleich hin, wenn du ein wenig Zeit hast.

Im Kaufhaus gab es eine große Auswahl an (selection of) Mänteln, darunter (among them) auch ein paar blaue und graue, die mir gefielen. Ich fragte meinen Freund, welchen er mir empfehlen würde. Er schlug vor (L 8.3.), einige von den grauen anzuprobieren (try on). Ich bat die Verkäuferin, mir einen von den grauen Mänteln zu zeigen.

Verkäuferin: Welchen möchten Sie anprobieren, den hier oder den da drüben (over there)?
Jim: Den neben (next to) den zwei blauen, bitte.
Verkäuferin: Bitte sehr (here you are). Wenn es nicht genau Ihre Größe (size) ist, kann ich Ihnen (noch) einige andere zeigen.

Ich verbrachte eine halbe Stunde damit, Mäntel anzuprobieren (L 9.2.6.), graue, blaue und auch einen grünen, aber keiner davon (= von ihnen) paßte (fit) mir. Diejenigen, die mir gefielen, waren zu eng (tight), und die anderen, die paßten, gefielen mir nicht (L 13.5.2.).

Komplexübungen zu 15.6.3. bis 15.6.8. und 15.6.10.

A. Setzen Sie je nach Kontext *all (of), none/not ... any, both, either (of), neither (of)* ein:

1. ... our friends are married but only two of them have children.   2. ...[769] of us got a ticket, because ... seats were taken.   3. That's ... I can tell you.   4. There are big shops on ... side of the street.   5. Jane and Joan wanted to become screen stars, but ...[770] of them succeeded.   6. Harry told us a lot of jokes, but I liked ... of them.   7. I need both books, so I can't give you. ...[771]   8. They made a lot of suggestions, but ... of them was acceptable.   9. Here are two dictionaries, you may take ..., it doesn't matter which one.   10. ... those who want to see the première should book tickets in time.   11. ... Frank and Fred had promised to help me, but ... of them did.   12. That's ...[772] of your business.   13. I've got two sisters, ...[773] of them are secretaries.   14. You can telephone me tomorrow or the day after tomorrow; ... day suits me.   15. Bob gave me several books; I read them ..., but I liked ... of them.   16. Mary is rather unhappy, ... of her expectations have come true.   17. Theodore likes to talk big, I don't believe ... of his stories.   18. We were shown two beautiful dresses in the shop, my girl-friend liked ...[774] of them, but they were so expensive that we didn't buy ...[775]   19. ... of the two boys was very intelligent, that's why Sue didn't marry ... of them.   20. ... matter is composed of atoms.   21. Some English words can be pronounced in two ways, ... pronunciation is correct.   22. Of ... the substances a plant gets from its environment, ... is more important than water.

B. Verneinen Sie die folgenden Aussagen mit *neither* **(im Objektfall auch** *not ... either*) **bzw.** *none* **(im Objektfall auch** *not ... any*).

Beispiel: *Anne talked to both my colleagues.* → *Anne talked to neither of my colleagues. / Anne didn't talk to either of my colleagues.*

1. I like both girls.[776] 2. Both these scientists are chemists.[777] 3. We knew all the people at the party.[778] 4. I talked to both the students. 5. All of us enjoyed the concert. 6. Both his boys are intelligent. 7. All my friends were present. 8. Both of the tourists spoke English. 9. All of them were interested in your lecture. 10. Both of Susan's brothers are sportsmen.

C. Geben Sie die richtigen Antworten in Sätzen mit *all, none, both, neither*:

1. How many of these countries are islands? – Spain, France, Egypt.
2. Which of the two picture galleries is in Dresden? – the Hermitage, the Louvre.
3. Which of the two writers is English? – Defoe, Dickens.
4. How many of these artists were painters? – van Gogh, Picasso, Repin.
5. Which of the two lakes is in Italy? – Lake Ladoga, Lake Constance.
6. Which of the two rivers flows through Hungary? – The Danube, the Tisza.
7. How many of these buildings are in Berlin? – The Zwinger, the Sans Souci Palace, the Thomas Church.
8. Which of these two plays is a tragedy? – 'The Merry Wives of Windsor', 'The Comedy of Errors'.

D. Geben Sie englisch wieder:

1. Ich habe jetzt nicht viel Zeit. 2. Wieviel verdienen (earn) Sie? 3. Wie viele Karten hast du gekauft? 4. Keiner meiner Kollegen kann Französisch. 5. Niemand kennt John besser als ich. 6. Meine beiden Schwestern sind noch unverheiratet. 7. Möchten Sie noch eine Tasse Tee? 8. Fred kennt viele Leute, aber er hat nur wenige gute Freunde. 9. Jedes Mitglied unseres Forschungsteams bekam eine Prämie (bonus). 10. Ich mag diesen Wein nicht, bestellen (order) wir eine andere Sorte.[779] 11. Ich kann meine Brieftasche (wallet) nirgends finden, ich muß sie irgendwo verloren haben. 12. Wir treffen uns alle drei Wochen. 13. Auf beiden Seiten der Hauptstraße sind einige Kinos. 14. Wir haben zwei Vorschläge gemacht, aber keiner wurde angenommen.[780] 15. Diese beiden Pullover gefallen mir, aber keiner paßt (fit) mir. 16. John hat zwei Brüder, ich kenne beide nicht.[781] 17. Der Film hat uns allen gefallen. 18. Wir haben keine Zeit zu verlieren, wenn wir (noch) etwas zu trinken kaufen wollen, ehe die Geschäfte schließen. 19. Peter hat viele Hobbys, für die er viel Geld ausgibt (spend). Deshalb hat er nur wenig Geld auf der Sparkasse (savings-bank). 20. Ich habe diese beiden Bücher gelesen, aber keins (von beiden) hat mir gefallen, beide waren ziemlich langweilig. 21. Wir sind beide zu spät gekommen.[782] 22. Meine beiden Brüder wohnen auf dem Lande. 23. Ich kenne keine der beiden Schwestern. 24. Fahren diese beiden Straßenbahnen ins Zentrum? 25. Dr. Smith ist ein sehr guter Arzt; jeder seiner Kollegen schätzt ihn (appreciate), und alle seine Patienten mögen ihn.

Ü 15.

15.7.
A. Übersetzen Sie:

1. The German engineer who developed the four-stroke internal-combustion engine was N. A. Otto. 2. A barometer is an instrument which measures the atmospheric pressure. 3. The play that first made Maxim Gorky internationally famous as a dramatist was 'The Lower Depths', which was produced and published in 1902. 4. The first place (that) tourists usually go to in Moscow is the Kremlin. 5. The Palucca Dancing School in Dresden has turned out a large number of prominent dancers, some of whom have become world-famous. 6. In Paris you can find several state-aided theatres, of which the best-known is the 'Comédie Française', whose tradition goes back to the 17th century. 7. Algae are plants of simple structure, the most primitive of which consists of a single cell. 8. It was the transistor that made possible the modern computer.
9. K. F. Braun, who shared the Nobel Prize with Marconi for the development of wireless telegraphy in 1909, also developed the cathode-ray tube, which was one of the most important preconditions for the modern TV tube. 10. The most famous pioneers of balloon development were J. and E. Montgolfier, who in June 1783 launched their first hot-air balloon, which covered a distance of 2.4 km. 11. The name of the English writer Shakespeare's plays were repeatedly attributed to was Francis Bacon. 12. The apparatus the German brothers Skladanowsky used for the motion pictures they presented on November 1, 1895 in what was the world's first public cinema performance, was the bioscope, a device they had developed themselves.

B. Erklären Sie die folgenden Substantive mit ... *somebody who/that* bzw. ... *something (that) you* ...

A baker – make bread;[783] a butcher – sell meat; a thief – steal things; a knife – cut things with;[784] a glass – drink out of; a patient – be ill; an actor – perform in a theatre; tools – repair things with; a dramatist – write plays; a teetaller – abstain from alcohol; a razor – shave with.

C. Korrigieren Sie die absurden Zusammenhänge, und entscheiden Sie dabei, ob ein bzw. welches Relativpronomen nötig ist.

Beispiel: *A typist – you write with it; a pen – she types letters* → *A typist is somebody who types letters. – A pen is something (that) you write with.*

a scientist – he mends the roof; a cartoonist – he writes plays; a tiler – he makes suits; a teakettle – you cut the grass with it; a plumber – he makes cartoons; a bed – you heat the room with it; a tailor – he does research work; a playwright – he lays pipes; a shopping-bag – you make tea in it; a stove – you sleep in it; a lawn mower – you need it for shopping

D. Setzen Sie *who*; *which*; *that* (L 15.7.2.); *whom*; *whose*; *what*; *whatever* ein. Entscheiden Sie dabei, wo das Relativpronomen entfallen kann.

1. The name of the girl ... lives next door is Anne; she is the girl ... Peter wants to marry.[785] 2. The ball-point pen ... was on my desk is gone. 3. Tell me about

...⁷⁸⁶ happened yesterday.   4. This is Mike, ... brother is a friend of mine.
5. Mary, ...⁷⁸⁷ I got to know last week, is a very nice girl.   6. John lent me 600 marks, ...⁷⁸⁸ is exactly the sum ...⁷⁸⁹ I need to buy a new radio.   7. I can't find the book ... I wanted to give you.   8. ...⁷⁹⁰ you have told me is very interesting.
9. Who is the boy ... is standing over there?   10. Dorothy tried on several sweaters, none of ...⁷⁹¹ I liked.   11. Margaret, to ... I introduced you yesterday, is a typist.
12. Peter told me a lot of things ... I hadn't known before.   13. John has four brothers, all of ...⁷⁹² are married.   14. Mr Ward takes a long walk every day, ... is very good for his health.   15. Did you achieve ... you were hoping for?   16. The only thing ...⁷⁹³ matters now is to arrive on time.   17. ...⁷⁹⁴ may happen, I won't change my mind.   18. This is all the money ... is left.   19. Fred told me about his trip abroad, ... interested me very much.   20. ... matters is to find a solution ... satisfies all of us.   21. This is a decision ... importance may not be realized by everybody at once.   22. The train may be late, in ...⁷⁹⁵ case we wouldn't catch the plane.   23. I'll never forget the day ...⁷⁹⁶ I met Barbara for the first time.   24. 'Is this the journal ... you want to have?' – 'No, I want to have the one ... is lying on the table'.   25. Dolphins produce ultrasonic pulses ...⁷⁹⁷ we cannot hear.   26. Torricelli was the man ... invented the barometer.   27. Galileo's ideas were far ahead of the age in ... he lived.   28. The Eiffel Tower, ... was completed in 1889, is 300.5 m high; it now has a big antenna ... height is 20.3 m.   29. Henry VIII, ... is known to have had six wives, reigned from 1509 to 1547.   30. The ship ... brought the first English immigrants to America in 1620 was 'The Mayflower'.   31. The first collected edition of Shakespeare's works, ... contained 36 plays, was published in 1623.   32. The name of the woman ... caused the Trojan War was Helena.
33. It was Odysseus ... suggested building the wooden horse by means of ... the Greeks won the Trojan War.   34. The two Americans ... made the first powered flight in 1903 were Orville and Wilbur Wright.   35. The aeroplane in ... Lindbergh crossed the Atlantic in 1927 was called the 'Spirit of St. Louis'.   36. It was the English admiral Francis Drake ... is said to have refused to break off a game of bowls ... he was playing the day ... the Spanish Armada was approaching in 1587.

E. Bilden Sie jeweils die beiden Sätze in Hauptsatz + Relativsatz um, und lassen Sie, wo möglich, das Relativpronomen weg.

1. Bob is an engineer. He works in our plant.⁷⁹⁸
2. Joan is an interpreter. She does free-lance work.
3. The suit was rather cheap. I bought it last week.⁷⁹⁹
4. This is Mr Miller. He is an actor.
5. Do you know the girl? Fred is married to her.⁸⁰⁰
6. There is still a lot of work. We must do it before we can go out.
7. There are some important problems. We must deal with them at once.⁸⁰¹
8. Mary had a date with John. I didn't like it.⁸⁰²
9. Sue is one of my fellow students. We talked to her at the party.⁸⁰³
10. Would you like to see these photos? I took them when I was abroad.
11. The man is one of my teachers. We met him at the cinema.
12. I liked the book. Harry gave it to me last week.
13. These two lab assistants are very nice. I work with them.⁸⁰⁴

14. The play was not very interesting. My friends took me to it yesterday.
15. What is the name of the girl? You said you were in love with her.
16. We had a very good tour conductor. With his help we visited all the places worth seeing.[805]
17. The lecturer mentioned a lot of authors. We had never heard of some of them.[806]
18. This is a detective story by Agatha Christie. I enjoyed it very much.
19. Some of the houses have been pulled down. They were rather old.
20. The fire destroyed part of the factory. It broke out yesterday.
21. We have got a new computer. It operates at a higher speed.
22. There are many causes of corrosion. Some of them are not yet fully known.
23. One of the chief things is to raise labour productivity. Automation can do this.
24. There will be a meeting tomorrow; the purpose of the meeting is to prepare the conference on biogenetics. The conference will take place at our institute next week.

F. Geben Sie englisch wieder:

1. Hast du dir die Zeitung angesehen, die auf dem Tisch liegt?[807]   2. Mein Freund Thomas, der verheiratet ist und zwei Söhne hat, wohnt in Halle.   3. Hier ist das Taxi, das wir bestellt haben.[808]   4. Ich habe einige Fragen, die ich Ihnen stellen möchte.   5. Das Kleid, das Jane gestern abend trug, muß sehr teuer gewesen sein (L 6.7.).   6. Das Haus, in dem Roger wohnt, befindet sich (= be) in der Straße, die zum Flughafen führt.   7. Manfred ist ein Kollege, auf den man sich verlassen kann.[809]   8. Wer war die Frau, mit der ich dich gestern gesehen habe?[810]   9. Peter hatte viele Freunde zu seiner Party eingeladen, von denen ich einige nicht kannte.[811]   10. Das Restaurant, in das uns Mike geführt hat (take), hat eine sehr gute Küche (cuisine).   11. Dies ist ein Foto des Hotels, in dem wir gewohnt haben (stay at).   12. Das Café im Fernsehturm, das ich noch nicht kenne, soll sehr teuer sein (L 6.5.3.3.).[812]   13. Harry hat zwei Brüder, deren Namen ich vergessen habe.   14. Dies ist ein Buch, das du lesen solltest.   15. Kennst du das Mädchen, mit dem Fred verlobt ist?   16. Das Thema, mit dem ich mich in meiner Diplomarbeit beschäftige, ist sehr kompliziert.[813]   17. Susan, mit der ich mich gern unterhalte, spricht gut deutsch.   18. Die Wohnung, die wir jetzt bekommen haben, ist größer als die, die wir vorher hatten.   19. Wo ist die Zeitschrift, die ich dir gestern gegeben habe?   20. Vor einigen Tagen traf ich Walters Frau, die ich nie zuvor gesehen hatte.   21. Mark hat ein neues Auto, das er vorige Woche gekauft hat.   22. Mary war pünktlich, was mich überraschte.[814]   23. Wer war der Herr, mit dem du gerade gesprochen hast?   24. Was mir nicht gefällt an (= about) Anne, ist die Art und Weise, wie sie sich kleidet.[815]   25. Ich war auf einer Dienstreise an dem Tag, als Thomas aus dem Ausland zurückkam.[816]   26. In dem Text kommen einige Wörter vor, deren genaue Bedeutung ich nicht kenne.   27. Das Projekt, über das bis jetzt keine Einigung erzielt (reach) worden ist, muß noch einmal besprochen werden.[817]   28. Etwa 50 Wissenschaftler, von denen mehrere aus nichtsozialistischen Ländern kommen, werden das Symposium besuchen.
29. Das Grüne Gewölbe (the Green Vault), dessen Kunstschätze (art treasures) weltberühmt sind, ist eine der größten Touristenattraktionen von Dresden.

30. Mexico-City, das eine Bevölkerung von fast 15 Millionen hat, ist die größte Stadt der Welt. 31. Pöppelmann, der den Dresdner Zwinger gebaut hat, war einer der berühmtesten deutschen Architekten des 18. Jahrhunderts. 32. Der Mont Blanc (L 20.1.4.), der 1786 das erste Mal bestiegen wurde (climb), ist der höchste Berg der Alpen. 33. Unter Charles I., der 1625 bis 1649 regierte (reign), kam es in England zu einem Bürgerkrieg (civil war), der 1642 begann. 34. Ernst Barlach, dessen Werke von den Faschisten verboten wurden (ban), war ein sehr vielseitiger (versatile) Künstler, der vor allem durch seine Plastiken (sculptures) bekannt wurde (L 4.6.3.).

G. Geben Sie die folgende Unterhaltung englisch wieder:

"Gehst du heute abend zu der Party, die Susan geben will?"
"Ich habe mich noch nicht entschlossen (make up one's mind); ich kenne nur wenige von den Leuten, die dort sein werden, und ich mag keine Partys, die bis spät nachts dauern (last)."
"Aber die Party, zu der wir vorige Woche gegangen sind, hat dir doch gefallen?" (L 12.1.)
"Ja (L 12.2.), einige der Leute, mit denen ich mich unterhalten habe, waren sehr nett. Das Mädchen, das mir am besten gefallen hat, war Mary, die neben mir saß und die sehr gut tanzt. Wenn sie zu Susans Party käme, würde ich auch gehen."

Komplexübungen zum Adverb (17.)

A. Wandeln Sie die folgenden Feststellungen in Sätze mit einem Adverb um.

Beispiel: *Her knowledge of English is good.* → *She knows English well.*

1. My friend is a very careful driver.[818] 2. Your wife is a good cook. 3. Mark is a hard worker. 4. Little Mary is always an attentive listener when I tell her fairy-tales. 5. Barbara is a quick thinker. 6. My brother is a fast learner. 7. I am an early riser. 8. Arthur's speech is slow. 9. Mr Dunford has always been a very exact interpreter. 10. Peggy is a good typist. 11. Your articulation is bad. 12. Jane is a good-looker.[819]

B. Entscheiden Sie, ob ein Adjektiv oder ein Adverb einzusetzen ist. (Beachten Sie die unterschiedliche Form und Bedeutung einiger Adverbien, L 17.3.):

1. Janet is a good interpreter, she speaks French very ... (good). 2. The film is ... (bad) synchronized. 3. Pierre speaks English ... (fluent). 4. Paul is rather ... (lazy), I can ... (hard) imagine that he will pass his exams. 5. Fred's arguments do not sound ... (reasonable). 6. Mike seems ... (angry), he must have had a ... (pretty) unpleasant talk with his boss. 7. This fabric feels rather ...[820] (smooth). 8. This meat salad doesn't taste ... (good). 9. You are looking ...[821] (sad), what has happened? 10. John looked ...[822] (sad) into his empty purse. 11. It was ... (general) agreed that the conference has been ... (good) prepared. 12. The play was ...[823] (fair) (good), but I wouldn't want to see it a second time. 13. I don't like this perfume, it smells too ... (strong); it smells ... (strong) of lavender. 14. I know

Ü 17.

Susan ... (fair) (good).   15. ... (Fortunate), the test has proved ... (successful).
16. There is no agreement in sight because opinions still differ ...[824] (pretty) (large).
17. The panel discussion was ... (pretty) interesting; the participants exchanged their arguments ... (lively).   18. A modern computer is a ... (high) complicated device.   19. Robots are being used in industry on an ... (increasing) large scale.
20. Whether idioms are used ... (correct) is ... (large) due to the situation in which they are used.

C. Finden Sie in den folgenden Sätzen entsprechend dem Kontext die richtige Form des Adverbs (L 17.3.):

1. John is very busy now, he even works ...[825] (hard) on Sundays. – Fred is not a friend of mine, I ...[826] (hard) know him.
2. It is ...[827] (near) impossible to solve this problem at once. – We came very ...[828] (near) to solving the problem.
3. The text was ... (pretty) difficult to translate. – Joan spends a lot of money on her clothing, she is always ... (pretty) dressed.
4. I haven't seen George ... (late). – Peter came rather ... (late).
5. The participants in the conference were ...[829] (most) physicists. – What I like ...[830] (most) about John is his frankness.
6. Harry wants us to come ... (right) after lunch. – You ... (right) assumed that Bob wouldn't pass the driving test.
7. John and Joan ... (most) sit ... (close) to each other. – Anne ... (close) resembles her sister.
8. You can't complain, you have been ... (fair) treated. – Don't trust him he doesn't play ... (fair).
9. What you have said is ... (high) interesting. – The cliffs rise ... (high) above the ocean.
10. Is the door ...[831] (fast) shut? – Don't talk so ...[832] (fast).
11. Your letter didn't reach me in time because it was ... (wrong) addressed. – I'm afraid I have caught you ... (wrong).
12. I was ...[833] (wide) awake when the telephone rang. – Opinions on fashion differ ...[834] (wide).

D. Setzen Sie das Adverb an die passende Stelle (L 17.6.):

1. The train has arrived. (just)   2. Have you been to Romania? (ever)   3. Mike's parents don't seem to like Susan. (very much)   4. Have you talked to John? (yet)   5. We have been informed about the arrangement. (already)   6. Don't disturb Mary, she is getting dressed. (just)[835]   7. I recognized Fred (hardly) when I saw him after ten years (again).[836]   8. We have found the mistake. (fortunately)[837]   9. The book is illustrated. (well)   10. You have translated the text. (very well)   11. The meeting was organized. (badly)   12. John interpreted at the conference. (badly)

E. Geben Sie englisch wieder; unterscheiden Sie dabei zwischen Adverb und Adjektiv:

1. Das ist ein gutes Buch. – Das Buch ist sehr gut geschrieben.[838]
2. Dies ist ein schneller Wagen. – Peter fährt oft sehr schnell.

3. Vergangenen Winter hatten wir extreme Temperaturen. – Die Temperaturen waren außerordentlich niedrig.
4. Es ist ein wirkliches Vergnügen, ihm zuzuhören. – Es ist wirklich angenehm (pleasant), ihm zuzuhören.
5. Der Film war schrecklich. – Der Film war schrecklich langweilig.[839]
6. Das Mittagessen war gut. Es war gut zubereitet (cook). Alle Speisen (dishes) schmeckten sehr gut.
7. Dein Wagen sieht noch ziemlich neu aus.[840] – Die neuentwickelte Maschine wird zur Zeit getestet.[841]
8. Hatten Sie eine angenehme Reise? – Ich war angenehm überrascht, als ich die Prüfungsergebnisse erfuhr (tell, Passiv).
9. Die Veranstaltung war schlecht besucht. 10. Deine Übersetzung ist völlig falsch.[842] 11. Ich treffe Peter oft und kenne ihn sehr gut. 12. Sprechen Sie bitte etwas langsamer.[843] 13. Der Vortrag war hochinteressant. 14. Wir müssen den Versuch sorgfältig vorbereiten. 15. Ich habe schlecht geschlafen,[844] weil es vorige Nacht im Hotel sehr laut (noisy) war. 16. Susan sieht heute sehr hübsch aus. 17. Es ist fast 10 Uhr, wir müssen sofort gehen.[845] 18. Deine Fotos gefallen mir sehr. 19. Wir müssen uns schnell entscheiden (make up one's mind). 20. Die Konferenz hat vorige Woche in Berlin stattgefunden. 21. Du wirst intensiv studieren müssen,[846] wenn du die Prüfung bestehen willst. 22. Dieses Bier schmeckt nicht sehr gut, es ist schal geworden (L 11.1.). 23. Vermutlich ist Harry krank. 24. Hoffentlich ruft Tom uns bald an. 25. Unsere Mannschaft spielt heute schlechter als vorigen Sonntag. 26. Wissen Sie zufällig,[847] wo Herr Martin wohnt? 27. Wahrscheinlich werde ich Mike am Wochenende treffen.[848] 28. Ich habe Walter gestern zufällig im Kaufhaus gesehen, er war gerade aus Tansania zurückgekehrt. 29. Ich sehe Tom ziemlich selten; in letzter Zeit habe ich kaum etwas (L 15.6.1.) von ihm gehört. 30. Unsere amerikanischen Geschäftspartner sprechen oft sehr schnell, so daß wir sie manchmal kaum verstehen können.[849] 31. Zieh deinen Mantel an, es regnet. 32. Das Radio ist zu laut, bitte stelle es leiser (turn down).

Komplexübungen zur Steigerung (L 18)

A. Übersetzen Sie:

1. Try to come as early as possible. 2. Jane doesn't know English as well as Mary. 3. Fred's eldest son is two years older than me. 4. Can you show me the nearest way to the airport? 5. John earns less money than his friend. 6. The weather is getting worse and worse, we shouldn't go any farther. 7. It was most considerate of you to send me a telegram. 8. Do you have any further questions? 9. The new method is simpler and more accurate than the old one. 10. The least you can do is apologize. 11. Fred always finds a way out even if the worst comes to the worst. 12. This year we have seen fewer films and less interesting ones than last year. 13. The situation has become more and more complicated. 14. The earlier somebody starts learning foreign languages the easier they will find it. 15. I don't like people who always take the line of least resistance. 16. Norman has promised to

Ü 18.

stick by me for better or for worse. 17. Bill always drives most carefully. 18. Proverb: The best things are worst to come at. 19. 'Have you heard the latest, Mary has had a divorce.' – 'Has she? The last I heard was that she was getting on pretty well with her husband.' 20. Galileo was as famous a scientist as Newton. 21. Light travels faster than sound. 22. Copper is about twenty times as abundant as silver, and the latter about twenty times as abundant as gold. 23. Robots are being used in industry more and more frequently. 24. The invention of the transistor in 1947 was one of the most important prerequisites for present-day computer development. 25. The earlier cancer is recognized, the more likely is the chance of successful treatment.

B. Ziehen Sie Vergleiche mit *than*; *not as/so ... as*:

Apples – oranges (cheap); roses – violets (expensive); New York – Chicago (large); Manchester – London (inhabitants); Hungary – Switzerland (mountainous); Belgium – France (large); the Danube – the Thames (long); Mont Blanc – Mount Everest (high); flying – going by car (fast); the Wartburg – the Trabant (spacious); a camp-stool – an easy chair (comfortable)

C. Ziehen Sie Vergleiche; verwenden Sie jedes Adjektiv bzw. Indefinitpronomen nur einmal:

bad – expensive – famous – fast – few – good – high – interesting – little – long – old – reliable – small – tall

1. Ted is John's ... brother. 2. Jean eats ... her friend. 3. Grapefruit is ... plums. 4. Fred is ... of my friends. 5. This is one of the ... films I have ever seen. 6. Luxemburg ... Denmark. 7. The Empire State Building is one of the ... structures in the world. 8. The Volga ... the Rhine. 9. Which is ... mountain in Europe? 10. Planes ... cars. 11. This is the book I like ... 12. I hope there won't be a change for the ... 13. Brahms wrote ... symphonies ... Beethoven. 14. Voltaire ... a philosopher ... Rousseau.

D. Geben Sie englisch wieder:

1. Heute ist das Wetter nicht so schön wie gestern. 2. Ist Jane ebenso hübsch wie ihre Freundin?[850] 3. Peter ist drei Jahre älter als sein Bruder. 4. John spricht nicht so gut Französisch wie Roger.[851] 5. Jean ist Mikes älteste Schwester. 6. Meine drei Tanten sind sehr intelligent, aber Tante Paula ist die intelligenteste (L 15.6.9.). 7. Können Sie mir sagen, wo der nächste Briefkasten ist? 8. Bob spielt gut Schach, aber sein Freund spielt (noch) viel besser, er ist der beste Schachspieler, den ich kenne. 9. Mein Bruder ist ziemlich klein für sein Alter; meine Schwester ist jünger als er, aber viel größer. 10. Anne ist sehr fleißig, aber Alice ist noch (= even) fleißiger.[852] 11. Wir kamen zu spät, obwohl wir so schnell gelaufen waren, wie wir konnten. 12. Ich mag Mike mehr als Jack, er ist viel zuverlässiger und weniger impulsiv.[853] 13. Gestern habe ich mich nicht wohl gefühlt, heute fühle ich mich noch (even) schlechter. 14. Fred ist sehr schlecht in Englisch, mein Englisch ist noch schlechter, aber Herbert hat die schlechteste Aussprache von uns allen. 15. Wir brauchen so viele Informationen wie möglich (L 19.4.1.) 16. Ich kenne keine Frau, die so unpünktlich ist wie meine. 17. Es waren dreimal

mehr Leute zu dem Vortrag gekommen, als der Redner (lecturer) erwartet hatte.
18. Gestern waren 10° unter (below) Null, heute ist es noch kälter.   19. Freitag abend war viel Verkehr in den Straßen, deshalb brauchten wir länger als sonst (= usual), um nach Hause zu kommen.[854]   20. Tomaten haben vorige Woche 5,– M pro Kilo (L 20.2.1.) gekostet, heute sind sie viel billiger.   21. Je früher du kommst, desto besser.   22. Sein neuestes Buch ist recht gut, aber nicht so gut wie sein vorletztes.[855]   23. Die Fernsehsendung (TV transmission) gestern abend war viel interessanter, als wir erwartet hatten.   24. Unser Nachbar ist doppelt (two times) so alt wie seine Frau, deshalb geht er nicht so oft mit ihr aus, wie sie es möchte.   25. Der Krimi (detective story) war viel langweiliger (boring), als ich gedacht hatte.   26. Heute waren nicht so viele ausländische Touristen im Kaufhaus wie gewöhnlich. Deshalb wurden wir schneller bedient (serve) als gestern.[856]
27. Joan geht oft mit ihrem Freund in ein Restaurant; sie ißt immer weniger als er, aber er trinkt viel mehr als sie.   28. Wir haben niemals eine Aufführung von "Hamlet" gesehen, die so faszinierend war wie diese.   29. Gestern war ich beim Arzt; ich dachte, es würde länger als eine Stunde dauern, aber ich brauchte nur weniger als 20 Minuten zu warten.[857]   30. Budapest ist eine der schönsten Städte, die ich kenne.   31. Welche Stadt ist größer, Moskau oder Leningrad?   32. In der englischen Literatur des 19. Jahrhunderts gab es viele erfolgreiche Autoren, aber keiner (L 15.6.10.) war erfolgreicher als Charles Dickens.

20.1.
Entscheiden Sie, wo der bestimmte Artikel zu setzen ist:

1. The sun rises in ... east and sets in ... west.[858]   2. Last year we spent our holidays in ... Caucasus.[859]   3. ... Rhine rises in ... Switzerland and flows into ... North Sea.[860]   4. Which bus goes to ... Oxford Street?[861]   5. ... Tower Bridge[862] was designed in 1894.   6. ... Lake Geneva is 582 sq km in area; ... Lake Constance covers an area of 538.5 sq km.[863]   7. ... Nile discharges itself into ... Mediterranean.   8. ... Matterhorn is considered to be the most beautiful mountain in ... Alps.[864]   9. Many famous Englishmen are buried in ... Westminster Abbey.   10. The first to climb ... Mount Everest[865] was E. Hillary.   11. Prof. Parker deals with ... history of science.[866]   12. After graduating from ... university Mike will work in ... industry.[867]   13. ... arithmetic, algebra and geometry are subdivisions of ... mathematics.[868]   14. ... subject of ... psychology is ... study of ... organisms' adjustment to ... environment.[869]   15. ... members of ... House of Lords are representatives of ... nobility, ... clergy and ... Royal Family.[870]   16. ... combustion takes only place in ... presence of ... oxygen.[871]   17. Throughout ... centuries man has put forward different speculations on ... origin of ... life.[872]   18. ... phonetics is ... science of ... sound.   19. ... love's a disease, but curable (Rose Macaulay).   20. ... road to Hell is paved with good intentions.   21. ... man is by ... nature a political animal (Aristotle).[873]   22. It's ... love that makes ... world go round (French song).   23. In ... capitalism, ... most of ... means of ... production are owned by private enterprise, in ... socialism they are owned by ... state.[874]   24. Since ... antiquity ... materialism and ... idealism have been ... two major approaches in ... philosophy.

Ü 20.

25. We'd better go by ... taxi. – Hurry up, ... taxi has come.
26. When did you leave ... school? – Peter's son attended ... school which is ... building opposite ... main station.[875]
27. Where did you put ... milk I have bought? – Susan often drinks ... milk.
28. Let's go to ... restaurant round ... corner; ... wine they serve there is very good. – I prefer ... wine to ... beer.
29. The concert will be transmitted by ... radio. – Yesterday we listened to ... radio all evening.
30. ... telephone was invented by Philipp Reis. – We received the message by ... telephone.
31. Mary likes ... art; she is particularly interested in ... art of ... twentieth century.
32. The tram stops right in front of ... church. – Lucy's mother often goes to ... church.
33. This problem should be discussed in ... public. – The park is open to ... public from 10 a.m. to 5 p.m.
34. I think we shall be able to translate the text with ... help of a good dictionary. – The thief opened the door by ... means of a skeleton key.
35. ... physics of low temperatures is called ... cryophysics. – ... optics and ... acoustics are branches of ... physics.
36. What does ... chemistry deal with? – ... analytical chemistry of ... transuranium elements began with ... discovery of ... first transuranium element, neptunium.

20.2.
Geben Sie den genannten Persönlichkeiten den richtigen Beruf, und verwenden Sie dabei den unbestimmten Artikel:

George Washington (American writer) – Titian (Roman emperor) – Copernicus (Greek philosopher) – Jean Marat (famous film star) – Nero (Italian painter) – Heraclitus (Polish astronomer) – Jean Marais (French politician of the 18th century) – Washington Irving (president of the USA)

20.1. / 20.2.
A. Entscheiden Sie, ob an den markierten Stellen der bestimmte, der unbestimmte oder kein Artikel einzusetzen ist:

A Short Visit to London

Mr Bertram, ... sales manager from Dublin, is on ... short business trip to London, ... capital of Britain. His friend, Mr Green, who is ... engineer in ... big London enterprise, meets him at ... airport and takes him to his home, which is about 20 miles from ... centre of London. He has ... little house in ... beautiful village, called Chalfont St. Peter, which is situated in ... County of Buckinghamshire.
On ... afternoon of ... following day Mr Bertram has time to go sightseeing with his friend. Mr Green suggests taking ... train rather than going by ... car, because ... parking is difficult in ... centre of ... town.

After thirty minutes they arrive at Marylebone Station, ... terminus of ... railway line. Then they take ... underground to ... Hyde Park Corner, which is near ... Buckingham Palace. There they want to see ... Changing of ... Guard, which always takes place when ... Queen is in residence. After watching ... ceremony they walk through ... St. James's Park to ... Houses of ... Parliament and have a look at 'Big Ben', ... world-famous 13.5 ton bell. On ... Westminster Bridge they take a photo of ... Houses of ... Parliament.
Mr Bertram says he would like to see ... home of ... Prime Minister. So they go back over ... bridge. A short walk takes them to ... Downing Street. Then they go on to ... Trafalgar Square to see ... Nelson's Column. They have ... cup of coffee in ... café and then take ... bus to ... St. Paul's Cathedral. After visiting ... Cathedral and ... Tower of London they go by ... bus to ... Piccadilly Circus and then take ... little walk through Soho.

B. Geben Sie englisch wieder:

1. Willst du mit dem Auto oder mit der Bahn fahren? 2. Ich gehe einmal im Monat[876] ins Konzert. 3. Harrys Frau ist fünfmal in der Woche im Theater, sie ist Souffleuse (prompter). 4. Der Lehrer gab uns eine halbe Stunde, um den Text zusammenzufassen. 5. Erzähle mir die Geschichte ein anderes Mal, ich bin in Eile. 6. Paul hat seine Freundin im Zug kennengelernt. 7. Susan hat heute Lust tanzen zu gehen, aber ich würde lieber ins Kino gehen. 8. Es ist schade, daß du nicht kommen kannst. 9. Ich sehe Mike nicht oft, wir treffen uns höchstens zweimal im Jahr. 10. Als Peter Mary traf, war es Liebe auf den ersten Blick. 11. Es war eine ziemliche Überraschung,[877] daß Liverpool vorigen Sonnabend sein Heimspiel gegen Leeds United 3:1 verlor; gewöhnlich ist es die bessere Mannschaft. (L 19.4.8.) 12. Im vorigen Jahr habe ich einen Teil meines Urlaubs[878] auf der Insel Hiddensee verbracht. Dieses Jahr werde ich die meiste Zeit[879] zu Hause bleiben. 13. Wir müssen das Manuskript spätestens bis Ende April einreichen.[880] 14. Roger ist ein ziemlich komplizierter Charakter;[881] einerseits ist er zurückhaltend, andererseits kann er sehr impulsiv sein. 15. Vieles klingt einfacher in der Theorie, als es in der Praxis ist.[882] 16. Im Laufe der Zeit haben sich die Ansichten über (view on) Mode immer wieder geändert (keep, s. 8.3.), und doch bewegt sich die Mode im Kreise (circle).
17. Die Schweiz ist ein Bundesstaat. 18. Die Normandie liegt im Norden von Frankreich. 19. Die Donau fließt ins Schwarze Meer. 20. Eisen findet man in der Natur in Form von Eisenerz.[883] 21. Die Biogenetik ist ein relativ neues Gebiet der Biologie. 22. Roboter werden zunehmend (increasingly) in der Industrie eingesetzt. 23. Die Menschheit braucht den Frieden, um zu überleben (survive).[884] 24. Die Entwicklung von Schlüsseltechnologien ist eine der wesentlichsten Voraussetzungen für (prerequisite for) die Erhöhung der Arbeitsproduktivität (labour productivity). 25. Der Mensch versucht seit Jahrtausenden, die Geheimnisse der Natur, des Lebens auf der Erde und des Weltalls zu ergründen (unveil). 26. Im Jahre 1987 fanden anläßlich der 750-Jahrfeier (anniversary) von Berlin viele festliche Veranstaltungen (festive ceremonies) in Anwesenheit hervorragender Persönlichkeiten (outstanding personalities) aus Ost und West statt.

20.1.
Setzen Sie, wo erforderlich, den bestimmten Artikel ein:

Automation

The term automation was coined in ... early 1940s to describe those processes in which mechanisms are used to perform tasks that previously required ... attention and control of ... man.

Throughout the centuries ... man has attempted to transfer some of ... burden of ... work to mechanical devices. However, ... widespread mechanization did not take place until ... beginning of ... Industrial Revolution in ... 18th century. What is called ... division of ... labour, i.e. ... restriction of ... activity of each worker to one specific task, led to ... machines being developed capable of performing these tasks, which were powered at first by ... newly developed steam engine and later by ... electricity.

The American inventor Oliver Evans created ... first continuous production line for grinding ... grain in 1784 – a cornmill in which all ... movement was automatic. Mechanization, ... precursor of automation, brought about a complete reorganization of ... methods of production – ... subdivision of ... production process into a number of well-defined steps and ... design of specialized mechanisms to aid in ... performance of each step.

While the term mechanization is often used to refer to ... simple replacement of ... human work by machines, ... automation implies ... integration of machines into a self-governing system.

It is ... presence of feedback systems above all that serves to distinguish ... automation from ... mechanization. Feedback means ... ability of a machine to regulate itself. It is ... aim of automation to operate ... technical equipment with a maximum of ... profitability, safety and reliability.

Automation contributes to relieving ... man of ... heavy and monotonous work or labour injurious to ... health.

Through automation ... human work can be saved or restricted to activities in ... fields of ... design, ... programming, ... supervision and ... repair. With ... help of process computers, rail vehicles, ships and missiles may be controlled automatically. In ... accounting, in ... banks, department stores and airline companies tasks of administration are performed by ... automata. Without self-operating equipment, ... television and ... modern communication engineering including ... transmission of news via ... satellite as well as ... space research would not be possible.

By means of ... microelectronics, automata which can learn have already become a possibility but ... operations they carry out are still based on purely factual logic.

From ... point of view of ... economy automation makes possible ... extension of ... production and an increase of ... labour productivity.

Thus, ... automation makes a decisive contribution to ... economic growth. Its effects extend beyond ... increase in ... industrial productivity to ... society itself.

Anhang

Komplexübungen

A detective story

(Schwerpunkte: Zeiten, Passiv, Infinitiv, Partizip, Gerundium)

Setzen Sie die Verben in Klammern in die richtige Form:

Joe Miller is a private detective in Los Angeles. He (have) a lot of interesting cases so far. Recently he (call upon)[885] by a hotel proprietor who wanted (have) his wife (shadow).[886] He (suspect) her of (have) an affair with an actor. The next morning the detective (stand)[887] near his client's house. At nine o'clock he (see) the woman (come) out. It looked as if she (go shopping)[888] because she (carry) a big shopping bag. Nevertheless he (make up one's mind) to follow her. She (begin/walk) down the street. After a few minutes she (stop) at a newsstall (buy) a paper. After (have a look) at the headlines, she (move) on. Suddenly she (stop) outside a bookshop. She (seem/wait)[889] for somebody. A man (come/hurry)[890] towards her. The detective (think) he (may) be the man he (look for). He (be) disappointed on (realize) that the man (walk) past her without (take notice of) her. Obviously, the woman only (want) to look at the books (exhibit) in the shop window. But the detective (not give up). He (follow) her into a department store where lots of people (crowd)[891] at the counters. For a quarter of an hour he (be afraid) he (lose track)[892] of her because she nowhere (see)[893]. When he (see) her again she (talk) to a beautician. Her shopping bag (seem/be) very heavy. Apparently, she (buy)[894] a lot of things. After (leave) the department store she (go) to a café where she (have) a cup of coffee. Then she (head) for home.

The detective (go on/observe) her, but she (not turn up) again. Evidently, she (decide/stay) at home for the rest of the day. Though (spend) a week (observe) her,[895] the detective (fail/find out) anything that (may/confirm) her husband's suspicion. (Tell) that he obviously (be) wrong[896] the husband (relieve). He appeared (regret/suspect) his wife.

Komplexübungen

Shakespeare

(Schwerpunkte: Zeiten, Passiv, Infinitiv, Gerundium, Partizip)

Setzen Sie die in Klammern angegebenen Verben in die richtige Form:

William Shakespeare, Britain's greatest dramatist, (live) from 1564 to 1616. He (be born) and (die) in Stratford-upon-Avon. Shakespeare (be) the third child of an apparently wealthy yeoman (engage, 9.1.1.) in the trade of a glover, who, in 1568, (elect) mayor of the little town (11.2.). He (attend) the local grammar school of Stratford. In 1582, he (marry) Anne Hathaway, who (be) eight years older than he and who (bear) him three children. Whether Shakespeare (leave) Stratford around 1586 because he (threaten) with punishment for poaching cannot (prove) definitely. At any rate, it may (take for granted) that he (move) to London at the age of 21 or 22 after his father (lose) most of his fortune. Shakespeare's first years in London (wrap in darkness)[897] but it (believe)[898] that he (join) a company of actors before long. He (mention) in a pamphlet by the author Robert Greene in 1592, who (term) him 'an upstart crow beautified with our feathers'. Hence it can (conclude) that he must already (attract)[899] attention as an actor and playwright at that time. The name of Shakespeare (find) in an account of the Treasury (Hofschatzamt) from the year 1594, (show)[900] that he (play) before Queen Elizabeth together with his friend, the actor and theatre-manager Richard Burbage, son of James Burbage by whom the first public London theatre (erect) in 1576. It (build) in a suburb of London because the town council would not allow any theatres (build)[901] in the centre, (consider) the amusements (provide) by them harmful to public morals.[902]

In the early 1590's Shakespeare (begin) to write plays. His reputation as an actor-playwright (bring) him quite a considerable fortune, which (permit) him to become joint owner of the Globe Theatre and the Blackfriars Theatre. It cannot (state) with certainty when Shakespeare (go back) to Stratford-upon-Avon. But after 1613, the year the Globe Theatre (destroy) by fire, he (know/have)[903] his permanent residence in his native town. In 1623, a collected edition of Shakespeare's works (publish), (contain) 36 plays. He himself probably never (think) of (get) his plays (publish)[904], they (write) for the theatre. According to the thinking of his time, the publication of plays (consider) detrimental to commercial success because there (be) no copyright that (protect) the author against arbitrary production of his works at other theatres. Moreover, it should (bear in mind) that plays (perform) and (look at), usually they (not read) at that time.

The theatres of that time were roofless except above the stage. When Shakespeare (write) his plays, the stage was almost bare. It (leave)[905] to the imagination of the audience to picture the scenery from the text that (speak). The stage (surround) by the spectators who (stand) in the yard or (sit) in the (encircle) balconies; sometimes they also (sit) on the stage. This arrangement (allow) direct contact (establish)[906] between the actors and the audience. The theatre-goers (make) to participate immediately in the action, a situation quite different from the picture-frame stage (Guckkastenbühne) of later times with the actors (behave)[907] as if nobody else (be) present and the audience (separate)[908] from them by an invisible wall. Performances usually

(take place) in the afternoon. The female parts (act) by boys. Obviously this (not suppose)[909] to be a handicap. If it had been, Shakespeare (not write) so many fascinating parts for women. It (be) not until 1660 that the first woman (appear) on an English stage.
Shakespeare's plays can (divide) into tragedies, histories, comedies and romances. Plays such as 'Hamlet', 'King Lear', 'Macbeth', 'Romeo and Juliet', 'Richard III', 'A Midsummer Night's Dream', 'What You Will', 'As You Like It' or 'The Tempest' (perform)[910] all over the world, and they (admire)[911] by theatre-goers for more than three centuries.

Die Anfänge der Eisenbahn

(Schwerpunkte: Relativpronomen, Passiv, Infinitiv, Partizip)

Die Ursprünge der Schienenbeförderung *(railroad transportation)* können bis ins 16. Jahrhundert zurückverfolgt werden *(trace back)*. Zuerst waren Schienenfahrzeuge *(railroad cars)* für europäische Bergwerke konstruiert worden. In englischen Bergwerken sollen die ersten Schienenfahrzeuge 1603 eingeführt worden sein (L 6.5.3.3.). Diese Wagen auf Eisenschienen *(iron rails)* mußten zunächst von Männern oder Pferden gezogen werden. Die Entwicklung der Eisenbahn *(railway)* begann, nachdem die Dampfmaschine *(steam engine)* erfunden worden war. 1803 baute der Engländer Richard Trevithick die erste Eisenbahnlokomotive *(railway locomotive)* der Welt. 1808 führte Trevithick in London eine Lokomotive vor *(demonstrate)*, die er "Catch-me-who-can" nannte und die Passagiere beförderte *(carry)*. Thomas Newcomen entwickelte um 1712 eine Dampfmaschine, die 1765 von James Watt beträchtlich verbessert wurde. George Stephenson baute die Dampflokomotive für die erste Eisenbahnstrecke *(railway line)* der Welt, die 1825 zwischen Darlington und Stockton eröffnet wurde. Die Stockton-Darlington-Eisenbahn, die als eigentlicher *(actual)* Beginn der Eisenbahnära *(railway era)* betrachtet werden kann, beförderte sowohl Fracht *(freight)* als auch Passagiere. Am 27. September 1825 fuhr *(run)* der erste Zug von Darlington nach Stockton mit 450 Passagieren bei *(at)* einer Geschwindigkeit von 24 km/h *(kph)*. Er wurde angekündigt durch einen Reiter *(man on horseback)*, der die Strecke *(track)* entlangritt und eine Fahne trug, auf der stand (= Präsenspartizip von read): "Periculum privatum utilitas publica" *(the private danger is the public good)*. 1830 wurden mit der von Stephenson konstruierten (L 9.1.1.) Dampflokomotive "Rocket" erstmals zwei größere Städte, Liverpool und Manchester, durch eine Eisenbahnstrecke von 64 km (miteinander) verbunden. Ein Jahr zuvor hatte ein Geschwindigkeitswettbewerb *(speed competition)* für Lokomotiven stattgefunden, der von Stephensons "Rocket" mit 58 km/h gewonnen wurde. Die erste Eisenbahnstrecke in Deutschland, die 6,1 km lang war, wurde bekanntlich (L 5.8.1.) 1835 zwischen Nürnberg und Fürth eröffnet. Drei Jahre später legten Züge zwischen Leipzig und Dresden schon eine Entfernung von 116 km zurück *(cover a distance)*. Auf dieser Strecke wurde die erste deutsche Dampflokomotive verwendet, die nach Entwürfen von Andreas Schubert, Professor an der damaligen *(then)* "Dresdener Bildungsanstalt", gebaut worden war. Wesent-

Komplexübungen

lich für (L 13.5.2.) die Entwicklung der Eisenbahn in Deutschland waren die Veröffentlichungen von Friedrich List, der als einer der ersten (L 5.6.) die ökonomische und politische Bedeutung dieses neuen Verkehrsmittels *(means of transport)* erkannte.

Zur (on) Entwicklung des Autos

(Schwerpunkte: Passiv, Infinitiv, Gerundium, Partizip)

Wie viele Erfindungen, kann (auch) die ursprüngliche Idee des Autos nicht einem bestimmten Erfinder zugeschrieben werden *(attribute to)*. Doch wird angenommen (L 5.8.1. oder 4.4.), daß der französische Ingenieur N.-J. Cugnot 1769 den ersten verwendbaren *(practical)* Vorläufer *(forerunner)* des Automobils entwickelte, ein dampfbetriebenes Dreirad *(steam-powered tricycle)*, das 20 Minuten mit *(at a speed of)* 3,6 km/h *(kph)* gefahren *(run)* sein soll (L 6.5.3.3.). Vor der Erfindung des Verbrennungsmotors *(internal-combustion engine)* wurden Dampffahrzeuge *(steam carriages)* weithin *(widely)* verwendet. Dampfomnibusse verkehrten *(run)* in Paris schon um 1800; in London sollen (L 6.5.3.3.) 1833 bereits über zwanzig solcher Busse in Betrieb *(in operation)* gewesen sein. 1876 konstruierte N. A. Otto einen Verbrennungsmotor unter Verwendung (L 9.2.6.) des Viertaktprinzips *(four-stroke principle)*, das 1862 von dem Franzosen Beau de Rochas patentiert *(patent)* worden war. C. Benz entwarf und baute 1886 das erste wirklich brauchbare *(useful)* Auto der Welt, ein dreirädriges Fahrzeug *(three-wheeled vehicle)*, das von einem Viertakt-Verbrennungsmotor angetrieben *(power)* wurde (L 9.1.1.). Im selben Jahr baute Daimler einen Benzinmotor *(petrol engine)* in einen vierrädrigen Wagen *(carriage)* ein. Der erste Automobilwettbewerb *(automobile contest)* war ein Zuverlässigkeitstest *(reliability test)* im Jahre 1894 von Paris nach Rouen, wobei der schnellste Wagen eine Durchschnittsgeschwindigkeit von 16,4 km/h hatte (L 9.2.7.). 1895 wurde das erste eigentliche *(true)* Autorennen *(car race)* von Paris nach Bordeaux und zurück veranstaltet *(hold)*. Die von dem Sieger *(winner)* erreichte Durchschnittsgeschwindigkeit (9.1.1.) betrug *(be)* 24,15 km/h. In den ersten Jahrzehnten des 20. Jahrhunderts wurde die Automobilherstellung *(manufacture)* durch Fließbandproduktion *(assembly line production)* revolutioniert. Das Auto hörte auf (8.7.1.), ein Spielzeug der Reichen zu sein, und wurde zunehmend *(increasingly)* ein Verkehrsmittel für die Bevölkerung.

Zur Geschichte der Luftfahrt

(Schwerpunkte: Relativpronomen, Passiv, Hilfsverben, Infinitiv, Gerundium, Partizip)

Der Wunsch des Menschen, sich den Vögeln gleich durch die Luft zu bewegen, läßt sich bis ins Altertum *(antiquity)* zurückverfolgen *(trace back)*.[912] In einer griechischen Legende wird uns von Dädalus aus Athen erzählt, der für König Minos von Kreta *(Crete)* das Labyrinth des Minotaurus *(Minotaur)* gebaut haben soll

(L 6.5.3.3.).[913] Nachdem Dädalus das Bauwerk *(structure)* vollendet hatte, sollte (L 6.5.3.1.1.) er auf der Insel bleiben.[914] Um zu entkommen, entwarf er für sich und seinen Sohn Ikarus Flügel aus Wachs *(wax)* und Federn *(feathers)*. Aber Ikarus flog zu nahe der Sonne, so daß er ins Wasser fiel und ertrank *(drown)*.
Schon um 1500 fertigte Leonardo da Vinci, dessen Erfindungsgabe *(inventiveness)* bekanntlich (L 5.8.1.) seiner Zeit um Jahrhunderte voraus war *(be centuries ahead of)*,[915] Skizzen *(sketch)* für den Bau eines Hubschraubers *(helicopter)* und eines Fallschirms *(parachute)* an.
Die berühmtesten Pioniere der Ballonentwicklung *(balloon development)* waren Joseph und Etienne Montgolfier. Am 5. Juni 1783 fand der erste Aufstieg *(ascension)* des von ihnen konstruierten (L 9.1.1.) Heißluftballons *(hot-air balloon)* in *(at)* Annonay in Südostfrankreich *(southeastern France)* statt.[916] Der Ballon stieg etwa 2000 m und blieb 10 Minuten in der Luft *(remain airborne)*, wobei er eine Entfernung von 2,4 km zurücklegte *(cover a distance, L 9.2.6.)*, bevor er landete *(touch down)*.[917] Am 19. September 1783 wiederholten die Brüder Montgolfier ihr Experiment in Versailles und schickten dabei (L 9.2.6.) ein Schaf, einen Hahn und eine Ente als Passagiere in die Luft.[918] Am 21. November des gleichen Jahres starteten *(take off)* Pilâtre de Rozier und der Marquis d'Arlandes im freien Flug *(free flight)* in einem Montgolfier-Ballon vom Bois de Boulogne in Paris. Nachdem sie eine Höhe *(altitude)* von mehr als 900 m erreicht und eine Entfernung von ungefähr 9 km in 23 Minuten zurückgelegt hatten, landeten sie sicher;[919] das war die erste bemannte Luftreise *(manned aerial voyage)* in der Geschichte (L 20.1.4.). Am 1. Dezember 1783 startete der französische Physiker J.-A.-C. Charles in seinem Charlière genannten Wasserstoffballon (L 9.1.1.) in den Tuilerien *(Tuileries Gardens)*. Sein Flug dauerte 2 Stunden, die zurückgelegte Entfernung (L 9.1.1.) betrug 43 km.[920] So wurde die Überlegenheit *(supremacy)* des Wasserstoffballons bewiesen *(establish)*. Jules Verne, einer der bekanntesten Science fiction-Autoren seiner Zeit, der selbst 1873 in einem Ballon aufstieg *(make a balloon ascension)*, popularisierte *(popularize)* den Gedanken des Fliegens einschließlich des Raumflugs *(space flight)* in einigen seiner Romane.
Das erste erfolgreiche Luftschiff *(airship)* wurde 1852 von Henri Giffard konstruiert. Ferdinand von Zeppelin war der erste, der große, starre Luftschiffe *(rigid dirigible)* baute (L 5.6.), die Güter und Personen befördern *(carry)* konnten.[921] Der erste Aufstieg eines "Zeppelin" fand am 2. Juli 1900 auf dem Bodensee *(Lake Constance, L 20.1.4.)* statt. 1929 flog das Luftschiff "Graf Zeppelin" in 21 Tagen rund um die Erde. Ein italienisches Luftschiff wurde 1926 von R. Amundsen benutzt, um den Nordpol zu erkunden *(explore)*. Die Entwicklung von Flugzeugen, d. h. von Luftfahrzeugen "schwerer als Luft" *(heavier-than-air craft)*, bewirkte, daß Luftschiffe von den dreißiger Jahren an ihre Bedeutung verloren (L 5.7.2.).[922]
Der Engländer George Cayley, der als Vater der Aeronautik *(aeronautics)* bezeichnet wird, baute 1853 das erste erfolgreiche Segelflugzeug *(glider)*, in dem sein Kutscher *(coachman)* den ersten bemannten Gleiterflug *(glider flight)* unternahm *(make)*. Der deutsche Ingenieur Otto Lilienthal unternahm ab 1891 mehr als 2000 Flüge in Segelflugzeugen, die er selbst gebaut hatte. Die Erfinder des ersten brauchbaren Motorflugzeugs *(powered aeroplane)* waren die Brüder Orville und Wilbur Wright. Am 17.12.1903 unternahmen sie vier gesteuerte Motorflüge *(powered and controlled aeroplane flights)*, der erste dauerte 12 Sekunden, der letzte 59 Sekunden

Komplexübungen 246

(L 9.2.7.).[923] Ende 1908 erreichte Wilbur Wright einen Rekord von 2 Stunden und 20 Minuten in Frankreich, wobei er eine Entfernung von 124 km zurücklegte (L 9.2.6.). 1909 erregte der Franzose Louis Blériot große Aufmerksamkeit, als er in 27 Minuten den Ärmelkanal *(The English Channel)* von Calais nach Dover überflog *(fly across)*.[924] Der erste Nonstopflug *(nonstop flight)* über den Atlantik von New York nach Paris, den Charles Lindbergh vom 20. bis 21. Mai 1927 unternahm,[925] dauerte 33,5 Stunden.

1947 wurde die Schallgrenze durchbrochen *(break the sound barrier)* und Überschallgeschwindigkeit *(supersonic speed)* erreicht. Der Gedanke des Vertikalflugs *(vertical flight)*, der, wie zuvor erwähnt, von Leonardo da Vinci stammt,[926] wurde Anfang des 20. Jahrhunderts verwirklicht (put into practice). Paul Cornu konstruierte den ersten Helikopter, der 1907 einen bemannten freien Flug in Frankreich durchführte – über einige Sekunden und bei einer Höhe von 2 m. Cornus Konstruktion erwies sich als (L 11.1.) unpraktisch und wurde aufgegeben *(abandon)*. Zwischen 1909 und 1910 baute der russische Ingenieur Igor Sikorsky zwei Hubschrauber, die sich vom Boden heben konnten *(lift off the ground)*, jedoch ohne Piloten. Der Tragschrauber *(giroplane)*, Vorläufer *(forerunner)* des modernen Hubschraubers, wurde 1917 von Bréguet entworfen. 1923 erfand der Spanier Juan de la Cierva das Autogiro *(autogiro)*, mit dem Helikopterflüge in größerem Umfang *(on a larger scale)* möglich wurden.

Einige Daten zur frühen Geschichte des Films

(Schwerpunkte: Relativpronomen, Passiv, Hilfsverben, Partizip, Gerundium, Infinitiv)

Der Film beruht auf (L 4.6.3.) der Verbindung mehrerer Techniken. Wesentliche Voraussetzungen für die Filmherstellung *(film-making)* waren die Fotografie, die in den dreißiger Jahren des 19. Jahrhunderts von Daguerre und Niepce erfunden wurde, und das Zelluloid, das J. W. Hyatt 1870 entdeckte.[927] Die Kamera kann auf Leonardo da Vincis frühen Entwurf einer camera obscura zurückgeführt werden *(trace back to)*. Der belgische Wissenschaftler Plateau stellte 1832 einen Apparat vor, der imstande (capable, L 8.2.1.3.) war, die Illusion von Bewegung zu erzeugen,[928] ein Effekt, der durch die Nachbildwirkung *(persistence of vision)* des Auges erreicht wird (L 9.1.1.),[929] d. h. durch die physiologische Tatsache, daß das Gehirn die Bilder etwas länger zurückbehält *(retain)*, als das menschliche Auge sie tatsächlich registriert *(actually record)*. 1891 erfanden Thomas A. Edison und William Dickson das Kinetoskop *(kinetoscope)*, einen direkten Vorläufer des modernen Filmprojektors *(film projector)*, durch den es möglich wurde, eine lebensechte Wiedergabe *(life-like representation)* von Personen und Gegenständen in Bewegung *(motion)* zu erhalten. Schon 1889 hatte Dickson einen Film auf Zelluloid gedreht *(shoot)*, der zeigt (L 9.1.), wie ein Arbeiter aus der Edisonschen Fabrik in die Kamera niest *(sneeze)*.[930]

Durch Verbesserung (L 8.2.1.4.) der Technik von Edison gelang es (L 8.2.1.1.) Auguste und Louis Lumière, den Kinematographen *(cinematograph)* zu konstruieren,[931] der als Kamera und Projektor verwendet werden konnte. Der Kinematograph, von dem das Wort "cinema" abgeleitet ist, wurde am 28. Dezember 1895 zum ersten

Mal öffentlich vorgeführt *(demonstrate publicly)*. Das Programm von zehn Filmen, die Alltagsereignisse *(everyday events)* behandelten, dauerte etwa zwanzig Minuten. Die Brüder Lumière sollten (L 6.5.3.1.1.) die Begründer des Dokumentarfilms *(documentary film)* werden.[932] Die erste Kinovorstellung *(film performance)* in der Filmgeschichte *(history of the cinema)* hatte schon am 1. November 1895 in Berlin stattgefunden, als Max und Emil Skladanowsky das von ihnen gebaute "Bioskop" *(bioscope)* vorführten.[933] Ihre Filme zeigten vorwiegend Jahrmarktattraktionen *(fairground attractions)*, zum Beispiel ein boxendes Känguruh, und Straßenszenen aus Berlin. Der Franzose Georges Méliès verfilmte als erster (L 5.6.) erfundene Episoden *(fictional episodes)*, wobei er Trickaufnahmen *(camera tricks)* wie die Zeitlupe *(slow motion)* nutzte (L 9.2.6.).[934] Unter den fast fünfhundert Spielfilmen *(feature-film)*, die er herstellte *(produce)*, war der erste Science fiction-Film, "Die Reise zum Mond" (1902), nach [935] einem Roman von Jules Verne. Der Western wurde von Edwin S. Porter mit "The Great Train Robbery" (1903) begründet, einer Geschichte von vier Banditen *(gangster)*, die einen Zug ausrauben *(rob)*.
Mack Sennett führte den Slapstick-Film ein, einen Komödientyp *(type of comedy)*, der durch turbulente Handlung und absurde Situationen charakterisiert ist.[936] In diesem Genre gewannen Schauspieler wie Buster Keaton, genannt "The Great Stone Face", und Harold Lloyd Weltruhm *(world-wide reputation)*, vor allem aber Charles Chaplin, der in seinen frühen Filmen, zum Beispiel "The Tramp" (1915), "The Kid" (1921) oder "The Gold Rush" (1925), soziale Probleme auf burleske *(burlesque)* Weise darstellte. Der amerikanische Regisseur David W. Griffith revolutionierte die Filmkunst *(cinematic art)*, indem er Techniken wie Nah- und Großaufnahme *(close-up)*, Aufblenden und Abblenden *(fade-in, fade-out)* entwickelte oder verbesserte (L 8.2.1.4.),[937] z.B. in seinen berühmten Filmen "The Birth of a Nation" (1915) und "Intolerance" (1916).
Der Stummfilm erreichte einen Höhepunkt zur Zeit des deutschen Expressionismus, als Regisseure wie Murnau, Wiene und Lang ihre besten Filme drehten *(make,* L 2.2.2.). "Das Kabinett des Dr. Caligari" (1919) von Robert Wiene, eine im surrealistischen *(surrealist)* Detail dargebotene (L 9.1.1.) Parabel über die Gewalttätigkeit *(violence)*, erzählt die Geschichte eines geistesgestörten Psychiaters *(demented psychiatrist)*, der einen seiner Patienten dazu hypnotisiert *(hypnotize into,* L 8.2.1.2.), Verbrechen zu begehen *(commit crimes)*.[938] F. W. Murnaus "Nosferatu" (1922), die früheste Verfilmung *(screen adaptation)* von Bram Stokers Schauerroman *(Gothic novel)* "Dracula" (1897), war der erste Vampirfilm *(vampire film)*. Sein Streifen *(motion-picture)* "Der letzte Mann" *(The Last Laugh,* 1924) handelt von einem Portier in einem vornehmen Hotel *(porter at a posh hotel)*, der aus Altersgründen *(for reasons of old age)* zum Toilettenwärter *(lavatory attendant)* degradiert wird und mit dem Verlust (L 8.2.1.4.) seiner Uniform auch seine Selbstachtung *(self-respect)* einbüßt *(lose)*.[939] Am Ende jedoch erbt *(inherit)* er unerwartet die Millionen eines Amerikaners, eine Parodie auf *(parody of)* das gängige Happyend *(conventional happy ending)* des Hollywood-Films.
1925 drehte der sowjetische Regisseur Sergei Eisenstein seinen berühmten Film "Panzerkreuzer Potemkin" *(The Battleship Potemkin)* über die russische Revolution von 1905, den 1958 eine internationale Jury von Kritikern zum besten Film, der je gedreht wurde (L 9.1.1.), wählte *(choose;* 5.8.).[940]

Komplexübungen 248

Der erste Tonfilm *(sound film)* war "The Jazz Singer", der 1927 in den Vereinigten Staaten entstand. Unter den bekannten deutschen Tonfilmen der frühen dreißiger Jahre waren "Der blaue Engel" (*The Blue Angel*, 1930) von Josef von Sternberg nach Heinrich Manns "Professor Unrat" (*Small Town Tyrant*), Fritz Langs "M" (1931), die Geschichte eines Sexualverbrechers *(sex offender)*, und G. W. Pabsts Verfilmung von Brechts "Dreigroschenoper" *(The Threepenny Opera*, 1931).

Computer

(Schwerpunkte: Relativpronomen, Passiv, Partizip, Hilfsverben, Infinitiv)

Man kann sagen, daß die Geschichte der Rechenhilfen *(computing aids)* mit dem Abakus *(abacus)* begann (L 5.8.1.), der im Orient vor etwa 5000 Jahren entstand *(originate)* und noch heute in einigen Ländern verwendet wird. Mechanische Rechenmaschinen *(calculating machines)* wurden während des 17. Jahrhunderts in Europa erfunden. Das erste derartige *(such)* Gerät war der Digitalrechner *(digital calculator)*, der 1642 von dem französischen Naturwissenschaftler und Philosophen Pascal entwickelt wurde (L 9.1.1.). Leibniz konstruierte 1673 eine verbesserte Form *(version)* von Pascals Maschine, die auch multiplizieren, dividieren und Quadratwurzeln ziehen *(extract square roots)* konnte. Der erste automatische Digitalrechner, die sogenannte analytische Maschine *(analytical engine)*, wurde in den dreißiger Jahren des 19. Jahrhunderts von dem englischen Mathematiker Charles Babbage entworfen. Dieses Gerät sollte (L 6.5.3.1.2.) arithmetische Operationen auf der Grundlage von Instruktionen, die durch Lochkarten *(punched cards)* eingegeben wurden (L 9.1.1.), ausführen; es konnte jedoch nicht verwirklicht werden *(implement)*, da die technischen Voraussetzungen *(prerequisites)* zu jener Zeit noch fehlten *(be missing)*. Von großer Bedeutung für die modernen Digitalrechner waren die Arbeiten (Singular) des englischen Mathematikers George Boole, der die symbolische Logik *(symbolic logic)*, jetzt als Boolesche Algebra *(Boolean algebra)* bezeichnet, entwickelte, eine grundlegende Vorbedingung *(precondition)* für die Konstruktion von Schaltkreisen *(circuits)*. Ein weiterer wesentlicher Schritt war die Einführung des Lochkartenverfahrens durch Herman Hollerith, einen US-amerikanischen Statistiker *(statistician)*, um 1890.

Der erste programmgesteuerte *(programme-controlled)* Rechenautomat wurde 1941 von Konrad Zuse entworfen. Die erste Generation von modernen Computern wurde 1946 an der Universität von Pennsylvania entwickelt. Der "Electronic Numerical Integrator and Calculator" (ENIAC) von J. P. Eckert und J. W. Mauchly war der erste vollelektronische *(all-electronic)* Digitalrechner, er konnte bis zu 5000 arithmetische Operationen pro Sekunde ausführen. Die zweite Computergeneration wurde 1959 eingeführt, als Maschinen, die Transistoren verwendeten (L 9.1.), in den Handel kamen *(become commercially available)*. Der Transistor war 1947 von Bardeen, Brattain und Shockley erfunden worden. In den Rechenautomaten der späten sechziger und frühen siebziger Jahre, der dritten Generation, wurden die elektronischen Komponenten weiter miniaturisiert *(miniaturize)*, was (L 15.7.4.) zu beträchtlichen Verbesserungen der Computer-Hardware führte.

Die Computer der achtziger Jahre sind oft als vierte Generation bezeichnet worden. Sie sind hauptsächlich gekennzeichnet *(characterize)* durch sehr hohe Integrationsdichte *(very large-scale integration)*, d. h. ein Schaltkreis enthält viele Tausende von elektronischen Komponenten auf einem winzigen Siliziumchip *(silicon chip)*. Seit Anfang der achtziger Jahre sind Versuche unternommen worden, Computersysteme zu entwickeln, die mit sogenannter künstlicher Intelligenz *(artificial intelligence)* ausgestattet *(endow)* sind. Solche Geräte der fünften Generation würden in der Lage sein, zu lernen und ihre Leistung *(performance)* auf der Grundlage eigener Erfahrung zu verbessern. Es wäre nicht mehr notwendig, ihnen Schritt für Schritt Instruktionen zu geben, wie spezifische Aufgaben auszuführen sind (L 5.5.), was bei den gegenwärtigen *(current)* Computern noch erforderlich ist.

In letzter Zeit sind rechnergestützte Konstruktionssysteme *(computer-aided design systems, CAD systems)* entworfen worden, die schon in vielen Zweigen der Industrie und Wirtschaft verwendet werden. In einigen Fällen wird der CAD-Prozeß mit rechnergestützter Fertigung *(computer-aided manufacturing, CAM)* integriert. Durch Verbindung (L 8.2.1.4.) der Konstruktions- und Herstellungsarbeiten *(operations)* erhöht das CAD/CAM-System die Produktivität beträchtlich und verringert die Zeit, die für die Entwicklung neuer Produkte benötigt wird (L 9.1.1.).

Zur Geschichte der Roboter

(Schwerpunkte: Relativpronomen, Hilfsverben, Infinitiv, Partizip, Gerundium)

Roboter sind Automaten (L 19.3.8.), die Bewegungen *(movements)* biologischer Systeme reproduzieren, d. h. sie können bestimmte manuelle Funktionen ausführen. Automaten faszinieren die Phantasie der Menschen seit vielen Jahrhunderten. Archytas von Tarent *(Tarentum)*, der eine flatternde *(fluttering)* Taube konstruierte, war einer der ersten europäischen Erfinder von Automaten. Es ist bekannt, daß selbsttätige *(self-operating)* Geräte im Mittelalter *(Middle Ages)* häufig gebaut wurden (L 5.8. oder 4.6.3.).[941] Unter den interessantesten (L 15.6.9.) war ein von Leonardo da Vinci entworfener (L 9.1.1.) Tierautomat[942] in der Gestalt *(shape)* eines Löwen, der sich bewegen und gewisse Handhabungen *(chores)* ausführen konnte.

Der Franzose Vaucanson stellte um 1738 einen Flötenspieler *(flute player)* her, der zwölf Musikstücke spielte, und eine künstliche Ente, die in der Lage war, sich wie eine lebende Ente zu bewegen und zu schnattern *(quack)*. Berühmt waren (L 13.5.2.) die Androiden *(androids)*, Figuren von menschlicher Form, die dazu gebracht werden konnten *(make,* L 5.8.1.) zu laufen, zu schreiben oder zu zeichnen, z. B. der 1779 von P. Jaquet-Droz gebaute (L 9.1.1.) Zeichner *(draughtsman)*[943]. In der zweiten Hälfte des 18. Jahrhunderts erregte ein von W. v. Kempelen vorgeführter (L 9.1.1.) Schachroboter großes Aufsehen.[944] Hinter einem Schachbrett *(chessboard)* saß ein als Türke verkleideter *(disguise,* L 9.1.1.) Android in Lebensgröße *(life-size android)*, der die meisten Spiele gewann. Unter anderem verloren Friedrich II., Katharina II. von Rußland, Voltaire und Napoleon gegen ihn. Doch erwies sich (L 11.1.) der Android als Schwindel *(fraud)*, denn in seinem Inneren *(inside it)* be-

Komplexübungen 250

fand sich ein perfekter Schachspieler, der die Figuren *(chessmen)* bediente *(manipulate)*.
Die bekannteste europäische Robotergeschichte ist die (L 15.6.9.) vom Golem zu Prag, einem Maschinenmenschen *(machine man)*, der von dem Rabbi *(Rabbi)* Jehuda Löw geschaffen worden sein soll (L 6.5.3.3.).[945] In Karel Čapeks 1920 geschriebenem (L 9.1.1.) Theaterstück 'R.U.R.' *(Rossum's Universal Robots)* wurde der von dem tschechischen Wort "robota" abgeleitete (L 9.1.1.) Ausdruck Roboter erstmals verwendet. Čapeks Roboter sind Androiden, die Arbeiter an Werkbänken *(workbench)* vollständig ersetzen *(replace)* und die als billiger Ersatz *(substitute)* menschlicher Arbeitskraft *(labour)* für eine amerikanische Firma Höchstprofite realisieren sollen (L 6.5.3.1.).
Unter den ersten ferngesteuerten *(remote-controlled)* Robotern waren der 1927 von R.J. Wensley vorgeführte (L 9.1.1.) "Mister Televox", ein Haushaltroboter, der z.B. einen Staubsauger bediente, ein Roboter, der 1932 auf einer Ausstellung in Chicago einen zwanzigminütigen Vortrag *(twenty-minute lecture)* über den Verdauungsprozeß *(digestion process)* hielt, und der 1951 in Bristol gebaute (L 9.1.1.) "Dynamo Joe", der radfahren konnte. Der "automatische radioelektrische Sekretär" *(ARS)* von B.N. Gruschin aus der Sowjetunion konnte unter anderem *(among other things)* telefonieren und Getränke einschenken *(pour)*, wobei er auf die menschliche Stimme reagierte (L 9.2.6.).[946]
Der industrielle Roboter von heute ist ein computergesteuerter *(computer-controlled)* programmierbarer *(programmable)* Automat, der auf bestimmten Anwendungsgebieten *(fields of application)* ein qualifizierter Arbeiter werden kann. In der Autoindustrie z.B. hat die Einführung von Robotern die Fließbandproduktion *(conveyor belt production)* beträchtlich automatisiert *(automate)*. Sie können unter anderem verwendet werden für das Schweißen *(weld)*, Montieren *(assemble)* oder Farbspritzen *(spraypaint)* von Autokarosserien *(car bodies)*.[947] Hochleistungsfähige *(highly efficient)* Roboter haben eingebaute *(built-in)* Sensoren, die es ihnen ermöglichen, Bewegungen zu korrigieren, die vom programmierten Ablauf abweichen *(deviate, L 9.1.)*.[948]
Visuelle Erkennungssysteme *(recognition system)* für Industrieroboter werden seit einiger Zeit untersucht. Roboter, die "sehen", "hören", "fühlen", "sprechen" können, sind kein Wunschtraum *(wishdream)* mehr.
Im Bereich *(department)* für technische Kybernetik an der Leningrader Polytechnischen Hochschule *(college)* wurde ein Serienroboter *(serial robot)* mit der Fähigkeit zu hören ausgestattet *(endow)*. Werden ihm Befehle *(commands)* gegeben, dann beginnt er, sich zu bewegen[949], und arbeitet nach den *(according to)* Instruktionen. Kybernetiker *(cyberneticist)* und Informationstheoretiker *(information theorist)* haben nachgewiesen, daß bestimmte Komponenten der Intelligenz (L 20.1.4.) von der Maschine imitiert werden können. So haben auch "denkende" Maschinen aufgehört *(cease, L 8.7.1.)*, eine bloße *(mere)* Utopie *(utopia)* zu sein.[950] Sie sind möglich, wenn leistungsfähige elektronische Rechner zur Verfügung stehen *(be available)*, obwohl Denken hier natürlich nicht mit dem schöpferischen Denken des Menschen identisch ist.

Schlüssel

Kapitel 1:
[1]Who is Peter's English teacher? [2]How many families live in this house? [3]Which of John's brothers studies chemistry? [4]Is Jack at home? [5]How much is this record player? [6]Can I speak to the manager now or is he busy? [7]Is Susan interested in sports? [8]Where do you work? [9]Where did you study? [10]Did you study ...? [11]Do you live near the place where you work? [12]Do you like to go/going to concerts? [13]Have you got/Do you have any problems ...? [14]Do you have breakfast ...? [15]Did you have a look at ...? [16]Did you sometimes have a talk with ...? [17]Which country are you from/... do you come from? [18]Which field of science do you work in?/In which field of science ...? [19]Who(m) do you turn to when/if you have any problems? [20]What (kind of) job do you want to apply for when you return home? [21]What does this film deal with?/What is this film about? [22]Who are you waiting for? [23]Who do you want to talk/speak about this matter to/with? [24]I don't/do not speak French. [25]I'm not good at mathematics. [26]I don't want to be an engineer. [27]I haven't got/don't have ... [28]Mike doesn't/does not often go to the cinema/to the pictures/to the movies. [29]He doesn't like to see films [30]They don't often go shopping [31]They don't go out with their friends more than once a month [32]Doesn't John work ...? – Yes, he does bzw. No, he doesn't. [33]Which of you can't/cannot translate the text? [34]Didn't you want to go to the theatre yesterday? [35]Please don't disturb me now [36]Don't be so impolite

Kapitel 2:
[37]A pilot flies planes [38]What are you doing there? [39]I'm writing a letter [40]We usually spend ..., but this year we are going ... [41]I don't meet Peggy very often, but I'm seeing her this afternoon [42]Susan has got a new dress, her friend is just having a look at it [43]Where did you get to know ...? [44]Didn't you want to tell ...?/Did you not want ...? [45]What did you talk about? [46]How long did it take you/... did you take to paper the room? [47]We were at the theatre yesterday [48]Jim got married five years ago [49]There were many wrong answers to this question [50]went window-shopping; were walking; stopped; were looking; got excited; was; liked; went; told; was standing; wanted; showed; was having; was counting; knew; was; found; was; did not have; left; noticed; looked/was looking; promised [51]... were having ... came [52]... phoned ... was seeing [53]... was very busy; ... was cleaning, ... was repairing ...; ... was doing ...; ... was reading; ... rang; ... put down ..., went..., ... picked up ...; ... wanted to visit; ... was talking ..., ... rang; ... brought ...; ... was cooking ..., ... came ... told ...; ... were talking ...; ... was waiting...; ... came ... invited ... [54]I have not read it yet [55]... have you seen ...? [56]I have been shopping [57]My friend has bought curtains ... [58]I have been waiting ... [59]I have been typing ... [60]We have had/have been having ... [61]... you have come ..., ... have been expecting ... [62]... have you had ...? [63]Has John gone ...? [64]I have not met ... [65]..., he has been seeing ... [66]What have you been doing? [67]I have been translating ... [68]I have translated ... [69]I have trusted ... [70]I have known him [71]... I have written ... [72]... he has been interpreting ... [73]I have been translating since eleven o'clock/for three hours [74]He has been a physicist since 1982 [75]I haven't been ... for five months/since

Schlüssel 252

March ⁷⁶I haven't been ... for one and a half years ⁷⁷... they have just got married ⁷⁸... he has been teaching for 15 years ⁷⁹Have you seen the film yet? ⁸⁰... have you had ...? I have had it for more than ... ⁸¹... I have been walking ... ⁸²... he has wanted / has been wanting ... ⁸³I have liked ... as long as / since I have known her ⁸⁴We met ... we have not met ... ⁸⁵... I have been here before ⁸⁶We have not seen ...; he went abroad ... ⁸⁷Peter has been an assistant ...; ... started work ... ⁸⁸Have you been to the cinema ...? ... I saw ... ⁸⁹Have you seen Mary lately? I last saw her some months ago. I wanted to visit her ... she has been away on a journey for some time ⁹⁰Do you like taking / to take photos? Yes, I do, but I began only five years ago ...; since then I have taken ... ⁹¹Peter didn't come (al)though we had invited him. ⁹²We had been driving ..., ... noticed ... were out of petrol ⁹³... was leaving ..., ... phoned. – ... had left ..., ... phoned ⁹⁴... was making ..., ... came. – ... came, ... made ... ⁹⁵I have lost ..., ... I am going to buy ... ⁹⁶Fred read ..., he liked ..., ... he is going to read ... ⁹⁷... he will be ... ⁹⁸... I'll go ... ⁹⁹... will you help me ...? ¹⁰⁰... she is going to buy ... ¹⁰¹... you will understand me ¹⁰²... I shan't / won't be back ... ¹⁰³... it's going to rain ¹⁰⁴When is Jane going to have ...? ¹⁰⁵I am seeing ..., I shall / will / I'll give ... ¹⁰⁶... Anne will be waiting ...; we shall recognize ..., she will be wearing ... ¹⁰⁷... you will be doing ...? ... I'll be having ... ¹⁰⁸You are certain / sure to enjoy ... ¹⁰⁹Jane is likely to be ... ¹¹⁰..., she is going to knit ¹¹¹... he will understand you ¹¹²Where is the meeting going to take place? / Where will the meeting take pace? ¹¹³... is going to get married / ... is getting married / ... will get married ¹¹⁴... is coming ..., he is going to repair ¹¹⁵What is Susan going to do ...? / What will S. be doing ...? / What is S. doing ...? – ... she will know it ¹¹⁶I began ..., ... I shall / will have saved ...

Kapitel 3:

¹¹⁷I would / should have accepted ... ¹¹⁸... she would have liked to be / to have been a dancer ¹¹⁹... I don't think she would have understood me ¹²⁰... it would have taken too long ... ¹²¹If the weather were better, we would make ... ¹²²Peter would be very disappointed, if you didn't invite him ¹²³If you knew ... you would understand her ¹²⁴If you had not been driving ... would not have stopped you and you would not have been fined ¹²⁵... Susan would have been very angry if we had forgotten ...? ¹²⁶If Mike hadn't gone ..., he wouldn't have seen Maud ¹²⁷If we had listened ... we would have taken ... ¹²⁸If we hadn't left ... we wouldn't have lost ... ¹²⁹If it hadn't already been ... they would still have served lunch ¹³⁰If it hadn't begun to rain again we would not have got soaked ... ¹³¹If I hadn't stumbled and sprained my ankle I would have been able to walk fast ¹³²If we hadn't got to the bus stop so late the bus wouldn't have gone yet ¹³³If we had not had to wait two hours ..., it wouldn't have been late ... ¹³⁴... I wouldn't be surprised if he were late again ¹³⁵... would not have happened ... had kept ... ¹³⁶... she would be glad if you met her ... ¹³⁷... if I were you I would buy it ¹³⁸... would not have been delayed if there hadn't been ... ¹³⁹What would you have liked to become if you hadn't become a chemist? ¹⁴⁰... you must tell ... ¹⁴¹... in case it should rain ... ¹⁴²... would not want ... if ... had not bought ... ¹⁴³If you would wait ... I'll try ... ¹⁴⁴If Mary should come ... I'll be ... ¹⁴⁵Should Tom arrive ... ¹⁴⁶If ... is hard of hearing he should wear ... ¹⁴⁷If you will cook ... I will do ... ¹⁴⁸If you should need ... you can / may contact ...

Kapitel 4:

¹⁴⁹A new youth club was opened last week ¹⁵⁰Peter must be taught a lesson ¹⁵¹... kilts are worn by ... ¹⁵²... the temperature must be kept ... ¹⁵³We have just been told ... ¹⁵⁴You will be met ... ¹⁵⁵Bob was given ... he had been bitten ... ¹⁵⁶The Eiffel Tower was built in 1889 ¹⁵⁷When did they introduce coffee ...? Coffee was introduced ... ¹⁵⁸Who developed the atomic model? The atomic model was developed by Niels Bohr. ¹⁵⁹No, they don't. Spanish is spoken in Chile ¹⁶⁰What is produced in this plant? ¹⁶¹The test has just been finished / completed ¹⁶²... must be followed exactly ¹⁶³Have you been told ...? ¹⁶⁴If we had been

told that some participants were / are prevented, we would have postponed ... [165]The series of tests must be continued as soon as the intermediate results have been evaluated [166]The fire could only be got under control after considerable material damage had been caused [167]... must be looked up ... [168]... will not / won't be turned down when it is talked about ... [169]... why hasn't a doctor been sent for yet? [170]... has not yet been dealt with / ... hasn't been dealt with yet [171]... has to be filled in ...; ... that can't be dispensed with [172]... the light has just been switched on [173]..., she should be looked after [174]... can be made up for [175]... should be insisted on [176]... who is looked up to by ... [177]This topic has not yet been talked / spoken about [178]The matter should be looked into carefully [179]I don't like / I hate to be made fun of (oder:) ... being made fun of (8.7.1.) [180]This matter should not be lost sight of [181]Some calculations remain to be carried out before final results can be put forward [182]It is (to be) hoped that ... [183]It is believed that ... [184]It has been decided ... [185]It has been estimated / It is estimated that ... [186]... is being repaired [187]... was closed [188]... was being demonstrated [189]... are packed [190]... are being packed [191]When was this church built? [192]... were / got destroyed [193]How was the pane broken? – How did the pane get broken? [194]John was / got caught [195]When did you get / become acquainted ...? [196]... I nearly was / got hit [197]When did Jane get engaged? [198]How long have you been married? [199]... got divorced [200]..., she never got used ... [201]... Have you got used ...? [202]Yesterday it was reported that ... [203]... have been cut off from ... [204]It is believed that ... [205]It is (to be) feared that ... [206]The population is being supplied ... [207]... doctors are being flown into ... [208]It is hoped that ... will soon be restored

Kapitel 5:
[209]so as not to / in order not to catch a cold [210]so as to / in order to make ... [211]so as not to / in order not to be heard by anybody [212]You had better discuss ... [213]... he would rather go ... than watch TV [214]Why not have ...? [215]You had better not use ... [216]Hadn't we better alter ...? [217]You'd better phone ... [218]Tom would rather buy a house than a car [219]John was nowhere to be seen [220]It is to be hoped [221]... to be mended [222]... is not to be had ... [223]... to be held ... [224]... to attend to ... [225]... to be checked [226]... the measures to be taken [227]It remains to be seen ... [228]... where to spend ... [229]... whether to accept it [230]... who(m) to invite ... [231]I didn't know what to say [232]Tell me when to telephone (phone, ring) you [233]... who(m) to go out with [234]I need a knife to cut the bread with [235]... to talk this matter over with [236]I haven't got a corkscrew to open the bottle with [237]... to drink the champagne out of [238]Be so kind as to lend ... / Would you be kind enough to lend ...? [239]... so as not to be late / ... in order not to be late [240]... though I'd like to [241]... so as not to be disturbed / ... in order not to be disturbed [242]... she didn't want me to think she was angry [243]Mother allows Jane to go dancing [244]Mary wants me to read ... [245]... made us submit ... [246]I want her to be informed ... [247]... will cause your article to be printed [248]I expect him to come [249]When do you want me to come? [250]You should cause the test to be repeated [251]... enables production to be stepped up [252]... showed himself to be ... [253]... I saw her leave / go away ... [254]... what made Peter leave / depart ... [255]Do you want me to make up my mind at once? [256]We want / would like our proposal to be discussed ... [257]You should make Fred apologize (oder:) You should tell / get (oder: cause / induce) Fred to apologize [258]Tell him to handle the typewriter carefully [259]I suppose (that) the data have been checked before / (formal:) I suppose the data to have been checked before [260]It's impossible for us to understand him [261]We have arranged for the Millers to stay ... [262]It is vital for them to be informed ... [263]Is it necessary for me to come or is it enough to telephone? [264]The text is too difficult for us to translate ... [265]Would it be convenient for you to visit ...? [266]... it is high time for us to reach ... [267]We have arranged for Professor White to take part ... [268]Dr Peters is known to be ... [269]You are not supposed to smoke ... [270]Am I supposed to clean ...? [271]... everybody except me was forced to lie down [272]They were told not to

Schlüssel

move ²⁷³We were not allowed to talk ... ²⁷⁴I was ordered to open ... ²⁷⁵I was compelled to put ... ²⁷⁶I was warned not to ring ... ²⁷⁷I was told to lie down ... ²⁷⁸We were made to tell them ... ²⁷⁹... we couldn't be expected to describe ... ²⁸⁰... I was told to return it ²⁸¹Dr Baker is considered / reputed to be an excellent surgeon. ²⁸²The newly developed drug / medicament was found to be very efficacious ²⁸³... is designed to accommodate ... ²⁸⁴... is intended to last ... ²⁸⁵Thousands of houses are reported to have been destroyed by ... ²⁸⁶... which are estimated to amount to ... ²⁸⁷The first radio programme is understood to have been broadcast ... ²⁸⁸to have happened ²⁸⁹to have drunk ²⁹⁰to have been injured ²⁹¹to be taken ²⁹²to be operated on ²⁹³to visit ²⁹⁴to have been improving ²⁹⁵to be discharged ²⁹⁶to be allowed to work

Kapitel 6:
²⁹⁷Harry may not be interested ... ²⁹⁸My uncle may be visiting ... ²⁹⁹You may not like ... ³⁰⁰John might know ... ³⁰¹Mary can't be ... ³⁰²We may not get ... ³⁰³... my brother may want ... ³⁰⁴he was not able to come / could not come ... ³⁰⁵... I was able to / could understand ... ³⁰⁶... we could overhear ... ³⁰⁷... I would be able to repair ... ³⁰⁸You ought to be able to solve ... ³⁰⁹... we were not able to / could not get ... ³¹⁰... to be able to speak ... ³¹¹... would be able to / could drive ... ³¹²I have not been able to contact ... ³¹³You might let me know ... ³¹⁴We might ask ... ³¹⁵You might try ... ³¹⁶Roy might be more considerate ³¹⁷... they will be ... ³¹⁸Anne will have come back ... ³¹⁹... he will be taking ... ³²⁰... he will sit for hours ... ³²¹... the water pipes used to / would freeze in winter ³²²Mr Brown used to be ... ³²³Didn't there use to be (Usedn't there to be) ...? ³²⁴... I used to / would drink ... ³²⁵Why didn't you want to tell ...? ³²⁶... he flatly refused to cooperate ³²⁷... he had wanted to ³²⁸We haven't been able yet to find the mistake ³²⁹Mary pretends / claims to be able to speak ... fluently ³³⁰Were you able to answer ...? ³³¹I may / can be wrong ³³²Susan may come ... ³³³Might I trouble you ...? ³³⁴I would have liked to see / to have seen ... ³³⁵I used to go skiing a lot ³³⁶Mary used to / would go ..., now she will spend / she usually spends ... ³³⁷You should / ought to read it ³³⁸Mary should / ought to be back ... ³³⁹Shall I order / Am I to order ...? ³⁴⁰... you are (supposed) to meet ... ³⁴¹... he is supposed to be doing ... ³⁴²John is said to be ill ³⁴³We are not to leave ... ³⁴⁴Shall I paint / Am I to paint ...? ³⁴⁵Anne is said to have inherited ... ³⁴⁶... you are not supposed to interrupt ... ³⁴⁷Peggy is to be back ... ³⁴⁸I was to have sent in ... ³⁴⁹You should / ought to consider ... ³⁵⁰I was to take off / to have taken off ... ³⁵¹We must hurry up / have (got) to hurry up ³⁵²Do you have to take ...? ³⁵³Walter doesn't have to come ... / needn't come / (auch:) doesn't need to come ³⁵⁴This problem has to / must be discussed ... ³⁵⁵The results will have to be checked ... ³⁵⁶... why the test had (had) to be interrupted ³⁵⁷You don't have to believe ..., do you? ³⁵⁸I need hardly say ... (s. Kap. 5, Fußnote 9) ³⁵⁹... he wouldn't always have to be told ... ³⁶⁰You needn't come / You don't have to come ³⁶¹... like to have / having to work ... ³⁶²I hope I won't / don't have to be operated on ³⁶³Why did the test have to be repeated yesterday? ³⁶⁴... he has never had to work ³⁶⁵When shall we / are we to come? ³⁶⁶I am to give a lecture ... ³⁶⁷We are to phone ... ³⁶⁸Bob was to accompany us ... ³⁶⁹... is to be opened ... ³⁷⁰... he is supposed to be ... ³⁷¹Anne is said to have got engaged ³⁷²The book is intended / meant to give a survey of ... ³⁷³... what this picture is supposed to mean? ³⁷⁴Did you have to wait long? ³⁷⁵My colleague may already have left ³⁷⁶..., he can't have seen us ³⁷⁷..., you ought not to / should not have thrown it away ³⁷⁸We couldn't have walked ... ³⁷⁹... must have happened ³⁸⁰One needn't have gone into all these details / All these details needn't have been gone into ³⁸¹Jack might have tried to phone us ³⁸²He must have forgotten it ³⁸³You needn't have taken ... ³⁸⁴The train can't have left yet ³⁸⁵Our conversation can't have been overheard ³⁸⁶it may have been misdirected ³⁸⁷He may not have liked the idea ... ³⁸⁸... he may have forgotten ³⁸⁹I should / ought to have known ... ³⁹⁰... could / might have been avoided ³⁹¹You needn't have waited ... ³⁹²You ought to / should

have been able to take ...   [393]he might have telephoned ...   [394]... it needn't have been talked about ...   [395]Peter needn't have passed the night ..., he could/might have stayed ..., if he had wanted to   [396]... is to be published soon   [397]... I was to marry her.   [398]... it should have /was to have arrived   [399]... we couldn't have walked ...   [400]she may have gone   [401]... which is said to be ...   [402]she could have told me   [403]I would have liked to go/to have gone with her   [404]she doesn't have to have gone   [405]she may be having/taking a walk oder: Perhaps she is having a walk   [406]She ought to be working ...   [407]She will have to/She has to take an examination

Kapitel 7:
[408]Jane says (that) she likes ice cream   [409]Fred said, 'I can't translate the text.' Fred said he couldn't/wasn't able to translate ...   [410]Alice said, 'I mustn't/I'm not allowed to watch TV ...' Alice said (that) she wasn't allowed/permitted to watch ...   [411]Bill said/told me (that) he had been working all day   [412]I said I knew (that) I had made a mistake   [413]Liz said she was afraid Ronald might have missed the train   [414]John said he would have to ask his wife   [415]... whether/if her parents had spent ...   [416]... what time Anne would come   [417]Tom asked me what hotel we/I would be staying at   [418]... whether/if she had to make up her mind at once   [419]... (that) he had bought ...   [420]... (that) she would visit ...   [421]... what I had told them   [422]... that he was late because he had missed ...   [423]... if/whether the guests had already arrived   [424]... he hoped we would/should be informed in time   [425]... who(m) he had talked about the matter to   [426]John said that Fred had moved ... John wanted to know if Fred had moved ...   [427]I said I was busy. Joan wanted to know if I was busy.

Kapitel 8:
[428]involved in solving   [429]responsible for leaving   [430]accustomed to staying   [431]admit having made   [432]specialized in producing   [433]used to speaking   [434]sorry for keeping/having kept you waiting   [435]hope of passing   [436]count on being received hospitably   [437]by getting up   [438]from drowning/being drowned   [439]without the disadvantage of ... being repelled   [440]fond of reading ...   [441]We look forward to seeing ...   [442]stop getting ... by asking   [443]denied having caused   [444]suggests redecorating   [445]criticized for not having handed in/not handing in   [446]escaped being hit   [447]feel like talking/feel up to talking   [448]objects to discussing   [449]a fuss about not having been given   [450]right in saying   [451]After leaving school ... he studied ...   [452]Aside from/Apart from taking lessons ... he learnt ...   [453]... but without finishing ...   [454]... before accepting ...   [455]On starting work... he was given ...   [456]... by introducing ...   [457]We suggest tackling   [458]I remember being/having been   [459]imagine ever being left   [460]... imagine yourself growing ...   [461]John is sure of getting ...   [462]I don't mind telling ...   [463]... he left without saying ...   [464]Instead of doing her homework Joan went dancing   [465]Harry's wife dislikes having to spend   [466]After trying ... I sent ...   [467]Dr Brown began his lecture by presenting ...   [468]Do you mind me/my opening   [469]Anne dislikes Henry (Henry's) going   [470]... can't prevent her (from) planning to sing ...   [471]Tom insisted on us/our coming   [472]We are surprised at John and Maggie intending   [473]We can't stop Peter (from) joining   [474]We wouldn't mind you not inviting Henry.   [475]... going ... watching TV.   [476]... to go ... watch TV.   [477]giving   [478]to give   [479]telling/having told   [480]to tell   [481]It is worth visiting the exhibition/The exhibition is worth visiting.   [482]It is no use queueing for tickets.   [483]I am busy preparing ...   [484]I'm interested in learning ...   [485]Would you mind/Do you mind me (my) smoking ...   [486]Excuse me/my disturbing you.   [487]Would you mind closing the door?   [488]What about/How about going ...   [489]I don't mind waiting   [490]I must apologize for answering ...   [491]You can rely/count/depend on me (my) informing you in time   [492]We dislike Alfred being so unreliable.   [493]she is used to/accustomed to being admired   [494]I regret having put you to trouble   [495]Anne is afraid of flying   [496]Our boss expects us to finish (5.7.)   [497]Bob is prevented from taking part   [498]She likes being told   [499]Before starting ... I expect to be

Schlüssel   256

given ...   [500]... resent not having been invited   [501]to prevent you (from) doing ...   [502]... I forgot to tell ...   [503]... try to paper ... we have never tried doing ...   [504]wanted to have; I tried to speak ... without managing to make myself understood, ... wasn't used to speaking German   [505]... remember me (my) lending him ...; ... forget to pay me back ... a way of forgetting things ... like to remember / remembering.   [506]... prides himself on knowing ...   [507]I seem to have lost it – try looking ..., ... have forgotten putting ...

Kapitel 9:
[508]... the science dealing with ...   [509]The results obtained ...   [510]The exhibition ... inaugurated by the mayor ... consists of ... finds excavated ...   [511]... the peace rally which takes place / taking place ...   [512]The problems which are dealt with / The problems dealt with ...   [513]... dangers which threaten / threatening ...   [514]The damage which is done / The damage done to the economy ...   [515]The efforts to reduce ... which are made in ... / made in ...   [516]The conference on ... which has been convened by UNESCO (20.1.4.) / convened by UNESCO ...   [517](When) speaking French I ...   [518]... fell asleep while doing his homework.   [519]Having parked our car we ...   [520]Having been cross-examined ... the accused ...   [521]The old office having become ..., the staff ...   [522]Given the right treatment, some forms ...   [523]... tons of it being used ...   [524]... while being transformed ...   [525]Being seriously ill Professor Baker had ...   [526]Having talked ... we were ...   [527]Being pressed ... I could not ...   [528]... to Mr Brown his address being unknown   [529]... near Tokyo airport with all the crew and passengers being killed.   [530]The necessary checks (having been) made, the analysis could ...   [531]Fission products ... being highly radioactive, they must ...   [532]play   [533]practising   [534](Nur:) We were left waiting ...   [535](Nur:) ... can be kept going ...   [536]I must have / get my teeth checked / I have to have / get my teeth checked   [537]The management is having enquiries made ...   [538]The librarian has had the last twenty issues of the magazine bound   [539]I shall have / get my paper typed   [540]... we'll have to have it towed off   [541]We should / ought to have it cut down   [542]You should / ought to have had them checked   [543]exceeding   [544]withdrawn   [545]engaged   [546]said   [547]damaged / to have been damaged (5.8.)   [548]... defined as (being) the time rate required ...   [549]presented   [550]published   [551]sung   [552]making   [553]besieging   [554]using   [555]being reflected and concentrated   [556]Judging from what ... this book is ...   [557]Having witnessed ... Peter was told ...   [558]... broke down, having had it serviced ...   [559]There being too many holiday-makers ... we'd better go ...   [560]The questions which arise / The questions arising ...   [561]The products which are exhibited / The products exhibited ...   [562]While I was talking / (While) talking ... I noticed ...   [563]As we had spent / Having spent ... we can afford ...   [564]... is in Berlin and studies ... / ... is in Berlin studying ...   [565]We spent the whole weekend papering ...   [566]After I had finished / After finishing (8.2.1.4.) / Having finished ... I went ...   [567]The problems discussed were ...   [568]... to keep the conversation going   [569]As I can't repair ... / As I'm not able to repair / unable to repair ... I have to / must take ... / Not being able to ... / Being unable to repair ... I have to / must take ...   [570]... caught Peter copying ...   [571]If one takes all factors into consideration / Taking all factors into consideration one can say ...   [572]Though Jack was asked ... he passed ... / Though (being) asked ... Jack passed ...   [573]We had a good time ...; we danced a lot, we looked at photos and talked about ... / We had a good time ..., dancing ..., looking ..., and talking ...   [574]Mary could not take part in ..., because she had been told ... to stay in bed / Mary could not take part ..., having been told ...   [575]I have often heard that Jim is referred to as a good organizer / I have often heard Jim referred to as ...   [576]Judging from what I have heard, the symposium ...   [577]If the new procedure is introduced ..., it can lead ... / If introduced ... the new procedure can lead ...   [578]As / Since water power is an inexhaustible source of energy / Water power being an inexhaustible ..., it should ...   [579]We must / have (got) to have our TV set repaired. (oder:) We must / have (got) to get our TV set repaired   [580]I had to have / to get my tonsils taken out   [581]Have / Get the minutes ... typed.   [582]dislikes having her photo taken.

Schlüssel

Kapitel 10:
[583]I suggest that it (should) be translated ...   [584]It is imperative that adequate precautions (should) not be neglected   [585]I wish I had ...   [586]He wishes he were (was) better ...   [587]I wish they liked each other   [588]I wish he were more polite   [589]I wish she didn't dress so loudly   [590]I wish he were not driving so fast   [591]I wish the bus would come   [592]I wish she wouldn't (didn't) always want ...   [593]I wish I wouldn't (didn't) have to leave ...   [594]I wish I had gone by car   [595]We wish we had rung him   [596]They wish they had never got married   [597]I wish he had been able to come   [598]He wishes he had had it corrected   [599]I wish he were (was) not so careless   [600]We wish he had kept ...   [601]I wish she didn't (oder: wouldn't) talk so much   [602]I wish they were not always quarrelling (oder: would not always be quarrelling)   [603]We wish it had been talked about ...   [604]I wish I had something to offer you   [605]I wish I had been able to help him   [606]She wishes she hadn't had to work ...   [607]I wish you wouldn't (didn't) have to leave ...   [608]She wishes she had had a new dress ...   [609]I wish I would get a new flat   [610]I wish I had a garden   [611]I wish I had chosen a different profession

Kapitel 11:
[612]... it is turning cold   [613]... when it was beginning to grow dark   [614]... it has got cool   [615]... has proved/turned out (to be) correct, Diana has become an actress   [616]... something must have gone wrong   [617]Who was elected/chosen sportsman ...?   [618]I can explain the matter to you   [619]We shall submit the matter to the manager

Kapitel 12:
[620]isn't she?   [621]aren't they?   [622]is he?   [623]doesn't he?   [624]does he?   [625]didn't you?   [626]did he?   [627]won't she?   [628]will you?   [629]hasn't she?   [630]will you?   [631]aren't I?   [632]couldn't it?   [633]didn't you?   [634]shall we?   [635]won't you?   [636]did they?   [637]did they?   [638]Your brother studies physics, doesn't he?   [639]Anne likes dancing, doesn't she? (oder: ... is fond of dancing, isn't she?)   [640]Harriet can type, can't she?   [641]Arthur can't drive, can he?   [642]Your girl-friend has got a dog, hasn't she?   [643]Helen had to repeat the examination, didn't she?   [644]Everybody is satisfied with this solution, aren't they?   [645]Kitty has had her hair dyed, hasn't she?   [646]Yes, I am   [647]No, they aren't   [648]Yes, I do   [649]No, he doesn't   [650]Yes, he has   [651]No, I don't   [652]Yes, I would   [653]Hemingway did   [654]Is he?   [655]Do they?   [656]Did you?   [657]Harry is an engineer and so are his two brothers   [658]'Neither/Nor does Jack.' (oder: 'Jack doesn't either.')   [659]'Neither/Nor were we.' (oder: 'We weren't either.')   [660]'So did I.'   [661]'So do I.' (umgangssprachlich auch: 'Me, too.')   [662]Donald hasn't got a car and John hasn't either (oder: Donald ... a car, neither/nor has John)   [663]Barbara doesn't know English, neither/nor does her friend. (oder:) ... and her friend doesn't either.

Kapitel 13:
[664]..., you are always forgetting something   [665]Mary does look elegant ...   [666]Mike was being impolite ...   [667]Do have another piece of cake   [668]... I do believe ...   [669]Do be a little more patient   [670]No sooner was the lecture over (had the lecture come to an end) than a heated debate began. (oder:) Hardly/Scarcely was the lecture over when ... (oder:) The lecture had no sooner come to an end than .../... had hardly (scarcely) come to an end when ...   [671]Only after a week did I notice ...   [672]It was not until the 16th century that the assumption ... was refuted ...

Kapitel 14:
[673]If I meet Jack tomorrow I'll give him the book   [674]When we see Helen on Sunday, we'll tell her the news.   [675]as/since/because   [676]unless   [677]until   [678](al)though   [679]now that   [680]even if   [681]no matter what   [682]rather than   [683]so that   [684]otherwise   [685](al)though   [686]both ... and   [687]if   [688]than   [689]as   [690]because   [691]therefore/that's way/so   [692]though

17 Übungsgramm. Englisch

Schlüssel

[693]that [694]either [695]such as [696]or [697]... as soon as we know details [698]... if you aren't on time / unless you are on time [699]... even if she is very busy [700]... no matter how late it is [701]... since I last talked to Maggie [702]... rather than invite a lot of friends

Kapitel 15:
[703]this [704]mine [705]his [706]the [707]A friend of ours ... [708]I've broken my ankle [709]Yours was the most interesting lecture / Your lecture was the most interesting one [710]... it is my brother's [711]... a friend of yours? [712]... a friend of my sister's [713]Whose slides are these? – They are Anne's. [714]Do you remember our first meeting? [715]We have convinced ourselves that ... [716]I hope you'll recover soon [717]I must deal with / (oder: concern myself with) this problem [718]Sit down and try to relax [719]We would like to talk to the director himself [720]each other / one another [721]oneself [722]yourself [723]himself [724]himself [725]Last night we enjoyed ourselves very much, telling one another about / talking about what we had experienced during our holidays [726]To understand one another it is important to talk to one another [727]any [728]some [729]anything [730]anybody [731]nobody [732]any [733]some [734]some [735]somebody / someone [736]anybody [737]some [738]any [739]something [740]somewhat [741]some [742]some [743]anywhere [744]somehow [745]somewhere [746]some [747]any [748]some [749]May / Can I offer you something to eat? [750]I don't have any further questions / I have no further questions [751]Richard doesn't work ... any longer / any more [752]... I can't find them anywhere [753]There must be some mistake ... [754]..., hardly anybody was listening, and ... nobody wanted to say anything ... [755]... there isn't any left [756]much [757]a lot of [758]less [759]a lot of [760]many [761]much [762]each [763]every [764]every [765]each [766]a new one. [767]some trendy ones [768]the one near the opera-house [769]none [770]neither [771]either [772]none [773]both [774]both [775]either [776]I like neither of the girls / I don't like either of the girls [777]Neither of these scientists is a chemist [778]We knew none of the people ... / We didn't know any of the people ... [779]..., let's order a different sort [780]... neither was accepted [781]I don't know either of them / I know neither of them [782]We were both late / Both of us were late [783]A baker is somebody who / that makes bread [784]A knife is something (that) you cut things with [785]... the girl who / that lives next door ...; ... the girl (that) Peter wants to marry. [786]what [787]whom [788]which [789]the sum (that / which) I need [790]what [791]which [792]whom [793]that [794]whatever [795]which [796]... the day (that) I met ... / ... the day on which I met ... [797]... pulses (which / that) we cannot hear [798]Bob is an engineer who works in our plant [799]The suit (that / which) I bought last week ... [800]Do you know the girl (that) Fred is married to? / (auch:) ... the girl to whom Fred is married? [801]... problems (that / which) we must deal with ... [802]... a date with John, which I didn't like [803]Sue, to whom we talked ..., is ... (auch: Sue, whom we talked to, is ...) [804]These two lab assistants, with whom I work, are ... (auch: ... lab assistants, whom I work with, are ...) [805]... tour conductor, with whose help ... [806]... authors, some of whom we ... [807]... the paper that / which is lying ... [808]... the taxi (that / which) we have ordered [809]... a colleague (that) we can rely on (auch: ... a colleague on whom we can rely) [810]... the woman (that) I saw you with ...? (auch: ... with whom I saw you ...?) [811]... a lot of friends ..., some of whom I ... [812]The café ..., which I don't know yet, is said to be ... [813]The topic (that / which) I deal with ... [814]Mary was on time, which surprised me [815]What I dislike about Anne is the way she dresses [816]... the day (that) Thomas returned ... (oder:) ... the day on which ... [817]The project, on which no agreement has been reached ...

Kapitel 17:
[818]He drives very carefully [819]She looks good [820]smooth [821]sad [822]sadly [823]fairly good [824]pretty largely [825]hard [826]hardly [827]nearly [828]near [829]mostly [830]most [831]fast [832]fast [833]wide [834]widely [835]... she is just getting dressed [836]I hardly recognized Fred when I saw him again after ... [837]Fortunately, we have found ... [838]The book is well written [839]The

film was terrible. – The film was terribly boring.   [840]Your car still looks rather new.   [841]The newly developed engine ...   [842]Your translation is completely/totally/entirely wrong   [843]Please, speak a little more slowly   [844]I slept badly last night because ...   [845]It's almost/nearly ten o'clock, we must leave at once/right away   [846]You will have to study hard ...   [847]Do you happen (oder: chance) to know ...?   [848]I'll probably see Mike .../I'm likely to see Mike ...   [849]... often speak very fast so that sometimes we can hardly understand them

Kapitel 18:
[850]Is Jane as pretty as her friend?   [851]John doesn't speak French as well as Roger does. (oder: John's French is not so good as Roger's)   [852]Anne is rather diligent, but Alice is even more diligent.   [853]... he is much/far more reliable and less impulsive   [854]... it took us longer than usual to get home   [855]His latest book is rather good, but not so good (not as good) as his last but one   [856]... that's why we were served more quickly/faster than yesterday   [857]Yesterday I consulted a doctor; I thought it would take more than an hour, but I had to wait less than twenty minutes

Kapitel 20:
[858]in the east ... in the west   [859]in the Caucasus   [860]The Rhine ... in Switzerland ... into the North Sea   [861]... to Oxford Street?   [862]Tower Bridge   [863]Lake Geneva ..., Lake Constance   [864]The Matterhorn ... in the Alps   [865]Mount Everest   [866]the history of science   [867]... from the university ... in industry   [868]Arithmetic ... of mathematics   [869]The subject of psychology is the study of the organisms' adjustment to environment   [870]The members of the House of Lords ... of the nobility, the clergy and the Royal Family   [871]Combustion ... in the presence of oxygen   [872]Throughout the centuries ... on the origin of life   [873]Man is by nature ...   [874]In capitalism, most of the means of production ..., in socialism ... by the state   [875]... leave school? – ... attended the school ... the building opposite the main station   [876]... once a month   [877]quite a surprise/rather a surprise ...   [878]... part of my holidays ...   [879]... most of the time   [880]... by the end of April at the latest   [881]... rather a/quite a complicated character (oder:) ... a rather complicated character   [882]... in theory ... in practice   [883]... in nature in the form of ...   [884]Mankind needs peace ...

A detective story:
[885]he was called upon   [886]to have his wife shadowed   [887]was standing   [888]were/was going shopping   [889]she seemed to be waiting   [890]came hurrying   [891]were crowding   [892]he might have lost track of her   [893]she was nowhere to be seen   [894]she had bought   [895]Though spending a week observing her, the detective ...   [896]Being told that he had obviously been wrong ...

Shakespeare:
[897]are wrapped in darkness   [898]it is believed   [899]he must already have attracted attention ...   [900]showing   [901]... would not allow any theatres to be built ...   [902]considering the amusements provided by them ...   [903]he is known to have had   [904]... never thought of getting his plays published   [905]It was left to ...   [906]... allowed direct contact to be established ...   [907]... with the actors behaving ...   [908]... and the audience separated from ...   [909]this was not supposed to be   [910]are performed   [911]have been admired

Zur Geschichte der Luftfahrt:
[912]... may/can be traced back to antiquity   [913]... we are told about Daedalus of Athens, who is said to have built ...   [914]After Daedalus had completed the structure, he was to remain (stay)/After completing the structure Daedalus was to remain (stay) ...   [915]Leonardo da Vinci, whose inventiveness is known to have been centuries ahead of his time ...   [916]... the first ascension of the hot-air balloon constructed by them took place at ...   [917]... covering a

Schlüssel 260

distance of 2.4 km before it touched down / before touching down [918]... sending a sheep, a cock and a duck as passengers into the air [919]Having reached an altitude of more than 900 m and covered a distance of ... they landed safely ... / After reaching an altitude of ... and covering a distance of ... they landed safely ... [920]... the distance covered was ... [921]... was the first to build big rigid dirigibles which / that were able to carry freight and passengers (oder:) ... (which / that were) capable of carrying ... [922]... caused airships to lose their importance ... [923]... the first lasting 12 seconds, the last 59 seconds [924]... (when) flying across the English Channel ... / ... when he flew across ... [925]..., (which was) made by Charles Lindbergh ... [926]The idea of vertical flight, which, as mentioned above, goes back to / derives from / stems from ...

Einige Daten zur frühen Geschichte des Films:
[927]... photography, (which was) invented by ... and the celluloid discovered by ... [928]... an apparatus (that / which was) capable of creating / producing the illusion ... [929]... an effect obtained / attained by ... [930]... showing how a worker sneezes ... / showing a worker sneezing ... [931]By improving the technique of Edison A. and L. Lumière succeeded in designing ... [932]The brothers Lumière were to become ... [933]... when M. and E. Skladanowsky presented the bioscope built by them. [934]... was the first to film fictional episodes, using camera tricks ... [935]... adapted from / based on ... [936]... type of comedy (that / which is) characterized by turbulent action and absurd situations [937]... cinematic art by developing or improving techniques ... [938]... parable on violence, presented in surrealist detail, tells ..., who hypnotizes one of his patients into committing crimes [939]... porter at a posh hotel, who is degraded to a lavatory attendant for reasons of old age, and who by losing his uniform also loses his self-respect. (oder:) ... porter at a posh hotel degraded to ... and losing his self-respect with the loss of ... [940]... on the Russian revolution of 1905, which, in 1958, was chosen by an international jury of critics to be the best film ever made

Zur Geschichte der Roboter:
[941]Self-operating devices are known to have been built ... (oder:) It is known that self-operating devices were built ... [942]Among the most interesting ones was an animal automaton designed by Leonardo da Vinci ... [943]Famous were the androids, figures ..., which could be made to walk ..., e.g. the draughtsman built by ... in 1779 [944]... a chess robot demonstrated by ... attracted a lot of attention [945]... a machine man who is said to have been created by the Rabbi ... [946]..., reacting to the human voice [947]... for welding, assembling or spraypainting car bodies / ... for the welding, assembling or spraypainting of car bodies [948]sensors which enable / allow / permit them to correct movements deviating from ... (oder:) ..., which make it possible for them to correct movements ... [949]If (it is) given commands it starts moving / to move ... (oder:) Given commands, it starts ... [950]Thus, thinking machines have also ceased to be ...

Häufig vorkommende unregelmäßige Verben

arise	arose	arisen	give	gave	given
be	was, were	been	go	went	gone
bear [ɛə]	bore	borne[1]	grind	ground	ground
beat	beat	beaten	grow	grew	grown
become	became	become	hang	hung[4]	hung[4]
begin	began	begun	have	had	had
bend	bent	bent	hear	heard [ə:]	heard [ə:]
bind	bound	bound	hide	hid	hidden
bite	bit	bitten	hit	hit	hit
bleed	bled	bled	hold	held	held
blow	blew	blown	hurt	hurt	hurt
break	broke	broken	keep	kept	kept
breed	bred	bred	kneel	knelt	knelt
bring	brought	brought	know	knew	known
broadcast	broadcast	broadcast	lay	laid	laid
build	built	built	lead	led	led
burn	burnt[2]	burnt[2]	lean	leant[2]	leant[2]
burst	burst	burst	leap	leapt[2]	leapt[2]
buy	bought	bought	learn	learnt	learnt
cast	cast	cast	leave	left	left
catch	caught	caught	lend	lent	lent
choose	chose	chosen	let	let	let
cling	clung	clung	lie	lay	lain
come	came	come	light	lit[2]	lit[2]
cost	cost	cost	lose	lost	lost
creep	crept	crept	make	made	made
cut	cut	cut	mean	meant [e]	meant [e]
deal	dealt	dealt	meet	met	met
dig	dug	dug	mow	mowed	mown[2]
do	did	done	pay	paid	paid
draw	drew	drawn	put	put	put
dream	dreamt[2]	dreamt[2]	read	read [e]	read [e]
drink	drank	drunk	ride	rode	ridden
drive	drove	driven	ring	rang	rung
dwell	dwelt[2]	dwelt[2]	rise	rose	risen
eat	ate	eaten	run	ran	run
fall	fell	fallen	say	said [e]	said [e]
feed	fed	fed	see	saw	seen
feel	felt	felt	seek	sought	sought
fight	fought	fought	sell	sold	sold
find	found	found	send	sent	sent
flee	fled	fled	set	set	set
fly	flew	flown	sew [ou]	sewed	sewn[2]
forbid	forbade	forbidden	shake	shook	shaken
forget	forgot	forgotten	shed	shed	shed
forgive	forgave	forgiven	shine[5]	shone[2]	shone[2]
freeze	froze	frozen	shoot	shot	shot
get	got	got[3]	show	showed	shown

shrink	shrank	shrunk	strive	strove	striven
shut	shut	shut	swear [ɛə]	swore	sworn
sing	sang	sung	sweep	swept	swept
sink	sank	sunk	swim	swam	swum
sit	sat	sat	take	took	taken
slay	slew	slain	teach	taught	taught
sleep	slept	slept	tear [ɛə]	tore	torn
slide	slid	slid	tell	told	told
smell	smelt^2	smelt^2	think	thought	thought
sow	sowed	sown^2	thrive	throve^2	thriven^2
speak	spoke	spoken	throw	threw	thrown
speed	sped^2	sped^2	thrust	thrust	thrust
spell	spelt^2	spelt^2	undergo	underwent	undergone
spend	spent	spent	understand	understood	understood
spin	spun	spun	undertake	undertook	undertaken
spit	spat	spat	wake	woke	woken
split	split	split	wear [ɛə]	wore	worn
spread [e]	spread [e]	spread [e]	weave	wove	woven
spring	sprang	sprung	weep	wept	wept
stand	stood	stood	win	won	won
steal	stole	stolen	wind	wound	wound
stick	stuck	stuck	wring	wrung	wrung
sting	stung	stung	write	wrote	written

^{1} aber: I was born in … ^{2} auch: -ed ^{3} AE auch: gotten ^{4} Unterscheiden Sie: I hung the picture on the wall. The picture hung above the couch. (aber:) The murderer was hanged. The ruined businessman hanged himself. ^{5} shine, shone, shone = scheinen, leuchten; shine, shined, shined = (Schuhe) polieren.

Übersicht zu den kontrahierten Formen

I'm = I am   I've = I have
I'll = I shall/will   I'd = I should/would; I had
you're = you are   you've = you have   you'll = you will   you'd = you would, you had
he/she's = he/she is, he/she has   he/she'll = he/she will   he/she'd = he/she would, he/she had
it's = it is, it has   it'll = it will
we're = we are   we've = we have   we'll = we will/shall   we'd = we would/should, we had
they're = they are   they've = they have   they'll = they will   they'd = they would; they had
verneint:
isn't = is not   aren't = are not   wasn't = was not   weren't = were not
haven't = have not   hasn't = has not   hadn't = had not
won't = will not   shan't = shall not
wouldn't = would not   shouldn't = should not
can't = cannot   couldn't = could not   needn't = need not
mustn't = must not   mayn't = may not   mightn't = might not
oughtn't = ought not   daren't = dare not

Die Form ain't (= am not, are not, is not, have not, has not) findet sich nicht im 'Standard English', aber häufig in der Umgangssprache, vor allem im AE: You/He ain't right. – I/She ain't seen him for a long time.

Anmerkungen:
- Kontraktionen sind auch mit Substantiven möglich, vor allem mit 's: My brother's ill. – John's been abroad. (Im gesprochenen Englisch auch mit 'll und 'd: My friend'll come tomorrow. – Mary'd be glad to come with us.)
- Bei have, be, will, shall, would, should bestehen für die verneinten Formen zwei Möglichkeiten der Kontraktion: I haven't seen this film. = I've not seen this film. – She isn't at home. = She's not at home. – We won't/shan't wait. = We'll not wait.
  Beachten Sie: I am not wird nur zu: I'm not
- Kontraktionen kommen **nicht** vor:
  - in bejahenden Kurzantworten (a) und allgemein, wenn das Hilfsverb ohne Ergänzung steht (b):
    Is Peter abroad? – Yes, he is. (a)
    Tom and Jane haven't come yet, do you know where they are? (b)
  - oder wenn die Feststellung besonders betont ist:
    I really don't know whether Mike is right.
- Kontraktionen sind besonders häufig im gesprochenen Englisch, auch bei der Wiedergabe von Dialogen in der Literatur sowie in Privatbriefen; sie sind nicht üblich in offiziellen Schreiben und in der Fachsprache.

Formen des Verbs im Aktiv

Infinitive Present Simple: to write
Infinitive Present Continuous: to be writing
Infinitive Perfect Simple: to have written
Infinitive Perfect Continuous: to have been writing

		I	we	he/she/it	you/they
Present	Simple	am writing	write	writes	write
	Continuous		are writing	is writing	are writing
Past	Simple	was writing	wrote	was writing	wrote
	Continuous		were writing	has written	were writing
Present Perfect	Simple	have written	have written	has been writing	have written
	Continuous	have been writing	have been writing		have been writing
Past Perfect	Simple	had written	had written	had written	had written
	Continuous	had been writing	had been writing	had been writing	had been writing
Future	Simple	shall/will write	shall/will write	will write	will write
	Continuous	shall/will be writing	shall/will be writing	will be writing	will be writing
Future Perfect	Simple	shall/will have written	shall/will have written	will have written	will have written
	Continuous	shall/will have been writing	shall/will have been writing	will have been writing	will have been writing
Conditional Present	Simple	would/should write	would/should write	would write	would write
	Continuous	would/should be writing	would/should be writing	would be writing	would be writing
Conditional Perfect	Simple	would/should have written	would/should have written	would have written	would have written
	Continuous	would/should have been writing	would/should have been writing	would have been writing	would have been writing

Formen des Verbs im Passiv

Infinitive Present: to be asked   Infinitive Perfect: to have been asked

	I	we	he/she/it	you/they
Present Simple	am asked	are asked	is asked	are asked
Continuous	am being asked	are being asked	is being asked	are being asked
Past Simple	was asked	were asked	was asked	were asked
Continuous	was being asked	were being asked	was being asked	were being asked
Present Perfect	have been asked	have been asked	has been asked	have been asked
Past Perfect	had been asked	had been asked	had been asked	had been asked
Future	shall/will be asked	will be asked	will be asked	will be asked
Future Perfect	shall/will have been asked	will have been asked	will have been asked	will have been asked
Conditional Present	would/should be asked	would/should be asked	would be asked	would be asked
Conditional Perfect	would/should have been asked	would/should have been asked	would have been asked	would have been asked

Register[1]

A

able: be ~ to 48, 49
about: be ~ to 24
accustomed to: m. Gerundium 65
Adjektiv: 103–105; als Subst. 104; Suffixe 104f.; Präfixe 105; Steigerung 111–113
Adverb: 105–111; Bildung 106; v. Adj. abweich. Bedeutung 106; ~ m. 2 Formen 107; Adj. anstelle d. Adverbs 108; Stellung 108ff.; Steigerung 114
advise: m. Obj. + Infin. 42; m. Gerundium 72
afraid: m. Gerundium o. Infin. 69
all: 96–97
allow: m. Obj. + Infin. 42; m. Subj. + Infin. 46; Umschreibung für may 51; m. Gerundium 72
another: 99; one ~ 94
any: 94–95; Zs.-setzungen 95
appoint: s. Ergänz. d. Verbs 83
Artikel: s. best. u. unbest. ~
as: (Konjunktion) 88; ~ ... ~ 113; not so/~ ... ~ 113; ~ well ~ m. Gerundium 67
assume: m. Obj. + Infin. 43; m. Subj. + Infin. 45
avoid: m. Gerundium 66

B

be to: 53–54
become: Passiv 35; s. Ergänz. d. Verbs 82
Bedingungssätze: s. conditional clauses
begin: m. Gerundium o. Infin. 69
believe: m. Obj. + Infin. 43; m. Subj. + Infin. 45
bestimmter Artikel: 121–124; ~ entfällt 122f.
better/best: had ~ + Infin. ohne to 38

both: 98; ~ and 98
busy: m. Gerundium 67
by: m. Zeitbestimmungen 21; 25; Passiv 30

C

call: s. Ergänz. d. Verbs 83
can: 48–49; m. Infin. Perf. 57f.
capable: be ~ of 48; 65
catch: m. Partizip 79
cause: m. Obj. + Infin. 42; m. Subj. + Infin. 46
certain: be ~ to 25; m. Gerundium o. Infin. 71
cease: m. Gerundium o. Infin. 69
choose: s. Ergänz. d. Verbs 84
come: m. Partizip 79
conditional clauses: 25–30
consider: m. Obj. + Infin. 43; m. Subj. + Infin. 45
Continuous Tenses (Verlaufsform): 14–25; im Passiv 34
could: 49; m. Infin. Perf. 57f.

D

dare: 38
deal: a great/good ~ of 96
declare: m. Obj. + Infin. 43; m. Subj. + Infin. 47; s. Ergänz. d. Verbs 83
defective auxiliaries: s. unvollständige Hilfsverben
demand: m. Konjunktiv 81
deny: m. Gerundium 67
depend on: m. Gerundium 64
design: m. Subj. + Infin. 47; 55
dislike: m. Gerundium 66

---

[1] Die Seitenzahlen beziehen sich auf den Leitfaden.

Register

do: Fragesätze 11f.; Verneinung 13; verneint. Imperativ 13; s. Frageanhängsel 84–85; s. Kurzantworten 85; emphatisches ~ 86; have done + Gerundium 67

E

each: 97; ~ other 94
either: 86; 98–99; ~ or 89; 99
elect: s. Ergänz. d. Verbs 83
enable: m. Obj. + Infin. 43
enjoy: m. Gerundium 66
Ergänzungen des Verbs: 82–84
estimate: m. Subj. + Infin. 47
every: 97; in Zs.-setzungen 98
excuse (for): m. Gerundium 64
expect: m. Obj. + Infin. 42; m. Subj. + Infin. 46; 54

F

fail: Umschreibung f. cannot 48
fairly: Gradadverb 106; 107
feel: 15; m. Obj. + Inf. 41; m. Subj. + Infin. 47; m. Partizip 79; m. Adj. 108; ~ like + Gerundium 67
few: 96
find: m. Subj. + Infin. 47; m. Partizip 79
finish: m. Gerundium 66
for: m. Perfekt 19, 20; (Konjunktion) 88
forget: m. Infin. o. Gerundium 70
Frageanhängsel: 84–85
Fragesätze: 10–13; indirekte Frage 62
Futur: 22–25

G

Gerundium: 63–72; nach Präpos. 66; nach Verb + Präpos. 64f.; nach Adj./Subst. + Präpos. 65; nach Verben 66f.; nach phrasal verbs 66; nach bestimmt. Wendungen 67; Obj. + Gerundium 68
get: s. Passiv 35; m. Obj. + Infin. 42; ~ + Obj. + Past Participle 80
go: s. Ergänz. d. Verbs 83; ~ on m. Gerundium 66
going to: 22–23
good: it is no ~ m. Gerundium 67
grow: s. Ergänz. d. Verbs 82

H

hardly ... when: 87
hate: m. Gerundium o. Infin. 69
have: im Fragesatz 11f.; m. Obj. + Infin. 41; ~ + Obj. + Past Participle 80; ~ got im Fragesatz 11f.; ~ (got) to 56f.
hear: m. Obj. + Infin. 41; m. Subj. + Infin. 47; m. Partizip o. Infin. 79
Hervorhebung v. Satzteilen: 86–88
how about: m. Gerundium 67

I

if: 26ff.; even ~ 27; ~ only 29; (Konjunktiv) 82
imagine: m. Obj. + Infin. 43; m. Gerundium 67
Imperativ: 13
Indefinitpronomen: 94–100
Indirekte Rede: 60–62
Infinitiv: 36–47; ~ m. to 36ff.; ~ ohne to 38; passiv. ~ 39; ~ m. Fragewort 39f.; ~ anstelle eines Relativsatzes 40; Obj. m. ~ 40ff.; for + Obj. + ~ 44; Subj. m. ~ 44ff.
in order (not) to: 37; in order that 89
insist: m. Konjunktiv 81; ~ on m. Gerundium 64
intend: be intended to 47; 55
Inversion: 87

K

keep: m. ing-Form 66; 79; ~ from m. Gerundium 64
know: 15; m. Obj. + Infin. 43; m. Subj. + Infin. 45
Konjunktionen: 88–90
Konjunktiv: 81–82
Kurzantworten: 85

L

leave: m. Partizip 79
let: m. Obj. + Infin. 41
lie: m. Partizip 79
like (Verb): 15; m. Gerundium o. Infin. 69; would ~ m. Obj. + Infin. 42

Register

like (Adverb): 114; m. Gerundium 67
likely: be ~ to 25
little: 96; Steigerung 112
look: m. Adj. 108; ~ like m. Gerundium 67
lot: a ~ of 96

M

make: m. Obj. + Infin. 41; m. Subj. + Infin. 46; s. Ergänz. d. Verbs 83
many: 96; Steigerung 112; a great/good ~ 96; ~ a 96
may: 50–51; m. Infin. Perf. 57f.
mean: m. Subj. + Infin. 47; 55; m. Gerundium 71
might: 50; m. Infin. Perf. 57f.
mind: m. Gerundium 66
much: 96; Steigerung 112
must: 55–57; m. Infin. Perf. 59

N

name: s. Ergänz. d. Verbs 83
near: Steigerung 112; be/come ~ to m. Gerundium 66
need: 38; 56; ~ not/don't ~ to 57; ~ not m. Infin. Perf. 59; m. Gerundium 67
neither: 86; 98–99; ~ ... nor 89; 99
no: 100; in Zs.-setzungen 100; ~ sooner than 87
nominate: s. Ergänz. d. Verbs 84
none: 100
nor: 86

O

Objekt mit Infinitiv: 40–43
one: 99; ~ another 94
order: m. Obj. + Infin. 42; m. Subj. + Infin. 46; m. Konjunktiv 81
ought to: 53; m. Infin. Perf. 58f.

P

Partizip: 72–80; z. Verkürz. v. Relativs. 73ff., von Adverbials. 75ff.; with + ~78; as + ~80

Passiv: 30–36; it + ~33; Verlaufsform im ~ 34; Handlungs- u. Zustands~ 34f.; get/become + ~ 35
Past Perfect: s. Plusquamperfekt
Past Tense: s. Präteritum
Perfekt (Present Perfect): 17–21
permit: m. Obj. + Infin. 42; m. Subj. + Infin. 46; 51
Personalpronomen: 90–91
phrasal verbs: s. Passiv 32
plenty of: 96
Pluralbildung: 115–117; regelm. ~ 115; unregelm. ~ 115f.; ~ n. d. Lateinischen 116, n. d. Griechischen 117; Besonderheiten b. d. Verwend. v. Sing. u. Plural 117–119
Plusquamperfekt: 21–22
Possessivpronomen: 91–92
Präsens (Present Tense): 15–16
Präteritum: 16–17
prefer: m. Gerundium o. Infin. 69
Present Tense: s. Präsens
prevent: m. Gerundium 64; 68
Pronomen: 90–103
prove: m. Obj. + Infin. 43; m. Subj. + Infin. 47; s. Ergänz. d. Verbs 83
provided/providing that: 88

Q

question tags: Frageanhängsel
quite: Gradadverb 106; Stellung d. Artikels 124

R

rather: Gradadverb 106; Stellung d. Artikels 124; ~ than 89; would ~ + Infin. ohne to 38
recommend: m. Obj. + Infin. 42; m. Gerundium 72; m. Konjunktiv 81
Reflexivpronomen: 92–93
refuse: 51f.
regret: m. Gerundium o. Infin. 71
Relativsätze: 100–103; bestimmende ~ 100ff.; erläuternde ~ 102
rely: ~ on m. Gerundium 64
remain: m. Partizip 79
remember: m. Gerundium o. Infin. 70
report: m. Subj. + Infin. 47; m. Partizip 79

Register

require: m. Obj. + Infin. 43; m. Gerundium 67; m. Konjunktiv 81
reziprokes Pronomen: 94

S

say: 60; be said to 45; 55
scarcely ... when: 87
see: m. Obj. + Infin. 41; m. Subj. + Infin. 47; m. Partizip o. Infin. 79
shall: (Futur) 22; (unv. Hilfsv.) 52
should: (Conditional) 25ff.; (unv. Hilfsv.) 53; m. Infin. Perf. 58f.; s. Konjunktiv 81
show m. Obj. + Infin. 43; m. Subj. + Infin. 47
since: m. Perfekt 19, 20; (Konjunktion) 88
smell: m. Adj. 108
so: in Kurzantworten 85; ~ as (not) to 37
some: 94f.; in Zs.-setzungen 95
stand: m. Partizip 79
start: m. Gerundium o. Infin. 69
Steigerung: synthet. ~ 111; analyt. ~ 112; unregelm. ~ 112f.
stop: m. Gerundium 65; 66; m. Gerundium o. Infin. 70
Subjekt mit Infinitiv: 44–47
Subjektfrage: 10; verneinte ~ 13
Substantiv: 114–121; Geschlecht 114f.; Pluralbildung 115ff.; Kollektivbegriffe 118f.; Bildung d. Genitivs 119ff.
succeed: ~ in m. Gerundium 64
suggest: m. Gerundium 67; m. Konjunktiv 81
suppose: be supposed to 46; 55; supposing that 27
sure: be ~ to 25; m. Gerundium o. Infin. 71

T

taste: m. Adj. 108
tell: 60; m. Obj. + Infin. 42; m. Subj. + Infin. 46
Tenses: s. Zeitformen des Verbs
that: (Relativpronomen) 101f.
the ... the: 113
there is no: m. Gerundium 67
think: m. Obj. + Infin. 43; m. Subj. + Infin. 45

try: m. Gerundium o. Infin. 71
turn out: s. Ergänz. d. Verbs 83

U

unbestimmter Artikel: 123–124
unless: 26
unvollständige Hilfsverben und Äquivalentformen: 48–59; can/could 48f.; may/might 50f.; will/would 51f.; shall/should/ought to 52f.; must 55ff.; must not 51; need not 57; unvollst. Hilfsv. + Infin. Perf. 57ff.
urge: m. Obj. + Infin. 42; m. Konjunktiv 81
use: it is no ~ m. Gerundium 67
used to: ~ + Infin. 52; be/get ~ m. Gerundium 65

V

Vergleich: s. Steigerung
Verlaufsform (Continuous Tenses): im Aktiv 14ff.; im Passiv 34
Verneinung: 13

W

want: m. Obj. + Infin. 42; m. Gerundium 67
was/were to: 54
watch: m. Obj. + Infin. 41; m. Partizip 79
what: (Fragewort) 10; ~ kind/sort/type of 10; (Relativpron.) 103
what about: m. Gerundium 67
which: (Fragewort) 10; (Relativpron.) 101f.
who: (Fragewort) 10; (Relativpron.) 101f.
whose: (Fragewort) 10; (Relativpron.) 102
why (not): m. Infin. ohne to 38
will: (Futur) 22; (unvollst. Hilfsv.) 51f.
wish: m. Obj. + Infin. 42; m. Konjunktiv 82
worth: m. Gerundium 67
Wortstellung: 9
would: (Conditional) 25ff.; (unvollst. Hilfsv.) 51f.

Z

Zeitformen des Verbs: 14–25

Bibliographie

Eckersley, C. E. and J. M.:
A Comprehensive English Grammar for Foreign Students
London, 1960
Hartley, B., P. Viney:
Streamline English
Oxford, 1984
Hornby, A. S.:
A Guide to Patterns and Usage in English
London, 1975
Lamprecht, A.:
Grammatik der englischen Sprache – Neufassung
Berlin, 1986
Leech, G., J. Svartvyk:
A Communicative Grammar of English
London, 1975
Quirk, R. et al.:
A Grammar of Contemporary English
London, 1976
Swan, M.:
Practical English Usage
Oxford, 1982
Thomson, A. J., A. V. Martinet:
A Practical English Grammar
Oxford, 1979
Thorn, M.:
Exploring English
London, 1979
Zandvoort, R. W.:
A Handbook of English Grammar
London, 1966